Getting it Together

Also by John Harvey-Jones

Making it Happen

Getting it Together

John Harvey-Jones

HEINEMANN : LONDON

William Heinemann Ltd
Michelin House, 81 Fulham Road, London SW3 6RB
LONDON   MELBOURNE   AUCKLAND

First published 1991
Copyright © John Harvey-Jones 1991

Reprinted 1991

A CIP catalogue record for this book
is held by the British Library
ISBN 0 434 31377 7

Printed in England by Clays Ltd, St Ives plc

To Betty

who, more than any other person in my life,
has helped me to 'get it together'.

1 A Prince's Life

It would never have occurred to my family that they did not have a clear and God-sent duty to provide leadership. Looking back, that statement itself places my memories in a specific period of time and shows the enormity of my forebears' misconceptions about the reality of life. Within the United Kingdom we 'knew our place', a suitably supine position somewhere in the great mass of the middle class; but, put us on a ship, with the white cliffs fading into the distance, and we were transformed. We felt that on our shoulders rested the heavy responsibility of bringing enlightenment and British values to those parts of the British Empire which in truth had been civilised whilst our forebears were still in woad.

Moreover, generation after generation of my ancestors had followed the same path. Serving miles away from home in alien and mostly inhospitable cultures. Separated from their children, their lives entirely governed by the rigorous and unreal concerns of duty, honour, good form and social decorum, changing for dinner even when on hunting expeditions many miles from another white man. Sadly, for all this dedication and service, success – in the sense of promotion and position – eluded almost all of them. We were truly the cannon fodder of empire, and our graves stretch from Canada to the Pacific in continuing testimony to the Captains and Majors of my family line. Indeed, in later life I was bemused to find that by some extraordinary macabre joke many of my forebears' graves were near to an ICI office or establishment overseas. It was as though generations of my family had striven to create a world fit for ICI to operate in.

My mother, Eileen Wilson, was extemely 'family conscious' and on her side the Minden Wilsons, who stemmed in the eighteenth century from Banffshire in Scotland, had always maintained a 'chronicler' who recorded the ever widening circle of those we considered to be within our family group. The Wilson ladies seemed to have a knack of marrying very interesting, and subsequently noteworthy people and this, combined with our 'chronicler's' skill and determination to encompass the furthest reaches of cousinship, still enables me to claim kinship with astonished meritorious individuals who have never heard of me. Our family tree encompasses such doughty individuals as Whyte Melville, Robert Louis Stevenson and Field Marshall Gerald Templer as well as a nodding acquaintance with Gordon of Khartoum.

My mother was the third of four children born to one in a long line of Major Wilsons. I knew little of my grandfather, but adored him. He had the ability to project warmth, fun and patience to a five-year-old in an unforgettable way. He in turn was the son of a Captain Henry Wilson. His great wish, as mine was to be later, was to join the Royal Navy, and he actually succeeded in obtaining a cadetship to the old wooden-wall *Britannia*, which in his day was the training ship for officers. Alas, however, although he possessed all the physical skills with which my mother's line was endowed, was an unerring shot, and had an excellent eye for a horse, he was not over-endowed with brains. In my time I never found the Navy to be particularly demanding in this area, so it must have been a truly exceptional achievement to be discharged from his cadetship because of his inability to keep up with the intellectual prowess of the others. I still do not know by what route he acquired the title of Major, but eventually he preceded my own entry into the chemical industry by becoming an indigo planter in Bihar in north-east India. The indigo planters led a rip-roaring life. In that, perhaps more typical area of imperial endeavour, my grandfather's lack of brain-power proved no inhibition to modest, albeit temporary, success. My mother and her brothers and sister were packed off to England to be educated and established the same sort of remote relationships with their parents which, to some extent, characterised my own upbringing.

In a surprisingly short space of time the growing of indigo for use as a dyestuff was supplanted by the British invention of synthetic dyes. I have often wondered where all the indigo went in those days. Nowadays blue jeans constitute the largest tonnage outlet for the stuff, but they had only just been invented at the time that my grandfather's planting career ended abruptly. This was caused largely by the development of the great German chemical companies, and their ability to export their products. In due course my grandparents retired to Devonshire where, the family legend has it, they succeeded in dissipating what family fortune there was. I can certainly attest to the fact that they lived well while they were doing it!

My first memory of any sort is, as many early memories seem to be, a sort of snapshot of a moment in time. I have no recollection either side of the specific event and I cannot fit it into any pattern. The incident must have taken place at Lynton in Devon and I remember being in a pram which was careering down a hill, my unfortunate nursemaid having lost her grip on the handle. I can recollect with surprising clarity being pursued by her and by a small black Scottish terrier called Jamie, until our downward progress was stopped by my running into a bank and overturning. At this time, when I must have been in my first couple of years, my grandparents maintained a full panoply of household help, as well as having a chauffeur-driven car. My mother's family had great confidence in their line. They saw themselves as continuously knocking on the door of the upper class, and set great store by their aspirations in this field. Despite their hopes, in an odd way they were not snobbish, believing that the true sign of gentlefolk was their acceptance of individuals as people in their own right, irrespective of their alleged station. This attitude was enhanced by their lives amongst the Indians, whose caste system was only marginally more formalised than the British one at that time.

My father, Mervyn Harvey-Jones, was employed by a succession of Indian states as an Administrator and shortly after I was born in London my mother and I returned to the backwoods of central India. In my early years I was lucky enough to grow up with Indian boys of a similar age and my parents had many more Indian friends than British. I have subsequently read a great deal about life in India in those days, and the picture painted is one of an enormous separation between the British and the Indians, except at the highest levels of Indian society. It is true that in that continent my family enjoyed access to a level of society which would have been denied them in Britain. Possibly in areas where there were many British people a gulf may well have existed but my family, except when serving in the Army, were invariably on their own, miles away from other Europeans. Although this separation from the mainstream of the ritualised routine of British society may have harmed our social aspirations, I have no doubt that our lives were much more enriched by the breadth of our involvement in our adopted home.

Of my father's family I know practically nothing. My relationship with him was always narrow and fraught with a feeling of artificiality. He never seemed to relax with me, and I don't think I ever felt comfortable with him. We met very seldom in my life, and sadly I still have less idea of the sort of man he really was than I have of most colleagues with whom I have worked subsequently. Except for his sister, who is now dead and was fleeting of memory, I am the last Harvey-Jones of our direct line. There was no chronicler on my father's side, and no great feeling of family. Such records as they had were either lost in innumerable trips between India and England or were burnt, with most of our other possessions, in the Blitz. Not for my father's side the annual tribute of all the children gathering for a formal lunch with grandparents. While in later years his family followed a rather similar pattern to my mother's, there was a significant difference. My father's line originally seems to have come from a much more poverty-stricken segment of our population. The Jones family lived, married and died in Birmingham, and the only records that I have been able to find show that some of them were silversmiths in the late 1700s.

From 1689, which is the earliest record that I have found, none of them seem to have ventured very far from Birmingham and its environs, until Alfred Jones was born in 1826. My great-grandfather and -grandmother seem, however, to have been truly remarkable people, real 'Empire-makers'. Alfred joined the Army in the ranks, which must have been a pretty tough life in those days. He rose from private to sergeant in six years, and met and married Mary Ann Harvey in Dublin. This was where the Harvey met up with the Jones. She must have been a most formidable woman. Between 1850 and 1871 she bore no less than eleven children, only two of which were born in the same place, and those in successive years. She bore him children all over India, in New Zealand, in Ireland and one, by some extraordinary coincidence my grandfather, was born in England. When one bears in mind the time taken to move from one continent to another and the conditions under which the wives of 'other ranks' in the Army travelled the world, one begins to get some sort of idea of her character and physical stamina. She had an ever-growing army of infants by her side and, plainly, no fixed home of any sort. Reflecting on the life that she and my great-grandfather led it is not hard to see where our family's resilience and 'stickability' come from. Alfred, moreover, made the massive leap from the ranks to become a sergeant and, even more astonishingly, became a major in 1870 – to found yet another line of middle-rank army officers. In turn his son, my grandfather, who I can remember having met only twice, joined the Indian army and rose to become a lieutenant-colonel, retiring to Nice in the south of France, and subsequently dying there.

My father was carefully groomed to pursue a similar career, and I doubt whether any other way of earning his living was even considered. Like my mother, and subsequently myself, he was shipped home to be educated. In his case, however, he had, thanks to the prodigious efforts of Mary Ann Harvey, a multitudinous array of uncles and aunts who apparently 'did their duty' by him. Alfred and Mary Ann's children plainly possessed many of the qualities of their redoubtable parents, for some of them were described as being extremely well-to-do. My father was brought up by one of his father's brothers, and although I know, from the little he ever told me, that he received precious little affection, love or warmth, he was educated to be a gentleman. He was taught to ride, shoot, fish, and pursue all the sorts of physical activities which were considered, in those days, to be the necessary passport to a successful position in British society. He had a natural ability at games of every sort, which undoubtedly helped, and was a fine, substantial figure of a man, who took great care to keep himself in trim.

He was educated at Wellington and subsequently went to Sandhurst, at both of which he distinguished himself. He was plainly a highly intelligent and broadly based man but inherited, or acquired through a lack of any affectionate ties in his youth, at least one flaw which was to cause him, and others, much unhappiness in his life. He found it very difficult to give of himself in any relationship. To me he seemed almost a cardboard cut-out figure, such was his fear of emotion and display, and his regard for decorum. He maintained an iron control of himself, and on the occasions when we were together I have no memory of there being any variation in his emotional state. He appeared neither to enjoy himself nor to show any signs of being cast down. He took everything that life dealt him 'on the chin', and absorbed any event, however bizarre, apparently without complaining, or needing to seek solace or comfort from anyone else. For him life was a series of rules, and the true man was he who followed them all with the dedication and single-mindedness of a monk. It may be that the emotional side of his life was released in the playing of his violin which, like everything else he pursued, was a solitary interest. Admittedly it would not have been easy to have played in trios or quartets in the Indian states in which he lived, but he showed no interest in joining an ensemble, shutting himself away in his room to play for himself for hours on end, always striving after the solitary perfection which would perhaps bring him some lonely satisfaction.

My father's life was, in all too many ways, a series of missed opportunities, and he never achieved a tithe of what I believe to have been his capability. From Sandhurst he joined the Indian Army, and served during the war in that most miserable of all campaigns in Mesopotamia. He was always a good soldier, but for some reason distinction eluded him. This seems strange as he was, after all, a third-generation soldier and had all the attributes which should have led to a successful career.

He met my mother in India and they were married in Simla in 1921. They have always seemed to me to have been the most ill-assorted couple and I still do not understand why they married. My father's interests were the macho stuff of the time. He was a superb and fearless shot with a wide renown in India for stalking and killing man-eaters and he excelled at the physical sports he loved. My mother, on the other hand, enjoyed very few sorts of physical activities; her pleasures lay very much more in the feminine side of life. She loved the theatre (of which there was none where we lived) and was fascinated by the softer, more intellectual side of life. Nor were they bound by a mutual physical passion. They spent long periods apart, apparently by choice, and I do not ever recall them sharing the same bed and very seldom even the same bedroom.

As I understand things, shortly after they married my mother's health failed and they were advised to leave India. My father resigned his commission and found himself back in England endeavouring to earn a living in London. It must have been a misery for them both. The awful comparison of suddenly being a nobody in England, the absence of security, household help, and so on, must have been very tough going. My father eventually got a job selling insurance, and I can think of no one less equipped to be a salesman. His extreme sense of honour and integrity, coupled with his inability to relate to others and his lack of background and integration into the British scene, must have made the job, never the easiest, a purgatory. However, he found it difficult to accept failure and would battle on against all the odds even when a lesser, perhaps more sensible man, might well have given up and changed tack.

I made my own arrival in the midst of this unpromising situation, and my place of birth is recorded as Hackney, which in 1924 one feels was not quite the social equivalent of Mayfair or Belgravia. I was, in the event, to represent my parents' only excursion into the joys of parenthood, but whether this was because of the impact I was to make on their lives, the absence of propinquity, or the dulling of passion I do not know. Apart from that one snapshot memory of my possible demise on Lynton Hill, there is a considerable gap in my memories from pram days to my emergence, intact, with my mother, father and nursemaid in central India some time in 1927. Either the fascinating world of insurance believed it could dispense with Harvey-Jones's help, or my mother's health improved. Whatever the reason, they felt able to elect once more for the life in India, in which they had both been brought up.

Contrary to most perceptions only some three-fifths of that mighty subcontinent was directly administered by the British. The rest of the country was still administered by the Maharajahs and other royal houses whose rule descended by inheritance, and who enjoyed powers of intervention and authority far surpassing anything we would recognise in Britain. While British control on such matters as defence and foreign relations was absolute, as far as the ordinary Indian was concerned the Imperial power operated at a considerable distance from their daily lives, which continued much as before. There were over five hundred Indian states, scrupulously divided by the British authorities into a rigid order of precedence, which had certainly not existed before our arrival, and disappeared totally after independence. The constitutional position of the states was complex, governed as it was by treaties of perpetual alliance and friendship between the states and Great Britain, represented by the Viceroy and, ultimately, the King-Emperor. Within an extraordinary wide range of freedoms the Rajahs could administer the states more or less at their own whim. Only considerable excess, or unbelievable maladministration, could provoke direct British intervention. The Viceroy was represented in the states by a political agent who was theoretically a liaison officer, but in reality exercised a good deal of influence behind the scenes. He was not involved in the actual running of the states, and was always very careful to treat the ruler with respect, both from the point of view of ceremonial matters, and also in reality. A political agent could be removed and replaced very easily, whilst the removal of a hereditary prince was a much more difficult matter.

The task to which my father addressed himself defied a neat description. He was appointed by the state council of Dhar state to be both the senior member of council (a rough equivalent to the job of a prime minister) and also the tutor and guardian of the young Maharajah, Bahadur, whose father had died when he was a baby. I am sure that the appointment required the blessing of the Government, but my father was in no sense a government servant, owing his loyalty, given with his usual total commitment, to the state and, specifically, to the boy to whom he was guardian. In later years this arrangement was to cause my father and my family considerable personal difficulties, but during the period of my residence in India with him everything seemed to sail serenely on.

Dhar state was a compact little kingdom of about 1,800 square miles, and formed a part of the central India agency, the political agent of which resided in Indore, one of the richest and most enlightened states, some five times larger than Dhar itself.

Everything in India was governed by protocol and precedence, and the states were divided into ranks described, in the terms of the day, as 'salute' states and 'non-salute' states. This signified the number of guns to be fired on welcoming the Rajah on an official visit or other ceremonial occasion. Since there were 118 salue states, with entitlements ranging from 21 guns down to a modest 9, I have always imagined that the first day of a Dhurbar, or gathering of the princes summoned by the Viceroy, must have been entirely taken up by the firing of salutes. The manufacture of saluting-gun ammunition must, in those days, have been a nice line of business.

Dhar was entitled to a respectable 15 guns, and was ranked sixth in the agency. Even Holkar of Indore, one of the Maharajas widely known in the world outside India, was only entitled to 19 guns, so we didn't do too badly. Bahadur himself was a Maharatta by origin, and about five years older than I was. He was a slender, sensitive lad, who seemed in a continuous state of bewilderment at the seeming impossibility of forming any sort of relationship with my father. He had an Indian companion of his own age, named Manka, who was a great favourite with my family and indeed, it seemed to me, was openly preferred to Bahadur, on whom our bread and butter depended. It was, in fact, considerably more than bread and butter that we received, for we all lived together *en famille* and thus enjoyed the services and opulence appropriate to the ruler of a fifteen-gun state.

When one considers the poverty of practically all of Bahadur's people, my memories of our lifestyle cause me severe prickles of conscience. I could not have done much about it at the age of four, however, and the gross differences between the style at the palace and the lot of his subjects was, in those days, considered an ineluctable fact of the order of things. We were, in contemporary terms, rather over-housed. The palace itself was a red sandstone building (not the marble edifice which, for many years, I thought it), and had an imposing demesne, well removed from signs of Bahadur's subjects. I have never been able to revisit it, and I know the tricks that memory and a change of perspective can bring. Nevertheless, I have mental pictures of the palace which certainly equate in size and grandeur to others I have seen during my more recent visits to India. The rooms were very high and large, for central India was extremely hot. The grounds were, in the later part of the year, scorched and dusty, with the exception of a small ceremonial garden, and the dust penetrated the buildings and the palace itself. It did this without much difficulty, since the windows were of the most rudimentary kind, and of immense proportions. We, that is my mother, father, nurse (for I still had an English nursemaid), Bahadur and Manka, managed to fill one wing.

To ensure that we were not too cramped, however, we also owned a large and rather more contemporary bungalow, in its own compound in Dhar, and an even larger one in Indore, where Bahadur was to go to school. Each of these bungalows was, as was the custom of the time, surrounded by many acres of its own land, at the outer edges of which lay the accommodation for large numbers of servants. My father had then, and retained until their deaths, a personal bearer called Cean Naat, and a Goanese cook called, at least by us, Jacob. They were the only human beings of whom I ever remember him speaking with affection, and he inspired in them total dedication. This was despite the fact that he appeared to treat them appallingly. He would bellow and shout at them, and they would smile seraphically and continue undeterred. Everyone else, including Bahadur, Manka and I, was terrified of him, and would try to keep out of his way. Cean Naat and Jacob appeared to lead charmed lives, and treated his tantrums with affectionate disregard. They shrugged off the tempests of his anger as lightly as one would a small April shower.

On the rare occasions when my father left India the two of them were discharged, allegedly for ever, and returned to their home villages. As infallibly as the dawn, however, they would be waiting at Bombay to meet the liner which bore him back from his visit to the United Kingdom. No one knew how they were able to find out his movements and plans from their remote homes, but some sort of bush telegraph, operating without the advantage of the telephone system, enabled them always to be there and they were, of course, immediately re-engaged with great smiles and banter as soon as seen. In the light of his real affection for them it seems the most extraordinary way of dealing with trusted servants. Nowadays we would have found some way of tiding them over the period, or at least given them the confidence of knowing that they would be re-engaged on our return. Not so in those days, although after this whole routine had been carried out four or five times it became recognised by everybody as a great joke, rather than a serious threat. The two of them took over all the organisation of our many servants, but my father's bearer was much more than a major-domo, excellent though he was at that task. He was in charge of the grooms, he loaded for my father on his frequent hunting expeditions, and was no mean shot himself. I would guess that he probably knew my father better than anyone else, including my mother, and equally well that he liked what he knew. My father never, to his dying day, referred to him without adding some adjective or epithet. 'That old rascal', or 'That old devil', or at the least 'Old

Cean Naat', but always with an affectionate ring. All this despite
the fact that Cean Naat was certainly younger than he was and
had entered his service as a young man of about eighteen. I
suppose the skills that he had learnt and acquired had been
taught him by my father, for certainly he seemed to be almost
perfectly created to look after his every interest. My mother and
I were always treated with warmth and respect by both of them,
but never with intimacy. We had managed to establish the same
sort of esteem and ranking in their regard as they had for my
father's guns or fishing rods, and we were treated with much the
same care. Never, however, would they reveal my father's feelings,
or help us either to please him or to avoid his displeasure.

In addition to the surfeit of houses, the household possessed
many other luxuries which I now recognise as having been quite
exceptional. The state, or more accurately the state as represented by our household, ran two royal cars. Both were Buicks
of American origin, with enormous running boards, convertible
canvas tops and mica side-screens. They needed the running
boards. Not only were the batteries carried on them, but also
each car had an immense, chromium-plated horn, shaped like a
snake, starting by the driver's seat, and emerging over the wings.
These were a constant source of curiosity and delight to a small
boy. Since the horn appeared to be, then as now in India, rather
more important than the engine or the steering mechanism, it
was in almost constant use as we made our stately progression.
They were, of course, the only cars in Dhar, and even in Indore
they were amongst a very small number. The highway code
barely existed in India, but even if it had it would have been
written much more from the point of view of the bullock cart
than the internal combustion engine.

In addition to these items of invaluable mechanical equipment
the running boards also provided the method of travel for the
mechanics who accompanied us on every journey. They were
certainly necessary, for a combination of unmade roads and Jehu-
like driving proved daunting even for the Buicks. I am sure that
we must have accomplished some journeys without a breakdown
or a puncture, but I have much stronger memories of endless

enforced stops by the road, while the mechanics and driver argued furiously, as only Indians can, both as to what was wrong, and whose fault it was. India had carried the principles of division of labour to a very fine art. Every individual seemed to be prepared to do only one job, and it was quite unthinkable to have any flexibility of work between them. The driver, therefore, drove, and even when he was the cause of the trouble there was no way in which he would involve himself physically in its rectification, although that did not preclude him from giving endless, increasingly loud, and bitter advice. With the knowledge I now have of organisation, I also recognise that it was unhelpful to have two mechanics, for the scope for debate, misunderstanding and sheer bad workmanship through the loss of tools, parts and so on was immense. Our mechanics were, however, absolutely adept at the 'lash-up' system of repair, and armed with string, electric wire, and the most primitive of tools and equipment, would cheefully repair almost anything, almost anywhere. None of these complicating factors detracted from the wonder of the cars, and the amazement of the crowds who would turn out to watch the royal *entourage* pass. I am still convinced that it was the interest and wonder of the Buicks that did it, although Bahadur was known and, as far as I am aware, respected by his subject people, through whose sacrifice our standard of living was maintained.

We also had more reliable and endearing methods of transport available. The state elephants may not have been able to match the top speed of the Buicks, but I'm pretty sure that they would have beaten their average. To my chagrin I never graduated to an elephant of my own, being allocated (within the strict rules of precedence) to the third or fourth down the line. Riding on an elephant was initially quite scaring for a rather small child, for we seemed an enormous distance from the ground, and lesser mortals such as myself were not allowed a howdah, out of which it was very difficult to fall, but clung on, as best we could, to a sort of flat bed fixed somewhat precariously to the animal's back. The gait of an elephant, as anybody who had enjoyed a ride at Regent's Park Zoo knows, is not the smoothest of methods of progress, although for traversing any distance it is certainly preferable to riding on a camel. There were, however, compensations for being small, for one of the elephants would pick me up in his trunk and place me down wherever required with amazing dexterity.

The task of administering the state did not seem particularly onerous to my father. All the work of the day was invariably finished by lunch time, unless we were on some ceremonial visit. The period immediately after lunch was hallowed, and woe betide the foolhardy individual who disturbed the senior member of the council's deliberations, which were usually carried out on the flat of his back in his bedroom. Sometimes, if sleep eluded him, he would play his violin. It was the early evenings which were really the highlight of his day, for it was then that the serious stuff of riding, shooting and occasionally swimming or playing tennis took place. Life must have been terribly boring for my mother. She was not interested in sport and did not enjoy hunting and shooting, although she accompanied us quite frequently. She felt the heat intensely, despite her Indian upbringing, and always seemed rather frail. Any frailness of body was, however, more than compensated for by a strength of determination and will which I was only to recognise later in life, and have seldom seen equalled. Her real interests being of a more intellectual kind, she was never happier than when reading, painting, or doing her embroidery. Books used to be sent out to her by the dozen, and she developed the habit of reading all the book reviews in the British papers, when they eventually arrived, and making lists of everything she would like to read. This habit continued all her life, and when I was clearing her things after she had died, I found long lists of books which she still intended to read. She continued plodding through these immense lists, with her usual dogged determination, even when there was plainly no hope of catching up.

So many things had to be sent from England, and the time which elapsed when ordering something from a catalogue, in those days usually that of the Army and Navy Stores or Gamages to receiving the eagerly awaited parcel, was never less than four months. The catalogues themselves were sources of wonder. They were all illustrated and offered what seemed to us the most amazing novelties and developments. Nowadays, when ordering a special offer from a colour supplement, all too often one forgets, within four or five weeks, what it was that one sent for. In those days, however, the contents of the order were emblazoned on our collective minds, and the excitement of all falling on the parcel when it arrived and seeing the reality of achievement is, I am sure, the basis of my almost childish love of Christmas now. Even my father was not impervious to these events, although he would often lose interest and leave us after his box of tennis balls, or gun-cleaning rod, had been disinterred.

Life was very predictable and we planned months ahead for anything outside our ordinary routine. Organising our trek to the hill stations in the hot weather began at least six months before the due date, and in many cases we organised ourselves a year in advance. I spent a good deal of time with my mother and my nurse, for the age difference between myself and Bahadur and Manka was, at that stage, significant enough for me to be a brake on many of their activities. It was my greatest (totally impractical) wish to be 'one of them', and I used to feel desperately left out on the occasions when they and my father would be busy with some manly pursuit which precluded my involvement. I realise how irrational these feelings were, but to a four- or five-year-old they were nevertheless painful in the extreme, and my mother and nurse's attempts to make up by paying me more attention, or copying the activity in a form more suited to my years, merely exacerbated the hurt and the difference.

To this day I can remember these disappointments, and the feelings of inadequacy they engendered, and these events added to my inability to communicate with my father. For instance I remember the shame, fury and distress I felt when my father promised that I could join the three of them for a game of tennis. In the event he forgot and made up the four with someone else who, I am, sure, enabled them to have a proper game instead of playing to a child's standards. But I could not see this, and remember sobbing my heart out with frustration and disappointment. He could not have known how much the carelessly given promise had meant to me, or the degree of betrayal and rejection I felt when he so easily forgot about me.

Bahadur and Manka were very different in their involvement with me. Despite the age gap they treated me as a younger brother and involved me in as many of their games and activities as was practicable. In fact I became a sort of mascot and played up to them a great deal. In later years we became real friends and the age gap became less important, but even then they showed tolerance and affection. I was also useful to them, for they felt pretty sure that my father's retribution would be less severe on me than on them. I therefore became a sort of scout to detect my father's moods and activities and a willing scapegoat when we incurred his wrath.

India represents so many of my first real memories that it must have moulded a great number of my future characteristics. I recall so clearly the incredible beauty of the jungle and the excitements in the family when we went for a picnic. Picnics there were much more the equivalent of the elegance of meals at Glyndebourne than the pack of sandwiches and thermos that we throw together for our days out now. Like everything else we did at that time, for us to eat *al fresco* and enjoy the unspoilt and untramelled scenery involved the efforts of a great many people. It was unthinkable that we should eat except at a table, and with the appropriate number of chairs. Cean Naat was the picnic expert, and always took ostentatious charge of his many minions, and slightly less ostentatious charge of us. There were a host of picnic baskets, wonderful wicker contraptions, superbly fitted with silver, china and real glasses. Although now and again we were allowed to eat the delicious Indian food, our regular fare was English style, and of a rather dismal standard. This sort of meal was therefore much more memorable and enjoyable for the difference in its ritual and appearance than for the food itself. To this day I still retain my childish love of picnics, and find myself irresistibly drawn to fitted wicker picnic baskets – I cannot feel really comfortable with plastic tablewear, or picnics made up of sandwiches and crisps. I have been firmly imprinted with the concept of right and wrong in the world of picnics, just like a bird emerging from its shell.

So it was with many other features of our lives, which were an extraordinary blend of simplicity and sophistication. My mother kept, and utterly adored, two totally unsuitable white bull terriers, who reciprocated her regard in equal measure. In addition they had a curious conviction that they had been sent to India to perform for the dog population the same enlightening role the British thought to apply to the Indians themselves. The problem was that the native dogs did not seem to share these views of bull-terrier supremacy – and there were an awful lot more of them. No damage or remonstration deterred our two from their self-imposed civilising task. My mother's life was one of continual patching up. Hardly a day seemed to go by without iodine, bandages, or even a sewing job to be done on them, and their original beauty began to turn more and more scarred and disfigured, until their heads and faces looked like a crosshatched etching. Perhaps because we represented the local first-aid post, but more likely because of their inbred sweetness of nature towards humans, they were the most wonderful companions and guards – and were seldom to be found far from one or other of us.

Even though we were interlopers in their country, and objects of curiosity to many in a state like Dhar, I remember no qualm of concern for our safety and security. Nor do I recall any attempts to lock things up or to foil, by physical means, what would have been a very understandable urge to transfer some of the opulence of our possessions to those in more obvious need. Partly this was because we had virtually no privacy. Even at night, particularly in the hot weather, there was a succession of servants outside the room, whose task it was to pull the punkah, a massive hinged fan suspended from the ceiling, which kept the air moving and provided the equivalent of today's air conditioning. The nights were always noisy in any event, since there is no such thing as tropical silence, but they would be interspersed by roars from the various rooms, exhorting the 'punkah wallahs' to greater efforts.

As well as the dogs, and my pony, which I rode in the full military regalia of tiny solar topee, jodhpurs and boots, it was in India that I first became aware of gardens and gardening. My mother was interested in flowers, and spent much time supervising the planning and layout of our garden and lawns. The heat, together with the problems of availability of water, severely limited the amount which it was practical to use for such decorative purposes, but we managed, at unbelievable cost, to maintain some green lawn and a few beds of cannas. We also had, adjoining the bungalow, a wire-covered conservatory which was lush with growth, and had, as permanent residents, some very colourful birds. I cannot remember at whose instigation it was that I innocently planted one of my earlier mango pips in this unfortunate location. With plenty of water, and the general conditions of growth in central India, it sprang away, and within a surprisingly short period of time was pressing against the roof and threatening to burst through the netting. I recall making the most unholy fuss at anyone who dared to threaten to cut down 'my tree'. I must have been a little horror, or my mother was (as indeed she was) super-indulgent because, rather than touch the tree, they ruined the conservatory by cutting a large hole in the roof, through which the birds promptly exited.

India also provided other tremendous excitements for a child of my age. In the hot weather we all decamped to the hill stations in northern India, where the seat of government was also transferred. In days gone by, quite obviously Bahadur and his predecessors would have stayed with his sweating subjects, but the practice of moving lock, stock and barrel to the Himalayas, so delectable to the British, was accepted by our Indian *entourage* as the most natural thing on earth. They joined in the spirit of the thing as though it were a centuries-old custom.

The journey was made by train. Dhar did not boast a railway station, but this insignificant fact did not dissuade us from owning a suitably grand railway coach. Bahadur's own coach, together with a large number of others for our family, Cean Naat,

Jacob, their subordinates and our general baggage train were all moved, incredibly slowly, up to the hills. Even express trains did not go very fast in India in the 1920s, and our progression was about twenty miles an hour, punctuated by continual stops to fill up the engine with coal and water, and the passengers with food, fruit, lime juice and even ice. The practice was to telegraph ahead from each station for whatever it was that one wanted to meet the train at the next. They were marvellous journeys. Life stopped its normal routine, and there was always something different to be seen. Since I could not read for myself, stories were read to me and people had time to play with me. The stations were constantly fascinating, for even though some things in India are similar whether you are in the north or south, it is the variety, colour and differences which strike the eye and the senses. The delicious iced lychees we bought on the platform at Lahore station remain, in my memory, the best I have ever eaten. They leave an echo of succulent excellence I have unsuccessfully tried to emulate ever since. It was from Lahore that we went to Simla, where I first saw snow, and experienced a 'British' Christmas, with relatives (my uncle and aunt), church, parties, crackers and large numbers of British people – including, for me, the totally new experience of meeting some other white children.

Sometimes we went on these trips on our own, while Bahadur and Manka visited relatives or friends, but more usually we were all together. I found it pleasingly reassuring that so much of the paraphernalia of our lives, both in the way of people and possessions, accompanied us wherever we went. It is all so different from my expectations today, where a small carry-on airline bag is all that I take with me on even quite long trips overseas. I somehow don't think it would have seemed quite right to Cean Naat.

One hot season our whole caravanserai departed up to the Kulu valley. The valley was a revelation to me. It was a great fruit-farming area, and apples, cherries and pears grew in abundance. At the top of the valley you reached Tibet, through the Shipki Pass, and there were always bands of Tibetans moving down to India with goods to sell and barter. They carried wonderful hand-woven blankets, crudely-cut and polished semi-precious stones, weird concoctions of rancid yak butter or blocks of tea, and other fascinating items that I don't think ever found their way in to Harrods or Selfridges.

It was there that I received one of the most memorable gifts of my childhood. I was given, by one of our neighbouring fruit farmers, my very own cherry tree. As long as we were there I could eat as many cherries as I chose, and offer them to my friends. Even I realised it would be impractical to move the tree back to the plains with us, but as a four-year-old I found the gift so exciting that I marvel at the imagination and understanding of little minds shown by that man, farming so many miles away, and on his own.

It was on this trip that my father, equipped with the most expensive split cane rod, applied himself to teaching Bahadur and Manka to fish for trout. Inevitably I found myself relegated to my nurse, Irene, and my mother's care, whilst my father and the boys, assisted by an assortment of native experts, mastered the art of white water fishing. This, yet again, increased my isolation from him, and my mother's attempts to fill the gap, although surprisingly successful, merely underlined what I saw as my rejection. Curiously enough, retribution struck him on this occasion for, determined not to be totally left out, I had prevailed on my mother to let me fish with a bamboo line, hook and worm bait. To everyone's amazement, including my own, our catch, without local help or special equipment, massively exceeded that of the three 'professional' rods. Far from seeing the humour of the situation, my father instantly took over our chosen spot, picked more for its ease of access than from any great knowledge of the habits of Kulu trout. However, the Lord was really smiling on me that day, for not only did they catch nothing in the spot we had been ejected from, but we did it again in the spot we moved to – landing our dinner as well as our lunch.

These events produced rage bordering on apoplexy, for my father's expertise had been impugned. Even this display of potential talent on my part did not persuade him that I might be properly taught and allowed to join my older brothers (for this was how I viewed them). It is such trivial events that I am sure developed so many of my future inner drives and fashioned my life in ways which neither he nor I could have imagined.

I was to leave India with a deep affection for that country and its people. I always feel at home there, although my command of Hindi has long since left me. I admire its people, and find the differences of philosophy and approach cause me constantly to re-examine my own beliefs and values. I find their willingness to accept the world as it is a very good antidote to the conviction in the West that things can be changed and manipulated to our own will.

Unfortunately, however, I left India with hardly any memories of my father which cause me pleasure. I never felt, or if I did I cannot remember, any warmth or love, or moments when I felt at one with him. Worse, I felt little concern or interest from him and, above all, no pride in my modest little achievements. Sometimes I wonder if this is jealousy? Jealousy of Bahadur and Manka who, both by their added years and by the nature of his job, demanded and got so much greater a share of his attention. I hope it is not, for I am not conscious of ever feeling anything but affection for the two of them, but one thing is certain – I was to spend a great deal of my life trying to earn my father's approbation, both consciously and subconsciously. If I received it I was never to know.

The irony of these matters is that, except for the material support which my father supplied with that scrupulous attention which his concepts of duty and responsibility demanded, he gave so little. Yet the influence on my life which I can ascribe to him exceeds that of my mother. My mother was selfless in her attention to me and in trying to make up for what she saw as his shortcomings and inadequacies as a father. She was generous in her love and ceaseless in her attentions. I never had any doubt that in her scale of concern she placed me well before my father, even though this may not have been a good thing. It is to her and to my wife that I owe practically every direct and loving influence that there has been in my life. Yet the determination to succeed, and the continuous need to prove myself in every area of my life, which has been the mainspring of my life, I am sure can be traced back to those early days. It was the only period when we were all to live together for any length of time. Now, when I look back, I can see more clearly that so many of the problems with our relationship were caused in turn by his own upbringing. His inability to give of himself, and his apparent insensitivity to the reactions of others were the product of the belief which had been inculcated in him that duty, control and the Victorian ideal of the 'stiff upper lip', were the true marks of manhood. Feelings were weaknesses which should be controlled and suppressed. Compassion and concern were 'feminine' characteristics which should only be expressed in action; actions which all too often were designed to temper the recipient in fire, rather than remove problems or provide consolation. Did he have regrets at the lonely path he chose to tread? I shall never know. I have met so few people who loved him, and none who felt that they understood him. He sought to be self-contained, and prided himself on his independence. He despised weakness of any sort and the part of life which concerns itself with the soft inner centres of our being was shielded in him as impenetrably as the core of a nuclear reactor is by protective and impermeable casings.

2 Return to England

Shortly after my arrival in India it was decided that Bahadur's education required the full public-school treatment, or its Indian equivalent. He and Manka were accordingly enrolled into the Dali College at Indore, one of the small number of schools in India modelled on the British tradition, and serving very much as the seed bed for the finest of India's youth. The school seemed characterised by a tremendously hearty emphasis on good sportsmanship and 'playing the game'. Bahadur hated it, but Manka, with his equable character, seemed to sail through it with ease, showing his ability to adapt, chameleon-like, to this change in environment and expectations.

The main effect on my life was that now our time was split between Indore in term time and school holidays in Dhar. Since Indore was the Senior State in central India and Holkar, the Maharaja, was a princely colleague of Bahadur's, we slotted easily into the social structure. The Europeans in Indore were a cosmopolitan lot, and amongst my parents' friends were Americans, a Danish lady, and a couple of Austrians, and I was also able to meet a few other children of expatriates. The social life was frenetic, and during term time my parents seemed to be forever donning evening dress and having me put to bed early. Some of the other differences to our lives gave me a small foretaste of life in England. Time was spent obediently lining up at the touch line to cheer whatever team the school was fielding at whatever particular sport. Besides the organised games of hockey and cricket there was much emphasis on tennis, riding and shooting, at all of which my father excelled, so that he was in great demand.

Despite the emphasis of the Dali College on the game itself being the thing, winning was important to my father and a defeat, or a missed shot, seemed almost a reflection on his manhood.

I guess Bahadur and I had more in common than I realised at the time, for he shared my own inadequacies on the sporting field. It was only by heartbreaking concentration that he was able to rise above the 'rabbit' status which was, and remained, my own sporting profile. My father found it difficult to believe that there were people less naturally skilled and more timorous than he. He mistook lack of ability for lack of effort, and was quite convinced that a more robust approach on our part would overcome what he saw as a major handicap for our respective futures. Neither Bahadur nor I ever conceived the slightest wish to ride in the Grand National, or play cricket for our country. I am still far from sure that those Indian princes who were world class sportsmen were able to administer their states any the better for these great achievements. Nevertheless, the British mores of the time clearly had it that financial institutions, industry, politics, literature and science would all be better if headed by Olympic standard sportsmen. It was to ensuring that we had adequate (winning) standards in the 'manly' sports that my father addressed himself, and by which he measured the achievement of his own professional goals. In this he followed the examples of his own upbringing. An upbringing considerably more successful in this respect than ours was. He would never tire of telling us how his uncle sent him back in disgrace from his first large shoot for failing to break his shotgun whilst crossing a ditch, even though he had the safety catch on. Not only was he publicly humiliated by being curtly dismissed before the guests, but as well as that his gun was taken from him, to be returned only after the end of the season.

Far from learning that such forms of punishment could, while possibly achieving the aim of deterrence, exact other, less desirable consequences, my father modelled his teaching methods on them, much to the horror of my mother and Irene. The two ladies found themselves continually consoling either Bahadur or me, whilst trying to explain the deep sense of concern for us both which led my father to use these unfortunate methods. From my point of view matters met their nadir when I was to be taught to swim. We had the use of a rather large, slimy, concrete tank in the residency grounds, which had the advantage of relative privacy (for total privacy in India was a contradiction in terms). I was, as usual, frightened, and excessively slow to embrace the joys of swimming. The water was too deep for me to stand and there were no comforting water-wings or rubber inner tubes to hold on to. My father soon got tired of my whining and crying and, picking me up bodily, threw me into the deep end of the pool. It is true that I swam, after a fashion, after sinking desperately below the surface a couple of times and then spluttering up gasping for air, but to his surprise the episode neither cemented my love for the water, which was to develop later, in gentler conditions, nor my regard for him. Indeed the thought crossed my mind subsequently that perhaps the whole event had been contrived in order for him to rid himself of an inconvenient encumbrance, so that I could be traded off for a more satisfactory model.

Our problems were made the worse by the fact that Manka was everything that Bahadur and I were not. He lacked the sensitivity which, in both our cases, was partly the cause of our problems, and which became heightened to the point of raw pain by our regime. He also had a natural ability at any sort of ball game. So good was he that, despite the tactlessness of continually vanquishing his friend and ruler, he left Bahadur leagues behind. Poor princeling. To be relegated so frequently to the company of a child five years younger than himself, and to be constantly seeking the support of the ladies of the family, must have put real burdens on his back. He adored my mother. I suppose that the fierceness of his attachment to her was in some way a compensation for his inability to reach the man in my father, and his fear of him.

Despite the unnecessary dramas of these early years, my life was one of security, privilege and almost ludicrous pampering. Indians love children and are incredibly indulgent of them. They are also demonstrative, voluble and tactile, and I was constantly being cuddled and petted by my mother's Indian lady friends, to whom I was a sort of mascot. In a way it was almost as though I was brought up in the atmosphere of a harem, for my contacts with my father were scheduled, and almost invariably of a formal type. Certainly I remember no cuddling from him, for he would have seen such activities as signs of weakness, and threatening the development of the sort of Ulysses figure he had clearly in mind for his son.

I found many compensations for what I lacked from him, however, in the wonderful opportunities, variety, colour and sheer excitement of India. Bahadur's elevated status helped to cut through the rigidity of the caste system; we went everywhere and encountered nothing but friendship, laughter and fun. In any other country with such extremes of wealth and poverty, envy would have soured these experiences in a way that would have been evident even to a child. In India, however, with its acceptance of fate, such emotions did not seem to be known. Everyone seemed to have time to spend – whether it was the groom squatting down to tell me great tales of horsemanship, or Cean Naat reminiscing about the man-eaters he and my father had shot, or Jacob showing me, in an indulgent way, the secrets and intricacies of the art of cooking – everyone gave him or herself to the small white boy who had so little to give in return.

Sadly the time was coming for me to leave and, though I would have been distressed if I had known it then, not to return for nearly forty years. I suppose one's childhood days always imprint themselves particularly strongly, yet for me the impressions gained from such an improbable perspective in my formative years forged a whole raft of beliefs and values which I treasure. A wholly different way of looking at things from the European approach. The vastness of the subcontinent compared to our own small country. The different views of time, both in relation to a sense of immutability, and the lack of a sense of urgency. The bullocks drawing water in skins from the wells of Dhar state, trudging up and down the inclines from the well head, were going about their business in the same way as they had for a thousand years. For a thousand years they had learnt the futility of abandoning that natural pace and rhythm which enabled them and their driver to maintain the flow of water, albeit pitiful, for long hours at a time.

My early thinking was influenced by such considerations and also, of course, very largely by the Indians themselves. Their warmth, their spontaneity, pride and dignity, their belief in their own skills and worth, and their endless love of talk, discussion and argument. It is, of course, impossible to lump together, in one generalisation, the vastly different races, castes, traditions and experiences that go to make up India. There is certainly violence in Indian life, but my early memories, and subsequent experience, hold Indians in affection much more for their gentleness and courtesy than for their darker side, which can evaporate as quickly as it arises.

I don't think there was ever any debate or discussion about my upbringing. It would have been inconceivable for me not to have been sent home to England to be educated, and indeed it was looked upon as a softness that I should have been allowed to stay with my parents as long as I had. I was, after all, over six years old. Both my father and mother had been wrenched from their parents and had grown up knowing little of them. I assume they found the experience satisfactory, for I can remember no suggestion that I could or should stay in India and join Bahadur in due course at his college.

My mother was duly delegated the responsibility to take me back to England and, within a reasonable space of time, set me up in a suitable prep school. She would then rejoin my father, Bahadur and Manka for the continuation of the even tenor of their existence. The preparations for our departure made a great impression on me. There were great steamer trunks to be packed, and enormously heavy leather suitcases, which were all labelled, in vast letters, 'H–J'. Above all I remember Bahadur's depression. For so long my mother had been his buttress, protector, confidante and consoler that he plainly felt as abandoned as I was to feel later, in very different circumstances. The day came, and the whole household accompanied us down to Bombay. The state carriage was attached to the train, and off we went. For me it would be the last time ever in such splendour. Cean Naat was in full command of the *entourage*. His total ability to command any number of people in any number of circumstances seemed to hold sway even in Bombay itself. The city was on quite a different scale to anything I remember seeing before, and the noise, hustle and bustle gave me a vivid foretaste of how different the world was from the provincial and insular calm of Dhar and Indore. Nevertheless the combination of my father, Bahadur's position, Cean Naat, and, I imagine, the application of a good deal of money, ensured that our departure from India was in the same style and with the same lack of simplicity that had characterised our lives there.

We were to return to Europe through the 1930s' equivalent of the Grand Tour. Something which, at the time, seemed wasted on me, but which must have had an effect, albeit subconsciously. Instead of embarking on a God-fearing P & O blue-ensign-flying Queen of the Sea, we were to leave India on an Italian liner of the Messagieres Maritimes line, for our approach to England was to be a transcontinental one, enfilading it, so to speak, from Italy. We were headed for Naples. The journey, in those days, would have taken some three weeks, involving calling, and coaling, at Aden and Port Said before reaching our goal. It was my second sea voyage and, in the light of my subsequent career choice, I would have imagined it making a vast impression on me. Not only that, but it was my first introduction to a host of other, powerful new experiences such as Italian cuisine and the company of Europeans only, and yet, in the kaleidoscope of my mind, it seems to have been totally wiped out. Not even a 'snapshot', either mentally, or in reality, remains.

In fact the first time that my mental shutter engages again, metaphorically speaking, is in Naples itself. Travel nowadays is so commonplace that it is difficult to recollect the struggles that were involved so long ago. We were an oddly assorted triumvirate. Irene, my nurse, friend and – increasingly in the years ahead – my surrogate mother, a Somerset girl of firm views and great practicality. My mother, assured of her position in life and society. Myself, a painfully shy, nervous, thin, small child, overly dependent on the imputed status I had enjoyed, and feeling, even then, inadequate against the criteria by which I felt I was judged. In today's harsher world one would have expected such a party to be ripped off at every turn, and for my mother and Irene to be fighting ceaselessly to preserve their honour. But if such matters did arise I was quite oblivious to any interruptions in the smooth flow of our lives together. My mother was an inveterate organiser and timetabler. We invariably arrived early for everything. Quite frequently so early that we caught the train before the one on which we had booked. Nothing was left to chance. Seats, taxis, porters, meals, and even, I suspect, the use of the lavatories, would have been pre-planned, booked, checked and double checked, well in advance. I suspect that Cean Naat's methods were less precise, relying more on force of personality, a great deal of shouting, and judicious application of money to achieve his ends. But Cean Naat was back in Dhar, protecting my father from the inconveniences of daily living, handing him his loaded, and probably aimed, rifle, only when the trophy was in his sights, and removing from him the heavy responsibilities of such tedious chores as putting the soda in the whisky.

My mother, however, certainly got us across Europe in style. I have no idea how long we spent in each place, but my mental camera was in operation with a vengeance from the day we landed. I recall Pompei, the view over the bay of Naples, Rome and the Coliseum, and the Leaning Tower of Pisa, as though they were on postcards. Indeed they may have been, except that my mental pictures don't line up with the sort of vistas and visions that sell in their thousands. I remember being hurried off the main street in Pompei to relieve myself, and also steadfastly refusing to walk around the Leaning Tower, such was my conviction that it had been preserved in that position for the sole purpose of allowing a significant part of it to fall upon me personally in the year of 1930. Above everything, I remember being petrified by the noise and the traffic. Even in Bombay, where motor horns were actually worn out – to the extent that they had to be replaced – through excessive use, the conduct of motor traffic and its speed were limited by what seemed to me to be the proper users of the road. Bullock carts, horses, rickshaws, bicycles and pedestrians, with an occasional elephant, were what I expected to see on a proper road. Noisy though such a highway was in India, things seemed to be conducted at the speed and sound levels of nature. Here in Europe I was aware only of the frenetic, smelly, frightening, jousting and apparently uncontrolled robots, jostling for space and advantage, and prepared to devour a small, frightened pedestrian on sight.

One particularly great excitement was my first sight of European shops. They exceeded even my active imagination, which had been stirred and prodded by an annual injection of Gamages', Army and Navy Stores' and latterly Hamleys' catalogues. I had pictured to myself these palaces of plenty, where things were actually sold at the price marked, and the advantage-seeking haggling and bartering stages of commerce were apparently unknown. My educational tour of the sights of the Renaissance was dominated by my fierce desire to see Woolworths, and what must have been a dreary insistence on this privilege, even when the nearest branch was some hundreds of miles away.

Our train journey also took us, albeit without the benefit of a state coach and via many cultural stops, to Brussels, where my mother had a widowed aunt living in the suburbs. In later life I have made constant visits to this post provincial of capitals. My perception of the place at the time was surprisingly accurate, and encompassed a rather dull, well-ordered, uneventful place, where our travels came to a temporary halt. Our heavy luggage had, of course, gone on in advance, and we were 'travelling light'. In those days even travelling light involved at least two large suitcases each, and movement under our own power was quite impossible. Moreover the pace of onward progress, and the lengths of our stays in any particular place, had been intricately worked out to enable our laundry to be completed, starched, packed and delivered back to us – for instant soiling on the next leg of our voyage. From our long years in India my mother had learnt to expect a ready availability of large numbers of people to provide our life-support systems. In 1930, sadly, such numbers were all too readily available in Europe which, to a child, showed almost unbelievable signs of prosperity, order and cleanliness. The modest hotels in which we stayed were overflowing with bellboys, chambermaids, waiters and so on. Each hotel carefully affixed its own label to our suitcases, so that the suitcases themselves appeared to almost disappear – becoming transformed into a sort of mobile patchwork or collage. The fixing of the labels was a sort of competitive art form to the porters at the hotels, and they invariably sought to obliterate those belonging to rivals that they considered unworthy or possibly, as I now realise, too worthy competition.

At last even our ability to *bummeln* around Europe brought us closer to our own shores, and the last leg of the journey was in sight. The cross-Channel trip, and the first sight of the white cliffs, looking disappointingly grey in the mist, was all that remained. Once in Dover my re-introduction to my native land was almost complete. Almost, but not quite. The train journey continued, and in our compartment a resplendent waiter served us the most wonderful meal. In fact it was my first really memorable meal, and I still view it as a sort of measure against which to judge everything since. It was that most magnificent of animals, a Southern Railway tea. Some things in life have a durability which defies progress. The teas served now still have some similarities to those served in those bygone days. However, in accordance with Hutber's law of business behaviour, which states that 'better means worse', today's British Rail teas, supported as they are by contemporary technological marvels, are a poor copy of the splendour that was served then. Delicious, de-crusted and delicate sandwiches, served on monogrammed china plates, and the *pièce de résistance* – a toasted teacake with strawberry jam. The last fully qualified seventh- or eight-generation teacake-maker seems to have died some years back. Despite the packaging, the capital investment and the intricate distribution of today's models they cannot, I fear, hold a teacake, so to speak, to the splendours I first met so long ago.

London itself proved to be even more terrifying than the other cities I had visited. I remember standing, rigid with fear, absolutely refusing to launch myself across the road, and holding my hands over my ears to block out the roars and rumbles of that aggressive mass of clanking, banging, racing steelwork. Initially we stayed at the Pembridge Gardens Hotel, which was to feature largely in my mother's family history as a sort of London trysting place. Almost any Wilson, no matter how remote, would head for this rather small, ordinary hostelry, as a homing pigeon to his or her roost. In later years my grandmother was to elect to live there permanently after my grandfather's death, secure in the knowledge that some relative or other would always be around. It became the scene for my grandmother's stately birthday parties, which all her children, together with a steadily increasing collection of grandchildren, attended. We sat at an enormously long lunch table, replete with two sorts of sherry, in a private room. To me the parties were mostly memorable for the almost total lack of unity amongst my uncles and aunts, which was exceeded only by the diversity and, in some cases, the distaste of their chosen partners for each other. Over all of this presided granny. She was a tiny woman who revealed an unrecognised gift for hedonistic pleasure only after my grandfather died. Thereafter she really led a smashing life, drinking (sometimes to excess), gambling (and quite often winning), and spending what was left of the family money as though there was no tomorrow – as indeed there would not be for her.

I could not have foreseen these future delights as we landed on the hotel, like particularly heavily laden swallows returning from warmer climes. We didn't stay long. Just long enough for me to achieve my ambition of visiting Woolworths in Oxford Street, which lived up to even my fevered expectations. Then we were off again, to land ourselves lock, stock, and now cabin trunks as well, on my maternal grandparents. Finding the north coast of Devon dull, they had moved to Teignmouth. Here they bought what I remember as an immense Edwardian house, called Stapleford, on the Haldon Road above the town itself. The gardens of the house were also large, and full of ancient, lushly growing rhododendrons. My grandparents employed a couple, Mr and Mrs Hobbs, of impeccable Devonian lineage, who seemed to combine in their two capable souls Cean Naat, Jacob and the dozens of their underlings. Hobbs (I never knew his Christian name – the use of which would have seemed to us all a gross familiarity), besides serving at meals and acting as major-domo, would appear in yet another disguise (leather leggings and peaked cap) to drive my grandparents' car. Mrs Hobbs was a large, loving woman, and a most redoubtable cook of the 'take twenty-four eggs' variety. My small appetite was a source of despair to her, and nothing would ever convince her that my problems were related to cubic capacity rather than lack of will, or even temptation. The two of them must have had other help, and certainly there were gardeners, but only the Hobbses engrained themselves in my memories and affections.

The train journey from Paddington, which I was to get to know so well, was a real excitement. There were the views, from the window, of the White Horse and the verdant, well-managed British countryside, the excitement of emerging from the tunnel after Dawlish, for the run by the sea, sometimes with the breakers spattering the windows. For years this scene was a part of the Great Western Railway's advertising posters, and it never ceased to delight and amaze me. When we first arrived at Teignmouth station there was a large party assembled to meet us. My grandfather and grandmother, Hobbs himself (in all his grandeur), a succession of taxis, and even a lorry to move us and all our equipment up the hill. Somehow the house seemed to expand to accommodate us all, with room to spare.

Life at Stapleford was, however, totally different from anything I had encountered before. Although my grandfather enjoyed occasional hallowed times when he shut himself away, in his household everyone did everything together. He and my mother shared the same sense of humour, with a marked sense of the ridiculous. He adored jokes of every sort, and it was at his knee that I first saw and learnt to appreciate the works of Heath Robinson. My mother and he were always locatable by the sound of her uncontrollable giggling and my grandfather's bellows of laughter. I don't think he was a great wit. In so many ways he was a simple and straightforward man, with a love of life and lack of pomposity which was infectious. He cannot have been particularly well-to-do, but showed a determination to maintain 'standards', and lived with a style which certainly eased life's pressures. The evenings were my favourite times with him. The whisky decanter appeared exactly at five in the afternoon, every day, winter and summer, and I would arrive with it. He suffered, and indeed that was the correct word, from gout and over the seven years until his death became steadily less able to get about, but I never heard a complaint, or saw him show any signs of pain or shortness of patience. I would climb on his knee, and he appeared to enjoy my company, telling me what I took to be outrageous stories of his life and experiences, but which I now suspect to be no more than the truth.

As in most families of the day, life centred around the men in the family, but Violet, my grandmother, enjoyed quite a different relationship with 'Bones', her husband, from that which existed between my parents. In reality she was the brains and determination behind the family, but she was always very discreet about it. She got her way either by ignoring everyone else, or by a sort of jollying process, which never degenerated into nagging. Although she was, I'm sure, his intellectual superior, she was careful not to make this obvious, choosing instead to share his pleasures and play her role in the lifestyle in which he was comfortable. At six foot two he was as large (albeit rangy and thin) as she was small and petite, and when they walked together she had to run to keep up with him. He was an impressive figure of a man even in old age, with a splendid full white beard and moustache, beautifully trimmed, and a fine shock of white hair above it. I was always intensely proud of him and loved to be seen in his company. I thought of him as a really great man and, in my imagination, I thought of us as 'pals'.

We probably did not stay at Stapleford long – perhaps a few months – but time, when one is six or seven, has a way of elongating so that each day or week seems like a whole separate existence. No one seemed to work, or have a gainful occupation, except the Hobbses. My grandfather, then sixty-five, had already been retired for eight years. There was some talk of him working with papers for the odd hour or two, and letters occasionally left the house but I don't remember him doing anything else. My grandparents enjoyed a modest social life, but were not pillars of the local scene. Life was spent at an even tenure, passing smoothly from Mrs Hobbs's 'gourmet' breakfast (complete with chafing dishes and choices of fish, eggs, kidneys and so on), to her gargantuan lunches, and on to her enormous teas. Yet, despite this cornucopia of indulgence, everyone remained slim, or even thin. We would go out on expeditions, driven in a stately way by Hobbs, and there were always excitements of one sort or another. Alan Cobham's air show at Haldon Aerodrome (my first sight of an aeroplane), the Teignmouth carnival, a stream of military bands playing on the promenade, trips across the bay in motorboats, sandcastle competitions and sand sculptures, Punch and Judy shows on the beach. The list was endless.

Amongst my grandparents' most prized possessions was a large beach hut near the pier. This was a square, wooden building with a proper four-pitched roof and a wooden floor. The hut could be opened at the front on to the beach, and had a canvas awning which could be spread to provide shade or shelter from Teignmouth's not infrequent, but pleasingly mild, showers. Inside, the hut was divided into changing spaces by canvas screening, and there was provision for primus stoves so that tea and other delights could be brewed up. It was possible, with a little pre-planning and a substantial amount of load carrying (rather reminiscent of the Sherpas in the Kulu valley), to set ourselves up for a whole day on the beach – the sort of day where each of us did what we wanted, reinforced by the proximity of the others, each equally engrossed in their own activities. Not only did the 'Sherpas' bring down food – milk, sandwiches (increasingly sand-anointed as the day proceeded) and the makings of delicious cream teas, but we also struggled down with books, rugs, knitting, embroidery, and even, on occasions, my mother's water colours and easel. The summer seemed long, cloudless and tranquil. Voices were never raised, and the whole environment was one of warmth and security. It was a new and seductive experience for me, and so greatly did I relish it that I felt I had no need for the company of other children. I continued, in this happier and more supportive atmosphere, to share my life with grown-ups and those older than myself, so making ever greater the eventual shock of my entry into life with my own age group, which was to occur sooner than I expected.

After a while with my grandparents, my mother took a flat in Holland Park Avenue in London, and she and I moved there with Irene. For the first time, although very briefly, I was to live with my mother in a home of our own, with our own furnishings and belongings. My mother and father had a horror of owning a house in Britain. All their lives they rented houses, and our possessions spent the greater part of their existence in the care of Saunders Repository at Ealing. Even when, bird-like, we landed for a brief stay in a temporary nest, we seldom if ever managed to get all our things away from the repository, and life would be interspersed with trips down to the warehouse, armed with lists of everything in every box, and complicated maps and identification systems for the relevant trunks, boxes and tin-lined cases which contained the worldly trophies of our existence. The Holland Park Avenue 'nest' was a maisonette at No. 159. The rooms seemed large and, by the standards of our Indian accommodation, of almost sybaritic luxury. My father's Indian experience had given him a knowledge and love of oriental carpets, which I now recognise as a considerable skill. Our main furnishings seemed, at that time, to consist of an endless selection of carpets of every colour, size and shape, matched only in their numbers by the skins and heads of the wild animals he had slaughtered. Both our floors and our walls were covered with rugs, as well as tiger, leopard and lion skins, carefully prepared and lined, with the heads invariably fixed in expressions of extreme ferocity as a tribute to my father's manhood and skill. These heads produced constant problems. If the skins were mounted on the walls the heads required specially built stands to hold them, so that they protruded at, in my case, head height. I was forever banging into them as they lay, snarling sightlessly into eternal space. When used to cover the floor, the skins were even more of a problem. The scattered heads in our hallway looked like nothing so much as a seaside miniature golf course, with the open mouths expecting to take delivery of a skilfully directed ball. If it wasn't the heads of the trophies that one fell over, it was the rugs, which skidded or rumpled up to catch the unwary, and life was a constant cacophony of the sounds of tripping, falling, sliding and dropping, as we negotiated our self-created assault course.

Most of the rest of my parents' possessions consisted of 'good' contemporary furniture, from Waring & Gillows and Maples. Almost the only pieces which impressed themselves on me were some very low and comfortable chairs (which were wonderful for my small legs, but must have posed real problems for adults) and my mother's elaborate equipment for tea parties. While the Harvey-Jones tea ceremony lacked the antiquity of the Japanese approach, we ceded nothing in its complexity and careful ritual. Afternoon tea appeared to me to be our main social event. These occasions served to really fix the imprint of my Southern Railways introduction to Britain, and established an affection and awe for a British tradition which has all but disappeared in my lifetime. The tea itself was always served from a wheeled trolley and consisted of at least two, and sometimes three teapots, to contain the various blends we served. Indian was considered to be very *infra dig* and Darjeeling was almost the only one allowed to cross our portals. Ceylon, in our tea world, might as well not exist, and our real concentration, apart from the ubiquitous Earl Grey, lay in various, very weak, Chinese types. The drinking part of the ceremony was complemented with a silver milk jug (always kept covered with a lace doily with blue beads attached, to weigh it down) and a magnificent silver kettle, fixed over a spirit burner, which played the role of a Samovar, but somewhat less efficiently. Interesting though the drinking arrangements were, to a small boy it was the cake stands which really concentrated the mind. Even for the occasions when my mother was entertaining only a single guest there were never less than two of these folding devices, loaded with four china plates each. Afternoon tea, as understood at that time, involved crustless mini sand-wiches – a real test of delicacy to avoid eating one in two mouthfuls – of types which appear to have followed the Great Auk into extinction. Cucumber, tomato, bloater paste, sandwich spread, sardine, and an infinite variety of other exciting gustatory delights – but with the marked exception of meat, which was not considered to be a suitable sandwich filling, or indeed a proper food to serve at tea time. All of these wonders were marred only by the paucity of both quantity and size. The sandwiches were, however, complemented by scones of various types, fancy breads containing dates and figs, and a whole raft of other delights, and all that before the onward march of the cakes. Cakes had to be of the slicing variety, both fruit and iced, although again fruit was considered to be a little less than 'smart'. Rene used to produce endless varieties on a theme. Lemon, Orange, Chocolate, Coffee, even Maple and Walnut, as well as Victoria sponges, Cherry cakes and Dundee cakes encrusted with almonds. How the poor woman found the time to make them, and how we disposed of these endless confections, are mysteries to me now, but then they were an essential part of our ordered existence, and when we visited elsewhere we expected, and were greeted by the same, albeit somewhat inferior versions, of our own customs. Although I believe passionately in progress and that, as a general rule, circumstances have got steadily better during my lifetime, the demise of tea, tea shops, and these pleasant conceits seems to me to be a real backward step. I am proud of the attempts made by Claridges and the Ritz to maintain our family traditions, but mourn the demise of Gunters, Lyons, Fullers, and the tea shops of my youth. Something seems to have gone awry with the laws of economics. Even though my family and I will still drive miles to a tea shop which provides even a travesty of yesterday's splendours, there are so few available now to meet what I am sure is not a unique, or idiosyncratic, preference.

Holland Park Avenue also marked my first, burgeoning acquaintance with white children of my own age. The house next door was occupied by a charming Irish doctor, who had two sons of about my age, with whom I used to play in the garden square.

Meanwhile my mother was carrying out her investigations to find a suitable preparatory school for me. For the time being I was enrolled at Norland Place School across the road, as a day boy. The school was coeducational, and catered for the sons and daughters of those who lived in the area. It was gentle, and for children of my age more like a play school than a place of learning. I have nothing but fond memories of the experience, especially as it was the first, and for many years the last time, that I fell in love. I formed an intensely private and violent passion for a girl called Ruth who was at least nine years old. I doubt that she was aware of the effect she had on a small insignificant boy looking hard for somewhere to divert a capacity for feeling quite out of proportion to his size and years. I can picture her still. Straight dark brown hair in a pageboy bob, the absolute pinnacle of female beauty (for a nine-year-old, that is). My adoration for this Helen of Troy buoyed up my daily visits to the school, and perhaps explains my affection for it. Of lessons I remember nothing. I was reading well by then, and had been from the age of four, but for the life of me I cannot recall a single class or a single teacher. My days were filled with delight by the luminescent beauty of this remote creature when I caught occasional glimpses of her around the building.

Weekends at Holland Park Avenue introduced me to other interests as well. Exercise was considered important, and Norland Place seemed to have no games facilities (another plus from my point of view!). Rene and I used to walk up to the Round Pond in Kensington Gardens on Sundays, paying ritual obeisance at the statue of Peter Pan on the way, and watching the boats, sometimes steam-driven models, on the pond. The approaches to the pond at weekends were filled with boys and men dragging behind them trolleys with model sailing yachts, some even with self-steering gear. There were also intricate models of liners, and even occasional warships. The older men, equipped with waders, could be seen up to their waists in the pond, adjusting their models for cross-pond voyages and even, on some occasions, circumnavigations. If the weather was wet we would go to the museums in South Kensington. Over a period of time we visited them all. The Victoria and Albert; the Natural History Museum – with its dinosaurs, and a rather smaller collection of the taxidermists' art than we had at home; the Imperial Institute, with its dioramas; the War Museum; and my favourite of all, the Science Museum. Years later this boyhood passion for the Science Museum led me to accept an invitation to become one of its trustees, and I was astonished to find how much had remained the same, nearly forty years later! I suppose museums should not change too much, but bearing in mind the march of science in those forty years it still surprises me to see so many old favourites. Rene must have been bored to salt tears, but to me the joy of turning handles and seeing the models move was never-ending. There was, in that magical place, every sort of model you could think of. Trains, stationary engines, factories, and models of every sort of ship from the day of the coracle onwards. Museum visiting didn't seem such a widespread interest then as it is now, for there was always room to spare, wheels to turn, and marvels to admire. This period of my life was an oasis of happiness and normality in what was soon to be a desert of misery. I felt secure, my own inadequacies did not seem to matter, and there was a whole new beckoning world to learn about. It was to vanish all too soon.

While I had been acclimatising to a form of life which compared well with my privileged life in India, and was blessed with neither a sense of time nor any forebodings, my mother had completed her enquiries. How she lit on Tormore school as a scene for my future torments I do not know. We didn't appear to know any parents of children who were there, nor had we any knowledge of the headmaster or his wife. The school had, for those days, its usual proportion of children whose parents were carrying the colonial burden overseas, but no more, I would guess, than others. Someone or something in the fates steered us towards this school, whose role in my life I still find difficult to assess. Such was my misery there that for many years I could not even bear to think back to it, as I was aware that I could bring no balance or fairness, or generosity of spirit to my view of the place. When I began to show signs of success in my later career, my old headmaster wrote to me, inviting me back to take part in various events there. While I hope I declined politely I could never, even as a grown man of some independence, bring myself to contemplate entering its portals again. I know I could not have forced out the circumlocutions and evasions of the truth which alone could have produced an endurable impact for the school and for myself.

At this stage I had no inkling of what lay ahead, although I know I felt foreboding once the preparations started. I refused to be cheered up by my visit to Swan and Edgar to be outfitted (with everything two sizes too large, of course, to allow for growth) in the school uniform. My mother, who was a most generous woman in most respects, had some curious foibles about clothes. I can never remember an occasion when she bought anything which fitted me at the time of purchase. Nor do I remember the passing of time ever achieving the moment at which these purchases, made with such foresight and care, caught up with where I was, physically speaking. I'm afraid that this habit, together with another curious quirk of motherly behaviour, have left me with a disregard for my clothing which even the Navy could not overcome. Indeed in later years the only adverse comments I can remember from that service, in the various reports which one was continually being given, referred to my inability, or unwillingness, to dress with that bandbox smartness which is the hallmark of the naval officer, even when going down with his ship (another desirable characteristic of the breed).

The other – complementary – quirk of my mother's, which was to lead me to this sad state of affairs, and I am sure was a contributory factor to my decision to join the submarine service, was her attitude to the 'best suit'. There were two important factors at play here. The first was that no matter how few of any article of clothing one had, as long as there were more than one, a best suit, a best shirt, a best pair of socks, etc., had to exist. The other factor was that once anything was designated 'best' no occasion was ever so grand, no society so demanding, no venue so outstanding, that it warranted wearing the best outfit. Indeed the attitude to best clothes was uncomfortably similar to my own attitude to the occasional bottle of outstanding wine in my cellar. I can never bear to indulge myself with such a bottle. To make matters worse I spend my time persuading myself that my guests and friends – even when I know them to be cognisant – would not appreciate such a treasure. The suits never got worn until I had grown out of them, and they were passed on to someone else. The wine doesn't get drunk until it is over the top, and even the act of swallowing it is a sort of penance. It is a retribution for meanness, and one would have thought that time and experience would teach me the error of my ways, but if so, not yet.

The preparations for school, once begun, increased at a startling rate. I was to join the school at the beginning of the autumn term. I had one last, halcyon, summer holiday with my grandparents at Teignmouth. They had sold Stapleford as being too large, and an unnecessary encumbrance, and had moved to a wonderful maisonette on two floors in one of the imposing Victorian buildings overlooking the crescent and the sea. The crescent, besides clock golf, tennis courts and the other luxuries expected of a seaside resort of that period, had at its centre a bandstand. When the bands were playing this was surrounded by an entire 'lawn' of green canvas deck chairs, mostly occupied by dozing, apparently elderly men and women, with hats pulled down over their faces. The bands changed every week, and covered the whole range and gamut of the regiments of the British Army. They played in resplendent dress uniform, and invariably started their concerts with their different regimental marches. Their closing theme, however, be they the Royal Artillery, the Rifle Brigade, the Devon and Dorset, the Warwickshire, or any other famous regiment, was always 'Oh Listen to the Band'. It was played sharp at ten, and night after night I would listen to the whole last concert, with the curtains drawn, in my bedroom overlooking the sea. I have loved military and brass bands ever since. My heartbeat increases, and I feel my pace quicken to adjust to the rhythm. I can barely bring myself to leave them, unless by chance they happen to play that particular tune. Even if it is self-evident that the concert is to continue, as far as I am concerned it is time to go.

The summer that year, in my memory, was the best of all. The sun shone incessantly, the bands played, the beach hut was still retained as an essential life-support system, even though our flat was only a couple of hundred yards away, and I discovered the irresistible delights of the penny-in-the-slot machines on the pier. Slot machines in those days operated more to appeal to curiosity than greed, and very few of them offered the opportunity of winning anything – even a second free turn. The majority were moving models of various sorts, where the penny suddenly brought the whole scene to jerky life and movement. The conjurer conjured, the ghost haunted, and tiny cars, trains or ships moved erratically across the plaster scenery. Some ships even sank, impaling themselves on plaster rocks to suffer a sad mechanical demise, always with their bows rising dramatically into the air, only to appear miraculously restored, from the far corner, on the payment of another penny. The pier was a wonderland, even though at that age I had to stand on tiptoe to be able to see, and could not always reach to insert the penny which, relying on the force of gravity to initiate the marvels, always had to be put in at the very top of the machine.

The summer holidays on this occasion did not seem to last forever, and all too soon we were back in the flat preparing for my leaving home. As in everything my mother did, order and method prevailed. All my uniform was laid out in the spare bedroom. I hated it already, and I had not even worn it. Every item was counted, recounted, marked with Cash's labels laboriously sewn on by Rene and my mother, and eventually packed away into a cavernous trunk.

My toys, with a terrible inevitability, were similarly marshalled, paraded and segregated into four heaps. One was to 'go out', which in those days meant that they were to be given to the Church Army, never to be seen by me again. One heap was to be packed away into a box for Saunders Repository, whence were also to go the tigers, leopards and oriental rugs, together with all my mother's props for her tea ceremony. Another heap was to fill a suitcase, to be looked after by the faithful Rene, who had accepted a pitifully small retainer to keep an eye on me and to provide a haven for me in my school holidays, and the last one, so small that it could not be dignified by being described as a heap, represented all I could take with me to the school. This process reinforced my fears and apprehension, which were to be massively increased when, two days before I was due to leave, I heard and saw my mother crying. In our family the showing of grief, even privately, was assumed to indicate a lack of moral fibre, but to cry before others was a sin which only the weakest would indulge in. I imagined at the time that she was dreading my leaving home as much as I was. It was only very much later that I realised that possibly the prospect of a lonely return to India, and an even lonelier existence once she got there, was the cause of this uncharacteristic behaviour. Be that as it may, the demonstration of her misery gave me the right to desert my infantile manhood, and to show my own feelings.

It is thus that my memories of my approach to Tormore start, with a long period of mutual tears and howls of misery. By the time she tearfully placed me on the school train, and had wrung the last unhappiness from the situation by waiting on the platform until the train had chugged out of the station, my crying muscles were in full spate and turned up to maximum volume. Since most of us in the compartment were in a similar boat, all starting a new experience, it would have been unreasonable to expect any of the other small boys to have any particular time or sympathy to spare for the snivelling and red-eyed wreck in the corner. It was at that time that I placed myself, with a tragic predictability, into a category of inferiority and inadequacy, which was to haunt my time at prep school. It was true that I differed from the others in one respect. I knew that my mother was due to sail for India within days, and had no idea when I might see her or my father again. Indeed, I would have been appalled if I had realised that it would be three years before we were together again as a family. After all, at that age it would have been equal to half my entire existence and would have seemed incalculable and interminable. The other boys were certainly in no mood to make allowances for my problems, and were already jostling for position in the pecking order which is such a feature of boys' schools and of which, in my innocence, I was totally ignorant.

Many of them must have felt as strange and out of their depth as I was, but they were more concerned with the future, while I was looking unhappily back to the past. In addition their backgrounds were all very similar. They all seemed to have homes in which they had lived continuously – most had brothers or sisters – and all had a certainty of their position and a relevance which eluded me then and to some extent does so even now. Their fathers had desirable jobs, which meant something to the others, while I could not then, or now, find any short way of defining what my father did. If I had had more guile or imagination I might have said the truth, that he was a big game hunter, and gained approbation therewith. However, it had never occurred to me that anyone's occupation mattered, or that one way of earning a living was 'better', on some mystic British scale, than another. The train journey to Deal put a new perspective on such adventures. Always before, they had been relaxed or exciting events, full of curiosity and new things to see. Now I sat frightened, huddled, miserable beyond belief, and realising that life as I knew it had gone. Kent is one of the most beautiful counties in Britain but that, and my subsequent journeys to Deal, put a sort of blight on it, which still persists in my imagination. The journey is, in reality, a short one, but on that day it seemed to last forever, the more particularly since I saw no relief in sight at the end of it.

My first twenty-four hours at Tormore still seem to me to be an eternity, and I can relive practically every moment of it. When we eventually arrived we were transferred to a coach, which brought us to the school. It was, in reality, a pleasant, creeper-covered red building of a sort of indeterminate 1900s period, but then it looked cold, forbidding and unwelcoming. We were shown to our dormitories where there were neither rugs nor animal skins to greet me. Rows of unforgiving metal bedsteads stood on cold bare boards. Our hand luggage was delivered to these doleful surroundings and, after briefly unpacking, we were taken down to the dining room for the first of a long series of apparently inedible meals. I could not have eaten anything if failure to do so had led to immediate execution, and indeed so unhappy was I that I could well have welcomed such a speedy end to my miseries. Then it was off to bed, where I struggled under the blankets. Ignoring the taunts and imprecations of my fellows I howled to myself until eventually exhaustion brought merciful release in sleep. School days had begun.

3 A Taste of Britain

It is, I am sure, normal for most children to find their first experience of boarding school a traumatic and unhappy one. Even from the safe distance of age I have not come across too many of those people who are reputed to look on their school days as the happiest ones of their lives. I am sure that my particular difficulties were exacerbated by the fact that I was being forced to adapt to too many changes all at once. There were the simultaneous problems of adjusting to the full impact of life in England (to which I had had a gentle and protected introduction with my grandparents and the Norland Place school) and also the problems of accepting a rigid, institutionalised way of life, which was so totally different from the uniquely individualistic nature of my early upbringing. In addition, as though to emphasise these other problems, I had the knowledge that my mother was about to leave me precipitously, and on a seemingly irrevocable basis.

My separation from my mother had a terrible feeling of finality and brutality about it, of which she appeared to be unaware. She left England about three days after I was sent to Deal, and so I had only one letter from her before she set off on the long sea voyage back to India. I knew that there was no way in which she could receive my piteous and copious cries for help for – at minimum – the six weeks it would take her to get to Dhar. Even if, as I realised was unlikely, she turned around immediately to come to my relief, neither she nor anyone else could come to my aid for a further six weeks. I could not expect any response to my misery from her in under three months. In the meantime my estrangement from our circumstances was enhanced by the sort of falsely jolly and optimistic letters I was to receive from her, writing of her conviction that I would have settled in and be enjoying the company of all my new little friends, in the time which elapsed before she could be aware of my situation.

My detestation of the other boys was matched only by their loathing and total contempt for my own small, foreign being. Tolerance is a rare virtue amongst the young. The objective of British institutions and schools in those days seemed to be to ruthlessly stamp out any signs of individuality or difference in order to produce a sort of homogeneous, clean cut, stiff-upper-lipped clone with the same clear and unquestioning view of duty and honour which my father exemplified so well. I felt, and indeed was, totally on my own, as a misfit of massive proportions. There may have been preparatory schools in Britain which cherished and nurtured the flickering flames of difference in their pupils, but Tormore was certainly not one of them. Success there consisted of conformity in every way, and even academic success, which was much prized because practically all of us were expected to sit for some scholarship or other, was tolerated only if accompanied by the whole range of other manly qualities.

The insistence on conformity ran through every value in the school, like the reinforcing bars in concrete. I fell foul of it almost immediately after getting up. I had led a spoiled and pampered life, where I was not required to eat unless I both wanted to and found the food on offer appealing. I was accustomed to helping myself, and while leaving food uneaten was viewed with disfavour once the selection had been made, this was treated more on the lines of the many small Indian children who were deprived by my actions than as a sign of revolution and mutiny. Breakfast showed all too quickly that these luxuries were things of the past. We filed in to the unfamiliar surroundings of the dining hall and went to our predetermined places, at large refectory tables with a member of staff at the head of each. Such was my continuing misery that first morning that my gullet appeared to have constricted and I could not have eaten even my favourite baked beans. The arrival of a vast soup plate with a congealed mess of grey lukewarm matter, coated with a near impenetrable skin, was unlikely, at the best of times, to tempt me. If I had ever had porridge before it had certainly not prepared me for this glutinous yuk, which had the appearance and some of the smell of a cow pat produced by a rather unwell cow. I politely, and with some foreboding, indicated that I did not want any. I was then impolitely and unambiguously informed that it was not a matter on which my feelings or wishes had any bearing, and that I was to eat it immediately. I got to know that plate of porridge pretty well, for it was to be produced at every meal that day, in the conviction that either I would be starved into submission or suddenly be brought to a realisation that this ageing plateful was really a gourmet's delight. I suppose the school looked on this act of gross insubordination as a test of wills which had to be won by them speedily if they were to maintain discipline over me in the future. For my part I was far too terrified and unhappy to have shown such spirit. I was just physically incapable of eating anything. To make matters worse I relapsed into tears again, to the delight of my fellow pupils. I stared desperately at my plate, choking back my sobs, and wondered how on earth I had landed in this hellhole. It was not surprising that the others withdrew from me at speed. With the inexorability of a Shakespearian tragedy everything that happened that day, and indeed for most of that term, continued to mark my differences and make my acceptance by my peers more difficult and less likely.

At our very first lesson I made another mistake which was to have even more long-lasting effects on my future, and has caused untold suffering to a succession of colleagues and secretaries over the years. By comparison with my fellows, had I but realised it, I was actually very well grounded in the basics of reading, writing and arithmatic. I wrote a fine, round, generous, joined up hand with fluency and, since I adored reading, I had a surprisingly large range of vocabulary. I had been taught to write on single lines, or unlined paper. At my very first lesson I was faced with a double lined exercise book. What was I to do with this new experience and unique phenomenon? I enquired and was told that, of course, you write between the lines. One of my many failings has always been a tendency to follow instructions literally and precisely. This is one of the reasons why, when my wife as navigator says 'next left', we invariably turn up some unsuspecting soul's drive – a habit described in my household as 'Get out the buns, we're coming to tea'. There was no way that I could force the uprights of my bold hand between what seemed to be ridiculously closely spaced double lines. Taking the instruction literally, the only way I could follow it was to print extremely small, increasingly illegible letters. That wish to please, and an unfortunate misunderstanding of what was required, is the basis of some of the worst handwriting I have ever seen. So bad is my hand that not infrequently I cannot read what I have written myself, particularly when writing in ships, planes, cars or trains. The sheer institutional cost of this error to the organisations that I have worked with, in terms of other people's wasted time in trying bravely to decipher the indecipherable, appals me. By now it must amount to many man or woman years, and is yet another accusation to lay at Tormore's feet.

Somehow I survived the day, including our first trial game of football – a game I had never even seen played before, since it was not a feature of Indian life. To add to my problems, cricket was the only game they played that I knew. I did not even enjoy it – but at least I knew the rules and had some, albeit rather basic, skills. None of my other, even poor-quality, sporting knowledge applied. Hockey was, to my surprise, looked upon as appropriate only for girls' schools, whilst tennis, probably sensibly, was reserved for the top form only. No one shot anything, (although the thought and wish to do so reappeared in my mind incessantly) and no one rode horses, or if they did, certainly not at school. Even swimming, where my father's unusual teaching methods had at least produced an ability to survive in the water, was only a summer sport. My initiation into the school's sporting life of soccer, rugger and gymnastics yet again emphasised my ignorance and low personal worth. One or both of my parents had put me down to be taught to box. Whether this was an uncanny prescience of the bullying to which I was to be subjected, or as a part of my father's wish to generally toughen me up, I don't know, but it was certainly money wasted. In the first place I have always had a dislike of being hurt. I would have expected this to be more widespread as a human foible than seems to be the case, but I certainly have a sense of self-preservation which precludes voluntarily inviting pain. At that time I was weedy, gangly and greatly underweight. Although in theory this gave me the advantage of reach, a combination of puniness, lack of punch, and any real feeling of aggression made it impossible for me to hold attackers at bay. Because of my height it always looked as though a large boy was being methodically pounded into the ground by a smaller one. Bystanders were inevitably more interested in my defeat than they would have been in any success I might have had. I also found that, despite those boys' books which invariably described their British heroes scornfully rooting 'lesser breeds' with a series of upper cuts or hooks, no one, at least in my school, fought in that way.

Many years later I was to learn that the headmaster had the gall to write to my mother after my second day at his school, saying that I appeared to be settling in all right. Oddly enough I have grounds for thinking that this was not entirely the cynical commercial initiative it might be interpreted as. Even though I could never bring myself to dwell on the realities of the school he ran, I know others who have. They were the favoured and successful few, in school terms, such as head boys or prefects, the survivors, in emotional terms, of our curious existence. It has been a comfort to me in later years that their memories, although they are gentler in their judgements and more forgiving than I, confirm the nature of the place, and the almost total lack of real understanding, on the part of the staff and headmaster, of our existence and feelings.

Without exception the major memories of all my contemporaries are of the bullying, and the systematic and grotesque cruelty of the older boys – veterans of twelve or thirteen – towards their cowed and unhappy juniors. I do not believe for a moment that this situation was a deliberately contrived one; it was merely a natural extrapolation of simplistic beliefs in discipline, and the perceived desirability to teach people early in life to 'take responsibility' for others. This form of responsibility involved no care, or involvement in the thoughts, sensitivities or feelings of the juniors. The task was simple. To ensure that the even seams of our corporate behaviour were not blemished, by intent or accident, through the breaking of the ranks of conformity. Deviations from such compliance were punished by endless beatings imposed, in the name of authority and discipline, by the seniors on the juniors. Such judicial sentences were perpetrated before all the rest of the elders and took the form of forty, fifty or even eighty blows on the bare bottom with a variety of weapons, of which the slipper was the most tender. The mercy was that since those who administered the punishment were relatively small and diminutive, lasting physical damage seldom ensued. The mental effects on the donors, as well as the recipients of these archaic forms of ritual are more questionable, and less easy to assess. In my own case it gave me a fear and distaste of corporal punishment which, despite taunts for my weakness, ensured that I did not indulge in these practices when my turn came to be a giver, rather than a receiver. I doubt whether, in this macabre *Lord of the Flies* existence, even those who were spared such experiences by my aversion to them thought the better of me. Such was the prevailing culture that failure to avail oneself of the prurient opportunities for an early initiation into sadomasochism was looked upon as odd, queer or weak.

The staff of this modern Dotheboys Hall were equally odd. The perspective of boyhood compresses age in a curious way, so that anyone over sixteen appears grown up, and anyone over twenty-five appears old. As has often been the case in boys' schools, the highlights of our teachers' lives seem to have occurred when they were at public school. The clocks of their growth as individuals were arrested at seventeen or eighteen and even thirty years later they seemed to believe that life as a pupil of Dr Arnold contained everything that a British gentleman needed to know of the great world outside. Foreigners of every hue and historical background were, by definition, inferior. If only the remaining two-thirds of the world not coloured red on our school atlases would gather their senses, they would accede instantly to British rule, humbly imploring our 'superpower' to take them under its wing. It was to produce boys with the wisdom, balance and power of leadership to receive others, be they Hottentots or Hungarians, into Britain's benevolent rule, that schools like mine considered they existed. And it was to this most honourable and least rewarding of tasks that the staff had pledged their loyalty and their lives.

Despite the impoverished appearance of our teachers, the frayed grey flannels, the moth-eaten umbrellas, the Harris tweed sports jackets earning their well-deserved reputation for longevity, it only occurred to me in middle age what an equally miserable existence they themselves led. They had all the trappings of the good life. They sported the odd gown, belonged to unlikely cricket clubs, and carried their old school ties with pride, and yet there was also something missing in their lives. For a start they had to eat the same food as we did, although they had the subtle advantage of serving themselves, and it was unlikely that we would raise a chorus of derision if they avoided the porridge, the brawn, or the dyed-bread breakfast sausage. Moreover they, and they alone, were served with toast, and actually had their own teapots and jars of marmalade. They were underpaid and overworked to a man, and one woman (we possessed, as a group, a rather unlikely French mistress, in the academic sense of the word). They also enjoyed another common characteristic. Perhaps because of all these factors they all lived on a very short fuse, and if baited long enough would lose their tempers with us to dramatic effect. We had a measured scale of these eruptions which had the accuracy of the Richter scale. We lacked the understanding of the process of induced volcanic activity, but we could instantly recognise the first signs of lava flowing. Being outside the fraternity of my companions, I was never a part of the elaborate rituals leading to explosion. When the desired effect was achieved it merely added to my fears because of the shouting, anger and physical violence. I also had the uncomfortable feeling that if a mob of such individually small children could wield such power, my own existence trembled on a hair spring. Perhaps to try to minimise these occasions, the school drove us mercilessly. The reputation of the school and its commercial viability, both of which were shaky at the best of times, depended totally on measurable academic achievement. The names of the boys who achieved scholarships were emblazoned on oak boards and written in gold leaf for all to see. Woe betide the year which did not look likely to fulfil its quota. If there seemed the smallest likelihood of such a disaster the staff swung into action and put even more pressure on the poor unfortunates who were not producing their allotted portion of glory.

Despite my loathing of the school I have to acknowledge its success in inculcating in me a habit of work which, once acquired, was well nigh impossible to break. There was constant pressure to perform and every moment of every day was filled. Even in our sports sessions there was continual exhortation to greater effort. Amongst the worst tortures were the cross-country runs, when the playing fields were frozen too hard for other activities. The whole school, ranging in age from six to thirteen, would stand, slapping hands and thighs against the cold, until the luckless master whose afternoon we were wrecking, blew his whistle. We would then erupt on to Upper Deal and speedily elongate into a sort of morse code of boys who, on a good day, would stretch out over a mile and a half on a five-mile run. I would trail and hobble towards the rear. Deal was the coldest place I have ever lived, until I visited the Antarctic. My hands and feet were a mass of painful, itching, burning chilblains. Even had I been in less pain, and had more enthusiasm, I would not have progressed at sufficient speed to keep the front of the school in sight, and on occasions I would fall so far behind that I was reduced to trying to decipher the paper trail which had long since been dispersed by the wind.

If I could not keep up in the running I could, once I understood what was required, cope with the work. Far from saving me from the contempt of my fellows this merely added to it. I was seen as a swot, and for what I am sure I was, a child desperately seeking the teacher's attention and approval. In time I learnt, by concealing my abilities, to achieve the desired state of intellectual mediocrity which enabled me to steer between the twin disasters of enraging the teachers, and infuriating the pupils, but initially I was unaware of such life preservers and just did my best. Despite this conspiracy to deprive the teachers of the rewards of their efforts they maintained their efforts to make us perform. What we collectively lacked in assiduity was more than compensated for by the hours we studied, and the amounts of work we were set and tested upon. The style of the teaching was very much a product of the times. The aim of the whole thing was for us to obtain an adequate pass in the Common Entrance exams, so that we could follow our preordained destinies and go on to the public schools which would complete the production system, to maintain the sinews of Empire. There was no thought at my school that any boy would let the side down so badly that he might pursue a career in business or, even more unthinkably, in industry. Our attentions were directed single-mindedly to arts subjects and the classics. Whilst we were taught adequate amounts of maths, algebra and geometry, there was no provision for science at all. We were all expected to achieve adequate standards of Latin, and the brighter amongst us, which I was not considered, were allowed to study Greek as well. History concentrated on the British Empire, and ignored such minor matters as the Industrial Revolution or the effects of economics on national politics. Europe featured in our thinking only as a good place to have a war, and our foreign languages were restricted to French, taught by a large woman named Miss Meredith. In fact she had real gifts as a language teacher, but these were disregarded because, when goaded beyond endurance, her loss of temper was the most spectacular of all our teachers'. So large was she that she could easly have obliterated any of us by the simple act of sitting upon us, but when in full flood she would pick up the child she had set upon as her prime target in one hand and box his ears with the other.

The first weeks at the school are seared into my soul with a clarity and force that time has done nothing to erode, and even now, sixty years later, the memories produce a feeling of sickness and self-pity. Night after night I would sob myself to sleep; it was only under the blankets in the freezing dormitory that I felt any semblance of being safe and secure. The bullying had started almost immediately and I found no way to deal with it. Futile attempts to defend myself merely increased the numbers who would join in to beat me up, while attempts at flight were almost as useless since, except for the lavatories, there was no safe refuge. I got to know the lavatories extraordinarily well, but there were limits to the time that could be spent in them. The problems with food continued, although eventually the staff began to take pity on me, and ceased filling my plate so full. The rule that what was served was eaten remained inexorable, and many times I found myself a meal behind the routine, so that I was still struggling to get rid of breakfast as others were falling upon tea with ill-concealed delight. Meanwhile I sent increasingly desperate SOS calls in my letters, which seemed to be consigned to oblivion for all the response I received.

Not surprisingly perhaps, during my time at prep school I succeeded in catching every childish disease known to man. I progressed through measles, mumps and chicken pox, but achieved my *summa cum laude* with scarlet fever. All of these were interspersed with colds, coughs and incessant chilblains. As I caught each disease in turn I would pray, with the desperation of the small, that perhaps this one would carry me away to the 'Green Hill Far Away' where people were nice to each other and there was, I assumed, the sort of warmth and love that I had mistakenly believed to be commonplace in the world.

It was at this time, when my life seemed pointless and miserable, that I sought escape through a singularly unfortunate route. My extreme unhappiness was exacerbated by the difficulties I was having in forming relationships of any sort with my companions. I craved any kind of contact with other people, which would help to assuage my loneliness. I appealed for pity and compassion for my situation and when asked why I should be particularly more deserving than any of the other unhappy little boys, claimed that one of my aunts had died. From my point of view she might just as well have done so, for all the practical or emotional help that she offered. I don't think, however, I made a conscious decision to tell what was, after all, a blatant lie, at the time. I suspect that it was partly in order to gain sympathy and partly to try to find some sort of respectable reason for my continual crying. Whatever the explanation, for a very short space of time it achieved the desired effect of easing the pressures upon me. Like all such devices, however, time speedily reduced the impact of the loss of one superfluous aunt, and I found myself forced to knock off another of my family. Eventually reality caught up with even my desperate imagination. It wasn't as though the Black Death was raging around the world. The unlikeliness of my entire family hanging up their boots, one after the other, at fortnightly intervals, struck home to even the few amongst my fellows who were inclined to be compassionate. Unfortunately the very few amongst them who were more sensitive, and might eventually have been prepared to put up with me, were alienated by this device. It is possible that it was this experience which sewed the seeds of a quirk of my values which developed later. I learnt then, the hard way, that it would have been better to try to face up to trouble head on, than to try to avoid it. I am still not sure whether this is as helpful in reality as it is in theory. A certain amount of cowardice and evasion does sometimes change the nature of the problem, since time and providence have a curious way of resolving so many things. However, over the years I have learnt to place an excessive regard on those who do not flinch from facing up to the realities of situations, and have the courage to tackle them directly.

It was right at the end of my first term at Tormore that I received any response to my miseries from my mother. I had started to try to conceal the extent of my suffering in a pathetic attempt to avoid causing her pain, but this laudable idea soon collapsed under the pressures I felt, and my letters became more and more cataclysmic in tone. Curiously I felt no bitterness or reproach to my parents for their apparent abandonment of me. I accepted without demur that they had no alternative, although even then I did not feel that the effects on me had been helpful. My mother sought to deal with my desperation and despair by pointing out the temporary nature of my situation. Three years, she wrote, will go in a flash, and in any case I would soon settle down and make the good friends who would ensure that the sun shone on my existence each day. It was a woeful misunderstanding, both of my situation and of how a child of six or seven perceives life. As far as I was concerned it had taken every part of my inadequate reserves of optimism, courage and pragmatism to survive three months. They were then and remain still, in my mind, the longest three months of my life. I became convinced that there was no way I could survive three years; moreover I had come to the conclusion that I had no capacity for friendship – indeed I still wonder if I have. I seemed to be unable to attract friends, and the biblical pictures of David and Jonathan revealed an apparent aspect to comradeship which I was never to achieve.

Eventually I managed to team up with someone else, and in later life I have had many associations with others which could be described as friendships. However, I experienced so much loneliness and introspection, in the midst of groups of my peers, that some essential elements which constitute the ability for friendship were, I believe, damaged beyond repair. I enjoy the company of others, and am concerned for them. I go to ludicrous lengths to try to repay a favour, or return a kindness – but the ability to share my deep inner feelings, and reveal the eternally soft centre of my being, is one which I simply do not have. It seems to me that deep friendships involve a degree of mutual regard, tolerance and trust which are either missing from my genetic coding or were killed, in their embryonic stages, at school.

Later in life I was to realise that there were some real compensations for all this. In the first place, and possibly most enduringly, I took refuge in reading and books. The school had a good library, with a wide range of books. I had always enjoyed reading, and during our time at Holland Park had belonged to a children's lending library which fed my voracious needs. There were wonderful things being written for children at the time.

Such things as *The Children's Newspaper*, *The Boy's Own Paper*, and such creative formulations of a generation's values as Arthur Ransome's *Swallows and Amazons*, Percy Westerman, Sapper's *Bulldog Drummond*, W.C. Johns's *Biggles*, and Richmal Crompton's *Just William*. All of these authors produced at least a book a year, and there was still the whole range of Victorian and Edwardian children's books to be enjoyed, with magical writers such as Henty and his myriad historical novels, all featuring believable (to the credulous), youthful heroes. There were books by Bartimaeus, James Jeans, Baroness Orczy, and Dornford Yates which fired the imagination and facilitated escape into worlds totally remote from the slightly seedy realities of my own battle for existence at Tormore. Not surprisingly I had no enthusiasm or taste for books about schools, and particularly disliked books about boys' schools. So Billy Bunter and Grey-friars played little part in my life – there was no way I could picture myself gallantly taking on the school bully, and showing him for the craven coward that such writers always assured you he was. What I wanted was a broader canvas, showing the exciting world outside, far away from England's shores, where even the most inadequate Englishman (readily indentifiable as myself) was respected by 'lesser breeds' before the law. The life of the lonely district officer, miles up the jungle, holding impartial sway over the lives and destinies of thousands, seemed ideally suited to the child who could not establish himself in the complex society of a British prep school. This habit of escape through reading has never left me, and I react fiercely to attacks on populist books. Better by far, in my view, to read and re-read books which may lack literary merit, but fire the soul and fill the mind with pictures, excitement and stimulus, than to restrict one's diet to a small number of 'good' books a year.

The other beneficial side-effect was perhaps more unexpected, but I am sure stemmed also from my lack of social relationships with the other boys. Whilst I had learnt not to try to excel in class, for fear of my peer group's taunts, I knew that I could not fight them and the staff simultaneously. Morever, I spent much of my time alone, and did not have much in the way of extracurricular activities. I therefore applied myself to my studies in a way which was slightly unusual. I worked extremely hard. The curriculum demanded it, designed as it was to force the dumbest of us to an adequate level of achievement. In addition, in many of my lessons I found the same escape from the horrible alternatives of lack of social contact with my colleagues that reading offered me. I actually enjoyed many of the lessons, which was a considerable achievement, since the style of teaching involved much learning by rote, and woefully little attempt to broaden the mind, or inculcate the spirit of discovery in us.

I realise that it would be unjust and ungracious to blame the school for all of my difficulties and shortcomings. Tormore was no better, and little worse, than most schools of its type. To my horror, despite my own experiences there, my two cousins, James and Christopher Wilson, were consigned to the school, and it did not have the same traumatic effect on them. I have since met men who were there at the same time as I was, and while their recollections tally with mine, they do not carry the same agonising imprints that scar me. I have to conclude that perhaps it was a combination of circumstances which caused my suffering. Too much feminine and too little masculine influence in my early years, too pampered an existence in India, too little contact with British children, all linked with the curious nature of my father and mother's relationship, which seemed to preclude our ever operating as a family group. On top of this there was the fundamental changes that a child of little more than six was expected to adapt to in a very short period of time. A different country, the loss of contact with both my parents together with all the familiar figures of my childhood, and the sudden shock of institutional life.

The term, as terms do, eventually ground to a close and Christmas approached. I had still not come to accept the school, nor had I found a *modus vivendi*, except to grit my teeth and try to get through one day at a time. I had hung on to the thought of my holidays as a beacon which was at least visible in my time span of imagination, and had come to think that perhaps I could avoid ever coming back. At last we broke up and I was put on the school train, to be met in London by Rene. How badly I needed the retreat she was to provide for my holidays. She lived with her sister and brother-in-law and it was to their house that we travelled. Doris, Rene's sister, was married to an army musician who was, at that time, the musical director of the Queen's Bays. That splendid cavalry regiment was stationed at Shorncliffe Camp outside Folkestone. Doris and her husband, Joey, lived in the sort of married quarters which don't seem to have changed since the heyday of military barracks and garrisons in late Victorian times.

Joey was a superb musician, and in many ways a most unlikely military figure. He directed band after band, ending his career with the Royal Horseguards, and he was a key figure in cementing my love for military bands, and for music. He knew all the contemporary composers, such as Eric Coates, and had very considerable skills at arranging music, as well as playing a vast variety of instruments. In those days bandsmen were expected to be skilled in at least two types of instrument. Kneller Hall, the Royal Military School of Music, seemed to provide the raw material for practically every band of the day, including all the jazz bands. As well as being first rate at his job he was a kind man, and his household represented a scene of harmony and contentment which could hardly have provided a greater contrast to my school life. Rene and Doris were wonderfully motherly figures. The house was always spotless, and both of them were superb cooks of the Mrs Becton type. It seemed to me that they were determined to make up for all the meals I had missed with the difficulties over the school food, which I described to them with feeling, if not with total impartiality. I do not know what arrangement my parents had come to with them all, but money was not plentiful in the household, and I imagine my board and lodging must have helped the family finances. The Director of Music occupied a curious position in the military hierarchy – somewhere between the socially conscious and secure Cavalry Officers, and the close-knit professional *camaraderie* of the Warrant Officers and Sergeants. The regiment was converting, with considerable reluctance, to mechanisation, but there was no doubt that the internal combustion engine represented to every member of the regime, from trooper to colonel, an abandonment of all that constituted the flower of the Army. It was unlikely that there would ever be another Charge of the Light Brigade. During my summer holidays the band spent a good deal of time on tour, playing for a fee in the same sort of bandstands which I had so enjoyed in Teignmouth, and of course Joey was with them. I saw less of him that I expected, for his band, even when at the barracks, was frequently playing in the evenings, and of course the days were filled with musical practice to keep up the repertoire, as well as incessant parades, drills and inspections.

As far as my adored grandparents were concerned, they evinced no interest in my well-being. My father's parents were living in Nice (then a place where one could maintain British standards of life quite cheaply), on their Indian Army pension. My mother's parents were still at Teignmouth. It was apparent that while I was acceptable to them as an undetachable appendage to my mother, grandparently affection could not extend to dealing with me on my own, or even if accompanied by Rene. There may well have been reasons for this which I didn't comprehend. My grandfather's health was failing, and he was increasingly chair-bound, whilst my grandmother, apart from exacting family homage from time to time, seemed self-sufficient and inward-looking. My other aunts and uncles, with the exception of Roy, were still in India. Roy was the brother who had 'made good'. Leaving the Army after the war he first of all trained as a wine buyer. Family legend has it that the job had been destined for my father who would, I am sure, have loved such a career, but was deprived of his chance by some obscure sleight-of-hand. Roy soon tired of the wine business, but carried with him throughout his life an awesome knowledge and appreciation of wine, from which, in later years, I was to learn much. He then married Ida, the daughter of Sir Frederic Hiam. For many years I considered her to be the epitome of female beauty and elegant dressing. Sir Frederic was a rich and progressive East Anglian farmer, and he introduced Roy into the farming world, where he prospered. Roy and Ida had four children of their own, and it is understandable that they did not volunteer to undertake the responsibility for another. The more particularly since Ida enjoyed a distant relationship with our side of the family, who I suspect she thought below her, while for our own part, revelling in our ancestry, we believed ourselves to be the superiors of the Hiams.

I was happy with Rene, who was loving and indulgent, and thrilled with my curious and unusual view of army life, but all these things re-emphasised the differences between me and the other boys. During the years I stayed with them Doris and Joey had a son, who increasingly provided companionship and a playmate during the holidays, even though he was some years younger than I was. Over a period of time I got to know, albeit somewhat superficially, the haunts of the Army in Southern England, as Doris and Joey moved from Shorncliffe to Tidworth, on to Aldershot, and then eventually to London, where they bought a house at East Molesey. This house was a brilliant logistical choice for Joey, who was on duty alternately at Windsor and at the Horseguards' barracks, in London. It must have been pleasant for Rene and Doris too, not to be living in army quarters for a change. I remember surprisingly little of these happy interludes – except strongly that they were so. It seems a poor return for all the kindness shown to me by Rene's extended family that my memory of the details of my life with them is so poor. I can only think that these happy memories were obliterated by the far stronger impressions of despair which were a constant in my life at that time.

In contrast to the snail-like progress of the autumn term the Christmas holidays seemed to fly past in a flash. By then it was apparent that there was to be no relief of Mafeking in my case, and that I was destined to return to the school. I can only guess at the reasons. Perhaps there were administrative difficulties involved in finding somewhere else, or possibly my parents were convinced that growing up involved learning how to cope with the worst that life could bring. I prepared myself suitably for the ordeal by starting to cry and sob at least two days before the off, and by the time I was forced on to the school train I had exhausted myself, and everyone around me. Rene tried in vain to cheer me up by preparing my favourite treats, but the contrast merely caused greater anguish and my gullet closed contemporaneously with the onset of my howls. Once on the train the boys seemed no more friendly and were no more willing to accept me as a member of the flock. There were, however, a number of new boys cringing and sniffling in their own miseries, who deflected some of the attention away from me. I wish I could claim to have had the courage to try to cheer them up – apart from anything else I badly needed to address my attentions outside my own miseries, but cowardice prevailed and I left them to cope as best they could.

One boy, however, was to save my sanity, and I owe him an everlasting debt of gratitude. Romaine Hervey was a clergyman's son. At the time I think his father was the Chaplain at Bryanston School. Romaine was accustomed to the institutional peculiarities of boys' schools, and appeared unmoved by the horrors that had so speedily eroded my own confidence. He has one of the best minds I have ever come across, and at Tormore was little short of brilliant, winning a scholarship to Winchester with apparent ease, to the awe of teachers and pupils alike. From my point of view, he had other inestimable gifts. He was almost as poor at sport as I was, but unlike me did not seem to think that this inability would totally blight his life. He was an equally voracious reader, and he had a fascination for science and technology. Those are, perhaps, rather grand words to describe the sort of areas of interest that we pursued together, but it was our joint experimentation and interest that led to my becoming fascinated by how things worked. Together we learnt the rudiments of electricity and wireless – making our own Crystal set. We studied simple mechanical devices, and we were forever planning great and improbable projects. The school thought him almost as great an oddball as they thought me. It was at least as much our rejection by the others as our attraction to each other which threw us together. We must have made an incongruous team. Romaine was speedily nicknamed 'The Professor', and consulted on any and every intellectual query from the sixth form down. I hung on to his coat tails, struggling to keep up with his thinking, and acting rather in the role of the unfortunate Dr Watson, to his Sherlock Holmes. At least I did not feel so totally alone, and my friendship with Romaine enabled me to survive, and even to begin to regain some of my self-respect. My self-confidence was to take a much longer time to revive, and it was only when I left Tormore that I would begin to have any renewed belief in my worth as an individual, or in my ability to achieve anything. But at least, for my remaining years at the school, I never again felt totally alone.

4 Dreadnought

In order to make the rest of my time at Tormore bearable I sought escape in the only way which seemed to be open to me, and began to spend more and more of my time in the realms of my imagination. Although nominally still a member of the school, the inner core of my being was utterly involved in my imaginary world, which came to be more and more real to me. While, thankfully, I have forgotten many of the details of the remainder of my time at my prep school, there were occasional happy times. Sunday evenings were spent with the headmaster's wife in her drawing room. Clad in our pyjamas and thick woollen dressing gowns (a survival necessity in Deal), we would sit on the floor whilst she read to us. This combined my love of books with the illusion of what I thought 'real' families probably did in the evenings, and gave me a comforting feeling of warmth and normality. In fact Sundays were relatively good days from every point of view. The food was better for a start. A rasher of bacon was served with breakfast, and lunch was some form of roast meat. The menu was totally fixed by the days of the week, and while occasional lack of availability produced some variety, there was no attempt to extend this rigid planning system beyond a seven-day horizon. After lunch we formed a long crocodile and went for a long walk. In winter we were muffled to the eyebrows with scarves, caps, gloves and heavy overcoats. Romaine and I invariably walked together, and spent our time happily designing improbable machines which would doubtless have given Heath Robinson a heart attack.

I had a good treble singing voice, and enjoyed singing, so

found myself in the school choir. I cannot claim that this increased my prestige in the eyes of my fellows. It was added to the list of my eccentricities, which inexorably added to their clearly defined view of my wimpishness. For me, however, that was a small price to pay for the pleasure of belting out hymns and psalms. Added to this was the certain knowledge that for an hour or so there was no prospect of being bullied.

There were other good times too. In summer the usual treat for some very special event, such as Empire Day or the King's birthday, was to give us a half-day holiday, and a picnic. There must have been about sixty of us, and we would all be loaded into a charabanc, together with vast baskets full of doorstep sandwiches, and unimaginable treats such as salad. Sometimes we were taken to the seaside, but more often to some favourite spot inland. Nowadays it would not be easy to find an accessible spot in the countryside in Kent for seventy people to picnic, play games and collect butterflies or wild flowers. But then there seemed to be no shortage of different places, all within twenty miles or so of the school. I recall those balmy sunny days with which retrospective memory blesses those times – but, above all else, I remember the sheer beauty of the Kentish countryside. Meadows ablaze with wild flowers, ancient lichen-covered trees, and pathways through woods which were still a wonderland of indigenous hardwoods. In one particular spot, near Betteshanger (which is now thought of more as a colliery than as a idyll of rural beauty), there was a tree of such magnificent spread that the whole school could sit under its protective arms to munch their ant-ridden packed lunches. Not that preparations for these excursions ever involved packing our meals individually. There was an arithmetical accuracy about the quantities that we brought with us, at least as much to ensure 'fair shares' as for reasons of economy, and all our food was distributed on the spot. All the jam sandwiches arrived in one mighty, jam-sodden, wasp-attracting, bee-buzzing hamper, while the breakfast sausage ones, which seemed to be more favoured by ants and midges, arrived in another. I had retained my affection for eating outdoors from my days in India, but while there was the same feeling of ritual to the preparations for such events, the equipment involved lacked the style and quality to which I still aspire.

These were not the only happy moments. In keeping with my total lack of skill, and hence enthusiasm, for ball games, there was never the smallest possibility that I would play cricket for the school. It was good news from every point of view. In the first place I was less equipped than most to withstand the obloquy that fell on the head of any player who let the side down. More happily, however, the non-playing members of the school were required to watch the team slugging out their diminutive test match with our deadly rivals. This gave us a whole afternoon and evening of peace. We lay on our rugs around the boundaries of the field and, apart from watching the clouds sail by, the occasional dragonfly or, on one unique occasion, an aeroplane passing overhead, had only one duty. We listened to the occasional clunk of bat actually contacting ball, and were required sportingly to give a desultory clap to particular prowess shown by either side. Fortunately for me this was invariably triggered by some happy enthusiast among us who hadn't made it to the first eleven. I was able to clap, and even utter the odd word of encouragement, without ever observing or understanding the game. Any performing seal would have been proud of my facility to clap and read simultaneously. A trick, I would claim, at least as difficult as clapping with a ball on one's nose.

Books (which were large items to carry around before the days of paperbacks) accompanied me everywhere, except to meal times. Here even my ingenuity had not found a way of smuggling one in, withouth the fear of being required to eat it, on discovery. Most of the time the teachers expected to see us carrying a book or two. But there were occasions, such as playing football, where this cover story really didn't 'fly'. To me the lazy and infrequent sound of a cricket ball being hit (backed by the weird honking cries of 'Over', or 'Howzat!') still represents the almost perfect background to a good read.

Meanwhile I began to progress through the multiplicity of forms, and variants of forms, which most small schools seem to believe necessary. With the knowledge I now have of school finances, I realise that, with the small number of boys, the school must have been struggling to keep going. Whatever concern I may harbour about the sensitivity of the school, its size – and economic necessity – certainly produced an academic performance from us all. I realise now that the size of classes was such that we enjoyed – or, more accurately, endured – a staff-to-pupil ratio which it would have needed almost sub-human thickness to withstand.

I enjoyed all my work except Latin, and that fact was to have a strong bearing on my choice of career. The irony is that as I have become more interested and involved in the concept of Europe as a single force, I have been grateful for what little Latin I did learn. Part of my difficulties stemmed, I think, from the fact that it was never represented as a language at all, nor was I told what tremendous use it could be in the learning of languages, or in an understanding of one's own. In those days, if you dared to ask why it was necessary to spend such long hours with *Kennedy's Latin Primer* (invariably, with sparklingly original wit, graffitied into *Kennedy's Eating Primer*), you were told it was to 'improve the mind'. Whether it did or not, Latin was still a compulsory subject for the Common Entrance. However, although Latin was compulsory also for the entrance exam to the Royal Navy, the Royal Naval College at Dartmouth had the (then unique) distinction of being the only public school I could find where the hated subject could be dropped once one had entered its portals and I made up my mind to go there.

In every other subject, despite my deplorable writing, I prospered and enjoyed the feeling of progress. I do not recollect being regarded as bright (except by my association with Romaine) but I managed to survive in the top quarter or so of each class, or subject – occasionally being carried away with myself and coming out top in something or other. Since such conduct was the immediate trigger for a mass beating-up by the dum-dums who, for their own deep psychological needs, were the bullies of the school, I continued to try to avoid attracting attention in that way.

In what was considered, by boys and masters alike, the most

important area of our existence – the pursuit of excellence in sport – I continued to show my unique inability to perform. One of the mysteries of my life was whether the headmaster really achieved the almost orgasmic delights he appeared to show when any of our school teams beat any other school at anything at all. Certainly the great man's normally slightly cold mien would soften, and smiles and chuckles of pleasure would emerge, as his tiny champions struggled to vanquish Betteshanger, or Dover College Junior School. Watching these gladiatorial combats and knocking ourselves out in enthusiastic support was an absolute requirement, and so weekend after weekend would find Romaine and I sitting, muffled to the ears, by the sports field. We stood, allegedly cheering our lot on, and trying to look as though we cared what was happening, but in reality earnestly engaged in designing the first schoolboy-sized airship or sometimes, with an ironic premonition of our mutual futures, a diving bell, or some other Jules Verne type underwater machine.

As time passed, and I progressed painfully to the higher levels of the school, the headmaster began an endless (unsuccessful) quest to find some form of sport at which I could represent the school. He plainly believed it would be good for my character and, perhaps more to the point, would provide an adequate justification for the fees which were being paid for my purgatory. However, the possibility of transmogrifying a sporting 'sow's ear' into some sort of purse (even if a silk one lay beyond his or my potential), was plainly too much to hope for. Eventually, with the perversity of fate which seemed to dog the whole of my existence at Tormore, he stumbled on the idea of making me play as goalkeeper for our various soccer teams. It was, from my point of view, a complete disaster. The nature of the goalkeeper's existence was rather different from the heroic exploits of those such as Gordon Banks. In the first place we seemed to play only on windswept, frozen and frosted fields, where the choice had to be made between immobility from wearing enough clothing to avoid freezing to death, or immobility due to cold. The latter alternative lay in some hope that there would be enough action around for me to avoid becoming encased in ice, like one of those

Siberian dinosaurs. I, and my chilblains, opted unhesitatingly for the Michelin Man approach which, of course, added to my already apparent ineptitude and lack of enthusiasm. The other problem was that failure to perform as the last line of defence was both immediately apparent, and disastrous in its implications. I do not know whether I was more frightened of stopping the ball and being hurt, or letting it through and being the unhappy object of derision and howls of fury and resentment from the rest of the school. Unlike Romaine and I, they all seemed to share the headmaster's view that competitive success against the other East Kent boys' schools was of far more importance than Adolf Hitler's unstoppable progress in Germany.

Poor headmaster. He was caught between choices and desires of his own making. They ensured that there was no way in which he could win, and in the event he lost both in his attempts to provide glory for the school and achievement for me. All that remains for all his efforts and trust is an improbable photograph of a thin (the food), nervous (the role), and unhappy (the norm for my existence) child in the back row of a photograph of the school for 1935. It was the sort of school where photographs of every sort of team that had existed since its inception were displayed in its halls and classrooms. This testimony to frailty, and wasted human effort, hung there until finally the school collapsed under its own inadequacies, and was subsumed into one of its much reviled rivals.

Preparatory school found me unprepared for many areas of real life. Despite the fact that the oldest boy was under thirteen years old, and that practically all of us were pre-pubescent, sexual curiosity was rife, indeed almost obsessive. Here my absence of parental guidance, and total isolation from elders or brothers who could have enlightened me, even belatedly, about the curious habits pursued by my peers proved to be a real problem. For some reason ignorance of simple biological facts in boys, youths or men, is taken by others of the male sex to betoken a lack of manhood, which I suppose in strict factual terms it does indeed indicate. Moreover, in the 1930s this was not an area where even my voracious reading was likely to enlighten me. Most of the books I was reading treated the idea of romantic attachments to the other sex as a distraction from the delights of duty, or of suffering incredible privations for King and Country. Even when affairs of the heart did obtrude the climax appeared to be a kiss on the lips. It was, I fondly imagined, this incredibly difficult transition from a graze on the cheek to full osculation which all the fuss was about, and at the time I confess I found it all very difficult to understand. The traditions of British schools, the Empire, and most of the books from which I derived my values and beliefs, taught that comradeship and manly affection between British gentlemen was infinitely to be preferred to 'dallying' or 'poodle faking' with the other sex, who were there, primarily, to provide us with something fearlessly to protect.

At Tormore these beliefs were manifest in frenzies of mutual or solitary masturbation. For those whose physical development had progressed far enough, the evening preparatory periods were spent playing with themselves, or even each other, under the tables at which we sat. Is it really possible that the invigilating masters were unaware of the throbbing of all those tiny penises? Or did they turn a Nelsonian blind eye, born of the conviction that such early initiations would bring out the 'right stuff' in future district officers in remote parts of the Empire? Whatever the attitude of the school, yet again my own inadequacies were all too apparent. I entered puberty late, singing as a treble in the choir at Dartmouth until I was nearly fifteen and, despite heroic and continued efforts to emulate the others, I was not physically equipped so to do. Since there was no one I could discuss this peculiarly personal problem with, and Romaine seemed uninterested in, and impervious to the continuous sexual circus going on around us, I was forced to the conclusion that yet again the fates had decreed that I should be different. Later this so-easily-implanted doubt proved to be a major concern for me, and this lack of experience, coupled with the loneliness of my unbringing, were factors in delaying the onset of my maturity. Sometimes I still wonder, in fact, when I *am* going to grow up, although I hope I have at least managed to overcome some of the sexual hang-ups over the years! I still look with awe at the social ease and accomplishments of others, and feel that my own view of the world is slightly infantile. Delayed development does, however, have tremendous compensations in later life, for I take an almost continuous childlike delight in new experiences and knowledge, which provide a crispness to life for which I feel deeply grateful. I cannot imagine boredom, or the possibility of even beginning to fathom enough of the depths of existence, and I believe that the very peculiar circumstances of my childhood have much to do with this.

During my time at Tormore my parents were to return to England on only two occasions. I cannot remember the moment when I first saw them again after our long, and to me, cruel separation. I do know that visiting me was not the first thing they did on their arrival in England. There was no nonsense of my being collected from school to meet the P & O liner on which they arrived. They stopped off in London to set up their opulent camp in their chosen domicile, before coming down to the school to see how I was. But this time I had overcome the initial horrors of my introduction and had finally managed to find some way of at least surviving, day by day. I had overcome, to a considerable degree, my habit of breaking into tears of self-pity, since I had learnt that such actions only increased my isolation and the pressures upon me. I was painfully shy and totally unsure of myself, as well as underweight and nervous. I was a pretty unhappy person. From the moment I arrived at Tormore until leaving and joining Dartmouth, I cannot recollect feeling any of that security which is the essential backdrop to contentment and enjoyment. Surely these cannot be accurate memories? It would not be possible for a child of that age to be continously miserable for five years, and there must have been some light to match the shade which I can recall so easily. Moreover I am lucky enough to have a pronounced sense of humour, and of the ridiculous, which must already have been present, at least in embryo, at that time. Somewhere along the path I have learnt to laugh at troubles and crises, a facility which has often proved to be a life-belt of preservation.

It must have been at this time that the seeds were sown which led to my joining the Royal Navy. As so often with decisions regarding one's personal life, the whole process was untidy and an improbable one. Some of the factors which influenced me were of a total lack of consequence in real terms, but they loomed large at the time. Originally I had begun to nurture a wish to become a lawyer. I envisaged myself proceeding through a preordained path from Tormore, via public school and university. Public school, in my imagination, seemed likely to be Tormore with knobs on, and the only real hope I saw ahead was to get over the 'growing up' bit as quickly as possible and emerge somewhere where being different was not an accountable sin.

I had produced these ideas when my parents, during our brief time together in London, asked me whether I knew what I wanted to do, and was speedily disabused of these simple dreams. It was explained to me that lawyers were not likely to be self-supporting until their mid-twenties, and that there was no way in which I could expect to be a burden on my family until that age. At this distance it is hard to say whether that really was the message that was sent out, but it was certainly the message that I received. In my childish way, therefore, I started looking, with an increasing feeling of urgency, at ways in which I could achieve self-sufficiency at an early age. There were, of course, other equally improbable strands in my unlikely decision-making process.

My constant retreats into the world of boys' books had clearly shown that almost alone of all careers, the Navy allowed (indeed expected) boys to be men. I realised, of course, that it was no longer possible to become a midshipman at sea at the age of twelve; in charge of a picket boat (manned by splendid 'salts of the earth' called Nobby and Whitey), fearlessly tackling pirates in the Arabian Gulf. But I did know that I could become a naval cadet at the age of thirteen (provided I could pass the exam), that I could give up attempting to learn the hated Latin and begin to study the stuff of life, like seamanship and engineering.

If I was to opt for such a choice, time was not on my side – even by the more leisurely, time-expanded perspectives of the young, in which a week was a long time, and a month eternity. The entrance exam for Dartmouth, where success was rewarded with a cadetship, was a special one, and the cramming we were already involved in for Common Entrance would not do. Special studies were considered necessary and specialist teachers who 'force fed' candidates, almost to the stage where the papers one took were free of surprises. Moreover, competition was intense. Many hundreds applied for the fifty or so available places each term and then – even if you passed the exam – the final selection was by interview. There were the most horrific rumours about this procedure, which it was almost impossible to prepare for. Although Tormore boasted a gold-lettered clutch of successful entrants to Dartmouth Royal Naval College it was not considered as a 'feeder' school, and the last successful entrant from our school had been well before my time.

My family contained no serving member of the Navy, although my adored grandfather had served briefly aboard the *Britannia* – leaving in circumstances which were shrouded in mystery before passing out as a midshipman. It was only through recent researches that I have discovered that Bones had abandoned his naval career because of his lack of intellectual accomplishment rather than for some heinous sin. I suggested to my parents the Navy might be a suitable alternative career and found, to my surprise, that it was not immediately welcomed as the panacea for their financial problems that I expected. Dartmouth was a considerably cheaper form of education than a public school and, although fees of £50 a term were levied, they were massively subsidised by the Admiralty. Moreover, when one emerged as a midshipman, at the ripe old age of seventeen, one was paid at the magnificent rate of five shillings a day. Since the five shillings was in addition to providing a roof, or more accurately a desk, over one's head, and enough food to sink a battleship, one could reasonably claim to be self-sufficient from then on.

I don't know why this startling solution to what I saw as the family's problems didn't go down well. Maybe my father thought it was a 'yah, boo, sucks' gesture to his professed unwillingness to support me in the career of my choice. Or maybe my mother, having seen my total inability to adjust to the enforced group living of a boys' school, feared for my life if I were to try for such a manly occupation. Be that as it may, my idea caused a massive reaction. Uncles and aunts were consulted, advice was sought, I was interrogated, and other alternatives were trailed before me. Not, it is true, very attractive alternatives to an eleven-year-old boy. Gentlemen, of which I was supposed to be one, were expected to follow a very limited range of acceptable careers, in my family. By some quirk of fate, despite all the hullabaloo, the Navy was within that narrow range of choice, which really boiled down to the professions (excluding accountancy, for which none of us were considered bright enough), the Church, the armed services and the home or overseas civil services. Anything else was considered eccentric and downmarket – a direction in which no Wilson or Harvey-Jones would deliberately head.

For once (and, with hindsight, to my considerable surprise) the opposition hardened what had been a tentative idea into a matter of conviction. The more the elders leant on me, the more fixed and obsessive I became in my determination to plough the seas. Since I have the greatest difficulty now in reconstructing my true reasons for this unlikely choice of future career (one, I should hasten to say, which I have never regretted at any time), I find it impossible to believe that my stubbornness was based on logic. Nor could my decision be claimed to be based on facts. It was, I believe, an emotional amalgam of many things. A sort of Mrs Beeton's cake recipe, with a dash of escape from school, a cupful of adventure and *Boy's Own Paper* romance, a tablespoon of my love for my grandfather, and an ounce or so of my reaction to the belief that my family needed my contribution to their finances.

Curiously, at Tormore the decision that I wanted to pursue a 'man's' career resulted in an easing of the pressures upon me. Probably it had more to do with the fact that there were other, more defenceless, targets to torment; or perhaps it was due to the fact that my peer group had reached the age at which they were the bullies themselves. In the first place I, as the only candidate for the Navy's entrance exam, began to receive individual tuition. This was a liberation in itself, for I was no longer afraid of over-achievement – if anything, quite the reverse. The pressures 'not to let the school down' began to build up in earnest. I worked with a will and, for the first time, with a goal which was self-evidently of my own choosing – no matter how ill advised it may have been. In addition, the world of my imagination took a whole new road. To this day I read every book I can lay my hands on about the sea and ships. I bless C.S. Forester, and his successors, and I never tire of reading about sailors and their lives, whether it be of past or present. Although so much of my time was spent cramming, I spent every spare moment reading and re-reading every book I could find that had anything to do with the sea, not only boys' novels, but also the more readable tomes on naval history. I lived continuously for tomorrow and, in consequence, today became more bearable and yesterday was pushed behind me. I still have the same propensity. It is always what lies ahead that fires me, although over the years, and with my wife Betty's influence, I have slowly accustomed myself to deriving the maximum from each event as I live it.

During my holidays I was sent to the crammers in London which were the 'predicting machine' for the entrance exam. For some procedural or bureaucratic reason, the exams were always of exactly the same type. Moreover, the exam setters seemed to be lacking in imagination for the same questions emerged over a five- or six-year cycle. Whatever the reason for this, it gave those who were especially prepared for the exam an unbelievable advantage.

The year 1937 was to be a turning point for me. A year in which everything seemed to happen. My parents were due home for the Coronation of George VI and I was to be allowed out of school for the whole of the Coronation week. I was also to sit my entrance exam for the Navy and be accepted for a cadetship. The exam itself was a totally new experience for me, in a number of ways. The setting, near Russell Square, was intimidating in the extreme and I can recall the apparently enormous size of the hall and the discipline of the proceedings. The cramming to which I had been subjected proved worth every penny, for the questions themselves were almost venally close to the predictions which I had been given. There was surprisingly little of a creative or analytical nature in the questions, which seemed more designed to test our degree of application to the syllabus and inherent ability to memorise, than our ability to apply logic. As I was later to learn, the Navy did nothing without reason, even though that reason may have originated in a different period and for a different cause. I suspected then, and believe now, that the aim of the whole process was to ensure the highest average standard of the lower echelons, and that there was a well-founded belief that the odd outstanding character would emerge. Little attempt was made then, or at Dartmouth, to foster individuality and nonconformity was not only frowned upon, it was eradicated – only to arise again, phoenix-like, at later stages in our careers. The design of the entrance exam was aimed, with the same single-minded concentration, on the ultimate objective – to ensure that the Navy was provided with the right sort of committed, hard-working, decent, averagely intelligent raw material to be moulded and formed as required.

The other new experience which the exams brought me was an introduction to commercial behaviour that made a great impression on me at the time and which I have never ceased to admire in later life. Lunch, in the area of Russell Square, and in the time provided in the break between papers, was not an easy logistical problem. It was, therefore, a master stroke by Gieves, the Naval Tailors, to take over the Russell Hotel, as it represented almost the only 'watering hole' within reach. Not only did they provide the lunch but at the same time they also took the opportunity to take the orders for the entire outfit which was needed if we were to pass the exam, and provided the tailors to measure us up on the spot, almost over lunch.

My mother had come over from India well before the Coronation proceedings, in order to see me through the exam which was to be the gateway to my improbable career. She was a deeply loving woman, who I am sure wanted the best for her son. It would have taken a parent of superhuman inviolability to resist the moral pressure to order the necessary uniforms, shirts, socks, underwear and sports wear that would crown their offspring's hoped-for success. Gieves made it quite clear that, in the unlikely eventuality of failure, the order would be cancelled. In any event, what doubtful parent or inwardly shaking candidate could allow of such a possibility? What, commercially speaking, was even more insidious was that it was made apparent that, when one joined the Navy, one started, so to speak, bare to the buff. Even if it was allowed that we might have somehow struggled so far with our own underwear and swimming costumes, it was explained that for the Navy's part they wanted no truck with such rubbish. We were outfitted totally anew as though we had been picked up as castaways wearing only a tattered pair of trousers. In order, so it was explained to us, to ease our problems, Gieves also opened an account in our youthful names. It was the precursor of what is now known as a budget account and, from the first moment I received any pay from the Navy to almost the day I left, my monthly payment to Gieves was always a prior charge. As a businessman now I admire the technique, but it also saved most of us from that most hideous of sins, being different. In only two cases in our term did parents, made of sterner stuff than most, insist on their commercial right to buy their son's outfits at tailors and outfitters of their choosing, rather than submit to the insidious blackmail of the Russell Hotel lunch.

It may be that the resultant kit was of better quality than Gieves's – it was certainly cheaper – but for the cadets concerned the resultant difference was purgatory. Even though boys of that age come in every shape and size, the Gieves uniform was what it said – uniform. We looked externally, and right down to our bare bodies (in many cases bare to the extent of a marked lack of body hair), as similar as any row of black and gold Mini cars. But in our term we had the misfortune of these two odd-balls not dressed by Gieves. It was a source of shame to us all. We would collectively surround the two miscreants, and endeavour to shelter them from the utterly critical views of the other cadets, and even more especially of the Officers and Masters. Gieves's opportunism, and my mother's determination to show confidence and support, saved me from this fate, even though I was, in practical terms, to pay for the decision for some twenty years thereafter!

If the exam was predictable, the interview was not. Not only had I never experienced an interview, but neither my school nor my family seemed to be able to offer any first-hand advice at all. I therefore went in cold, so to speak. In fact so 'cold' was I, that I was shivering with fear and apprehension. I imagine that it is very few twelve-year-olds, and possibly pretty odious ones at that, who can project self-assurance at an interview. However, I added to these problems by my own chronic shyness and perpetual self-doubt and denigration. Almost the only thing I had going for me was my encyclopaedic knowledge of Percy Westerman and his ilk, but even there I wasn't too confident that the elderly and terrifying members of the board appreciated the finer points of such writers for the young. Unlike the exam, which was corporatist, the interview was very definitely individualistic. We were ushered into a waiting room, handed pen and paper, and invited to write an essay. I brightened up a bit at that as I rather fancied myself as an essay writer but I had not bargained for the subject. I was asked to comment on Dr Johnson's much-quoted aphorism 'Patriotism is the last refuge of a scoundrel'. Aphorism it may be, but I didn't understand it then – and I don't understand it now. The meagre amount of courage I had managed to draw up disappeared through my diminutive shoes as I wrote three pages of unadulterated waffle, explaining what a splendid thing patriotism was and what scoundrelly things scoundrels were. As though that weren't bad enough, I was then made to wait outside the interview-room door, rather as I had, in the past, waited outside the headmaster's study – and with the same overriding lack of enthusiasm.

Eventually the door opened and a white-faced twelve-year-old shot out, as though propelled by a catapult, and dashed past me without giving me a chance to make any sort of enquiry. I waited until I heard a very unreassuring bellow, in a voice accustomed to carrying to the foretop against a force nine gale, commanding me to come in. I was in a sort of daze from then on. The interviewing board consisted of three Godlike individuals, and the head member, to my juvenile eye, seemed to be encased in gold braid from head to toe. I waited until asked to sit, and was mercifully invited to do so before my legs gave way altogether. The only good thing, in retrospect, was that I was far too frightened to attempt to lie or bullshit. I was convinced that these omniscient individuals knew, or would find out, everything about me and so I replied in the best way I could to a bewildering series of questions. Predictably there were questions about my parents (not easy to describe in a sentence), about my sporting achievements (a sentence was too long for this one), and my reasons for wanting to join the Royal Navy. To my amazement the idea that I was looking for a life of adventure, and service to my country, didn't evince the cynicism and hoarse laughs it would now. In fact I was made to feel that those were the most natural and manly aims, which any normal Englishman would both understand and wish to emulate. I didn't feel I'd got many marks for my father's curious occupation, and I was sure my honesty at my sporting ineptitudes was a major minus. However, it was in the general knowledge part of the interview that I really felt I'd blown it.

I still cannot understand the necessity for a putative naval cadet to be able to discern the difference between an African and an Indian elephant. I suppose if one's navigation is very seriously out (as I have to admit that mine was to be from time to time), the ability to discover one's whereabouts by the characteristics of the flora and fauna could be helpful. Suffice it to say that, despite being the only candidate or member of the interviewing board actually to have ridden an elephant of his own, I got them the wrong way round. I went through the interview in a sort of haze and, unlike the conventional wisdom that these things are all over in a flash, my flash seemed to go on forever. When it was eventually over, I staggered out to be greeted and revived by my mother. I am convinced that her presence was the only thing that saved me from throwing myself under a bus. To my utter amazement I passed both the interview and the exam, going in to Dartmouth at about number twenty out of fifty-six in our term.

All of this was over before my father and Bahadur came to join us for the Coronation, and that summer was a magical interlude. The worst was behind me, there was no more swotting to do, and the end of hated Tormore was in sight. My name was painted in gold as another entry on the pitifully short list of naval cadetships; even the limited remaining time at school was bearable. I don't know whether the records show it to have been an exceptional summer, but my memory certainly has it as such. My parents were not due to return to India until the autumn, and I had the whole summer holiday to look forward to.

As well as the Coronation itself, there was, for an embryo naval person, an even more exciting event – the Naval Review. At some time in India my parents had provided hospitality to Bruce Fraser, who eventually became First Sea Lord, but was at that time commanding one of the Navy's four aircraft carriers. He invited us all to join him for the review as his guests, and I was almost sick with the excitement and anticipation. It gripped my imagination in a way that nothing else could have done, and was the most marvellous experience. It was hard for the mind to encompass the thought that, in addition to the apparently interminable lines of sparkling ships off Spithead, there were still many other ships of the Royal Navy going about their business in the naval commands which then ringed the globe and served the Seven Seas.

The ships, as befitted a peacetime Navy, were immaculate, even those which had been brought out from reserve for the occasion. They seemed to stretch for ever, for these were the last days when the ships of the Royal Navy outnumbered those of the next two largest nations' fleets put together. A smart ship is a refined sensual pleasure. Even though warships are designed for functional rather than artistic purposes there is an intrinsic beauty in well-engineered design which speaks for itself. More-over, in those days when showing the flag and ceremonial duties were considered important parts of the Navy's function, ships still had teak decks, holystoned to a gleaming white, and brassware was buffed and polished till it shone like gold.

The Naval Review was the last time so many ships were gathered together in one place. The Royal Navy was supplemented on this occasion by warships of every nationality, which had come to pay their respects to the new king. To a boy of thirteen there could have been no more heart-swelling experience, and no greater confirmation of the correctness of my childish decision to pursue a naval career. The whole thing breathed power, organisation and patriotism. Percy Westerman's world of adventure lay only just over the horizon. I could not wait to join up at Dartmouth, and was totally convinced about my good fortune at having the opportunity to serve in such a plainly unvanquishable force. So mighty and powerful did they look that it was impossible to envisage (leaving aside the doubtful taste of so doing) one of those men-of-war sinking ignominiously below the waves.

Before starting at Dartmouth, however, there was another most important experience awaiting me. For some weird reason, which I never quite understood, it had been decided that we would all spend my summer holidays in France, in Brittany. For almost the first, and sadly the last time, I was able to spend a long period in the embrace of an entire family. Those six weeks of holiday seem, in the concertina of time which occurs with memory, to last as long as the whole of my time at Tormore. Such was the intensity of experience and my rediscovered ability to enjoy new sensations that, over forty years later, I could still retrace our steps and adventures. It was the last time that Bahadur and I were to be together and the disparity of our ages had been eroded by our being at the opposite ends of the teenage spectrum. Our closeness may also have been increased by his awareness that I had actually chosen my career and calling – an opportunity denied to him, whose destiny had been preordained. We enjoyed being together and began to share confidences, as well as our guesses about what our parents would come up with next. He felt then just like the brother I had never known, a feeling which I have not been able to recapture since. That year was, in every way, the beginning of my rebirth. It was almost as though I had been in a deep frozen state of suspended animation during my prep school years, and that wonderful summer was the resuscitation and the commencement of growth again.

The reasons why I took so happily to life at Dartmouth still elude me. On the face of it I should have had even greater difficulty coping with the ferocious discipline and multitudinous rules and restrictions than I had experienced when trying to settle in with my peers at Tormore. The reality was that the whole group of us was equally uncertain in this environment. Nothing that we had experienced before prepared us in any way for Dartmouth, with its curious combination of public-school life together with the tradition and discipline of the country's premier service. Not only did we all start equal but the feeling of comradeship amongst us was so strong that those of us who stayed in the Navy preserved the 'term' spirit as a sort of overlay, which transcended the wide differences in level which we were to achieve. Moreover, the close understanding between us helped during the whole complex series of sailing and specialisation courses which provided the backdrop to our lives for the next six years. When we eventually emerged we were carefully trained, fashioned and honed to the status of professional officers in what prided itself as the most professional of navies.

Even though our first two terms at Dartmouth were spent in a special house for the most junior cadets, there was no delay in making clear what was expected of us. On arrival at Dartmouth from London, by train, we were formed up into a pretty messy squad, and marched up the hill to the college. It was a steep climb and our progress was not helped by our stumbling incompetence at keeping step. When we reached the main building, we were marched to our house and reunited with our belongings. All of our personal possessions were stowed in the sea chests of venerable antiquity which stood at the bottom of our beds and which were opened for inspection every evening at 'rounds'. Within the chest, the flap of which lay down like a table, there was an exact prescribed place for each item of our kit, which in turn had to be folded, pressed, piled and presented with an exactitude which defied belief. Some (though my wife would claim not many) of those habits remain with me still. The way in which I fold a suit into a suitcase marks me as an ex-Dartmouth cadet as surely as if the fact were tattooed on my forehead. The smallest failure to match up to the standards was punished with a beating, as was any transgression of the myriad rules which governed every waking moment. Not only were there vast numbers of college rules to be obeyed, such as the requirement that everything be done at the double, but there were an even larger number of arbitrary rules handed down through generations of cadets. These involved, as in most public schools, the rights to use certain paths, and such items as the length of the lanyard which we wore around our necks. Whilst this nearly throttled us in our first term, by the time we were ready to leave the college it hung down to our navels in a wondrous sign of maturity and seniority. These latter rules were enforced by the cadets themselves, through the system known as 'Guff'. Any senior cadet could 'Guff' one his junior, by so little as a term, if found in dereliction of the rules. It was certain that any transgression observed by a cadet captain would be reported, but one could not be quite so positive about the reactions of others of one's seniors. The world was definitely a first-term cadet's enemy, as his perpetually aching bottom (from the constant corporal punishment) kept him well aware.

Despite the overwhelming odds against doing everything right I found the system infinitely preferable to that at Tormore. Here at least it was predictable and, in its own curious way, fair. Bullying was punished as rigorously as any other misdemeanour. In any case we were worked so hard and felt such common cause against the rest of the college, that we did not have inclination, energy, or time for those indulgences which had so marred my earlier education.

By the time we fell, exhausted, into our bunks that first night we had begun to get some inkling of what lay ahead. 'Call the Hands' was at 0600 the following morning. There was no lying in bed enjoying that happy half state between sleep and waking, for the last out of the dormitory was appropriately punished. The very first action was to put us, still half asleep, through a cold plunge. This was a large, square, lead-lined cistern containing about eighteen inches of unheated water. Indeed at the height of winter, despite its being inside the buidling, it was occasionally necessary to break the ice before the first cadet could get in. Total immersion was required, and woe betide any of us who were suspected of shirking this unpleasant ritual. I have never been fond of cold baths, but I can honestly say that the plunge was a worse fate by far. It was actually quite difficult to get the whole of one's head and body under the water, since the plunge was not large enough to allow one a sort of racing dive. There seemed no way of achieving the desired result without unbearably prolonging the experience by a sort of slow, agonising descent. Then it was 'doubling' to the parade ground and physical jerks and drill before 'doubling' into breakfast.

Maybe it was the unaccustomed exercise, the contrast with Tormore, or the lack of compulsion, either in the helpings that we were given or in the necessity to clear our plates, but I had no difficulty with the food at all. It was, in fact, standard naval fare, heavy in calories and fats, but of excellent quality and quantity. The Navy school of cookery had particular techniques with all sorts of things I have never found replicated elsewhere. Their way with a roast potato, for example, would shame any five-star hotel. I simply do not understand why naval cooks so seldom seem to find their true vocations in such centres of excellence.

Despite the quantities of fattening food served us, I never succeeded in putting on weight, and remained skinny until after I got married in 1947. Bearing in mind that I now find it almost impossible to reduce my weight, something drastic must have happened to my metabolism when Betty took a hand in my affairs. The curriculum at Dartmouth was carefully tailored to the perceived and professional needs of a naval officer, excluding rigorously the 'frivolities' which were in those days considered to be the hallmark of an academic man. I have often, rather disparagingly, claimed to be trained, rather than educated, because of this emphasis on specificity of subject, and the way in which the subjects were taught. The passing out exam at Dartmouth was considered to be the equivalent of matriculation, but fell far short of that standard in a number of ways. For example, the basis of celestial navigation was spherical trigonometry, a subject which was taught well and exhaustively. Calculus was, on the other hand, barely explored at all, except by those who specialised in the sciences. Our history lessons concentrated, to an almost ludicrous degree, on naval history and, as far as I can recall, there was no attention at all paid to economic history, which had, after all, a not inconsiderable relevance to the root causes of so many naval conflicts.

I suppose that this compression of our academic education was enforced by the need to teach us so many other subjects which are not a feature of normal public-school life. By the time we left to go to sea we had learnt the basis of seamanship on wonderful old models, some of which dated from before the 1914 war. We knew our Morse code, our signal flags, and could read and send semaphore. We had been taught the skills of the parade ground, and could shoot a rifle. We could sail, row and repair a motorboat (a feat which we were required to exercise on more occasions than I care to recall). We could man a mast, and were, to a man, taught ballroom dancing, so that our nation need never be ashamed when we showed the flag in the country clubs of the world. We could sew, darn a sock, play squash, fence and swim. We could play, with varying degrees of skill, almost every game known to man, and we knew the appropriate number of guns to fire in salute to every potentate we were likely to encounter.

In addition to all these skills which, at some time or other, were all to be of real practical value to us, we were given the equivalent of an engineering apprenticeship. As with sport, I was to find yet another area of my brain which is clearly missing. Here, though, there was a difference. I loved engineering, and was constantly fascinated by the theories of triple reduction steam engines, and Parsons' turbines. However, when it came to the practical side of things, my interest and enthusiasm were not enough to compensate for this missing ingredient of my make-up. Our first term's work was the inevitable task of filing a keyway through a block of brass. This was followed, equally inevitably, in the second term, by filing the shoulders down level, so that a perfectly flattened block was available for another thirteen-year-old to repeat the whole exercise. It remains a puzzle to me that, despite nearly six months of twice-weekly filing sessions, my keyway resembled the cleft of Cheddar Gorge in its pleasing inconsistency, and my 'flat' block emerged with the sinuous waves of a belly-dancer in full flight. One would have thought, and indeed I have been told, that any idiot can be taught to file straight. Despite the combined weight of the entire engineering department at Dartmouth this idiot couldn't, and still cannot. My failure at this simple task was swiftly followed by my producing the wrong size of pattern in the pattern shop, dovetail joints that gaped and yawed in the shipwright's shop, castings that were flawed in the foundry, and bolts that were cross-threaded in the machine shop. Theory, fine. Ability to criticise other's effort, exemplary. But for example, look elsewhere.

It is still my shelf that falls down, or isn't true. It is my picture which, painstakingly hung on a carefully inserted rawlplug in the wall, crashes to earth with a resounding thump in the middle of a dinner party. Thank heavens that I was blessed with a bride of the most exemplary, fastidious and painstaking practicality, although I was completely unaware of this additional bonus during our courtship. Without her no picture would remain hung on our walls, no shelf would stay up and no repair would be made to last more than the most ephemeral period. Not only do I not possess the engineering equivalent of green fingers, but I am accident prone to boot. It is always my bolt, carefully placed for re-assembly, that rolls into the inaccessible sump of the machine, or my nut which, seized solid, will resist even the administration of WD40, until it eventually fractures under my exasperated hammering. To the Navy's credit, they never gave up hope, and were surprisingly forgiving of my ineptitude. It is all the more ironic since I have made most of my working life with machinery of every sort, and share the fascination and pleasures which all engineers derive from a perfectly balanced bearing, or a mechanic's skill at making a fitted piece to microscopic tolerances.

Dartmouth, despite its insistence on our single-minded attention to the task in hand, and its intolerance of any lack of compliance with its view of the correct way to do things, performed wonders on my behalf. The never ceasing pursuit of perfection, and the conviction that we could always do better, sets enduring standards. The pressures under which we were brought up, the intensity of our efforts, and the sheer hours expected of children, continuously stretched our abilities as well as our beliefs in, and understandings of, our own capacities. Behind every minute of every day lay an overt as well as an unspoken conviction that we were the chosen beings. Nothing in the world could possibly represent a greater honour or a more satisfying life, than to serve in this, the mother of the world's navies. Such was our conviction in our service that it never remotely occurred to us that there could be any other country capable of challenging our self-evident superiority. We found it difficult to imagine that we could, or would, ever tangle with a worthy foe. In addition we ascribed to our officers and superiors qualities and wisdom that, with the benefit of sad experience, were unlikely to be present in the abundance that we believed in. Anyone who doubted the value of starting cadets so young, cannot have appreciated the unswerving loyalty and belief in our cause that was engendered. It was not, in any event, a cynical age, but cynicism in that Navy would have felt akin to treason. For the task that lay ahead of us, this almost Messianic belief in our service and our system had both good and bad points. On the plus side these convictions led us unhesitatingly to stifle individual doubts or fears, and our only concerns were the personal ones that we might, in some way, be inadequate to live up to the standards of our peers. On the minus side, we lacked objectivity, and the lessons we had to learn were the harder for it. We doubted the capacity of others, who had not had the benefits of the careful selection, followed by the expensive, time-consuming training, to do as well as we could, and we were frightened and intolerant of experimentation and novelty.

In my later life I was to be taught to treat such approaches and such self-sacrifice in the pursuit of perfection on a single parameter as being misguided and even irrelevant. The realities of life are, of course, that both approaches are necessary. The painstaking and character-testing striving after perfection in the single path is just as important as the soaring imagination which jumps far ahead by a different approach. But seldom are the two skills encompassed in a single person. Somewhere an angel sat on my shoulder and whispered in my ear that, if the end could not be achieved by the sweat and strain of marginal improvement, there had to be another, and not necessarily worse way.

Dartmouth emphasised the fact that we were growing up, and were expected to make choices on our own account. We were allowed to choose the forms of exercise and games that we played, with a complicated system of points allocated, for example, for half an hour of squash, or a period of swimming. There was, as far as I can recall, no compulsion (although a certain amount of moral pressure) to indulge in the masochistic pursuit of sports at which one had no ability whatsoever. Since there were facilities to enable us to follow every game known to man (except golf), this left opportunities for even the most deficient sporting individual to find something he could do. Certain matters, as befitted future sailors, were obligatory. We were all required to learn to row the heavy naval cutters, whalers and gigs, with which the college was supplied in abundance. We were expected also to master the art of rigging them and sailing in the ample waters of the Dart.

The whole boating side of things was a paradise for a boy. The closeness to the elements and the simple loveliness of the river, with its plethora of oak and other broad-leaved trees sweeping down to the water, and the towering hills which enveloped us on every side, gave an introduction to that identification with nature and natural things which is the greatest gift a sailor receives from his calling. This feeling of being part of the natural system of things, and a humbling realisation of how insignificant that part is by comparison with the forces of wind and weather, storm and natural calamities, come from our association with the elements and the realisation that you can accommodate, but never vanquish them.

The top dozen cadets in each term were streamed differently in the last year in the college, being selected for one of two alpha classes, one specialising in the sciences and one in the arts, which included languages. At this stage an attempt was made to emulate university life, as we were allowed a good deal of free time, and use of the excellent library to study subjects of our own choice which had been agreed with our tutors. At Dartmouth there was no shame associated with academic success and derision was reserved rather for the dumbos amongst us than for the swots. The reverse, however, was equally untrue – brainpower on its own was not enough unless accompanied by an elusive attribute defined as 'Officer-Like Qualities'. Describing these was rather like trying to describe an aura or a mood. They were instantly recognisable, and the whole of our elaborate system was designed to produce them (if missing) or to enhance them (if present). Yet they were unquantified, unqualified, and totally subjective. Moreover, there was a certain degree of self-fulfilment about the concept. If it was believed you had them, even if you yourself felt that they were absent, they suddenly arrived, or at minimum appeared to visit. I spent twenty years of my life trying to acquire them. I ruthlessly prevented the promotion of those without them, and I was privileged to serve a few who had some of them, and yet this holy grail remains as elusive to me today as it did at thirteen. The curious facet of OLQ was that they were not wiped out by grotesque idiosyncrasies. Drunken exploits enhanced the mystique to a degree, although sottish behaviour removed it instantly. Intolerance, arrogance, lack of sensitivity and boorishness were not hindrances, nor were they believed to be even mildly incompatible.

With much effort I can, I think, describe some of these desirable traits, which still seem to me to derive from Kipling and *The Boy's Own Paper*, as much as military theory or psychology. As Professor Norman F. Dixon MBE has shown so brilliantly in his book *On The Psychology of Military Incompetence*, the qualities so sought after were a lopsided bunch, which contained the seeds of their own destruction. But to a boy they were a beacon, and a beacon, moreover, which has warmed and guided much of my life. Besides the obvious (and in my experience rare) qualities of courage, steadfastness and integrity, they contained a concept of duty which appeared simple but was of immense subtlety and complexity, as many fighting men of all nations have found. It was the monarch from whom we derived our commissions, when we eventually earned them, and it was to him, or her, that we owed our allegiance. We had other duties as well, which were drummed and beaten into us. Our duty to our service (an entity and standard even vaster than our sovereign, with almost as long a lineage and, it seemed, a less chequered basis of steady commitment and performance). We believed we knew that the Navy had never failed our country, or its leader, and carried the responsibility of ensuring that those hundreds of years of faithful service were not let down by inadequacy or lack of grit on our part. Just to ensure that our kit-bag of duty was not flopping around with any unfilled corners or empty spaces, our duty to our ship and shipmates and, above all, our duty to those entrusted to our care was added in. This constant emphasis, year in and year out, on the primacy of our duty to our subordinates, was the greatest single factor of OLQ. Belief that it was a privilege to have the opportunity to lead, certainty that effective leadership had to be earned by example, and proper concern for those for whom we were responsible, were hammered relentlessly into us from the very first days. Small as we were, if we were the coxswain of a boat, or in charge of a group of our peers, woe betide us if we did not shoulder the greatest load. We were taught to be last to leave the scene of action, having made a final check that all was in order. We were expected to be the last to receive the cup of cocoa or boxed lunch, and then only when we had ascertained that everyone else was provided for. In later years this principle was enforced with equal rigidity, and in many cases much more discomfort. As a midshipman in charge of a ship's boat, soaked to the skin and chattering with cold, it was all too tempting to avoid being the last to climb the boom and seek the shelter and warmth of the gun room. Once on board, there was a fierce urge to rush below, rather than miserably to ascertain that the four or so sailors of one's tiny command were provided for. The Navy's attention to the details of the techniques of leadership and command was rigorous, consistent and omnipresent.

Superiors were merciless in their criticism of their juniors. And this, all too often, in public and without regard to the problems that were created by so doing. There was no question of being taken discreetly aside and remonstrated with – a bellow of apparently incoherent rage was usually the chosen vehicle for reproof. Since the Navy collectively believed that perfection was, in itself, not good enough, there was always plenty of admonition flying around. The energy which was expended was prodigious in its pursuit of apparently meaningless achievements such as the correct cheesing down of the halyard, or the exact width of the folded shirt in our sea chest. I am not, by my nature, a perfectionist, nor am I switched on by detail. My pleasures are derived rather in the broader achievement than by the excellence of execution of the intermediate steps, and I am still puzzled that I found this new, and for me unnatural environment so totally to my liking. It may have been the illusory belief that, once mastered, the meticulous performance of all these individually tiny duties would deliver my dreams of distinguished participation in adventures and triumphs over the king's enemies; be they Arab slave traders, or an ill-judged (and plainly unnecessary) Colonial insurrection.

Life at Dartmouth proceeded on its highly structured, deeply rewarding route, but I also had two pieces of good fortune in my academic studies, which were to have a lasting influence on my later life. The first of these was in my choice of languages. After an initial grounding in French, at which I was moderately proficient, we were allowed to switch to German or Russian. The teaching of Russian at that time was a surprisingly imaginative option for the Navy to introduce; it was taught by a charming and likeable Russian called Nicholas Sollohub. There was little doubt in my mind, however, that, despite the attractions of learning such an esoteric subject from such a kindly teacher, a knowledge of German was likely to be of more immediate application. War with Hitler's Germany already seemed probable and my tutor, when I discussed the choice with him, had no doubt about steering me towards learning German. How lucky I was. The language itself grabbed my interest and affection almost immediately. I even liked its grammar which I found, in typically Teutonic style, more disciplined, orderly and predictable than its French counterpart. I was not to visit Germany, to my enduring sadness, until after the war, and so missed the opportunity of seeing the country in its heyday. Yet I read so voraciously and was taught so well that when I did at last arrive in the chaos and wreckage of the Germany of 1946, I felt that I could recognise what it had been before the destruction of its fabric and what appeared, at the time, to be the destruction of its people. This introduction to the language, and subsequently its people, provided a richness and breadth to my later life which has been one of the guiding factors in my affection for Europe as an ideal. It was the beginning of a lifetime's love affair with a country that I think of as a second homeland. This provides a curious balance with my Indian affiliations, and is almost as strong a contrast with the way of life in the UK.

The other, even more unlikely, coincidence was the arrival at Dartmouth of Professor C.N. Parkinson, later to be world-renowned as the progenitor and discoverer of Parkinson's Law – a law the workings of which I was to study at first hand for most of my naval and industrial life. His influence on me took a different form at this stage. He was our professor of naval history. The subject was of absorbing interest to him, and his enthusiasm served to intensify my own. Apart from the detailed knowledge which we both possessed of the tactics of practically every naval battle from the Armada onwards, the passion and eagerness he showed for his subject opened important doors for me. He was always probing into the human aspects of the conflicts he described so vividly. It was from him that I learnt to look beyond the mechanisms of the events and to try to understand the reasonings and thinkings of those who set such affairs in motion. He was also the first person to draw my attention to the impact of technology on history, and the complexities of the interaction between technological possibilities and the human ability to adjust to them and harness them to the achievements of desired ends. He was very young then although, being prematurely balding, he appeared to us of immense age and authority. The sense of humour from which he was later to reap such well-earned rewards was already, and irreverently, present. He seemed, at the time, to be almost the only person at Dartmouth who saw the humorous side of our professional prides and pomposities. In addition therefore to the pleasure I derived from learning my craft as a sailor, there were three academic subjects (for I always enjoyed English) which I actually looked forward to with interest and pleasure.

This whole period of my life was made even better by the fact that I was reunited with my mother again. Ostensibly, at least, it had been decided that she should stay behind in England to support me in my entry into the college. Somewhat naively I wonder whether this may have arisen from a belated realisation of the catastrophic effect of my introduction into Tormore. In reality I think that there were other, more apparent reasons why a return to India at that time might not have been either welcome or sensible. My father's contract with Dhar state was coming to an end, as Bahadur was reaching the age at which he could be responsible for his own affairs. My father would therefore be seeking another appointment with the next princeling in need of the Harvey-Jones treatment. I do not recollect there being any suggestion that he might seek a less unusual occupation but I suppose that, if one has been used to being a sort of surrogate prince, other more mundane tasks must lose a lot of their charm. I imagine that competition was pretty intense for what I, perhaps unjustly, thought of as a fairly simple and straightforward, but well-rewarded, job.

My mother, however, was obviously not thought to be a necessary part of the job-seeking process. I still find this odd. To my certain knowledge Bahadur adored my mother as much as he feared my father. Surely any objective view of the pair of them would have seen their respective contributions as complementary and necessary to each other. Possibly, in that era, the Raj still in its heyday, it would have been looked upon as a sign of almost unbelievable weakness to acknowledge that a woman could make a valuable contribution to the upbringing, education and values of a young boy being developed to rule a country. Yet one of the facets of Indian life which I admire is the strength of the contribution of the women in their society. Although few would claim that India is a matriarchy, women have always seemed to me to play a very substantial role as involved influencers of their menfolk. When I first left India I was too young to have any understanding of these matters, but I do know that my father's selection as guardian for his next ward was made without the participation or involvement of my mother. Most likely, I believe, the seeds of the dissolution of their marriage were beginning to sprout. They had always seemed an unlikely pair, bound together more by perceptions of social conventions than shared interests or passion. Their interests lay at such totally opposite ends of the spectrum that it must have made life particularly difficult for a couple who spent much of their time virtually alone together, isolated even from the curious Indian version of English society.

I suspect that my mother was only too glad to have a respectable set of reasons which enabled her to remain in her beloved London. After all, plainly Bahadur did not need her any longer as he would shortly, on normal Indian form, be entering into a suitable arranged marriage. My father's next victim (a young princeling in the state of Junagadh) was not yet selected, and her presence was certainly not needed until he was, so the coast was clear. For my father's part I don't think he would have been too perturbed at her absence. The idea they they might have divorced and gone their separate ways would have been socially unthinkable, and filled both of them with horror. Yet, provided the fictions of marriage were maintained, it seems that they were content to allow each other considerable freedoms. In reality I believe that each was constraining the other. My father had, I am sure, his fair share of physical and sexual needs, but I suspect that they were just that. He never seemed, in the whole of his repressed, duty-ridden, wasted and slightly dismal life, to need an emotional relationship with anyone else. He found the odd attempts to create such a bond embarrassing and beyond his capability of response. What my mother had to offer in abundance was not for him, and what he had to give, in full and overflowing measure, was not for her. It was a little tragedy of its time, and one which wasted too much of two lives.

Their loss, however, was emphatically my gain. For my mother set up house in London, renting a flat in Drayton Gardens, South Kensington. To her it was unthinkable that she should live far outside the Royal Borough of Kensington and its environs. A selection of their furnishings were removed from store, although in the light of the, alleged, temporary nature of her stay my father's sporting trophies were allowed to rest in peace, and it was possible to enter the flat without following the whole gamut of big-game shooting from coast to coast of the Indian subcontinent. One of the by-products of my parents' curious existence was their horror of the responsibilities associated with home ownership, neither ever evincing the slightest wish to own a house of their own. It seemed that at some time or other in their lives they had either had, or known someone who had had, a 'bad experience' with a house. Initially this was an attitude which I inherited from them and, sadly and stupidly, this lost Betty and me our chance for an early entry onto the housing ladder. Both my parents were convinced that no sooner did you own a property than financial disaster would strike. It would require a new roof (the ultimate disaster, apparently leading to immediate bankruptcy). Wet rot, dry rot, death watch beetle – all these would strike with single-minded determination the moment that the deeds changed hands. Partly, in their case, this may have sprung from the fact that they came from a long line of rootless souls who did not seem to feel the desperate need among my own family to put our roots down. Put Betty and my daughter Gaby and me down in a blank green field in the middle of nowhere and we dig in like moles, so determined are we to belong, and to have the illusion of permanence.

What I was lacking, except at the college, were friends of my own age, and particularly girls. My mother's circle of elderly friends certainly did not encompass such rare creatures. Puberty was inexorably setting in and, in my almost monastically segregated existence, I became more and more avidly interested in the sexual side of life. In its way it was as unnatural an unbringing as I had had in India, and was to create unimagined difficulties for me when I started to meet girls as contemporaries. My shyness and lack of self-confidence with the opposite sex was intensified, and took years to overcome. It also meant that it was a very long time before I was able to see girls as people and friends, as opposed to the objects of my unrequited and intensifying prurience. In later life I ascribed this lopsided approach to the British system of segregated, single-sex education and certainly, from my endless discussions on the subject with my colleagues at the college, I was not alone in having difficulties in this adjustment. However, in retrospect I suspect that the curious circumstances of my upbringing were as responsible as my pseudo public-school education for turning a normal heterosexual and basically interested and friendly boy into an approximation of a sex maniac. Happily more enlightened times, and changes in our society, seem to have produced better adjusted teenagers who appear to be able to cope with these aspects of growing up. Suffice it to say that, by the time I found myself as an officer at sea, entrusted with the protection of the realm, I was gauche, sexually ignorant, boorish and crude in my views of women and their place in the world. When my wife eventually helped me to grow up, I found, albeit belatedly, the immense satisfaction that friendships with women brought into my life. I had been largely deprived of this because of my strange upbringing. It was a sad loss, and I am the poorer for those wasted years.

I spent my term times at Dartmouth and my holidays with my mother and, for the first time I can remember, my life seemed to settle into something which approached normality and stability. The two major uncertainties which still troubled me were the alleged possibility that my mother would have to return to India once my father had landed his next state, and the increasing likelihood of war.

Even to me (the lowest possible form of naval animal life) it was apparent that, despite Mr Chamberlain's bits of paper and promises of peace in our time, a conflict with Hitler was becoming inescapable. To a boy of my age, war promised adventure on an even greater scale than that envisaged by my mentors, Percy Westerman and James Jeans. We had no idea of the real circumstances nor would it have been possible, in all we were taught, to give us any inkling of what it would be like to be trapped, without possibility of escape, in a small, frail vessel, which was being slowly demolished by shot and shell. We none of us knew how soon those awful realisations were to come. In the meantime our excitement, and the anticipation of being able to practise our craft for real, and to serve our country as our generations of forebears had done before us, knew no bounds.

I was on holiday in London with my mother when the end came. We listened, in stunned silence, to Mr Chamberlain's precise and unemotional words. They were followed, almost immediately, by an air-raid siren, for which we were ill prepared. We were at war. Life would never be the same again, and my short-lived stability had gone as quickly as it had arrived.

5 The Blooding

Things barely seemed to change at Dartmouth at all. The two training cruisers were removed from their tasks and sent to join the Fleet. This meant that, as midshipmen, we would progress directly from the college to our ships, but otherwise the advent of war seemed almost an anticlimax.

At home my mother and grandmother displayed the sort of illogical behaviour engendered by generations of army service. Although neither had any relevant skills for the war effort, and would have been far better deployed away from the capital, both decided to stay put and 'do their bit'. This quixotic view, which was to cause all three of us to endure the worst of the Blitz in London and would cost my grandmother her life when the Guard's Chapel was bombed, was based on a refusal to be 'forced out by Hitler'. When, much later, my mother left London for the remoter climes of Perthshire, despite the excellent family reasons for the move, she viewed her departure as a victory for the Nazi cause on a par with the fall of Tobruk. Both of them joined the Women's Voluntary Service and were in no time engaged in the myriad activities which that excellent organisation undertook. We had moved to a basement flat in Campden Hill Court, which was as close to being an air-raid shelter as one could have wished. Its only disadvantage was the uncomfortable possibility that the six floors above us could, inconveniently, collapse upon us.

I spent my summer holidays with my mother in London. August and September in 1940 were the height of the Blitz, and as a holiday resort London lacked a certain something. Day and night seemed to invert, for practically all night was spent either being bombed or helping out, as best I could, with the innumerable incidents and interruptions to the normal life of the city. There were fires to be put out everywhere, and I remember helping to dig out survivors and wounded and even, occasionally, corpses from the collapsed buildings. A partly trained, able-bodied sixteen-year-old was a welcome addition to practically any of the hastily created teams who were trying to cope, and there was no shortage of useful things for me to do. My main impression of those events was the incredible messiness and chaos. None of the crisp organisation that accounts of such events, and films, suggest. Rather a sort of haphazard scrabbling to do anything which appeared to help. Activity helped to quell fear, and one was soon so engrossed in the action that there was really no time to think of the bombs coming down around one.

Returning to Dartmouth at the end of this memorable holiday seemed almost like a rest cure, but we all felt a desperate need to get to sea and contribute what we could to the struggle. The war at sea had intensified considerably and whilst we no longer believed that victory would be so swift that we would 'miss the war', it began to look entirely possible that we might miss it for other reasons. None of us doubted that, if the UK was indeed invaded, the Navy would continue to fight from whatever bases we might command, but it was obvious even to us that we needed to be actually aboard a ship if we were going to be able to be part of that fight.

I achieved my aim of becoming an alpha student, and so was able to spend my last year with free study periods, limitless access to the library and a host of other academic privileges. It was at this point that I learnt how to learn as well as how to work. The freedom I was given and the personal encouragement to choose a subject and organise the consequent study was a wonderful basic skill to be given, and still seems to me to have been a most unlikely one to achieve in such a structured environment.

My other ambition – to become a cadet captain – eluded me. I was bitterly disappointed, but plainly 'Robbie', our house officer, did not see in me the Officer-Like Qualities necessary for such an appointment. It was the first failure I had experienced in attempting to meet one of my personal objectives (if one disregards my total failure to escape from Tormore) and I did not take it well. Even now I find myself hoping that I concealed the strength of my feelings, for to show that one expects to achieve what was plainly impossible only adds to the apparent failure. However, within myself I conducted an endless self-criticism. Interestingly enough, I did not seek to externalise my failure. Such was my simple faith in the fairness of the system that it never occurred to me that the fault could lie with anyone except myself.

My time at Dartmouth was drawing to a close. We were allowed to put our names down for the naval station in which we wanted to serve and the other cadets we would like to be with. The choice for a sailor in early 1941 was wider than one would have thought. Initial appointments were to cruisers and larger capital ships, for although destroyers carried a single midshipman the aim was to try to continue our training afloat. At that time the main war (from a naval point of view) was in the Mediterranean and, to a man, we all made it our first choice – after that personal perference could play a part. I felt a great need to see my father again, imagining that now I was a man (in my eyes at least) I would form the sort of relationship with him that I had manifestly failed to achieve so far. He was still in India, having taken on what was to prove his last appointment, in the state of Junagadh.

I thought of transferring to the Royal Indian Navy, and sought Robbie's advice. He was appalled. Joining the RIN was obviously, in his eyes, rather akin to becoming a soldier of fortune in South America, and he virtually forbade me to make such a request. He made it abundantly clear that it would go no further than his waste-paper basket if I were so misguided as to persist. This advice was undoubtedly correct as far as a naval career was concerned, and I have sometimes wondered what would have happened to me after Partition in 1947 if I had joined the RIN. At the time, however, it appeared pretty harsh, and seemed to lack any understanding of my personal concerns. This incidentally remained a feature of naval man-management during the whole period of my service, showing itself at its most unfeeling when Gaby, my daughter, got polio. The attitude which was generally applied was that we belonged to the Navy body and soul, twenty-four hours a day, seven days a week. We were not entitled to any leave, which was viewed as a privilege rather than a right, and our personal lives were considered to be irrelevant and rather weakening distractions from our calling. Such things were to be pursued in such odd moments as the Navy failed to fill up with useful work. Useful work could merely be to stay on board one's ship, be it a birthday, Christmas day or the birth of one's child. It was considered unarguable that the Navy's smallest whim should take precedence over any family matter, no matter how vital.

When this, admittedly rather half-hearted, attempt failed I tried another approach to the problem, which was to put my name down for the East Indies Station. At that time this covered the whole area from India to the date line. (Incidentally it also happened to be an area where two subsequent German friends of mine were creating merry hell with their armed merchant raiders.) Four of us had agreed to try to serve together, and to my considerable gratification the others were all quite happy to apply to serve in the East Indies. It was, therefore, a source of some surprise to us all to receive on 1 September 1941, our appointments as midshipmen, to join HMS *Diomede* at Bermuda on the West Indies Station forthwith. I had succeeded in adding another ten thousand miles or so of separation between myself and Junagadh and gave up any hope of seeing my father during my adolescence, which I had an increasing feeling might be a rather shortened experience. One of us, Claude Kerr, fell by the wayside, and it was on a wet and windy September morning that Robin Usher, John Elgar and I reported to Gourock Pier to embark on the troopship which was to carry us across the Atlantic to follow our ordained fate.

I got two shocks in fairly quick succession when we joined the *Pasteur*. This French luxury liner had been seized in 1940, and was serving as a troopship across the Atlantic. I had 'passed out' well at Dartmouth, receiving the maximum seniority, and found myself as senior midshipman of our gang of six. This presented few problems with John and Robin, for we were equally innocent and ingenuous, but we had been joined by three midshipmen of the Royal Canadian Navy who were not only considerably older than us, but also considerably more worldly wise. Naval discipline being what it was, they had no option but to accept my quavering leadership, but my own knowledge of my inexperience and inadequacies did little to reinforce my self-confidence or leadership abilities. The second shock was of a more basic kind. The *Pasteur*, as well as carrying very large numbers of trainee RAF aircrew who were going to the Empire training schools in Canada, was also carrying a number of wives and children to join their husbands over there. As trained sailors, we were expected to work our passage and, besides abandoning our cabins and comfortable berths for hammocks in the passageways, were put on the watch-keeping rota to help out on the bridge. That meant that at dead of night we would be feeling our way around the ship, for of course she was darkened to avoid attracting the attention of submarines. Within a day of sailing we found these trips to and from the bridge enlivened by the necessity to circumnavigate (or, on occasions, leap over) couples indulging in the most intimate (and to us only imagined) delights. I was so innocent and naive that I was shattered to discover that married women, separated from their husbands, felt free to pursue their carnal interests with other than the partners to whom they had given their vows. It is difficult nowadays, when every ten-year-old views such matters with cynical realism, to imagine the ignorance and simplicity with which the three of us had embarked upon our journey into life. My Canadian colleagues were, of course, neither surprised nor scandalised, and instead became preoccupied with getting a bit of the action themselves.

The *Pasteur* transited the Atlantic in seven days. We had only one submarine encounter during which, to our great excitement, we were able to watch our escorting Canadian destroyers dashing around and dropping depth charges.

Halifax, which we were to revisit more quickly than we imagined, was a considerable disappointment. The harbour was fantastic and crammed with ships of every size and shape assembling for a convoy-run to the UK, but the town did not live up to our expectations of the New World, or to the lyrical descriptions of their native land given by our three homesick companions. We quickly left for Bermuda – desperately trying to catch a glimpse of our future ship, only to find a bare anchorage, for the elusive *Diomede* had left the day before for the Pacific. By then we were beginning to feel unwanted, and to make matters worse our meagre financial reserves were beginning to erode. Budgeting for an indefinite, and apparently continually extending period of time on the princely sum of £10, with total uncertainty and the fear of ending up with nothing at all, proved a further quick lesson in adult responsibility.

Off we went back to Halifax. When we got there we discovered that *Diomede*'s next allied port of call was to be Esquimalt on Vancouver Island (exactly the other side of Canada) and we were to journey over by train to join her. My Canadians were overjoyed, dropping off the train at various points and promising faithfully to join us on the due date. My fevered imagination and an awareness of my responsibilities caused me to wonder what fate awaited a senior midshipman who lost half his command within six weeks of his appointment, but I need not have worried. Royal Canadian Naval discipline prevailed and they turned up, albeit bog-eyed, hung over and at the last moment, but a very welcome sight.

I should have been worrying about other matters, however, for while we were given our railway tickets and instructions to report to the naval base at Esquimalt in two weeks' time we were given no vouchers for meals, nor were we given any travelling expenses or advance of pay. Our pay at that time was five shillings a day, so there wasn't a great deal to advance on, but almost anything would have helped the logistical nightmare that I had landed us in. We solved our problems by eating our way across Canada on a somewhat improbable diet of five-cent pieces of apple pie and free iced water. Every time the train stopped, the duty midshipman would dash for the station buffet and race back clutching our pie ration. Our fellow passengers watched this procedure with increasing incredulity but total disregard. They may well have imagined that, as refugees from rationed Britain, we were exhibiting uninhibited cravings for the pride of Canadian cuisine. In any event we managed the six-day journey without the inconvenience of any form of meat or vegetables crossing our lips, and it was a great many months before I could look a piece of apple pie in the face again.

Even the food problem could not detract from the wonders of that journey. Quite apart from the breathtaking beauty of the trip from coast to coast and the comfort of the train, by means of this trip I gathered a comprehension of the size of North America and the sparseness of the population in Canada that no amount of flying could ever have given. Long train journeys are the most marvellous way of seeing a country in its totality. Neither people nor wildlife pay any attention to trains, which seem to be accepted as a part of the background in ways which roads never achieve. We were, moreover, traversing Quebec and Nova Scotia at the end of September, just as the maples were at their last fiery burst of colour before the winter. Villages seemed to be an extension of the woods they nestled in, and the sheer size overwhelmed one as the train proceeded through the same sort of scenery for hour on hour, interspersed from time to time by the flying feet of the duty pie-man.

At last we were able to join our ship, and we realised how lucky we had been. She was almost the smallest cruiser to carry a gun room of midshipmen, and the six of us were 'it'. On board there were already two sub-lieutenants, who shared our cramped quarters and were responsible for us. The sub-lieutenant in charge was a Royal Navy Reserve officer, having already done his time as a cadet in the Merchant Navy, and was a first-class practical seaman. He also brought with him the taste for the rough life which sailors are meant to enjoy. Whichever port we visited, he would unearth the brothels and bars with the certainty of a well-trained gun dog putting up game. Such was the single-minded intensity with which he pursued his hobbies that he would discover his necessary service stations in even the most demure and prim localities, finding levels of debauchery in small terraced houses, which I am sure the neighbours would have been amazed to know of. I and my colleagues were far too frightened and unsure of ourselves to follow this unlikely Pied Piper, but he found ready playmates in two of our Canadian colleagues, and the three of them devoted themselves to a sort of sexual circumnavigation of the Americas.

Diomede's job at that time was to cover the west coast of North America and the canal area from the expected attack of a German raider and, later, to protect the South American trade routes. We were accompanied by a tanker and replenished at sea, staying on patrol for at least a month at a time. Our ship had no radar and we relied entirely on Intelligence and our eyesight, spending most of the time rolling around at five to ten knots and not really going anywhere at all. To my surprise I loved the routine that others found boring. The steady watch-keeping, standing to at dawn every day and watching the sun rise in the Pacific, the slowing of the pace of life so that even the smallest variant in weather, sea birds, or the occasional sighting or pursuit of a ship, were savoured and enjoyed. I even learnt to enjoy the constant scanning of the horizon while on watch – a skill which was to stand me in good stead in submarines. Sighting ships at sea is an art. Good eyesight, which I had, was a necessity. To actually pick out the smudge of smoke, the hairline shape of a masthead breaking over the horizon, or the faintly differing blackness of the silhouette against the blackened sea and sky is an acquired skill, and very largely the result of concentration.

In my submarine days I was scientifically taught how to maintain a lookout, but at that time one learnt on the hoof. It amazed me then, and still does, that despite the number of lookouts and the obvious pressures to see before you were seen, nine times out of ten the sighting was made by the officers or the signalman, not the lookout. *Diomede* was blessed with two extraordinary petty officers, both of whom had a lasting effect on my view of life. There was a Yeoman of Signals who carried the largest telescope I have ever seen. Looking through a telescope from a rolling platform is difficult enough, but Yeoman Blye could see things which, even when he pointed them out, were only discernible by others long after his initial sighting had taken place. He was a short, tubby, totally imperturbable man, who had already retired. I never saw him lose his composure, and he had the ability to inspire total affection and esteem in everyone on board, from the captain to the boy-seamen. He was efficient in an effortless and totally reliable way. I never heard him raise his voice to any of his people. The other was the Petty Officer of my division. Like Blye, he had been a peacetime regular as indeed, at that stage in the war, practically all our POs had been. He possessed many of the same qualities but he was, in addition, a natural seaman. He always knew the right thing to do and had always done it at least once before. But even more to the point (and this was the true hallmark of a real sailor) he never took a short cut or a chance. It was not for nothing that the Navy prescribed exactly what to do in every situation. The vast number of different knots and hitches all had to be used in particular circumstances for particular needs, and while the wrong hitch would hold most of the time, once in a blue moon it would fail, and someone would be hurt. Being a sailor means constant and continuous attention to detail, for the forces with which you are dealing are so much greater than your own physical strength. The weights you move, the force of wind and wave, the massive impetus of a swinging boat, the problems of securing a cruiser's anchor chain to a buoy, all these are greater than man-size problems, with which men must cope. Experience, confidence, expertise and sensitivity to the forces at work are what make the sailor, and both these men had all of these skills in abundance. I was lucky to serve with them. They were unfailing in the sheer decency they showed me, and their polite but firm refusal to allow me to do, or ask others to do, stupid things was a lesson I have never forgotten. Their corrections were never an overt challenge to my authority, slight as it may have been. None of those who served under me can possibly have had confidence in this callow, nervous, rather childish youth, even though the naval system gave me not only the power, but the responsibility to decide matters which could have been vital.

For a while we continued our gentle progression through the eastern Pacific, but then our lives changed abruptly – the Japanese attacked Pearl Harbor. In no time at all we found ourselves in command of a combined task force to occupy the Galapagos Islands, where, rumour had it, the Japanese were already ensconced. The Americans stormed ashore in style, to the amazement of the turtles and iguanas whose tranquil lives were so noisily interrupted. We were then relieved by a sister ship and sent back to Bermuda to refit and replace the *Dunedin* (another D-class cruiser) which had been sunk in mid Atlantic with horrendous loss of life. Almost all the crew had managed to abandon ship but only 70 of the 350 survived four days in rafts in the barracuda-ridden area in which they were floating.

The German submarine campaign in the Caribbean and West Atlantic had just begun, and there was a desperate shortage of warships of any sort. Hunting submarines with a cruiser was a pretty futile exercise, for our equipment and experience was minimal. However, we did our best. Despite being at war, and constantly exercising, life settled to that curious, slowed-down version the sailor knows so well, where everything has an added emphasis and one's enjoyment is derived from small pleasures. Two I remember in particular. On my seventeenth birthday my father had shown one of the only flashes of interest in my upbringing of which I was aware. In those days everyone who purported to be a gentleman had his own gunsmith, tailor, hairdresser and tobacconist. My father, as a 'macho' man, was a pipe smoker and had (or imagined he had) his pipes made for him by Loewe in the Haymarket, who also blended, packed and sent him his own personal smoking mixture. On my birthday I received a tiny, almost straight-grained pipe and two ounces of his 'special'. It was a shrewd move on his part, for I have never been tempted or interested in cigarettes and over the years I have derived endless, and pretty harmless, pleasure from my pipe. There is a tempo and ritual to pipe smoking which cannot be rushed. If you pack it carelessly, or are in too much of a hurry, it will not draw properly. 'Puffing furiously at his pipe' as my boyhood heroes were often described as doing, is not an option. It is, for a start, very difficult to do, and the ridiculousness of the operation soon occurs to even the most savagely inclined individual.

I soon abandoned my father's mixture, if only for logistical reasons and the inordinate expense, but I was never to settle totally happily with the naval tobacco, even though it was unbelievably cheap. During my midshipman's time I attempted all sorts of sailor-like activities. I did a good deal of fancy ropework and, largely I think to emulate the sailor on the John Player's packet, made up my own 'Pusser's Prick'. In those days one could either draw one's tobacco issue as a made-up mixture in vast tins (known as 'Ticklers') or one could draw a bunch of actual tobacco leaves, stalks and all. An elaborate ritual then followed, which was just the job for a South Atlantic three-week patrol. The stalks were stripped out, the leaves, liberally soaked in rum, were assembled on a piece of canvas, which was then screwed up tight with tarred hemp under all the pressure one could exert, using a technique called a Spanish windlass. The end result was a cone-shaped, perfectly regular stick of tobacco, which was reverently put aside to mature for an agonising three to six months. At the end of this period it was as hard as a policeman's truncheon. The approved technique was to take the extremely sharp knife which no sailor was ever without, cut off a plug at a time and slice and shred it. Real toughies were reputed to chew the stuff but I cannot imagine the constitution which could actually masticate it and survive. Even the smoke nearly finished me, when the day finally came for me to sample my handiwork. I was the nearest I had ever come to being seasick – and in a flat calm to boot. This experience taught me very swiftly that there were clear limits to what I was prepared to do to establish my manhood, and that tamping a pitifully small pipe with tarry, black, evil-smelling, rock-hard tobacco trimmings did little to enhance the image of a green-faced, watering-eyed, sickly seventeen-year-old.

The second experience was not marred by such foolish attempts to improve on a good thing. Life near the equator in a blacked-out ship with little ventilation was a misery, and we were allowed to sleep on deck. At sea there are no midges or mosquitoes – only the inevitable crew of cockroaches which, before the advent of DDT, infested every inch of an aged cruiser and used to take what seemed like a personal delight in dropping from the deckhead onto the perspiring body in the hammock below. Sleeping on deck, with the cooling breeze generated by the ship itself and the glorious array of stars in the velvet-like sky which seems only to occur in the tropics, is a sensual experience beyond compare. The sound of the sea lapping down the ship's side as we churned on our mission; the low chatter of the watch-keepers, huddled around their guns; the occasional flashes of phosphorescence as porpoises or fish came to investigate the alien intruder; the unaccustomed comfort of a safari camp bed, by comparison with the enveloping, shroud-like feel of a hammock; all these combined to make the nights a time of delight and reflection.

Above everything these patrols, which were viewed by so many as monotonous and God-forsaken, gave one endless time for thinking about the fundamentals of life and its curiosities. The midshipmen were kept busy, for every moment of the day was filled with instruction of one sort or other. We were also watch-keeping on the bridge, one watch in three, as well as taking part in interminable exercises to ensure that the ship was up to snuff for the moment when we met the enemy. Which, in the way of such things, we didn't, of course. We didn't see a single enemy surface ship – not even a blockade runner. We picked up survivors of attacks from time to time, but a real life encounter, where we would be tested for better or worse, eluded us. To make matters worse, *Diomede* developed a defect in her port engine and broke down. We had been patrolling out of Monte-video in Uruguay for some time, with an occasional foray to the Falkland Islands, the first of a number of such visits during my naval career. It was, therefore, back to Montevideo that we limped to repair ourselves, for although the Uruguayans were as

pro-British as the Argentinians were pro-German, at that stage
of the war neutrality still prevailed. The engineers had a miserable time, but for the rest of us it was heaven on earth.

We were welcomed everywhere. Uruguay was a wonderful
country. Democratic, and without the obvious extremes of
wealth and poverty I found so distressing in Brazil and the
Caribbean. They seemed to have everything – abundant food,
space, culture, and mutuality of respect. They were not apparently corrupt or belligerent people and were economically secure,
liked and trusted. Out of the whole of South America it was my
dream country and it seemed the country least likely to develop,
or to sustain, an extremist regime – and yet it happened.

The midshipmen were invited to spend a week on a six-
thousand-acre *estancia* up country, and we got an idea of what
life could be like on one of those vast estates. It was marvellous
to ride out with the gauchos, sleeping on the pampas, wrapped
in blankets under the stars, catching, killing and barbecuing a
sheep for the evening meal – still the best lamb I have ever tasted
– and sharing their maté tea drunk from a gourd through a silver
pipe and strainer.

Despite our best efforts we could not repair the turbines, and
returned to Rosyth rather ignominiously on one engine, with our
port screw disconnected and trailing.

Due to a combination of circumstances I had quite a lot of
leave at this time and spent, in all, nearly seven weeks in London.
For three of these I was being treated for shingles (which I
viewed as a sort of moral failure – and a very painful one at that),
but the remainder of the time I was foot loose and fancy free. I
had, for a midshipman, quite a lot of money saved and was ready
to spend it. A feature of the wartime Navy was that, once afloat,
there was very little to spend one's meagre pay on. During the
whole of my naval career I never drank at sea. In harbour,
midshipmen were not allowed to drink spirits, and at that time I
did not like beer, so my bar bills were negligible. My tobacco bill
was tiny since, despite my lack of enthusiasm for Ticklers,
economics won the day. I had a full kit of uniform, and so really
there was nothing to spend money on. Our runs ashore were

innocent, for I was far too uncertain of my self to follow the sub-lieutenants on their carnal tours of the knocking-shops of South America. I therefore arrived back in England both virginal, and with nearly a year's pay under my belt.

This leave and some of the following year, during my sub-lieutenant's courses, represents all that I was to enjoy of a conventional adolescence. I have always wondered whether my apparently infinite delay in achieving the sort of maturity I see in others of my age is due to this, or to some other quirk of the genes. Despite having been at sea for a year I was still very much a little boy at heart. I was convinced of my inadequacies and had very little feeling of self-worth. I was painfully shy and with-drawn, rather earnest and priggish, and terrified of the opposite sex. I saw these creatures of fantasy alternately as objects of my extreme sexual desire (which for lack of outlets burned at a constant near-critical heat) or as pure goddesses to be worshipped from afar. My seven-week leave did nothing to resolve these conflicts – rather the reverse.

I was invited by my smart cousins to join the fringes of debutante society. There was still a superfluity of young 'gals' and a marked absence of the young men of means and breeding with which they consorted. The Navy has always produced a curious social passport into British society. A regular or reserve commission is seen as indicating a degree of acceptability afforded only to the smarter regiments. I found myself, fam-iliarly, out of my depth in this world of the smart set, where everyone knew everyone else, their homes, parents, brothers and sisters. I had no tales of derring-do at sea, and had so far avoided being shot at or personally attacked. Even though my months at sea had reached into my soul in a way which has never left me, I was uneasily conscious of being an oddball in this respect, and also of not having had a 'good war'. In our block of flats I did, however, meet a wondrous creature who was my first, chaste, but deeply loved girlfriend. She was adopted and had similar problems of social uncertainty to mine. Those were the days of ballroom dancing, and we would go out together night after night, walking home in the early hours of the morning, and lingering on the way for increasingly passionate kissing and caressing. I was so heavily imbued with the apparent values of my father and of the Navy that it never remotely occurred to me that I might have anything to offer in my own right. The latter's belief that one's worth as an individual was a direct reflection of one's worth to the Board of Admiralty certainly reinforced our family prejudices. The more so since I found it difficult to persuade myself that my commission in *Diomede* had resolved many of Their Lordships' problems.

When my leave came to an end I was appointed to join *Ithuriel*, which was refitting in Portsmouth dockyard. This was a real fighting ship which had covered herself in glory by ramming and sinking an enemy submarine (and managing to do so under the watchful eyes of a film crew) at the conclusion of the second Malta convoy.

Life became much more adventurous from then on. We were frequently in action against both submarines and aircraft. Our actions against aeroplanes were pretty ineffectual because our main 4.7-inch guns would only rise to a maximum elevation of about 30 degrees, so that effectively we only had 20-ml Oerlikons. These had a very short range, and depended entirely on the shooting capacity of the gunner, since there was no radar control. Time passed very quickly under the circumstances, particularly since mostly we were working 'watch and watch', which meant that we had a maximum of four hours' sleep at a time. Fate seemed invariably to ensure that during one's sleeping watch the enemy would seek to make life difficult for us. Gone were the long philosophical sessions and sensual enjoyments of the sea and sky, to be replaced by the scrabble to keep fed, washed and adequately rested to do one's job. The gunner and I shared the after part of the ship as our action stations, and made a good team. He had all the knowledge and I had all the energy and enthusiasm! One of the problems of being so far away from the bridge was that most of the time we had no idea what was going on until we were told to open fire, prepare a depth-charge pattern, or whatever. The good side of things was that I spent the whole time with my sailors, and there was no one else to talk to. I got to know them better in these circumstances than would have been possible in a larger ship. In reality most of them were only a little older than I was, and almost equally inexperienced, but their different, less sheltered backgrounds gave the impression of wisdom far greater than mine.

We were destined to join a fighting force called Force Q, of three light cruisers and three destroyers, set up to intercept convoys running from Italy to Bizerta on the north coast of Tunisia to keep the Africa Corps supplied, and were to operate from Bône, the closest port to the front line still in allied hands. Bône, as I was to recognise very quickly, was under continuous air attack, and so the idea was that we stop over only prior to carrying out our attacks. We spent quite a bit of time doing destroyer-like things until towards the end of November, when we arrived at that hapless harbour to fuel and wait for the expected convoy. The Germans, however, spotted us almost immediately on our arrival and we were raided continuously. *Ithuriel* was secured alongside an ammunition ship (which didn't seem to me the most felicitous arrangement) and about 2 am one morning a large bomb fell about three yards off my gun, and exploded underwater. We were all blown off our feet and when we picked ourselves up it was obvious that both ships had been damaged. I went below and got the wounded and shocked crews out of our magazines and supply rooms, and tried to find out the extent of the damage. In the darkness we assumed only that a large amount of the side plating had been blown in and once we had got everyone out the problem was to shore up the bulkheads to enable them to withstand the sea pressures. This we did with baulks of timber, pads of wood and wedges of various sorts and sizes. I got a sort of instant, on-the-spot, course in damage control, and the ship continued to sink slowly and inexorably, but with considerable dignity. The dignity wasn't helped too much by the arrival of the French fire brigade, complete with brass helmets, to assist with pumping us out. The other ships also sent across pumps of various sorts, but to our dismay even the massed pumps of Bône did not prevent our Turkish home settling further and further down. By the morning the truth dawned upon us. The bomb had broken the ship's back, and she was unsaveable. All we could do was to ignominiously beach her off the entrance to the harbour, having removed every bit of recoverable equipment from her.

Life then became very trying indeed. The rest of the force left Bône precipitously, one destroyer light, and there was only a tiny force of motor minesweepers left behind. The harbour was being bombed continuously and we, as spare hands, found ourselves in great demand for a host of most un-sailor-like activities. We became instant bomb-disposal experts, a task I disliked only marginally less than the day we were required to provide two platoons, of which I was in charge of one, to fight off an alleged force of six hundred paratroopers intent on recapturing the benighted place. I shudder to think what would have happened if our less than enthusiastic sailors had fallen into the path of six hundred of the German best, but fortunately for us this did not occur. Cowardice alone made it clear to me that life at sea was better, safer, cleaner, better fed and altogether more my style than this miserable *apologia* for a soldier's war. I therefore asked the captain whether I could apply to join one of the other ships when the fleet next appeared and he agreed to this if I could find one to take me.

There was only one chance. One of the destroyers was Australian, and so could not take me, but I knew that *Quentin* had no midshipman. Sure enough, when in early December she entered harbour, this very dishevelled midshipman arrived on board to see if he could join. The captain, in his kindness, suggested I join on his next return but, hoping to put my front-line experience behind me, I pleaded successfully to be allowed to sling my hammock that day. So it was that I trooped on board *Quentin*, with what little of my gear had been salvaged from *Ithuriel*, at 1400 hours, in time to sail by 1430. I was given a bunk aft, and an action station on the quarter deck gun again, which I was at from 2000 hours onwards. It was an eventful night, and the closest to an, admittedly rather one-sided, surface battle I was to experience. Our five ships intercepted the convoy which had four supply ships, three destroyers and a number of E-boats, and sank the lot. We engaged them from about two miles' distance, and sank the destroyers and several E-boats, before putting paid to a number of supply ships. These were sunk from a range so close that we could see our shells hitting the targets and exploding. It was a lot too much like slaughter for my liking, and one of the supply ships, carrying petrol, exploded and disintegrated before our eyes. By 0300 it was all over and we turned to run for the protection of our own air cover before it grew light. The night had been infinitely preferable to being bombed at Bône, and I felt excited and pleased with myself as I collapsed into my bunk. I felt less excited and far from pleased however, to be woken at 6 am by being thrown from my bunk with the sort of crash and explosion I recognised from *Ithuriel*. As always, all the lights went out, and I could hear water pouring in the other side of my cabin wall. To make matters worse, the floor had buckled and I could not open my cabin door.

Since Dartmouth days I have never been one of those who linger between sleep and wakefulness, and this was certainly no time for such luxuries. The ship was listing fast and I had visions of being trapped as we turned turtle. Naval doors had panels which were removable, for just such occasions as these, so, pausing only to collect my cap – since I realised that none of the crew would know who I was, I broke my way out and up to the quarter deck. I had been sleeping in my underpants, and that and my cap were for a long time my only naval equipment. We were plainly in a mess. The ship had stopped and there was a large hole by the engine room. The rest of the force were just visible as they disappeared over the horizon, leaving our sister destroyer, the *Quiberon*, to do what she could for us. As a veteran of one sinking (although I doubted whether a French fire engine would arrive to help on this occasion) I knew what to do. I collected a few rather unhappy sailors and set to, shoring up the bulkhead between the cabin flat and the place where our engine room had been. We soon started to run out of timber and I sent one of my people to collect some more. When he didn't return I went up to investigate, to find to my dismay that the last of the crew were just transferring from the fo'c'sle on to *Quiberon*, which had come alongside. Never has a midshipman in underpants and cap moved faster. I shot down and collected the rest of my faithful band and we made it in record speed up to the bows, just as *Quiberon* shot astern, having collected what she thought was everyone. We just managed to jump for it, and were helped aboard by the Australians, who caught me by the scruff of my neck. The area we were in was no place to linger. The enemy were determined to finish off the job they had begun, and friendly air cover was only available ten miles further in towards Bône. Where we were – about twelve miles out from the island of Pantelleria – was still occupied by the Axis and very definitely their territory.

So, after the shortest commission in my naval career, with a sinking heart and no kit at all, it was back to Bône – the hellhole I had got away from with such relief less than twenty hours earlier. Luckily for me, I was considered a part of *Quentin*'s crew, and was ferried back to Algiers, where we were employed on odd jobs for a while until we could be returned to the UK. I must have been a weird sight, for apart from my naval cap I was entirely kitted out by the Army. Needless to say neither they nor we carried such necessities of modern war as spare pairs of midshipmen's white patches, and even if they had I doubt whether I could have sewn them on. I therefore enjoyed a brief period of anonymity – especially as, as far as the Admiralty was concerned, I seemed to have completely disappeared. Eventually we were shipped back to the UK, on a troopship, and after kitting out with a hand-me-down officer's uniform from a WVS bureau I was appointed to the *Duke of York*.

The *Duke of York* was the first 'big ship' that I served upon. The experience decided me that it was not one I wished to repeat – in such a vast ship, so far removed from my previous experience, that I might as well have been in a barracks. However, I only had to endure three months of it, and then, having completed my time, was posted as acting sub-lieutenant, for courses. This was when one learnt the solid professionalism of one's calling. I spent the next months at the various naval schools, learning gunnery, torpedo work, electrical and electronic matters, signals, navigation and so on. Each course culminated in an exam, on the results of which more seniority could be earned. At the end of the courses we were allowed to volunteer for our chosen specialisations. I did sufficiently well on my courses to be able to take my pick and hovered between the Fleet Air Arm and submarines. The Fleet Air Arm would have meant even more lengthy training, and I already felt that the war was passing me by. So I opted for submarines, and what a splendid choice it proved to be.

My wish to join the submarine service had its roots in a number of things which were apparently unconnected with the sterling traditions of that fine organisation. While my boyhood reading had given me a vividly enhanced picture of what the life might be like, when I first volunteered, I had never actually been on board a submarine. I had not even met anyone who followed the 'trade' and therefore had no one who could describe the realities of what I was letting myself in for.

I can, with the benefit of hindsight, detect three main trends which led me to the choice, none of which was particularly noble. The first was my general feeling that I had had a pretty soft war, despite my progressing inexorably up the ladder of seniority by my application to the various educational aspects of my career. I was determined to try to prove myself, not only to others, but to the inner forces which compelled me as an individual. Somehow a year of swanning around South America didn't quite seem to me to do the trick. Even my more active life in the Mediterranean had been marked by its brevity and abrupt ending. This contrasted with the prolonged experience of action at sea which, to my rather naive view, constituted the life of a true naval professional. It was a totally false picture. In fact the reality of naval warfare is that it is composed of a life of continuous drudgery, interspersed with brief moments of too much excitement. My experience in the *Duke of York* should have given me a better perspective, but I wanted to be a hero, and was not prepared to see the truth. Submarines were reputed to be in almost continuous action. Even though this was not and obviously could not have been the truth, at least the ratio of action to inaction was much higher than in surface ships.

The second reason was an even more ignominious one. I have always disliked loud noise – perhaps a legacy of the relative silence in my early upbringing in India. I found it extraordinarily difficult to concentrate on other things when standing by guns in action. I tried every sort of ear plug to deaden the effect but if I had succeeded in shutting off the noise which distracted me I could not actually have done the job, since I would have been hermetically sealed in a world of my own. This fear meant that I was always tense, waiting for the fire gong which preceded the violent explosion of the guns going off only a few feet away from me. Others did not seem to share my problems and revelled in the ear-splitting cacophony of surface ship warfare. *Ithuriel* and *Quentin* had added to this dislike, for in both cases the ships had been hit within only a few feet of me.

It was obvious to me that it would become more and more difficult for me to do the complicated calculations which were required in order to aim the guns if I was always terrified of them actually firing. This problem was yet another I could not share with anyone else. I was ashamed of being frightened and disorientated by explosions. Over the years I tried hard to deal with my fears, but right to the end of my naval career I always sought action stations below decks rather than above. I used to sweat with fear and anxiety before a gun action and submarines seemed to offer me an honourable way out of this dilemma.

The third reason was only marginally better. My experience of surface action in ships had shown me, all too vividly, the fate of the wounded aboard a ship in action. There is no safe place for them, and it is a particularly vicious form of agony for a wounded man to be ditched into the sea. I would always have chosen to accept death rather than extreme pain – and very few sub-mariners were wounded. Either you all went or none of you, and while the form of death might not have been what one would have chosen, the pains were at least as much mental as physical.

I had rather more confidence in my ability to withstand the former than the latter. It was on such unpromising grounds that in 1943, together with a number of my term mates from Dartmouth, I reported to the submarine training establishment at Blyth in Northumberland. The reasons for my volunteering may have been poor, but the results were emphatically not. I can trace so many of the things which influenced my views and approach in later life to my time in submarines.

Blyth was then a busy east coast port and mining town, shipping coal to the power stations of London and the South. It was my first introduction both to an industrial town and to the North East of England. Eventually this was to be the area in which I have lived for the longest consecutive period in my life, and I have a deep and abiding love for it. The training course was short and intensive, and from the very first we all felt ourselves to be somehow different. Submarines had a mystique, together with a reputation for all the manly qualities I most craved to be seen to possess. Almost everyone's initial reaction on learning that you were a submariner would be to announce that it was something they could not possibly do. The image of a claustrophobic life of hardship and challenge was so strong that people viewed the submariner's lot with the sort of awe and disbelief that I reserve for those who pursue the hobby of pot-holing today. The reality, for a gun-shy, scruffy nineteen-year-old, totally lacking in self-confidence, could not have been more different.

The hallmark of the submariner of the time was a vast, supposedly white, polo-neck sweater and a generally crumpled appearance. One of the luxuries we forewent was stowage for clothing and personal possessions. This suited me perfectly, for I had already lost most of my things, and so had the minimum of items to stow. Life on board was a perennial picnic. Stowage for food was limited and cooking facilities were minimal and primitive in the extreme. Water was also in short supply, except the salty sort, so beards were *de rigueur*. The officers shared a washbasin and toilet, so there was neither opportunity nor facility for such niceties as showers or baths. Discipline aboard a submarine was about as far removed from that on the *Duke of York* as life on Mars would be. Professional failure at tasks one was given was leapt upon instantly and mercilessly. Such discipline, however, was reserved for matters of importance, rather than for the rather petty misdemeanours which I had fallen foul of in the past.

My time at Blyth was among the happiest of my life. Not only was I serving my apprenticeship and enjoying the reflected glory of the service which was viewed, not least by itself, as a *corps d'élite* – but I also met the girl who proved to be the love of my life.

My wife and I have discussed many times our first, unpromising, meeting on the dance floor at the Old Assembly Rooms at Newcastle, a trysting place, I may add, that I visit on each occasion that I visit that city. I have no doubt that she is right when she says that she went out with me more because she felt sorry for me than because it was love at first sight. I was a gawky, uneasy, brash young man, with little idea of how to woo such a sophisticated and beautiful creature. Moreover I felt myself to be in a hurry, since I knew that my time at Blyth was limited, and pictured myself in some remote part of the world thereafter.

She was a Wren radio operator, based at Tynemouth and working a watch-keeping rota in the port station, under the fort, at the entrance to the Tyne. On the night of our first meeting she and a number of other off-duty Wrens had been detailed to attend the dance which was to seal my ultimate fate so happily. As I gazed across the room, the first thing I became aware of was the most glorious pair of legs, which belonged to the most exquisite creature I had ever set eyes upon. I knew that I was a good dancer, but to this day I don't know how I plucked up the courage to ask this rather unwilling attendee to be my partner. The dancing may well have helped, for it is bad enough to be ordered to go to a dance on your evening off, without having your feet and ankles mutilated to boot.

It certainly cannot have been my conversational ability, for I was so thunderstruck to be holding this vision in my arms that I all but lost the power of speech. To add to my fumbling uncertainty, she appeared to be everything that I wasn't. She seemed so socially adept, and to come from just the sort of well-to-do and secure background which I so plainly lacked. She had masses of friends, professional parents (both of whom did describable jobs) and, very understandably, hosts of admirers.

I did not rate my chances very highly, but I do know that it was that much-derided 'love at first sight' as far as I was concerned. Over four years of heartache and pursuit were to pass before we married and I guess it was during those four years that I was to grow up. For a young man who had spent practically all his life concealing his feelings and operating, as a consequence, on a very limited range of emotions, the whole experience was a bombshell.

I shall never know how I managed to pass my training course at all when, for the first time, the whole of my being was totally involved (albeit unskilfully) with someone else. In all honesty, I do not believe either of us could describe our experiences together as a courtship – and whatever it was, it was conducted under very great difficulties. Betty's watch-keeping rota placed major constraints on the times that we could meet – even if she had been madly keen to do so. In addition the vagaries of a very inadequate public transport system, and the distance from Blyth to Tynemouth, added to my difficulties.

In addition she herself was proof against the thunderbolts of puppy love from which I was suffering. Being the kind person she is, and possibly out of a feeling of wartime duty, she put up with me rather than lived for me. Even this modest response was more than enough to keep the fires of my passion at a continuous rolling boil of desire and expectation. However, even the most muted form of consummation lay far into the future for, to my utter despair, she was whisked away before the end of my course, to train as a Wren officer. Quite apart from the physical separation, this also dashed my hopes even further, for Wren officers were goddess-like beings, far beyond the reach of mere sub-lieutenants – even ones who possessed social attributes of a quite different order to mine.

Once she left, I besieged her with letters. It was only really the lack of response to these that began to bring home to me the very tenuous hold I had on her affections. My wife could never be described as a keen letter-writer. Her approach is that if she does a job it has to be done properly, so you either get nothing at all or *War and Peace*, which has to be sent by parcel post. Not altogether surprisingly, there were not too many of these packages coming my way. I don't know whether it is a trick of wartime or a feature of being nineteen, but time seemed to expand. When I look back on my life, the relatively short period that I was at war seems to occupy a totally disproportionate amount of my memories. It was, possibly, the added emphasis with which we led our lives. I have never subscribed to the views, expressed so many years later, that the possibility of the atom bomb extinguishing us all led the young to feel a greater necessity to make hay while the real sun shone. I do not believe that we were all contemplating imminent death, but days did seem to count, and we played on the whole keyboard of experience and emotion. At that time I was very taken with the idea that true feelings of enlightenment could be reached through the powers of the intellect and, within the limited means to hand, I sought to reach out for such delights. Like many teenagers of the time I was absorbed by the publications of PEP (the forerunner of the Policy Studies Institute), the first Penguin books, books on modern artists, the publications of the Nonesuch Press and a host of other broadening and worthwhile influences. Maybe I hoped to be an intellectual – if only as an escape from the alternative models of success in society – even though, looking back I can see that I lacked the basic qualities for such an ambition. Perhaps the relative success I had had with my studies, however hard won, had fuelled my belief in my intellectual capabilities. My eventual path was, in the most unlikely of ways, to be so totally different. Not, as I now realise, inferior, but using a curious amalgam of ill-considered skills which would not have won any of the prizes so esteemed either by my generation or by myself as a young man.

It was the puncturing of such postures, and the deep satisfaction that my modest success in becoming a competent submarine officer gave me that was to be the key to so much of my future direction. I completed my submarine course, and despite the distractions of my obsessional love, contrived to do well and was then appointed as fourth hand on the *Trusty*. As so often in my naval career, I joined her in dock.

Yet again the curious spirals of life were to give me short-lived experiences which would echo through the years. Even though we were at war and the shipbuilders were the key to our survival, I found Wallsend a tough experience. The rugged independence and unique strength of personality of the craftsmen who worked on the *Trusty* were a lesson in themselves. I could not believe that these sturdy individualists could possibly fail to share my own conviction that getting my particular submarine to sea was a sacred trust. The idea that they saw their hard-won demarcations and rights as in any way of comparable importance to the major matter of vanquishing the Axis powers through the activities of the King's well-trusted submarine service, was incomprehensible to me. Yet, they were, at the same time, such normal, proud and skilled souls – struggling eternally to complete their particular part of a job – always held up for materials or the relevant craftsmen, and never a manager or supervisor in sight. When the shifts clocked off – for, war or no war, clock off they did – they would leave the yard for the mean streets and pubs which surrounded Swan Hunter's. Often I would accompany them, for my sub-lieutenant's courses, coupled with being taken in hand by a connoisseur uncle, had given me a rudimentary ability to sink a pint. My technique was something between a throat-opening pour and an officer-like gulp, but at least I had finally learnt to drink beer, an accomplishment which was to bring me much pleasure through the coming years. I was still painfully thin – and no amount of stodgy naval food or pints of beer appeared to fill out the slight form in its ill-fitting inherited uniform. Maybe dockies and naval officers sharing a drink was a sufficiently novel experience for us all to gain from the experience, I certainly know that I did. It was not easy, since understanding the Geordie dialect was a difficult art to acquire – even with the help of the wartime Newcastle breweries.

Be that as it may, *Trusty*'s refit was my first introduction to the working North East, and it struck chords which have resonated ever since. Over forty-five years later, I still follow the fortunes, or lack of them, of Swan Hunter's with a fierce possessiveness. I know what those men are capable of and grieve that we have contrived to give so much of what was within our grasp away to others, for few proud ships are now built on the Tyne. Soon, however, we were completed and off to sea again. The captain of the *Trusty* was a retired submariner of vast experience and, it seemed at the time, advanced years, whose nickname was 'Ginger'. We were a most unlikely bunch of officers, varying from the experienced to the jejune. The captain, in particular, had some individual idiosyncrasies which I might now admire, but viewed then with something approaching horror. Here was this inheritor of Nelson's tradition, a worthy follower of the World War I VCs, a leader of the *corps d'élite*, captain of one of our few submarines (only ninety in all, even at the height of the war) which formed the sharp spearhead of our aggressive thrust – and this man's hobby was knitting. As our vessel teetered from crisis to crisis and our inexperienced crew (helped by their even more inexperienced fourth hand) lurched from near disaster to near disaster, Ginger would remain stoically behind his curtain, knitting one and purling two. In retrospect I can see this as a heroic act of *sang froid* which should have instilled in all of us a sense of calm and confidence, but for some reason it didn't. In later years I was to serve with submarine captains who shouted, screamed or appeared to lose all control, and one at least who seemed to me to be totally mad. Strangely, these wildly different and inappropriate styles of leadership had nothing like the devastating effect of Ginger's laid-back and admirable *insouciance*, coupled with the dextrous skill with which he plied his needles. God knows where the products of these prodigious labours ended up, but today one of my proudest possessions would be one of his creations. He was not a fancy knitter. Not for him Fair-Isle patterns, or even (although on one occasion I thought I saw the beginnings of a cable) Aran. Just solid, repetitive, apparently endless, totally formless sheets of white hand-knitted material which were presumably sent to the WVS, for the solicitude of sailors in greater need.

Apart from the rather different approach of our captain from the heroic exemplars I had had in mind, *Trusty* met most of my other requirements. We patrolled off Norway, and occasionally deep on the North Atlantic in order to intercept *Tirpitz* if she were to make a break for it. The life was a hard one, for submarines were forced to surface every night to charge their batteries. Watch-keeping on the conning tower, only feet above the freezing cold water was, at the best of times, a miserable experience. We wore oilskin suits which were designed to keep as much water out as possible but, in the wild weather conditions we encountered nothing, except a diving suit, could possibly have kept us watertight. In these conditions a two-hour watch was not something to be looked forward to. Added to all these physical discomforts was the mental pressure of the responsibility that one carried. There were only four of us on the bridge at a time, and more often than not we were lashed to the superstructure to avoid being carried away by the waves. The survival of the submarine and every man on board depended on our alertness, and on our ability to see the enemy before he saw us. The good news was that anything you spotted was at least certain to be unfriendly, but the bad news was the difficulty of maintaining concentration, and seeing anything at all through salt-encrusted, wet and obscured naval-issue binoculars. We carried tissues which we used ineffectively to try to dry off the lenses. However, most of the time it was anyone's guess whether the lens or the tissue was the wetter, and our pathetic attempts to clear them all too often ended up with even worse visibility than before.

By contrast the days were, at least in relative terms, a delight. There was virtually no insulation in a submarine, so if the sea temperature was near freezing it was rather like living in a fridge. In the tropics the reverse situation occurred, and we used to keep watch wearing only the briefest of underpants, sweating continuously. Despite the cold, and a marked resistance to dispense with our thick sweaters even in bed, the boat somehow contrived

to be cosy and cheerful. Massive wodges of corned beef sandwiches and hot soups and drinks appeared at meal times, and
were wolfed down by even the most fastidious of us. We were
dry, moderately warm, and full of that cosy feeling of shared
experience and adventure which accompanies the best Boy Scout
camps.

Most of *Trusty*'s few operational patrols were of short duration
and usually occurred if there was a scare that some ship or other
of the German High Seas Fleet was trying to break out. I wasn't
sorry, therefore, to be transferred into an S-class submarine
called *Sturdy*, and then on to join the smallest of our range, a
five-hundred-ton V-boat called *Voracious*. We were bound back
to the Mediterranean to join the squadron based on Malta. The
Voracious was the most modern version of the small inshore
submarines which had wrought havoc in that sea in 1941 and
1942. She was ideally suited for the conditions we encountered.
Painted the dark blue which blended into the Mediterranean sea
so much better than the grey of the northern boats and the dark
green of the Pacific submarines, and carrying a crew of only
forty-two (including four officers), she could manoeuvre on a
sixpence. The Mediterranean waters were very confined, and
mostly we operated close inshore. Our particular theatre of
operations was to be the Aegean, which was still held by the
Germans and posed all sorts of challenges and opportunities. We
were based ashore at Malta and were one of the few ships using
that island. We had to sail in and out through an extensive
minefield and, although distances were not great, managing to
find the swept channel and meet our escort at the end of a patrol
was a real test of navigational skill and luck. There was no way
into the Aegean except by running the gauntlet of the German
and Italian minefields which formed an allegedly impenetrable
barrier between the islands, and an awful lot of the excitement of
operating there came from our attempts to thread our way
through these minefields, either on the surface or submerged.
There were myriads of theories about the best way through the
fields. We used to traverse them at about two and a half knots,
with a short transmission unit fitted on our asdic which, when

all went well, would pick up a mine about fifty yards ahead. We would then change direction until we found another one ahead of us, and so on. We attempted to plot the mines we picked up in this way. Once through the fields, however, we were in a happy hunting ground, albeit one with strong elements of the absurd.

The patrols were eventful and full of action – though of a fairly minor sort, for most of the big targets had long since gone. Although many of our actions used our solitary gun or involved placing demolition charges, we did get to fire an occasional torpedo and had our share of counter-attacks, both with bombs and depth charges. Submarine guns were a simpleton's delight, even for someone like me who detested the things. Since they filled with water when we were submerged they had to be of the sturdiest and least elaborate construction you could imagine. Although it would not be true to say that Nelson would have felt at home with them, certainly any turn-of-the-century gunner would have instantly recognised them. They were coated in heavy non-floating grease, which in itself was enough to put off any self-respecting shell. They were not really terribly deadly, even at their effective range, which was only a few hundred yards. From the submarine's point of view, a submarine gun attack was a really great production. Since a submarine is at its most vulnerable on the surface, the whole objective was to get up, get done and get back down as quickly as possible. Everything was made ready for the attack. The Gun Layer – the only sailor on board with any training in the art – was allowed a brief peek through the periscope and then we prepared to surface. The boat was forcibly held down until the last moment, and shot up like a cork, while the gun crew opened the hatch before we had surfaced and raced up with the water pouring in. We would fire the gun as fast as we could until we had done the necessary damage, and then dive as quickly as we had appeared. For some reason, in this situation the explosion of the guns did not create in my mind the inability to concentrate which I had always experienced before. It is true that there was only one small gun but I was at least as close to it as I had been to the destroyer's.

Maybe the necessity to concentrate single-mindedly on the task in hand helped, whether it was conning the ship, or maintaining the vigilant lookout which was our only defence. In any event, submarine gun actions – and I was to see plenty of them – were the only gunnery experiences I ever enjoyed.

One of the distinguishing features of any submarine-trained man is his ability to sleep instantly, anywhere, for any length of time and at any time. Our sailors slept on top of torpedoes, mess tables, or any other relatively flat surface. As an officer I started my submarine sleeping career on the same mess table that served as the only focus of our entertaining ability when in harbour. It was either that, or when one of us was on watch, the 'hot bunk' principle, which was all too literally just that. The lack of anything except the simplest washing facilities, and the general fug of a submarine crew, living on the air they had fortuitously carried underwater with them, created a degree of insensitivity to some of the finer points of life and smell. No wonder that after a patrol my idea of heaven was a turkish bath, which at least left one with a transient belief in cleanliness. The resultant sweat used to horrify even the hardened attendants by its leaden colour and the ingrained dirt which emerged. Sheer heaven was to follow this with two or three pints of cold beer (to top up the liquid loss) and a full night's sleep on cool linen sheets.

The Aegean war came speedily to a close as, island by island, our people ejected the German and Italian garrisons and we found forward bases closer and closer to our prey. It was at this time that I visited Khíos, Mitilíni, Lesbos and some of the other haunts of antiquity and modern package holidays. Although we had little enough time, we were seeing them in almost ideal circumstances, on foot and with the minimum number of other people. They were unforgettable. To add to their delights the islands had many things that Malta did not – like olive oil and wine. Even with the limited carrying capacity of a submarine, we had a fair amount of 'trade goods' to offer in exchange. It is surprising the effect that the urge for private enterprise of forty-two sailors can have on a five-hundred-ton displacement submarine. Under normal circumstances, when such a vessel is dived and trimmed, even one sailor moving from forward to aft has to be compensated for by pumping water in the opposite direction. When forty-two sailors' illicit and heavy acquisitions of wine and olive oil have been brought on board, a V-class submarine is liable to sink like a stone to the bottom, while the pumps labour to pump out enough sea water to compensate for contraband. This indeed happened, to our excessive surprise, on our very first call on a Greek island, and to our lesser surprise and greater preparation thereafter. At that time the Aegean submarines must have represented a considerable distortion in the Maltese trade figures.

There is nothing more useless than a submarine without a war to fight, and so it was no surprise to us when we were ordered to Ceylon, to join the Far East Fleet at Colombo. I remember two incidents on the passage – both to my discredit and both a part of the accelerated course in growing up which was a by-product of my time in submarines. The first occurred in the Red Sea when our main cooling water inlet got blocked and the submarine came to an unexpected and slithering halt in the brilliant sunshine and flat calm of that most sheltered of seas. We had been followed by shoals of curious sharks for some time. They doubtless were looking on us as some sort of dinosaur-like throwback to their ancestors. When we stopped they hung around, as sharks will, in ever-increasing numbers. Presumably they were expecting that the death throes of the biggest meal they had ever seen were not far away. It became obvious that somebody had to go over the side and pull out whatever was blocking the inlet, about eight foot underwater. The captain (for plainly his duty was to stand by his ship), asked for – nay, demanded – a volunteer, and looked expectantly around. It was a Hollywood scene, but with the difference that not one of us saw any percentage in going over the side, relying on the dubious marksmanship of our fellows to keep what we were sure were man-eaters at bay. Whenever I see films of intrepid scuba divers bashing terrified sharks on the nose I blanch at the memory, but in 1944 we took an altogether less robust view of the relative power of man and shark. I quite quickly learnt why anyone volunteers for anything. It is because you are more scared of your peers realising your own state of abject terror than you are of the task that you believe to be ahead. Thus it was that, with a line around my armpits and in a muck sweat of fear (calculated to attract the most docile shark) I found myself over the side, struggling to remove a mass of something from the inlet. To add to my distress I was convinced that, as well as being surrounded by sharks, the unknown object blocking our inlet was probably an irate octopus or else a poisonous Portuguese Man of War. Whatever it was there certainly was a lot of it, and it took me many terrified dives to remove it all. Alas, however, for Percy Westerman's pal (hero Jones) the reality was an ignominiously large wodge of cotton waste, thrown overboard by one of our people. Far from being the object of praise, concern and admiration that I had imagined, I instantly found myself a source of derision and mirth. Why was I taking so long? What was I frightened of? If they had known what a meal I would make of it every single last sailor would have done the job better and quicker. But of course they didn't, and they hadn't, and every last one of them had had the presence of mind to avoid volunteering for the job in the first place. You only need to learn this lesson once, particularly if you learn it in such a graphic fashion. Although I was to volunteer to do stupid things for bad reasons again, at least I did so in the full knowledge of my own motives and with a suitable cynicism abut the probable outcome.

The second incident was at Aden, and I have to admit was sadly the first of more than one similar, but unforgettable, event in those early years. The fourth hand, John Marks, and I went ashore with our petty officers to their club. It was our naive intent to have a couple of drinks and then go on for a good meal ashore, and we were decked out in what passed for our finery. At that time this meant crumpled whites and white buckskin shoes. Both John and I had had the odd drink with our petty officers before, but always on a one-to-one basis. This was the first time that we presented ourselves as twin targets for the combined strength of the six POs who actually ran the ship. Even the most bloodthirsty referee would have put a stop to the contest long before we lurched out into the warm starry Aden night, allegedly to seek food, but in reality to crawl away and die. Die we did. The dawn broke to find me, on my own, clutching miserably to a mooring buoy on a jetty which seemed to be about a mile long. Of John there was no sign, but the buoy and I were covered in wet, clammy and sticky tar, most of which had left the buoy for the more sympathetic surface of my only white uniform. A long, winding trail of tar down the jetty bore witness to my agonised progress, which had obviously been made on my hands and knees. Looking more black than white I arrived on board, still at something between a creep and a crawl, and braced myself to comment, through gritted teeth and heaving stomach, on the splendid night we had had. The lesson was clear – *caveat emptor* – but particularly *caveat* petty officers *en masse* plying innocent young sub-lieutenants with alternate mixtures of cherry brandy and whisky – followed by crème de menthe and gin – known in the trade as 'Port and Starboard Lights'.

While the others viewed the prospect of Colombo with gloom I had my own reasons for seeing it in quite a different light. From one of the rare responses to my barrage of importuning missives, I had learnt that Betty had been posted to Colombo, having completed her officer's course as a Wren Signals Officer. While I had few illusions that I represented her ideal of romance I knew, as firmly and irrevocably as before, that she was still the girl of my particular (and very frequent) dreams. I had somewhat more confidence in myself with my track record as a proven submarine veteran with combat experience, and felt that on that score at least I could hold my own with any competition. In the softer arts of courtship I had no more idea than before. Although I had had a number of fumbling dates I remained a man of the most manifest lack of experience, and my conversation tended to the leaden rather than the light. Even without the excuse of submarining, my appearance was scruffy rather than bandbox and, all in all, I cannot have represented much of a catch. Moreover, the competition to date a Wren officer was intense even in Britain – in Colombo it would obviously be frenetic. However, none of this did the slightest thing to prevent my heart singing as each turn of the screws brought us fractionally nearer to my heart's desire.

I contacted Betty at once, and to my joy and amazement was not instantly rebuffed. There followed for me the most wonderful, six-week-long, romantic interlude. Whenever *Voracious* was not at sea, and Betty was not on watch, we would be together – swimming off the beach at the Galle Face & Mount Lavinia – or dancing, night after night, at the Silver Fawn nightclub. I had the accumulated riches of nearly a year's submarine pay. All my accelerated promotion had resulted in my receiving my promotion to Lieutenant. In peacetime one was expected to serve in this rank for eight years before becoming a Lieutenant-Commander, which for many officers was to prove to be the summit of their careers. In a submarine the rank had a pleasing anonymity, since many of our boats were actually commanded by lieutenants. In my case there was a minor snag. I had not had the foresight to order the shoulder boards for my new-found rank, and it took me quite a while to find somewhere in Colombo to purchase any. Meanwhile, therefore, I had to rely on borrowing the First Lieutenant's, if he didn't happen to be wearing them. Depending on the whereabouts of the First Lieutenant I would, therefore, sometimes appear as a Lieutenant, and sometimes as a Sub-Lieutenant, to the great confusion of others.

For me those six weeks in October and November of 1944 were a period of idyllic happiness. I lived for the moments that we were together, and the settings and surroundings could not have been more wonderful. The beauty of Ceylon, the warmth of my beloved, the lack of career or wartime pressures, the range of Betty's friends (who accepted me as one of their gang), all combined to give me a taste of what I imagined heaven could be. In the 1970s I contrived to stop over in Sri Lanka again to pay a sentimental visit to our beach, and I found that it stirred me in just the same way. Not only was my future wife beautiful, but the sun suited her ideally. Her hair became almost ash blonde, and her love of swimming and relaxing on the beach turned her skin to a marvellous muted tan. She was beautifully dressed as well, having had the foresight to bring with her a selection of evening dresses, the memory of which still makes me gasp. I could not believe my good fortune to be the chosen escort of this infinitely desirable vision. We seemed to get on famously, and she showed concerns about me which I had never experienced before. It may have been self-protection on her part, but when she collected her month's pay and gave me a number of white uniform shirts I felt that I had finally arrived. I was shattered by this gesture, which I took as a troth of love, rather than a comment on my sartorial standards, and my besotted state became even more enhanced. No shadow spoilt this interlude. I did not realise that Betty was on the rebound from a love affair with a married man in Liverpool, and had sought a foreign posting to get away to a less complicated existence. As far as I was concerned the good Lord had ordained that I should have another chance to try to win her heart, and I used that chance to the best of my ability.

Our time was broken by her getting an attack of dengue fever, and spending a while in the hospital. I was there for every visiting hour I could manage, and felt as though the end of my world was nigh. When the end of this world did occur, however, it was for altogether different reasons. The submarines operating off the Andaman Islands from Trincomalee were at the extreme of their range. The patrols were long and arduous and it had been decided to reinforce them by giving each of them an experienced watch-keeper. Thus it was that, with a breaking heart but still full of hope, I was appointed to HMS *Sea Scout*. The S-class boats were almost half as large again as the Us and Vs, but were still small submarines by most other countries' standards.

From a professional point of view, I was delighted to be going back to operations again, despite my broken heart. The war in Europe was almost over, and for a career officer it was plain that the Pacific was the place to be. At that time none of us had any idea how quickly hostilities with Japan could end, and most of us expected that at least another two or three years of hard struggle lay ahead. *Sea Scout* was based at Trincomalee, whither I was despatched to join her. She had yet to do her first patrol, and I was to serve aboard her until I returned to the United

Kingdom after the war ended. She was, without exception, the unhappiest ship I have ever experienced. Some years later I was convinced that Herman Wouk's book *The Caine Mutiny* was based on my experiences in *Sea Scout*. The character of Captain Queeg was a dead ringer for that of our own captain at the time.

We were all of us very young – possibly too young for the responsibilities that we carried – and the physical conditions in a small submarine in the Indian Ocean and the Pacific placed great strains upon us. If you have to live in a confined space, such as a submarine, and don't get on with your colleagues, there is nowhere you can go to get away from them. If you collectively dislike your captain, and he appears to reciprocate your distaste, you have no recourse but to grin and bear it. Our captain was both highly ambitious and constantly tense. Far from helping our confidence as a crew by emanating an aura of calm control, even the smallest incident was exaggerated by him. On one epic patrol, of over fifty days at sea, we arrived back with *all* the officers allegedly under open arrest – about the most serious form of disciplining an officer can face, and a certain blight on any future career prospects. Once we were back at our base nothing came of the matter, but that was little consolation at the time, when this added pressure was piled on to the stress we felt already. For a minor misdemeanour one of my fellow officers (now sadly dead) had all his shore leave stopped for three months. I would have thought this form of punishment medically unwise, leaving aside the question of its appropriateness or fairness. Life was certainly never dull, but the result of all these odd quirks of behaviour was to bind the other officers together into a granite-like block of resistance.

The more we combined, the more isolated the captain became, and the more he responded by ludicrous impositions of his authority. Many of these, so many years later, seem laughable and childish, but at the time they were viewed by us as anything but that. On one patrol he decided that the entire ship's ration of sardines (a much prized wartime treat) were to be retained for him alone, and that none was to be issued to anyone else. To make sure that this somewhat unusual, not to say one-sided, decision was upheld, the cases and tins of sardines were counted every other day. Needless to say there was no way that one man, on his own, could eat his way through fifty mens' rations of even the most delectable of foods, and we returned from our long patrol with three-quarters of our allowance untouched. The fact was that every single uneaten tin of sardines was begrudged by every one of us on board. The action was looked upon as being quixotic, selfish, and frankly a little bit mad. In harbour we avoided him like the plague, and even at sea we kept our dealings and conversation with him to the minimum. When you live so closely with one another in a submarine, conversation is bound to flag eventually. If you have spent twenty-four hours a day, day in and day out, cooped up with four or five other people in a space smaller than a railway compartment, you find you know each other's views and thoughts on most subjects distressingly well. The only new things to happen are the shared experiences of wind and weather and action. You are even out of touch with the radio news, and have probably read every book on board (possibly more than once!). You might just as well have fallen off the edge of the world, and this experience has given me a great deal of sympathy with those who face a year or so at a time aboard a space shuttle.

On our first patrol, even though I found the atmosphere of our submarine to my distaste, I was buoyed up by the anticipation of getting back to Colombo and Betty. We received well-earned leave after each patrol, except the fourth hand (who at that time was still serving his sentence), and I looked forward to a renewal of my previous romantic nirvana. When I did eventually arrive at Colombo, however, my dreams were abruptly shattered, and I got another sharp lesson in the realities of life. I found that my hitherto unknown rival for her affections had followed Betty out to Ceylon, and was well ensconced in the place that I had hoped to occupy in her heart. I was shattered and inconsolable. Having so briefly had a foretaste of heaven seemed almost an additional cruelty. Colombo, without the Silver Fawn, without the lazy evenings on the beach, without the closeness, the caring, the chattering and the warmth, without the innocent (as indeed they were) caresses, seemed to mock my every waking moment. My leave was a shattering experience. The contrast between what Colombo had meant to me before and what it was now was almost more than I could bear. Suddenly my eager hopes had been removed and I was devastated. I felt more lonely and abandoned than I can ever remember being in my life.

The war went on, and I went with it. *Sea Scout* was ordered out to Fremantle in Western Australia. We carried out an Andaman patrol on the way out, and then carried on the long trip, past Singapore and through to Perth. Once we arrived, the fourth hand (who by then had served his sentence) and I went on leave together. I wanted to see the gold-mining town, Kalgoorlie, and so the two of us, accompanied for some reason by the gun layer, went off to investigate. To describe Kalgoorlie in 1945 as friendly would be the understatement of the century. In fact it was so friendly that our gun layer is still there. When we returned to our ship sans gun layer the roof fell in. It was then relatively easy to replace a submarine officer, but a submarine gun layer was totally indispensable, even though the difference in our training and pay was immense.

Sea Scout then carried out some patrols from Perth, refuelling at Exmouth Gulf on the way into the South China Seas to the Lombok or Sunda Straits. The Japanese knew full well that these routes were the only way in, and therefore patrolled them relentlessly. The distances were so great that it was impossible to traverse them, submerged, in one day. On our first attempt we were detected early on, and spent a day and a half underwater, trying to evade the continual attacks. Although we had a couple of flasks of oxygen to enrich the air on such occasions, when dived we basically lived on such air as we had taken down with us. By the end of this time, the longest period submerged I was ever to experience, we were all beginning to suffer from oxygen depletion and get a small taste of what it must be like to be trapped at the bottom of the sea. Curiously it wasn't too unpleasant an experience. The mind increasingly loses its ability to follow logical progressions, and indeed one gets an extra feeling of confidence that one is in command of all one's faculties, even when it is apparent that one is doing stupid things. An order to put the helm to port, for instance, would result in the helmsman turning it smartly to starboard, and arguing interminably that he had done what he had been asked. When we eventually surfaced the following evening I was, as usual, the surfacing officer of the watch, which meant that I and the captain were first up, and had the job of sweeping the horizon to make sure we weren't sighted by the enemy. The air poured out of the submarine with a rush, for the pressure had been building up the whole time we were down, and was actually black in colour – and evil smelling. I was more surprised, however, by the effect of the fresh, sweet, tropical, ozone-rich air, which momentarily made both of us feel quite drunk. Perhaps it is this experience which has made me value so highly the pleasures and scents of being in the fresh air, be it the sea, the moors, or just enjoying the fresh smell after mowing the lawn, or the grass after rain.

Shortly afterwards the Americans captured the Philippines, and we were off again, leaving the paradise of Perth, which was then every man's picture of a civilised home town. Our submarine was, by then, under the general command of an American submarine admiral, James Fyffe, who inspired in us Brits the same conviction and belief that he so readily conjured up from his compatriots. From our point of view, while we never doubted our cause, the sheer demands on us grew greater and greater. American submarines were three or four times our size, and had been developed over the years with just this sort of war in mind. They had range, relative comfort, and space. We were determined to compete and were trying to keep our ends up in boats designed for the coastal waters of the North Sea and the Mediterranean. Seventy days at sea for an American submarine was approaching the limits of endurance, but for us it was well over what we could take. The Americans on extended patrol received mail drops, fresh provisions and even ice cream from their colleagues, but for us it was quite different. We set off with what we had, and that was it. The patrols extended, the danger never lessened, but all of us got more tired, less understanding and less conciliatory, and the levels of internal contention invariably heightened, even in happy ships. When I compare our lives with the lives of those who had to endure real extremes of pain and hardship, many of whom I was to meet in later life, I realise how comfortable a time we enjoyed and how much more we could have taken. But all human experience is relative, and in our minds we were having a tough time. Any Chindit would have thought our lives soft in the extreme, and any Japanese prisoner of war would have thought himself blessed beyond reason to have exchanged places with us, but for us the going was tough.

We were by then patrolling from Subic Bay. Our patrol areas were in the Gulf of Siam, and it was there that we were on patrol when the atom bomb was dropped. We were in position to intercept the expected Japanese re-supply efforts when the planned invasion of Malaya occurred in just a few days' time. It is interesting to look back at how we viewed things at that time. Despite all our optimism, we expected the defeat of the Japanese to be long, bloody and attritional. The Pacific theatre was the only area of water where I was terrified of being taken prisoner, for no submarine prisoner survived, even death only came after much degradation and suffering.

This fear of the Japanese was to colour my thinking and approach to the country and its people for many years. Fear is difficult to forgive and even more difficult to surmount without the corrective feeling of superiority, which was never to be my lot. When we heard of the first bomb our universal feeling was one of disbelief, tinged with a dawning of hope. There can have been few serving men in the Pacific theatre who did not fall on their knees with thankfulness when the second bomb forced surrender. I am sure that there are many more of us alive today as a result of that agonising decision, and those equally blameless sufferers who were killed or maimed at Hiroshima or Nagasaki. Like many of us there, I was to visit Japan and both sites later, almost as an act of expiation. But no amount of philosophical reflection can change those instantaneous judgements. The possibility of atomic warfare, as of all technical advance, was inevitable and unstoppable. We can argue endlessly about the moral issues, and I am grateful that the decisions were not mine. If we could balance what we then believed would happen, against what did, every one of us today would have joined the cheers and delight of my submarine crew when we were told that the war was over.

6 Introduction to Muscovy

Despite the fact that the war was officially over, we lacked conviction that the message would have permeated to all the Japanese commands and nor did we take it for granted that such an instruction would be obeyed if received. We returned to Subic Bay after our shortest recorded patrol in the Far East, and after a few days 'turn-around' we joined the naval force which was to assist the surrender of Hong Kong.

Here the submarines were the only ships to be berthed alongside the dockyard and for some days we had the place almost to ourselves. The fourth hand and I had blued some of our savings on a Triumph motorbike which had made the journey lashed to the upper deck. Fortunately we had not had to dive, and after a good clean up we found ourselves the proud possessors of our own transport. This was how we came to be amongst the earlier visitors to the prison camp at Stanley, where most of the European families had been interned, and heard first-hand accounts of the privations and cruelties they had suffered. Our regard for our enemy was not enhanced by this experience and it was to be many years before I could eradicate these memories and think of Japanese men as normal human beings. Another unusual and startling experience at that time confirmed the gap of culture and values that separate us. When we came to clear the barracks which had been occupied by the Japanese, under practically every mattress we found a staggering collection of the most extreme pornographic photographs. Many would now be greatly valued as collector's pieces, and had plainly been greatly prized by their erstwhile owners. Most dated from the turn of the century and were clearly of French or European origin. I would not for a moment suggest that a clear-out of a British barracks would not reveal a similar fascination, but it was the ubiquitous nature of the interest and the unbelievable quantities which we found so surprising.

Apart from suitcases full of such dubious items, our sojourn in the docks also gave us the happy opportunity to roam the yard and top up our naval stores, and stocks of paint. At first there was no normal life in Hong Kong at all and, in the absence of any more suitable vessels, the submarines were used as surface anti-piracy patrols through the Lamma channels and the outlying islands. Junkloads of Japanese soldiery were making their some-what inexpert way to Hong Kong to surrender – obviously concluding, probably correctly, that they stood a better chance of avoiding mistreatment at our hands than if they fell in with the Chinese.

It was about as bad a use of a submarine and trained crew as one could imagine, but it was a change for us and kept us occupied while we eagerly awaited our instructions to return to the UK. *Sea Scout* had, by then, been away from the UK for nearly eighteen months and so we were high on the list to return. Our voyage home, on the surface and in safety, should have been a delightful cruise. Unfortunately relationships between the wardroom and the captain had reached a degree of sourness I can still hardly credit. Such was our loathing of him that we sailed the whole way home with him 'in Coventry' as far as we were concerned. He spent most of his time in solitary splendour in the wardroom, whilst we found any space we could. I was signals officer and so spent a lot of my passage time in our tiny radio room, enjoying the company of our telegraphists, for the contin-uous barrage of instructions and intelligence transmitted to us during the war had switched off like a tap.

It was the closeness of my contact with the sailors of the submarine service, and my realisation of their capabilities as people which, more than anything else, formed my belief in the un-ordinariness of so-called ordinary people. The knowledge of the deprivations of their lives before the war, and the low expectations they had of achieving success – or even self-sufficiency – influenced me greatly. I felt that it was terribly wrong that apparently only under the impetus of war were they called upon to give of a substantial part of their capabilities. Moreover, I had seen again and again how our people grew in stature when great expectations were laid upon them. Even the very few who, for their own reasons, did not want to be responsible for others, bloomed when expected to perform greater tasks than they believed that they could undertake. Despite our wide differences in background, education and upbringing, every one of us relied equally on every other member of the crew. Any one man can sink a submarine. No matter how many checks are put in, carelessness, inattention to details and any deviation from the meticulous following of routine and drills can have literally fatal results. Not only did we have this degree of interdependence – which I have shared with others practically all my working life – but in terms of abilities there was little to choose between us. In those days everyone on board lent a hand with anything and everything. The torpedo officer heaved and hauled on the tackles to handle the massive weights of our spare fish in the fore ends with the rest of his team. The officers were expected to (and could) do every job on board, except those mechanical tasks relating to our diesel engines – and yet our sailors, time and again, could do their own jobs far better than we could. Everyone in such a small team knew the best and most effective worker for every task and he was frequently not the most senior – just the best. We all took justifiable pride in our skills, and a good submarine crew, working together, was a joy to see. Each man covered for the other. It was never necessary to shout or push others around. Each of us had only such validity in the eyes of others as we earned by our diligence and ability. Moreover, living so closely together we knew each other's moods, quirks of character and senses of humour in ways which far transcended rank. We did not all have to like each other (though mostly I think we did) but we did have to learn compassion, forbearance, tolerance and the ability to accommodate others' views and opinions. One learnt not to believe that one always

knew best, and to realise that often one's opinions were preju-
diced and one's knowledge inadequate. While all submarine
people were proud of their calling, life in a submarine was a great
leveller and an even greater destroyer of pomposity and personal
pride. Besides growing up during this time, I inherited from my
shipmates so many of the beliefs I now hold dear, and which
have guided me in the wide variety of jobs I have done and the
situations I have encountered.

We arrived home at Gosport and I was left to pay *Sea Scout*
off. Fort Blackhouse, the submarine headquarters, was a curious
place to be at the beginning of 1946. A high proportion of the
submarine officers had been regulars and volunteers, while our
crews had increasingly been pressed men and wartime sailors
only. Conscription was still in force and a submarine service had
to be kept in being, but from the point of view of our sailors
there was little attraction in the life. They had not enjoyed the
common force of wartime service and their thoughts were, almost
from the day they joined, centred solely on the time they would
obtain their discharge. My first months of peacetime submarining
as the First Lieutenant of a training submarine were the most
hair-raising of my entire career. Again and again silly mistakes
would be made and we would find ourselves careering to the
mercifully shallow bottom, with our pumps screaming to stop
our descent. Moreover, I was lonely. My friends had gone
elsewhere and Portsmouth was not the happiest or easiest of
hunting grounds for female companionship. Betty had vanished
from my world, and the only girls I knew were in London, which
seemed a long way away.

At this time a chance event occurred which once again was to
alter my whole direction. An innocent-looking Admiralty Fleet
order appeared asking for volunteers to learn Russian at Cambridge University. I happened to read it after a particularly hair-
raising squeak with my inexperienced and uninterested crew. I
had no particular interest in Russian, although it was already
appearing that our erstwhile allies stood a fair chance of being
our future enemies. But I was more than interested in getting to
Cambridge. I had always yearned to go to university and, while

plainly this was not going to be a normal undergraduate life, it represented the nearest approximation I was likely to find. Moreover, I thought, six months would give submarines time to settle down and I could return to a more stable, ordered and hopefully less hazardous existence. I never even stopped to think what I was to learn Russian for. If I had any mental picture at all it was a vague vision of liaison duties or interpreting at flag showing visits. To my amazement, I was accepted for interview and requested to go to the Admiralty in Whitehall to be seen by a commander in Naval Intelligence. Even when I met Commander Anthony Courtney I still did not link that bluff former boxer with the murky world of Secret Intelligence – or indeed any intelligence at all.

The selection of the ten volunteers to acquire civil service interpretership after a six-month concentrated course at Cambridge seemed to owe as much to a wish to test the abilities of our teachers, as to the aim of producing an end product. We were a wildly assorted group with no apparent common factor uniting us – except a shared determination to spend a jolly six months at the university and a completely undeveloped interest in actually learning the language. One of us, who was later to become First Sea Lord, already showed his acumen by having a Russian mother and a degree of familiarity with the language. As for the rest of us, we would just as readily have volunteered to learn Swahili – and might have found it easier. We had all had an active war and had left our years of book learning well behind. Memorising long lists of vocabulary, written in an incomprehensible script, was not what we had had in mind. We soon learnt that we were the 'trial batch' and that Professor Lisa Hill and her staff were competing for the prize contract to teach the services the linguistic skills on which our National Security would depend. They therefore did not approach with our own lighthearted attitude the task of beating into our befuddled brains a smattering of the language. We were in for a rude shock. The first of our small group was unceremoniously ejected within three weeks, never to be seen by any of us again. He may, for all I know, still be carrying out his duties as a guard in some remote naval penal colony. A combination of this horrific example and Lisa's boundless patience, energy and sheer persistence persuaded us that our course was not going to be the skylark we had expected. It was not a skylark in a number of other ways as well. In its wisdom, the university was prepared, as a National Duty, to allow us to use its teaching facilities but, at that time, neither the university nor any college was prepared to allow us to join as members. We found ourselves, therefore, in a sort of half world.

We found digs which were more accustomed to the shenanigans of former public school boys than the grizzled, battle-hardened veterans we considered ourselves to be. I was the youngest of our group, four of whom were married and set up houses in the area with speed and alacrity. The remaining three of us stuck together and tried hard to achieve a happy balance between learning enough Russian for survival and enjoying the opportunities afforded by a quasi civilian life. By the time we started, most of us had blued the bulk of our wartime savings and so found ourselves in the midst of the financial struggle for existence which every student knows so well. Our landladies strictly forbade cooking in our rooms, so in order to allow for the modest degree of social intercourse which we saw as the essential rights of man we had to find the Cambridge equivalent of the Canadian Pacific Railroad five-cent apple pie.

The excellent coffee stall in Cambridge market, which still exists, proved to be our saviour – producing vast rolls and butter and mugs of tea which kept us going during most of the day. I am sure that modern nutritionists would not view our diet as being one calculated to increase our intellectual activities, but we got by. An even bigger problem was that, even for me as a submariner, we were all accustomed to an open-air life. We found it difficult to acclimatise to the confines of the lecture rooms, or swotting miserably in our digs. We eventually found a *modus vivendi* which we could endure, by using our afternoon break punting or walking up the Backs and to Granchester. One of us would do duty as puntsman while the others struggled to learn Russian grammar or verbs, but at least we were in the open air and on water.

The course was not exclusively for naval personnel; there were also some Army and RAF students as well. In fact we had only been going about a fortnight when there was an enormous influx of slightly bemused-looking soldiery. Well they might have been, for it transpired that on the Friday they had been collectively struggling to learn Japanese. Come Monday, by the edict of someone at the War Office, they found themselves dedicated to the pursuit of Russian. With surprising speed, despite our dedication to the good things of life, we found ourselves skilfully trapped by Lisa into becoming interested and involved in our studies. Although at the time I felt it a poor substitute for actually studying at a university, it did reinforce my Dartmouth experience of tutored study in engendering in me at least the rudiments of an ability to teach myself and learn on my own. We were helped immeasurably since the Russian department included a number of ex-service officers who had a degree of sympathetic understanding of our struggles.

Although I was still not in touch with Betty, who retained her grip on my heart, I was involved in a fairly active life of pursuing eligible young ladies in the hope at least of finding someone who could tap my emotions in some way. I bounced from girl to girl, never finding that elusive formula for transcendental happiness which I had known. I always backed off at the later, or in one case latest, stages of entanglement. I did not really ever expect to see Betty again. Although I had heard nothing of her getting married to my rival (who must surely have divorced anyone in the world for the sake of this paragon), I assumed that they were still together. I therefore made only the most desultory efforts to track her down again. Despite my feeling of hopelessness at ever achieving the heights of my romantic ambitions, I could never quite bring myself to settle for anything less. My attitude to this was diametrically opposed to my normal approach to a problem. In general I have either to be struggling actively to achieve my aims or, if I can see no way forward, I will generally bring myself to accept the less preferable alternative. In this vital area of my personal life and development, I could not apparently do either. Possibly the pain of my rejection made me unwilling to face up to the possibility of a repeat. If this was so, I found nothing to admire in such an approach. The man who fears to hazard all for the right cause had no place in my boyhood books, nor in my simplistic models of the sort of man I wanted to be. Thinking over the situation, as I did constantly, I felt that I was so generally inadequate that it was no surprise that I had not proved worthy of her continued affections. I had deserved her rejection and, indeed, had not deserved the period of intense happiness which preceded it. Such thinking was entirely in keeping with my very low level of self-regard, and yet in my heart I cannot have truly accepted it or I would have settled more readily for one of the others I wooed so half-heartedly.

Our six months passed in a flash – in contrast to my wartime experiences, which seemed to take forever. We sat our civil service exams which, to my amazement, I passed. In the late summer of 1946 I emerged as a Russian interpreter, second class. We all believed that the exams had been a fiddle and, with one exception, were in reality quite inadequately prepared to act as professional linguists. In addition our training had been, inevitably in the very short amount of time we had spent, very specific to our naval needs.

Imagine my surprise when I found myself, within ten days, posted out to Germany and loaned as an interpreter to the pool of those unfortunates who were struggling to serve the Allied Control Authority in Berlin. It was my first experience of the difficulties of International Collaboration and it was a lesson I was not to forget. At the end of the war it had been determined that Germany would be placed under military government – apparently interminably. Each of the main allies, Britain, the USA, France, and the USSR, administered a zone and in addition played a role in the military authority located in Berlin which dealt with the myriad of problems which required resolution on a countrywide basis. The attempts to agree and coordinate such measures were taken to the smallest details of administrative life. They all had to be agreed by all the chosen representatives of the Allied Commanders, through the medium of endless and tedious meetings.

I have always considered that I contributed more than my bit to the collapse of this unlikely and highly impractical way of running a country. On my first day's duty, proudly wearing my naval uniform (in itself something of a rarity in those high-flown circles) I found myself detailed off to interpret for the British representative on the Milk Pasteurisation Sub-Committee of Agricultural Control. Beyond a smattering of grammar and the invaluable knowledge of the Russian for cow and milk, I was somewhat ill prepared for the intricate wheeling, dealing and in-fighting which ensued. The national representatives were them-selves a somewhat ill-assorted and ill-balanced quartet, and the fact that the available interpreters gave them a minimal chance of mutual understanding acted as a *coup de grâce*. That night in my cabin at the comfortable house in Grünewald which was the naval mess, I diligently mugged up all the words I thought might help to reconcile the irreconcilable. The following day, instead of cows I found myself giving my all to the cause of steel production – and so it went on. The meetings were very formal, and every statement had to be consecutively interpreted into the other two languages. Because it was formal conference work, the national in question was always interpreting into the foreign language, so everything depended on knowing the subjects and the specialised terms associated with it. The standard of the interpreters varied enormously and, while I suspect I represented the lowest marker, many of my Russian colleagues were at least as ineffective as I was. At the top end of the proficiency scale were the Americans, most of whose interpreters were of dual nationality. To add to the frustrations of the job, such was the formality of the proceedings that one was powerless to intervene to head off the disasters which one saw coming. The day that the Russian delegate's comment that his American colleague was a 'Mother F—ing liar' was interpreted verbatim predictably gave us all the day off. But these occasions were sadly heavily outnumbered by the times when at least two of the four delegates were groping hopelessly for the meaning of the sonorous and long-winded declarations being made by the others.

There were differences enough in ideology, objectives, style, perception of the task, and readiness to shoulder responsibility, but when the deliberations occurred in a sort of non-listening Tower of Babel, it was small surprise that the system was ineffectual, and only added to the self-evident suffering of the Germans. This was the time of non-fraternisation so we only had minimum contacts with the Germans. It would have taken a hardened stomach and total disregard for others not to be aware of their travails at this time. Berlin was an unbelievable mess – not only had it been extensively bombed but it had all too literally been raped and pillaged by the Russians on their advance to the West. In the midst of these people struggling for survival the allies, many of whom had not been involved in the fighting, lived in an ostentatiously arrogant and luxurious style. The naval parties who had taken over the posts and naval establishments of the *Kriegsmark* had selected their messes and accommodation with care and an eye to the future. We were housed in a splendid house in the Grünewald and had access to unlimited transport. The best hotels had been taken over as officer's clubs, where luxuries unheard of by the Germans were served to all and sundry. Drinks were cheap, and the country had already moved onto the cigarette economy so that, for a no-smoker like me, almost anything or anyone could be bought for the price of a few duty-free packets. I was certainly no prude, nor was I oblivious to all these delights, but I could never come to terms with the unbelievable gulf between the most junior of the victors and the most distinguished of the vanquished.

My education progressed in the broadest of terms, for I was taken in hand (in every meaning of the word) by an older Canadian lady who was also working as an interpreter. Not only was she more experienced in every way, but she had the great advantage, as a Ukrainian, of speaking both languages effortlessly, so that she had boundless energy and enterprise to pursue her other interests which, for a short time, included me.

Trying to understand why the Navy employed me on such unmilitary tasks I can only assume that I was in a sort of 'park and polish' stage for the next delights they had in store. Within eight weeks I was unceremoniously hauled out of the Allied

Control Authority, where I had done my worst, and from the arms of my Ukrainian lady where I had done my rather inadequate best, and sent off to Hamburg to the Naval Headquarters. Berlin had been a sort of extension of university. I wasn't viewed as a part of the naval establishment and was left to get on with my own tasks in my own way. Hamburg was a different kettle of fish. We had an Admiral, barracks, parades, a staff and the whole shebang. A shebang, moreover, of which I had no previous experience, for submarine admirals were very much 'one of us', and we were viewed by the staff as the justification for their existence. Here, although the Navy had a multiplicity of tasks to perform, the administration was king, and I got a rather biased foretaste of the directions in which my profession was moving. Luckily for me I had re-entered this life in a sort of twilight world, for we Intelligence people, although owing allegiance to our admiral in Germany, were also responsible to a multiplicity of people and organisations, including the Russian section of the Naval Intelligence Division in the Admiralty under the ubiquitous Tony Courtney, who was to be my *éminence grise* for the next five years.

Hamburg proved to be only a staging post, to my relief, before I continued to my presumably preordained position at Wilhelmshaven. I have written of this exercise elsewhere, but at the time I had no inkling that that unlikely and unloved town would prove to be the point on my main line which diverted me to a host of future destinations of which I could not have imagined. The naval base at Wilhelmshaven had been the largest naval dockyard in the world, building, amongst many other mighty vessels, the *Tirpitz*. The town was a purpose-built one, erected to serve the Navy during both world wars and the preparations for them. Like many towns which were developed over a short period of time, it showed all the disadvantages of the concepts of town planning at the turn of the century. The town itself, by comparison with Berlin, Hamburg and Bremen, was relatively unscathed, although the dockyard buildings were extensively damaged. The latter were a considerable shock to me, for I had failed to realise how difficult it is to destroy a machine shop from the air. Even though the roofs of many of the shops had gone and walls had been blown in, the machine tools remained – row on orderly row, just waiting for the word to produce an instant supply of items of the highest possible quality (as we knew to our cost). I was seconded to HMS *Royal Rupert* under the command of a legendary captain, Eric Condor – who is still revered in Wilhelmshaven today. There was already an intelligence officer on his staff, a cousin of mine, who was engaged in the distasteful job of denazification and keeping an eye open for a highly improbable resurgence of German naval power. Unlike the army, the German navy had resisted the Führer's instructions and had maintained its independence from the Nazi party until late in the war. Indeed, it was Admiral Raeder's stubbornness in refusing to force his officers to belong to the Nazi party which, among other reasons, led to his replacement by Doenitz. However, Doenitz's inheritance of Hitler's mantle in 1945 had created an impression of German naval participation in the affairs of the Third Reich which was not entirely based on the facts. The naval war had been a 'clean' war, unmarked by the savagery and sadism of much that had happened ashore and, with some right, they felt that, as a force, they had never been defeated. They retained that spirit and belief in the honour of their calling, and I was to find many friends amongst their ranks.

Condor had put the yard itself to work under its German admiral, to manufacture anything and everything which was needed for the reconstruction of a shattered country and, despite all the difficulties of fuel, energy, transport and raw materials, it was humming along as a creative enterprise. Its days were, however, numbered, for it had been allocated to the Russians as a part of the reparations package to restore the damage caused in that country. There was a deep irony involved in these decisions. The reparations delivered exceeded in quality anything the Russians had ever had, or were likely to have had. Yet, on the other side, the removal of all the pre-war and wartime plant from Germany ensured that, once rebuilding began, that country would have the most modern, efficient and purpose-built industrial infrastructure in the world.

My task was to act as the Liaison Officer for the Russian

mission who were to arrive to 'supervise' the loading up of the Wilhelmshaven yard. I was also required to keep an eye on them to ensure that there was no subversion or sabotage, and to find out what I could of the destination and future of the yard when they received it. From Condor's point of view the task was a nuisance, an interruption and an obstruction to his plans for the rebuilding of the town to perform a peaceful and constructive role. Above everything he didn't want a lot of hassle. The job had to be done but if I could have waved a magic wand and caused it all to disappear that would have been his ideal.

Magic wands, like everything else, were in short supply at Wilhelmshaven and I speedily got an idea of what I had been let in for. I was twenty-two years old and had never worked in a dockyard in my life. Besides me, there was an engineer from Rolls-Royce, a naval constructor, the entire administration infra-structure of the yard and my team of Russians. A more unlikely band would have been difficult to imagine. The leader, Major Bardini, was a multilingual KGB officer and the nearest approach to a smooth Russian I have ever met. He was a cultured and cultivated man with a weakness for the ladies which was to prove a problem for him. The others included a Soviet captain who became a particular friend of mine. He had endured the whole siege of Leningrad and was prone to devastating moods of depression, fuelled by a hatred of Germans, the like of which I had never encountered before. We used to sit up late at night, knocking off a bottle of schnapps, and I relived every chilling day and night of the siege with him many times. The only naval man was a major in the Naval Infantry, who was looked on by the rest of the team as a sort of Master Mariner of vast nautical experience – a delusion he did nothing to enlighten them about. He was a simple man, but boastful to boot and claimed a degree of heroism I had real reason to doubt. He flashed a whole battery of gold teeth at an astonished world. To my dismay his one remaining rotten molar developed an abscess and I had to take him to our dentist. Despite multiple injections, and the fact that the tooth itself was by then virtually waving in the wind, it could only be parted from him by physically restraining him in the chair for the few seconds it took for the unfortunate dentist to detach it. The whole process had been accompanied by bellows of fear which could have been heard in Moscow, I am sure. To cap it all, I had to listen to him regaling his colleagues in the bar with accounts of his courage and bravery.

My team included two Russian sergeant drivers, because the Russians would not allow any German to drive their BMW cars. All of us were accommodated in a single barrack block, but we ate in the mess with, but apart from, my fellow naval officers. Most of the time I lived as a Russian, but from time to time I retreated gratefully to my own kind, in order to attempt to recharge my batteries. Only Bardini spoke anything but Russian, and although I started trying to teach them some English they showed interest, but little aptitude or application. They started in a paroxysm of mistrust, spending the first week continually trying to prove that we all had the simple aim of cheating them and depriving them of their rights, and they were particularly suspicious of me. Moreover they found it impossible to believe that any of us had actually done any fighting. It was a trying time – somewhat akin to trying to gain the confidence of a headhunter in New Guinea, but without the red beads.

After a time they accepted me and even spent considerable efforts discovering my true 'Russian' characteristics. One of these, which gave them particular pleasure, related to a mind-boggling bender on Red Army Day, from which I awoke in the early hours face down in the snow. Far from this being the cause of shame which my British naval officers would have considered it to be, had they known, my Russians saw it as the true compliment of one striving to attain 'Russianness'. The other reason for my further acceptance was, to me, even more idiosyncratic. I was going out with two girls at the time – one a gorgeous slim Pole who, despite being in a displaced person camp near Oldenburg, managed to look like a top model every time I was with her. The other was an altogether much more robust girl. She had a great sense of humour and was splendid company, but no beauty. She was well built in every way and made few concessions to femininity – preferring tweeds to silk. On one occasion, when we were discussing the national characteristics of our respective countries, Bardini remarked how atypical I was of his experience of the British and how similar I was to his fellow countrymen – a great and undeserved compliment. He culminated his vodka-induced flow of rhetoric by commenting how I even shared their taste in feminine beauty. I thought instantly of my beautiful Pole, but was stunned to hear him go on to say how, like me, they liked their girls strong, with powerful legs!

As the suspicions eased away and my Russians realised that, whatever else I was doing (which was quite a lot), I was as determined as they were to see that the dockyard left us for Mother Russia, our relationship became much warmer. Whenever they left for one of their periodic visits to Berlin to report, in a secure way, their activities – official and unofficial – they would invariably bring me back a present of some sort. On one occasion it was a small dog, christened by them Muishka or Little Mouse, who became our collective mascot. On another it was two sets of improbable and unaesthetic Russian longjohns, made of an indestructible cellulose fabric and dyed in fetching tones of pink and blue. One of the curiosities of my colleagues, besides their habit of ladling marmalade into their morning tea or coffee, was a predilection to bathe in their underwear, the soap being applied to the outside of this all-enveloping covering. By this means they avoided sullying their skins, which I assume were only cleaned down when they visited the steam baths in Berlin on their three-monthly visits.

It was apparent that the steam baths were not the only visits they made, for, despite the bans on fraternisation, one of their number arrived back with an unmistakably socially transmitted disease. This gave me another interesting vignette on the problems of being a Russian in 1946. The disciplinary punishment for such a dire transgression of the rules would have been horrific. Moreover the eventuality was not one which the poor man could discuss with any of his colleagues. In his despair, watching the progressive deterioration of his genitalia, he found me the only worthy recipient of his confidence, and I was expected to resolve the situation which, with the help of the base doctor, I duly did. Even though we liked one another on an individual basis, the Russians, unless they wanted something, always looked upon us as potential enemies. We were allies in name only. To a man they refused to believe that we had contributed anything to the defeat of the Axis and privately and publicly they denigrated the assistance we had offered them. Since I had lost four friends in the Arctic convoys I did not find this attitude an endearing one.

The task itself was a nightmare. The Russians expected the dockyard to be transferred right down to the last paper clip. Any minor item which went missing was viewed as a combination of sabotage and international incident. Moreover the Germans lacked any remote enthusiasm for the job, reasoning, correctly, that the yard would be used to arm the Soviets against the naive allied victors. In addition they had the practical problem that there was no work in the area and knew that in completing the task they were sending away their only means of earning a living. The Russians continually changed the specifications, as more and more impractical and bureaucratic instructions poured in to us. At no time during my tenure of office did any senior Russian come to see what was happening for himself. It was all done by inflexible, monolithic and snail-paced remote control. It quickly became apparent that their intention was to exactly replicate Wilhelmshaven on the shores of the White Sea. Obviously all the equipment was going to arrive at its destination long before the civil engineering would be done. We were required, therefore, to load each machine tool into an enormous double-skinned packing case, mounted on gigantic wooden runners, so that the whole edifice could be dragged across the tundra. The cases themselves were lined with tarred paper and were clearly going to represent home to some unfortunate employee once the machine tools had been removed. The Russian specifications also forbore to require any expansion slots when the tools were bolted onto their massive runners, an operation which we carefully carried out, under their supervision, in our heated packing hall. The conditions of the tools cannot have been too good after standing for a North

Russian winter or two, interspersed by the short, but surprisingly hot, summers which are a feature of the country.

Although I dealt extensively with the German management of the yard, I took great care not to get onto personal or friendly terms with any of them. Not only was it prohibited (although many of the occupying forces, armed with their cigarette rations and such temptations as coffee and chocolate, sought solace in German arms), but I also knew that such actions would lose the rather shaky trust I had established with the Russians. It is difficult to give a fair account of what a ghastly time this was in Germany. The winter of 1947 was one of the worst in memory. The sea froze off Wilhelmshaven and the canals were impassable. Everyone, apart from the occupying forces, was suffering unbelievable shortages of everything – food, clothing, heat, power and even shelter. None of the pertinences of civilisation were available in adequate quantity for the Germans. The currency was worthless and everything was done by barter. Queues would form up outside my cousin's office of Germans seeking to denounce husbands, brothers, sisters and sons as Nazis, in the hope of some meagre reward. The fabric of German society seemed to me to have been totally destroyed and I could not believe that the country and its people could ever rise again. Even within families, all too often it became every man for himself. Honour and honesty seemed to have gone out of the window with the occupation. Many of the occupying forces ignored these privations and lived lives of ridiculous ease and privilege without the slightest compunction, regarding them as the well-earned spoils of the victor. I could not do this and my curious position as a sort of filling in a triple-decker sandwich between the Germans, the British and the Russians forced me to see each party's point of view in this Kafkaesque situation.

Even though I gained from the experience, and life had some hilariously funny interludes, I hated it, and swore never to return once I was able to get away. Anything more remote from the simple, clean and natural life of a sailor at sea could barely be imagined. Everyone had an angle – half of the people were engaged in a desperate struggle for the simplest forms of personal survival whilst the other half were, with some honourable exceptions, pursuing personal gain and hedonistic aims. I began to look on submarining, even with unwilling and untrained sailors, as a form of recreation and release from an experience which I found difficult to cope with on an emotional plane.

Just when my morale had reached almost its lowest ebb, a wonderful thing happened. Betty, whom I had long ago abandoned all hope of seeing again, got in touch with my mother. At least I knew where she was and, even more importantly, that she was not attached to anyone in particular. I wrote immediately and, when not rebuffed, started to plan for our next meeting. I spent that awful winter at Wilhelmshaven lurching from one manmade crisis to another and longing to be with Betty again. She was living in Halifax, where she was running one of her mother's businesses, and in April I journeyed there to see her. That day Halifax seemed to me to be imbued with a wondrous glow and an aura of loveliness which I still ascribe to it. It was as though there had been no *interregnum* in our relationship, and the difference between the romantic beaches of the Galle Face and cold, wet, dark and dirty Halifax on an early spring day were barely discernible. It would not have mattered to me if I had been at the bottom of a coal mine and I doubt that I would have noticed. I was even more besotted and in love than I had been before, and this time I was determined not to lose the happiness that seemed to be within my grasp.

In those days professional naval officers were not allowed to get married before the age of twenty-five. Should they do so, as well as incurring Their Lordships' displeasure, they received no marriage allowance, quarters or recognition of their insubordinate state. However, there was no way I was going to lose another two years in order to satisfy the Second Sea Lord's antiquated view of an appropriate age of consent, and we planned to get married as soon as possible. 'Planned' is perhaps an over-ambitious description of a decision which, fortunately for me, seemed to take itself for both of us. We emphatically did not sit down and work out where we would live – or on what. In any event, Betty could not have come to Wilhelmshaven, even if I had been of the magic age. We knew we did not want to waste more time and that we wanted to make our lives together. It was the turning point of my life – the moment at which I felt myself emerge from a seemingly endless process of growing up. The knowledge that Betty wanted to share my life gave me, in one wondrous step, the first flickerings of the self-confidence which I had always lacked.

If we had no idea of the simple administrative things of life – such as housing, money or even location, Betty had even less idea of what she was letting herself in for. As a Wren officer she thought she knew the Navy and its ways, but neither she nor I had any inkling of the life that lay ahead. She is fond of saying that she married a naval officer, and would never have married a businessman. However, I was not following a normal naval career (if there is such a thing) and even the next ten years were as different from most people's pictures of life in the Navy as one could have. We decided that we wanted to get married in three months' time and, despite some opposition, prevailed on our families to go along with us despite their misgivings at the very short period of our engagement. Right up to our wedding day both families resolutely refused to see that, from our point of view, we had already spent four years of courtship and regretted the time we had wasted.

At about this time I was summoned to the Admiralty in Whitehall to see Tony Courtney, who was still heading up NID 16, the Russian section of the Admiralty. I was interviewed by a Wing Commander and a Lieutenant Colonel of the 'Cherrypickers' in the catacombs under the Cabinet offices. The interview was the first of many I was to experience later, where if they did know what they wanted they certainly weren't going to tell me what it was. In fact I left with even less idea of what was expected than when I arrived and could make no judgement as to whether I had done well or badly. They had asked many questions about the Russians, about whom my knowledge was very much a worm's eye view of a singularly small sample. I later found out that even this inadequate insight into Russian psychology was encyclopaedic by comparison with the practical experience of my colleagues, who had never had anything at all to do with our perceived antagonists. Despite my youth, by comparison with the other service representatives, and the paucity of my knowledge of the inner workings of Intelligence work, or of the Russian approach to this problem except at the lowest level of field operations, I found myself appointed as the naval member of a mysterious organisation known as the London Controlling Section. Like so many clandestine organisations, this was the inheritor of a large and highly successful wartime set-up, which had commanded the skills of many well-known men from a wide range of activities and backgrounds. This pale shadow of past glories consisted of three of us. We occupied the offices which had been Churchill's command centre, and are now open to public view. Frequently, when I was requested to work overnight, I would snuggle down in the great man's bed, for everything – except what was needed for our interloping activities – was retained exactly as he had left it.

The work was fascinating, but the insight it gave me into the ways by which our country was governed was even more dramatic. Within days of starting work, with no real introduction to the complexities of our tasks, I was asked to draft a paper for ultimate submission to the Chiefs of Staff, on what the British policy should be on a certain subject. It felt a bit like my debut at the Allied Control Authority and I not only felt inadequate, but knew that I was quite unfitted to perform the task. I took some comfort from the thought that mine was only the first draft, and that obviously the paper would be seen by an endless succession of experts before submission, so little real harm could be done. I did not relish the idea of being exposed to ridicule for my naiveté and lack of understanding. What actually happened was deeply worrying to a twenty-three-year-old with an almost sublime faith in the leadership of our country. Apart from a couple of corrections to the grammar, my paper sailed through the various committees and working parties. It shot into and out of the dockets, in-trays and minutes of Staff Offices of all three services, as well as the Foreign Office, MI6 and MI5, and within three months I found myself the architect of our country's declared policy. I had always imagined the great men striding up and down their offices formulating in their infinitely wise minds the complex intersecting grand designs which would then be turned into action plans by serfs like me. Not for a moment had I dreamed that the leadership applied from the top took the form of largely negative interventions on the ideas flowing from below. Moreover, during the next two years of my stint in the Cabinet offices I was to find that, all too often, these 'original thoughts' emanating from below were guesses as to what the great men were thought to want to hear. A good deal of policy seemed to be formed by a sort of osmotic process and progress was made more by the establishment of case law than anything else. This did not preclude endless and bitter inter-service warfare, which seemed to take precedence over the common goal of resisting the onward march of Russian influence. This used to be particularly frustrating for our little band, since we were as one in our views of how to discharge our own particular responsibilities, but getting all the agreements which were necessary before we could proceed often proved impossible for reasons totally unconnected with the merits of our suggestions.

Despite the frustrations it was a curious, demanding, stimulating and fascinating job. I met, on a professional basis, the most extraordinary cross-section of the leaders of our country at that time. I saw in action the Prime Minister, the Foreign Secretary, the Chiefs of Staff, Lord Portal, Sir Henry Tizzard, some of the outstanding scientific brains of the country, and a wide range of the Foreign Office staff as well as the then heads of the Secret and Security Services. Moreover, inadequate though I felt my training and background to be, when I saw these leaders I was the best apology for an expert we had to hand. Quite apart from this insight into the machinery of government, with its missing cogs on so many of the wheels, the experience of meeting legendary people at the very top gave me another astonishing correction of a widely held and personally cherished misconception.

The whole of my enthusiastic reading, training and experiences during the war had set firmly in my mind the view that great leaders were in some way different in kind and quality to the 'hoi polloi' like me. I was convinced that these differences were of a fundamental type, that they possessed intellectual and conceptual abilities and insights of a breadth and significance not vouchsafed to the ordinary mortal. In short, I believed in Supermen and Superwomen. There may well be some around and certainly history and science do point to some people who seem to have had this quite different capacity from that of their fellows, but so far, personally, I have not come across one of them. What I have seen is people with the same frailties and quirks of human nature as the rest of us, struggling manfully with bigger jobs than we have. Even the size of the job is something to which anyone can become accustomed. It is surprising how easily one slides up the scale of worrying firstly about tens of pounds, then hundreds, then thousands, and eventually refusing to become involved with matters affecting less than a million. Usage is a great familiariser, almost too much so, for as the scale of the problems with which you deal gets ever larger it is all too easy to forget that everything ultimately ends up with individual men and women doing different things in different ways.

One of the fascinations of my work at that time was the continual see-sawing between minutiae and massive affairs of state. There was always a temptation to try to see in all these things a single, totally integrated seamless coat – without bits sticking out, or errors in its execution. One of the things I brought to the task was my practical experiences of the Russian ability to cock things up. This was an ability of a totally different order to our amateurish efforts. Indeed during my time trying to organise things with, through or for the Russians, I learnt that positive written confirmation of some intended event invariably meant it would not happen. In the early days at Wilhelmshaven I used to believe that a series of telexes promising the arrival of a specific Russian ship at a particular time was sufficient pre-warning to justify arranging for berths to be cleared, warehouses filled and stevedores prepared for day and night work. Experience and wisdom soon taught me to treat such official pronouncements with contempt and only to start planning when a ship actually started through the Kiel Canal. Even then one could never be sure that a last-minute diversion would not abort all one's needless exertions.

Time and time again I would find that we would ascribe to the Russians degrees of premeditation and intricate organisation of interrelated but disparate events, in widely disparate parts of the world, that we, with all our sophistication, would have been hard put to pull off. It may be that it is better to overestimate one's competition, but all my experience of the Soviet Union has always been the same. Things can only be made to happen as a result of almost unbelievable use of human energy and resources. The inertia in the system, the multiplicity of decision points, the draconian punishments for failure and the poor rewards for success, all militate against efficient operation. This experience was to be reinforced many times over the years, and proved to be just as relevant when I was dealing with the USSR on industrial matters as it had been in those years immediately after the war. One of the greatest doubts about Russian ability to change and adapt must rest on those deeply ingrained patterns of behaviour which are not, in themselves, uncomfortable, but sap the will to stand on one's own feet and make one's own way.

My work at that time was fascinating and exciting. I was right in the front line, and the tasks I undertook seemed as relevant and important to the security and well-being of my fellow citizens as had my efforts during the war. In fact I began to feel quite superior to my colleagues in submarines, endlessly training and preparing for the war which I was engaged in preventing. The fact that I could not then or now talk about my work, and enjoy the reflected glory of being associated with it, did not worry me for I had an implicit belief that the evil of Nazism had been transferred lock, stock and barrel to communism. It seemed even more dangerous if one compared its seductive theories with the rather crude leaps of faith necessary for a belief in *Mein Kampf*.

Despite these views, there seemed to me then and thereafter something missing. My time with the Russians had given me a great affection for them. I found their simplicity, their jolliness and ability to laugh at themselves, even their inefficiencies, endearing. While all of them believed, despite all the evidence to the contrary, that they lived and worked under a superior system (had they not won the war, in their belief, single-handed?), none of them seemed to want to rule the world. I had met many Germans who seemed to believe that such was their innate racial superiority, they would have been the rightful rulers of the world had not everyone else, inexplicably, ganged up on them. My Russians, however, seemed much more imbued with their Marxist belief that in our death throes we capitalists would seek to exterminate them as guardians of their holy grail of belief. Indeed they looked upon the German attack as a sort of false start to such an attempt.

Few of them seemed to believe that it was necessary to expand their influence by force and war, for they cherished the thought that the superior fairness of the Soviet system, with all its government-imposed freedoms, would triumph by its own logic. Many of the freedoms they believed in so strongly were, to our eyes, ludicrous in the extreme. For example, they viewed the very different viewpoints espoused by the Western press as clear evidence of propagandist manipulation by newspaper tycoons, by comparison with the government-preferred truthfulness and similarity of *Pravda* and *Izvestia*. They really did look at the other side of the looking glass, but they were not zealots. As a people, their aim was to start to rebuild their homeland, ravished and devastated as it was. Given the poverty of their resources, the ineffectiveness of their organisation and the size of the task, it was obvious that they had more than enough to do for many years to come.

Holding these beliefs, why did I accept so readily that they were our enemy, in the same way that Germany and Japan had been? I think it was a self-fulfilling result of the work I was engaged in. As soon as one saw and experienced the activities of the Soviet secret agencies, the apparent similarities to the Nazi regime became inescapable. The curious thing is that Soviet intelligence capability was far superior to that of the Nazis. For a start, far more effort was devoted to it, and it was able to call on the millions of sympathisers of all nationalities across the world, in a way quite outside the potential of the Nazi command organisation. It was, I think, the internal security role, the willingness to resort to extremes of sadistic pressures, and the indifference to human life and suffering, which bridged the parallel. It was my knowledge and experiences of these unpleasant manifestations of a police state which overcame my reading of the characteristics of the ordinary Russians and led me to believe that the work I was doing was worthwhile. This was just as well, for it was to occupy most of my life from 1946 until 1957.

Despite the clear evidence there is now that so much of my efforts were wasted, and my increasing doubts about both the ways and the means, I still cannot regret those years, and the experiences which I gained. Although I increasingly found myself attempting to fight fire with fire, I do not recall any actions of which I feel ashamed. While perhaps the crusade I thought I was embarked upon had false goals, and certainly never did retake Jerusalem, who is to say what might have happened without our efforts? It is only now, over forty years later, that the tide is turning and the basic inconsistencies in the Soviet system are shaking apart the mechanisms of repression. At minimum, we prevented the tide moving still further up the beach and in this battle our little group played a vital role, against very substantial odds. There were so few of us and so many of them. The good news was that, as I was to discover later, too much incoming information swamps the analysts and there is still no interpretive device to compete with the single human brain. To this day I cannot imagine how the Russians, with their lack of organisation can begin to interpret the mountains of information and misinformation they so diligently collect. I know we could not use such depths of 'cover' to our advantage, and I believe it must be very difficult for them to do so.

Meanwhile Betty and I were starting our married life together. We got married in great style, largely for the benefit of Betty's parents, in Harrogate in late July. Our wedding was memorable, as all weddings should be, but in our case for some rather idiosyncratic reasons. Betty had lived in Harrogate for only the briefest of times and so, together, she and I knew hardly any of the vast numbers of guests who thronged the bride's side of the church – contrasting rather markedly with the rather sparse numbers of family and friends that I managed to rustle up to occupy the pews on my side. Betty's mother and father, both business people of long standing in the area, made the most of the whole thing, with marquees, crates of champagne and unsparkling speeches. My best man was a fellow Naval Intelligence officer and we paraded around with swords and medals in the appropriate manner although, to Betty's lasting infuriation, my mother would not let me wear my 'best' uniform. Even my wedding did not seem to her to be an important enough occasion for this hallowed garment to be worn, and it remained in London, in a box under my bed. The nature of my work made it impossible to have the usual raised swords of my fellow officers and a line of cloaks and daggers would have seemed in doubtful taste. As always in the great moments of my life, my employers (in this case the Cabinet Office) came up absolutely to my expectations. We were involved in a rather tricky operation at the time and so I was very graciously given the Saturday off to get married, provided I was on duty by Monday morning. Our honeymoon (if you could call it that) therefore took place on Saturday night at the Station Hotel at York – a hostelry for which I still have an unaccountable affection and which does not seem to have changed at all.

To put the cap on it all, my brother-in-law had unwittingly (he swears) put empty champagne bottles instead of full ones in our going-away car and, on our return train journey to London on Sunday I could only obtain a seat for my wife. I do not recommend standing for hours in the corridor of a British Rail train, unable even to feast your eyes upon your beloved, as the best start to married life, but such was our euphoria that it barely broke our stride. My mother had moved to Melbury Road off Kensington High Street, and made the top floor of her maisonette there available for us; it was there that we started our lives together. The gesture may have been well meaning and was certainly financially helpful, although of course we paid rent, but accepting it proved to be an error of judgement on our part. Although in theory we lived separately, in practice we had little privacy and my mother's jealousy and possessiveness soon intruded on our lives together. I tried, ineffectively and unfairly, to hold a balance between the two of them and thereby placed pressures upon us all that we could have done without. Moreover the arrangement, which was so seductively easy, prevented us using the small amount of capital that we had to put down on a house. We did indeed debate this but a combination of my family's terror at the responsibilities of home ownership and a total lack of helpful advice from Betty's stepfather, who certainly knew what would have been a sensible course of action, led us to abandon the idea. It was a sad error, which was to haunt us until after I left the Navy.

Despite these intrinsically poor domestic arrangements and the inevitable adjustments involved in sharing one's life for the first time, we enjoyed our lives to the full. I found that the girl I had married was a very different being from the one who had enraptured me at the Old Assembly Rooms in Newcastle. Not only was she, in my view, even more beautiful now, but she revealed totally unexpected and highly developed domestic skills. She was, for a start, a superb classic cook, and it was no time at all before, thanks to her, I overcame my childhood revulsion of onions, and my meals became immeasurably tastier! Our little flat sparkled and she was determined to make it ours, energetically seeking out bits of second-hand furniture, redecorating and cleaning like a being possessed. It was as well she did, for we speedily found out the impossibility of living on a lieutenant's pay in London. Since I was two years under the age which the Admiralty considered the bare minimum for the assumption of marital responsibilities, we received no London allowance. Our tiny little nest egg, which I still wish we had put to the downpayment on a house, eroded at a frightening rate. I was quickly reduced to walking from Kensington to Whitehall in order to save the fare, and taking a sandwich for lunch, or meeting Betty in the park for a picnic, to save my mess bill.

Nevertheless, thanks to my wife's frugal skills, we managed to live surprisingly well – and even to entertain. This was the heyday of the cinema and we were regular visitors to the luxury of the Kensington Odeon. Although we had no spare room, we had splashed out on an excruciatingly uncomfortable bed-settee so that our visitors could stay overnight. This gargantuan piece of furniture, which was moved up to the fourth floor of our building by an army of removal men, managed, notably, to be almost as uncomfortable in its role as a settee as it was as a bed. Neither of these faults prevented it being in almost continuous use in both roles as our friends took advantage of a free pad in Kensington.

We had the small memorable adventures that one has as a young couple, and despite Betty's experience of living in Britain, by comparison with my institutionalised past, managed to make some hilarious mistakes in our attempts to save money. We would walk miles to save a copper or two, and viewed the Kensington shops and their prices as being akin to ordering deliveries from Fortnum and Mason. Saturday afternoons (for in those days we worked Saturday mornings) would find us in Hammersmith or Shepherd's Bush markets, trying to find the cheapest possible produce. As time went on, the problems of our shared *ménage* became more and more inescapable. My wife and my mother had equally strongly held views on almost everything, but they were all too often diametrically opposed. I worked long hours and, coupled with the hour or so it took me every morning and evening to get to work, Betty spent more time alone in the flat, with my mother fulminating a floor below, than she did with me. If you add to all this our financial struggles, the whole package must have seemed a poor reward to the girl for losing her independence. By contrast, it was obvious that I was not suffering too much. From having been underweight and nervous, the first six months of marriage saw me ballooning up in weight in an almost unstoppable way. In reality I went from pitifully underweight to slightly overweight, but the change was all too obvious – adding as it did to our financial stresses by the need for a certain amount of re-kitting.

Further complications arose for us. The partition of India had found my father in as unenviable a position as it would have been possible to conceive. He was senior member of the council of Junagadh and under contract to the Nawab. Junagadh was ruled by a Moslem family, but the majority of the state was Hindi. At Partition it was granted to India, and the family, with my father's help, very prudently fled to Karachi. The Nawab was famous, or infamous, for his love of dogs and for the state wedding he held for the nuptials of two of his favourites – including parades, bands and all the appropriate paraphernalia. The chartered aircraft took off bearing my father's employer, his wives, the son to whom my father had been guardian (still my friend to his recent death) and a large number of dogs. My father remained, administering the state on behalf of his employer, who continued to send instructions to him as though Partition was a minor administrative inconvenience. The Indian government, both to avoid any action by Pakistan and, I imagine, with some impatience at my father's view of his contractual obligations, invaded the state with landing craft and the full force of his old comrades in arms, the Indian Army.

My father was given twenty-four hours to leave, forbidden to take any possessions and found his funds blocked. He was, after generations of colonial work by my family, shipped home to Britain as a distressed British subject, which indeed he was. He joined our *entourage* at Melbury Road, which placed even further stresses on our fragile family group. I was convinced then that, at the outbreak of war, my parents had decided to call it a day as far as their marriage was concerned. Now they were two sad people, bound purely by my father's sense of duty and my mother's determination to maintain her status. The arrival of this sad, unemployed, ill-adjusted but decent man in our midst was shattering. He and I were strangers and had no basis to build where there had been nothing before. Moreover he felt his position desperately, for everything on which his life had been based had been removed. At the time I did not realise the courage he showed, or the miseries he must have felt. Overnight he had lost all the power, the adulation and comforts he had accepted as his rightful due, to find himself an unwanted squatter in a small flat, with a woman with whom he shared neither mutuality of regard nor love.

In addition, England as he knew it had gone. No tender enquiry from the Palace or the India Office – no Rolls-Royce and no concern. Even his achievements were looked upon almost as having been British exploitation, and as something to be ignored rather than praised. He and Betty struck up the nearest approach to a human relationship I ever witnessed on his part, but even that innocent and, I am sure, sincere action merely added to the tensions in our *entourage*. My mother's well-ordered existence – the theatre twice a week, meals at her favourite cafés every day and a calendar of minor social engagements stretching weeks ahead – vanished with everything else. There was no money coming in, no payoff, no redundancy and not even access to the money my father had accumulated in India. Their savings in the UK were intact but inadequate, and between them they had few relevant skills to earn a living in the Britain of 1948, which was thronged with their like.

Betty and I had, by eating our way all too literally through our savings, lost the possibility of moving out, and of course my time at the Cabinet Office was beginning to come to a close. The Navy, despite the fact that I was seconded to, and paid by, the Cabinet Office, still insisted on 'commissions' of between two and three years, so that a move was a certainty in 1949. The ironies of life meant that April 1949 would also see my official recognition as a married man, so that we would have rather more freedom to choose. There was nothing we could do for my parents. Their gulf was unbridgeable and we could not have functioned as a family even if we had wanted to. It was, therefore, a relief to us when I was summoned across to the Admiralty again, to be informed by the ubiquitous Tony Courtney that he was going to Germany as Staff Officer, Intelligence and he wanted me to take over at Kiel.

My many requests to be spared a return to that unhappy country were ignored, but I was well aware that, if ordered, I had no option but to go. My attitude on this was viewed with total incredulity and lack of understanding by my superiors and indeed I felt it was almost taken as some sort of moral weakness. As usual, once the die was cast, yesterday was too late and within days I found myself handing over at the Cabinet Office and bidding farewell to Betty for what I thought would be only a few days. Germany called and I was back in the Navy again.

7 I See the Sea

Despite my unwarranted misgivings about returning to Germany, everything seemed to have miraculously worked out for the best. The Navy would produce a house for us, and it seemed as though we had every chance of balancing our precarious budget at last. Moreover, I would be my own boss, the headquarters was a conveniently long way away and, best of all, I had another shore posting, so at last we could be alone to enjoy our married life. Predictably there was a fly in the ointment. Even though the house we were to occupy would stand empty, there was no way the Navy would allow Betty to join me until my twenty-fifth birthday.

Neither Tony Courtney nor I had expected this intransigence – for Naval Intelligence had its own ways of getting round most things – but this problem was apparently insuperable. We pleaded; we pointed out the extra expense involved in putting me up in a mess, while the Naval Officer in Charge's house stayed empty; we argued the social advantages of having my wife to represent the Senior Service; we argued the loneliness of my harrowing tasks, and my need for the support of my beloved, all to no avail. A naval regulation was a naval regulation, and hot-blooded whipper-snappers who could not defer their marriage until after their twenty-fifth birthday could and should be taught the consequence of their open mutiny.

Thus it was that far from starting life anew and together, I found myself starting anew and apart. In the event it gave me a chance to get my office and duties sorted out before Betty's arrival on the scene. My predecessors had been naval officers first, and intelligence officers second, despite the fact that the

Kiel office had hardly any classical naval responsibilities. Although we were nominally responsible for the Kiel Canal, that splendid outfit ran itself with the usual superb efficiency of any German organisation unless it was 'helped' by the allies. We represented the Navy's most advanced eyes and ears on the Baltic – an area where we kept no naval presence since it was believed it could easily be blockaded in – but where there was a fairly substantial Soviet fleet based on Leningrad. In those days the build-up of the Soviet navy was in full swing, but the northern fleet at Murmansk was quite a bit smaller than the Baltic fleet which still remained as the *corps d'élite* of the Soviet sea-going forces. There was, therefore, plenty to watch and listen to and I and my tiny team of three were able to fill every hour of every day doing something useful. We were collecting a vast amount of information, and very soon I began to feel that I knew the Baltic fleet rather better than I did my own service. I even began to recognise some of the foibles and thought-processes of individual Russian commanding officers.

In addition to the fascination of the work, I had really fallen on my feet as far as facilities were concerned. The substantial naval presence in Germany at the end of the war had been progressively scaled down, but at that time we took over all the assets of the *Kriegsmarine*. As proud bases such as Kiel were reduced to one young lieutenant, a naval writer, and a couple of civilians, we still retained the best that the Germany navy had had. Although the yachts had all gone, I still retained a magnificent admiral's barge, fine offices together with a flagpole and a yardarm – just in case I wanted to string anyone up – and a couple of splendid cars with German drivers. My drivers were both former career sailors, one a former lieutenant and the other a coxswain. The latter was one of the nicest men I had ever met – almost a dead ringer for the senior ratings I admired so much in our own service. Nothing ever phased him and he had a wonderful dry sense of humour which, combined with a seaman's philosophical view of life, gave me a totally different view of many of my fellow men, Germans and British alike. Küchler and I became firm friends, and when Betty joined me she formed the same regard for him. Some time later I had to prepare my plans for the eventuality that the Soviets invaded and I had to stay behind. Despite the fact that by then I had a vast array of German friends and acquaintances, many of whom I had been able to help in one way or another, it was to Küchler that I decided I would turn. I was secure in the belief that he would never betray me, regardless of the circumstances – a trust I was not prepared to give to many of his former superior officers.

Although my primary task was to watch the activities of the Russians, I was also required to keep an eye on the activities of former German naval personnel. They were having a very rough time, especially the most senior ones, because of the popular perception of their willing involvement with Nazism. The younger career officers had helped one another and were to be found busily and fruitfully engaged in the rebuilding of their country, but the admirals had the greatest difficulty finding work, and I knew two who were relegated to working as car-park attendants and watchmen. Their former subordinates, rather touchingly, still treated them with the respect due to their naval rank, and I was careful to do the same.

Over the next three years I was to get to know most of the surviving German senior naval officers and liked and admired them greatly. Some time later the Imperial Defence College was visiting Germany and I found out the major engagements fought by the British naval members. I was able to produce somebody from both sides of practically every surface engagement and I then organised a most memorable evening where I paired them with their German antagonists. Within minutes of the first schnapps, the cutlery was steaming ahead and reliving the turns and twists of the battles they had fought so few years ago. The air was full of 'I couldn't understand why you turned to port then,' or 'Why did you make smoke?' Both services had prided themselves on their professionalism and enjoyed the same ideals of service. The sea is in any event a clean environment and always provided a common enemy which punished sloppiness or lack of care and attention regardless of race or flag. This creates a common bond amongst sailors and the similarities between us seemed far greater than our differences. It was sad that it was so difficult to find any survivors from submarines for the reunions. Unfortunately their skirmishes had all too often led to their demise.

The months passed agonisingly slowly until at last my birthday and my wife arrived simultaneously. It was quite the best birthday I have ever had, and we took up the reins of married life with gusto. Our home was a small commandeered German house and our neighbours were all German. The property had been owned by Herr Boetel, to whom it would revert when the British moved on. For the first time we had a garden, which Herr Boetel helped us with, and we all shared the produce. It was still hard to obtain fruit and vegetables and they tended to be of poor quality. Our own rations were delivered weekly, including our meat ration. Meat was still well-nigh impossible to obtain on the German market. The cigarette economy was still in existence but not to such an extent as in 1947 and the shops were beginning to regain something of their appeal. Things were slightly easier in Britain, but both countries were still preoccupied with provision of the simple necessities of life rather than the pursuit of luxuries.

In addition to all the other novelties for a relatively newly married couple setting up on their own, we acquired a maid/housekeeper of dismal mien but nice disposition. Guthe was an East Prussian who had somehow managed to trek to the West faster than the Russians advanced. She arrived as a displaced person, and she seemed to have a great deal of difficulty acclimatising herself to the West German way of life. Despite all our efforts to joke with her she appeared to be dedicated to a Prussian melancholia, coupled with continuous anxiety that her services were not adequate to our needs. In truth they were not – even though we required little enough. However, we were so concerned with her apparently irremedial gloom that we greeted her efforts with all the enthusiasm one would reserve for the triumphal homecoming of a gold medal Olympic winner. We speedily learnt to accustom ourselves to a rather limited culinary repertoire of *bauernfrühstuck* (bacon and potato omelette), and *königsberger klopse* (meatballs), neither of which helped to put a stop to my burgeoning corporeal expansion.

Our problems were not eased by Guthe's inability to speak almost any language at all. Her German was inaudible and incomprehensible even to some Germans, while English was a flight of fancy far beyond her wildest dreams. Betty flung herself into the task of communication with her usual gusto – but with permanent damage to her command of the pure and elegant German she could otherwise so easily have mastered. My wife is a gifted actress and had the most perfect pronunciation and intonation. In any event, in a surprisingly short space of time Betty and Guthe were chattering away in a manner which put my pathetic command of the language – accumulated so painfully since the age of fourteen – to shame.

In addition to our drivers and two splendid German secretaries, I commanded a naval writer and two civil servants, one of whom was the most accomplished linguist I have ever met. 'Mac' acquired languages with the ease with which dogs attract fleas. It required only the most specious of reasons for him to devote the six weeks or so of evening study necessary for him to get a sound working knowledge of Magyar or Pushtu. The area I was in charge of, as well as the entire Baltic Sea, covered the whole of Schleswig Holstein from Flensburg in the north to Lübeck and Travemunde in the east. For good measure we also took in the island of Fehmarn in the east and the Frisian Islands and Sylt in the west. Over the next year I was to grow to love the historic beauty of the area, and to know every fishing village and creek. Despite being much further north than Wilhelmshaven, this area seemed much less harsh and forbidding. There were lakes, woods, hills and, for post-war Germany in 1949, surprisingly little residual damage. My duties were of the most varied type imaginable, and every day brought a new challenge or opportunity. We worked hard to ensure that no scrap of information eluded us, spending time debriefing and interrogating the refugees who still flooded across the frontier from East Germany and Poland, questioning the fishermen, or meticulously tabulating and recording all the data pertaining to Soviet merchant or war

ships leaving the Baltic by the canal or by the straits of Kattegat
or Skagerrak.

We dealt with sailors who had jumped ship, literally throwing
themselves overboard into the canal and swimming for a more
hospitable shore. We made the arrangements for the occasional
warships traversing the canal or visiting the harbour, and their
entertainment. From time to time even weirder tasks befell us,
such as the occasion when one of the salvage teams, raising the
many wrecks of the German navy, pulled up a sunken submarine.
This was not uncommon, but this particular submarine was
found to have contained a very large crew and, on closer
inspection, the remains of a number of women. There was still
continual questioning as to whether Hitler had genuinely per-
ished in the bunker or whether the whole affair had been an
elaborate deception to enable him to flee the country, to fight
again another day. The head of American Naval Intelligence in
Germany was convinced that the whole bunker thing had been a
put-up job which it was his destiny to unravel. After announcing
the discovery of a number of passengers aboard the wreck, I
therefore received a signal asking for permission for a scion of
US Naval Intelligence to investigate my findings. The day
dawned and a splendid and unconcerned American, a sort of
chief mortician's mate, arrived to survey the bodies. I have never
much enjoyed the grizzly side of life and reluctantly accompanied
my companion, who greeted the sight of the bones recovered
from the sludge which filled the boat with great enthusiasm.
Calipers, rulers and so on were applied to even the least likely
fragments, before he was prepared to accept that we did not have
the Führer's fibula and tibia in our possession.

Practically all contact with my superiors was in writing. As
long as nothing too untoward happened and there was a regular
flow of reasonably accurate reports, they seemed as happy to do
without me as I was to do without them. My pay and rations
arrived reliably and there was a pleasant social life in Kiel with
the widest range of amenities that any couple could ask for. We
also had access to an absolutely splendid *schloss* in the country at
Westensee, which was yet another relic of the Navy's past

predominance. It was still used occasionally as a 'safe house' when we had 'visitors' from the East, but for the vast majority of the time it was available for us as a weekend country retreat. The aristocratic owner continued to live there and was extremely anxious that the Navy should not relinquish its title to the house. If it did so, she would have had a number of displaced persons billeted upon her, and they were likely to be less understanding than her infrequent and undemanding naval visitors. However, for me the real advantage of being in the Navy in Germany related to the availability of boats. We had inherited the whole of the *Kriegsmarines* stock. Even though this had been winnowed down as the naval presence in Germany reduced, we were still handsomely 'overboated'. At Westensee the lake boasted a splendid motorboat for aquaplaning or water-skiing as the fancy took us.

Although the work was responsible, demanding and secret, in reality there was little or no physical danger in the tasks we performed. We were always on our own territory, and even though the Soviets and East Germans operated in West Germany with relative impunity there was hardly any of the type of behaviour portrayed in so many spy books. This did not, however, stop us enjoying the full range of melodrama that intelligence work seems to attract – so one got all the trappings without the realities. However, at about this time I became involved in a new venture which was to have a profound effect on my own ideas and more particularly on my understanding and affection for the Germans.

In the Baltic the Russians were operating a number of former German E-boats which they had received as reparations. We still possessed two of these superb craft, which had been built at the Lürssenwerft yard at Vegasac on the Weser river and were powered by twin Mercedes high-speed diesel engines. We decided to strip one of them down and increase her power. With the combination of her low weight and enhanced power she would be able to show her heels to any other surface ship then afloat. She was to be manned by a hand-picked German crew. Since Germany was still demilitarised, it was essential that she operated under a British officer and, from time to time and as appropriate, carried a British Chief Petty Officer Telegraphist.

We had our pick of all the surviving E-boat aces, but particularly wanted one with experience of operating in the Baltic. Thus it was that I met Hans Helmut Klose, who rose subsequently to be the Admiral Commanding the German Fleet, but was then an unemployed former Lieutenant-Commander. He would later become my daughter's godfather and one of my closest friends of any nationality. The running of the operation was shared equally between us, although the ultimate responsibility lay with me. We selected a fantastic crew – every man of which was later to find success in the new German navy or as one of the new breed of German businessmen. All of them were imbued with a fierce detestation of the Russians, some of them having been born in East Prussia, and the territory which until recently comprised East Germany. We ran the ship as a German naval ship, designed and procured our own uniform, and set ourselves up ostensibly as a German fishery protection vessel. It is fair to say that I remember very little actual fishery protection. West German fishing vessels had a healthy respect for the Soviet navy and steered well clear of areas where they might fall foul of them. The Russians regarded the Baltic as their back yard and were very quick to enforce their self-assumed rights both within and outside their unilaterally-appointed twelve-mile limit.

Living so closely with my German crew, where the relationship between officers and men was so close, taught me a great deal. We all messed together, went ashore together, knew each other on Christian-name terms, and yet discipline, when needed, was first class. Not only did we have numerous adventures together, but we also shared many experiences of a more mundane but, to me, equally revealing kind. For a start there was the refitting at the Lürssenwerft, which was trying to eke out a living by building small yachts and commercial vessels. The yard had designed and built the original *schnellboote* (torpedo boats) and retained a fierce pride and dedication to their craft. Our boat was beautifully conceived, designed and balanced, and a far better sea boat, with its round bilge and sophisticated hull design, than the hard-chine British-designed motor torpedo-boats. Most of us believed that it would be only a matter of time before a new German navy was formed, and the yard were determined to show what they could do. The two Lurssen brothers became friends of mine and did an unbelievable job for us, producing a finish worthy of a royal yacht. Meanwhile we stayed in a local pub, which gave me an introduction to a German life which was vouchsafed to few British people in Germany at that time.

When we recruited our crew I was struck by the differences in approach from the way in which a British ship would have been manned. After selecting the first lieutenant and the chief engine-room artificer, the next man chosen was the cook. What a choice he was, too. When not at sea the crew were put up in a barrack block at Blankenese in Hamburg, where I was shortly moved, and the cook performed even more lavishly ashore than afloat. After the captain, the cook was without question both the most popular and the essential member of our crew and they would all help him. They would become quite upset if he had to do the sort of chores which Royal Naval cooks were expected to do for themselves and which were usually considered to be below the dignity of the average sailor. The remainder of the crew were selected with equal care for, in addition to needing masters of their craft and self-disciplined men, we had to ensure that there was no risk to our security.

In addition to the recruitment of the crew and the refitting of the boat, we also had to procure spares for the engine and arrange for the tuning-up. The high-speed diesel line at the Mercedes-werke at Stuttgart had long since closed down, but after a couple of visits their engineering director took on the task with the same enthusiasm and vision that we had met at the Lürssenwerft. Within no time they had re-assembled for us the same top team that had engined the whole E-boat fleet. When the day finally came and the boat was ready for sea trials we were amazed and delighted to see what we had achieved. Although we carried dummy torpedo tubes we had no real armaments. We had a few small arms and an anti-tank launcher, in case we were hove-to by somebody, but otherwise it was her speed that we relied on

– and could she shift! Her top speed was no problem, the difficulties lay with our almost total inability to move slowly. Even with only one engine operating, throttled right back, we were continually breaking ten knots in calm seas. In really bad weather this minimum was too high, unless we were running before the weather. We were to find this out the hard way. On one of our trips, with the coast of Lithuania as a lee shore, we could not steer off-shore without breaking up. Reading the weather accurately became even more vital for us than it was for most light craft. Moreover, in bad weather we could not use the speed which was our protection to give us the advantage over any hostile pursuers. However, in calm weather the thrill of tearing across the Baltic at fifty knots, with the wake stretching behind us like a straight line to the horizon, took some beating. The ingrained belief we all had in the importance of the work we did continued to give us all a heady sense of accomplishment.

Practically all our work was secret and, although others have written of some of our exploits and their outcome, I would not wish to breach the trust that was placed upon us. Suffice it to say that the Baltic was our oyster and we roamed it at will. Our cover enabled us to shelter at Bornholm in Denmark and Gotland in Sweden, and we came to know every inch of the Baltic coast and every defence which the Russians maintained, in a particularly intimate way. Life at sea never goes as planned and we encountered more than enough excitements to last the average lifetime. These shared experiences gave us a deeply held personal regard for one another. The Chief Petty Officer, John Maye, remains my friend to this day and we have never lost touch with each other. He also became a convert to the German way of life, falling in love with and marrying a charming Austrian.

Although the command of S.208 speedily became my main task, in terms of importance, there were still all the other facets of my responsibilities to carry out. We had said goodbye to Kiel with regrets, but Hamburg was to bring us a whole range of new experiences. When we first arrived the Admiral and his staff were still in residence and, even though my activities were so different, we were still expected to play an appropriate naval and social role. By then Betty was appearing regularly on the British Forces Network Radio, doing plays and readings, and also did some radio work in English for the Nord-West Deutsches Rundfunk. We had a lovely house in the woods near the headquarters, a marvellous housekeeper, a dog – our first dachshund – and our very own transport, a pre-war Austin Seven. From my point of view the only thing needed to change this heaven into paradise was for the headquarters to move away – and sure enough they obligingly did so.

Thus it was that in 1950 I found myself, at the age of twenty-six, as the naval officer in charge of Hamburg, Germany's greatest port, and yet again conveniently out of range of day-to-day supervision or interruption. Once more I had my pick of the departing Navy's facilities – ending up in a splendidly unique house by the Alster, with my office and modest staff within half a mile. From my predecessor, David Wheeler, who had shared the responsibility of setting up the E-boat operation with me, I had inherited a vast range of contacts from within the former German navy. In order to develop these we used to host German naval reunions for the admirals and captains who had remained on the northern seaboard. They were all honourable, dedicated, and decent men and I became more and more convinced of the accuracy of Hitler's distrust and dislike of the German navy. Although the five years since the war had been fearsome levellers in a social sense, I was always impressed by the respect these men still commanded from their subordinates, most of whom had prospered far better in the nascent revival of Germany then beginning. Betty and I led an almost bohemian social life – her friends came increasingly from the world of radio and theatre, while mine came from the former German navy and from the intelligence community. Our house seemed to be continually full, and we were both intensely busy and very happy. Time fled by.

The patrols that I undertook in S.208 were invariably of quite short duration – we could, after all, cover the whole Baltic in twenty-four hours of hard sailing if we needed to – and it was only if we were weatherbound that I was away for any length of time. Our involvement with the British Forces Network, besides yielding us some marvellous friends, also led to my first faltering introduction to the medium of radio. It proved to be a godsend for, while Forces Radio had much of the best of BBC professionalism, it also had a devil-may-care attitude to experiment and risk. My contributions, sandwiched in between my other overt and covert activities, took the form of book reviews and occasional contributions to documentary programmes. The British Forces Network was a formidable breeding ground for talent, and a surprising number of today's familiar names had their grounding there. It also had another characteristic which endeared itself to me. There was no correlation, except perhaps an inverse one, between military rank and the contribution that people were asked to make. Our rather grand-looking house was thus as full of corporals, aircraftmen and sergeants as it was of German, and occasionally British, admirals and captains. Our every need was catered for by our German staff and we maintained and enjoyed a standard of living we have hardly attained since.

To crown everything Betty became pregnant again. We had had a series of miscarriages and were beginning to fear that she might not be able to carry a full-term pregnancy. The naval doctor, who was doing his national service and could, therefore, be presumed to have both more practical experience and interest in gynaecological problems than the usual seaborne saw-bones, decreed that she was to spend the later months of her pregnancy in bed. Even with all the help we had, it was a daunting prospect for a fit, fun-loving and active twenty-nine-year-old but, with her usual determination, she followed the instructions to the letter. To our delight British Forces Radio happily accepted that our house be used as a recording studio and so she was able to continue her radio work. Eventually our daughter was born, in the British Military Hospital in Hamburg. At the critical time I managed to be absent – involved in an operation somewhere. A friend of Betty's went with her to the hospital and I only got to see my newly arrived daughter some hours after her delivery. I felt intensely proud of my wife. The baby was beautiful, and we called her Gabrielle, which coincidentally happened to be the name of the charming German nurse who had attended Betty during her delivery. We were overjoyed, and it seemed to us that we had everything that any young couple could wish for.

We were living a privileged life in a country we liked and Betty was as successful in her interests as I was in mine. I knew I was good at my job, which I still believed to be a key element in the preservation of freedom. This time probably represents the apogee of our lives together; there seemed to be no clouds on the horizon and we lived in and for the moment. Of course we had no money and no home to return to in England, but life was too full for such considerations to concern us greatly. In customary naval fashion we were, however, to receive a rude shock. The Powers That Be had decided, probably rightly from their point of view, that I was in danger of becoming so specialised that I could no longer pursue a conventional naval career. I imagine that my next appointments were intended to give me the best chance of a re-entry into a normal naval career path, but for us, they represented a savage interruption in our lives when we were least prepared for it. I was notified that my time in Hamburg was over. Betty and Gaby were to return to the UK, and I was to be given a sea appointment.

Gaby had just been christened in the Mission to Seamen Church in Hamburg with Helmut as her godfather and Betty's closest friend as her godmother. She was just five months old and we were to be uprooted and sent back, in the height of winter, to an indeterminate fate in England. A greater contrast from our luxurious life in Germany would be difficult to envisage. We were seen off from Hamburg main railway station by all our friends and the whole crew of S.208 singing sentimental farewell songs. Almost from the time we left the station we were in trouble. Gaby took as poorly to the prospect of leaving Germany as Betty and I did. She yelled and cried at this unwarranted intrusion into her well-ordered existence, and was desperately sick over and over again. We were separated on the ferry, Betty and Gaby sharing a cabin with a number of other officers' wives and I being bunked with a bunch of soldiers.

We had decided to stay with friends of our own age who had a flat in Sydenham while we found our bearings – and this was not an easy problem to solve. I had no idea where I would be sent and in any event we had virtually no capital to put down on a house. In those days you required key money even for rented accommodation. Almost as soon as we had received our baggage and car from Germany, I was given the unwelcome news that I was to be posted to the recommissioning of HMS *Amethyst* in the Far East.

This meant a probable two-and-a-half years away and, moreover, a return to active service, for there were wars in both Korea and Malaysia at that time.

We were both aghast at this news. At that time Betty could not drive and neither she nor I saw much future in her going to live with her parents. They had now retired to Cornwall, and in any event evinced no enthusiasm for such a solution. My mother had moved to a small one-bedroomed flat and, apart from our friends Pam and Don Liddiard, at Sydenham, practically all our friends and acquaintances lived in London. With time moving against us we searched desperately for somewhere for Betty and Gaby to live. Despite the illegality of the system it was then impossible to rent without paying key money. We had agreed that Pam should have the use of our car provided she chauffeured Betty from time to time. Finally, with only days to go to my departure, we found a pretty unsuitable upstairs flat on Sydenham Hill. Pausing only to hand over most of the rest of my savings for key money and leaving my wife and daughter, with my remaining £50, sitting dismally in a half-empty flat up three flights of stairs and miles from the shops and public transport, I set off to go to war.

As so often in our lives together we seemed to shift from heaven to hell in one mighty bound. Betty was struggling to cope with Gaby on her own, without any of the facilities we had come to rely on. I was worried sick at my own inability to provide the necessities of life for them, and dreading our being parted for

1 As a baby, with my mother

2 On horseback,
with one of our servants
and the dogs

3 With Bahadur
and Manka

4 With our Buick car
in India around 1935

5 My father

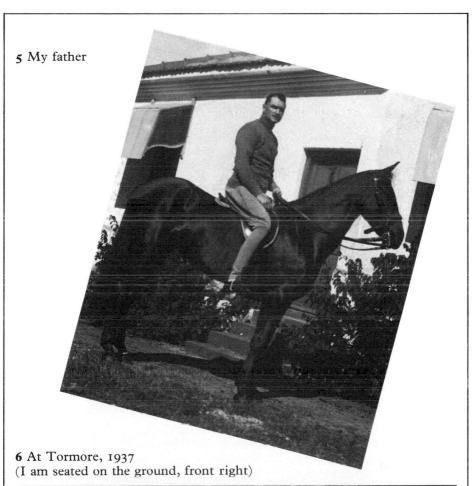

6 At Tormore, 1937
(I am seated on the ground, front right)

7 A new cadet at Dartmouth in 1938

8 At John Elgar's wedding

9 Betty in 1941

10 Our wedding,
26 July 1947,
with Betty's sister, Pamela

11 Betty and Gaby, 1951

12 1954

13 St Austell Bay, Bermuda, October 1954
(I am second from the left, front row)

14 Gaby, in late August 1955,
aged almost four

15 The Wilton site at night

16 Stonegate Mill, Yorkshire

17 1970: opening for the Directorate

18 A visit to Mond division in 1983

19 An ICI publicity shot, 1988

20 Betty, 1978

such a long period of time. To make matters worse, I had little confidence in my ability to do the job to which I was being appointed. I had last served in a surface ship as a midshipman in 1943, some eight years earlier, and never in peacetime. I was not used to the ways of the peacetime Navy, and the only sailors I had dealt with since the end of the war had been personal friends and mates rather than subordinates. My own concerns and worries made me unhelpful and unsympathetic to Betty's problems and I am sure that by the time I left, despite the enormity of the tasks ahead of her, she was glad to see the back of me.

Our depleted finances were further strained by the need for me to re-outfit. Full white uniforms were not the order of the day in a submarine and although I had retained my sword and telescope there was little that I still possessed or could wear that was appropriate for my new job. I had not lost the dramatic increase of weight that had come with my happy newly married state, and the uniforms which swam on me at under nine stone did not fit so kindly on my tubby and ill-distributed ten-and-a-half-stone figure. Leaving my wife and baby to fend for themselves, worried and concerned about almost everything, and with a trunk full of second-hand uniforms, I duly reported to the troopship *Empire Fowey*, to find that I was the naval officer in charge of the Naval Draft being shipped out to the Far East. There were just over one hundred of us carrying the reputation of the Royal Navy – in a ship containing 1,300 soldiers and airmen and run more like Aldershot barracks than a warship. We were a motley crew. None of us was likely to serve together again, and we were thrown together in whatever unlikely proportions the drafting requirements of the Far East fleet required. In the unlikely event that the whole crew of our troopship were suddenly struck down we would have had great difficulty steaming on our way for we had more stokers than seamen and barely enough officers to man a watch-keeping rota. By contrast the Army, as ever, were travelling in tightly knit units carrying with them all the regiment's pride and familiarity with each other which is their hallmark.

As soon as we had boarded and slung our hammocks I went

down to the mess deck with the CPO who found himself, willy nilly, my coxswain and staunch right hand. I introduced myself, explained where I was from and where I was going, and told my ill-assorted bunch that although we were numerically the weakest by a long chalk, as sailors we were in our own element. I was determined that we would show the other services what being a sailor meant, and that aboard ship we had to be the best. Our mess decks had to shine, our drill and command of our own environment had to be the best, and we had to have the best discipline and behaviour. Ashore it was another matter. As far as I was concerned we all carried our traditions once we stepped aboard a ships boat, but excepting only that they had to catch the ship before we sailed, they could behave ashore as sailors always have.

They certainly took me at my word. On board we were, to the chagrin of the troops, invincible. We won every competition despite our lack of numbers by sheer grit and determination (aided by a resistance to sea sickness which was, after all, a part of our heritage). Ashore, however, it was a different tale. My chaps would arrive back if they had to crawl – and many did – but their battered and bruised visages and monumental hangovers clearly indicated that our superiority depended to some degree on our familiarity with our own element, the sea, coupled with gladiatorial rules which evened the numerical odds.

The voyage, which lasted nearly twelve weeks, taught me a lot. It renewed my faith in the spirit of the Royal Navy and gave me another lesson in team-building. Right until I left the Navy I would meet others who had been a part of our draft and they would always reflect joyously on how we saw off the Army.

Eventually, a greatly lightened *Empire Fowey* – for we dropped off troops and some sailors at almost every port of call on the way out – arrived at Kure in Japan. This was then the rear headquarters of the Commonwealth forces in Korea. We bade farewell to our friendly competitors from the Army and set off on our individual ways to join our ships. *Amethyst* was at Sasebo and it was there that I journeyed to find my predecessor understandably champing at the bit to get away and ensure that he did not miss the returning trooper. The passage of time, coupled with the various bits of accelerated promotion I had received, enabled me to join *Amethyst* as a Lieutenant-Commander, the make-or-break rank in the Royal Navy.

I joined as the First Lieutenant, the second in command responsible with the Engineer Officer for the actual running of the ship. I soon found, reassuringly, that despite my nearly ten-year absence from surface ships the thoroughness of my basic training, combined with a slow rate of change of matters naval, enabled me to cope with the multiplicity of my duties without too much difficulty.

Amethyst spent most of her time on East Coast patrol off the Korean coast, supporting the troops with pretty inaccurate bombardment from our four-inch guns and from time to time taking part in raids behind the enemy lines. Anyone who experienced the Korean War cannot have been surprised at the problems that the Americans encountered in Vietnam.

It seemed to most of us at the time that if the United Nations Forces and the Chinese had withdrawn, the Koreans would have settled down in no time at all. We used to find ourselves sometimes as 'anchorman' on the front line, and, as far as we could see, the Koreans on both sides had usually established a *modus vivendi* quite effortlessly until our arrival on the scene. This was invariably the sign for a frenzy of slaughter as they fell upon each other to demonstrate their enthusiasm for the war, and desisting only from time to time to fire in our direction.

As wars go, it was a most unsatisfactory one. Although the evidence of North Korean aggression was there for us all to see, few of us saw the war in terms of protecting our homeland or loved ones. Korea did not seem then to have any economic importance to the Commonwealth, and few of us relished the systematic demolition of what was in those days a pitifully poor country.

Amethyst was also a marked ship. She was famous for fighting her way from entrapment down the Yangtse river with great loss of life. The publicity which still attached to the ship since the Yangtse incident ensured that we only had to fire a gun and the newspapers back home would rabbit on about '*Amethyst* fighting (or thundering) back'. This was thoroughly unhelpful on two counts. Firstly, our families in England were constantly convinced that we were fighting for our lives twenty-four hours a day, seven days a week, and secondly the constant publicity was resented by the rest of the fleet. In consequence, whenever we were in port with other ships my people were in far more danger in the bar-room brawls than we usually were while we were engaged with our official enemies. The doctor seemed to spend his whole time patching up our crew, who whenever we left port presented a mass advertisement for Elastoplast.

We worked and played at a stirring rate, and life was never dull. *Amethyst* spent most of her time on detachment so that there was not too much of the fleet escort stuff. She was a noteworthy ship in another respect as well. No longer in her youth, and having led a hard life, the old girl showed her age in curious and sometimes disturbing ways. For instance, when one of our sailors dropped a heavy weight from about three-foot height it disappeared through the upper deck which was meant to shield us both from the elements and the enemy.

The fame of the ship, as well as the fact that we still had on board some of those who had lived through the Yangtse incident, gave us a tremendous morale, but controlling our people was a bit like trying to drive an eight-in-hand. We seemed to attract the scallywags and misfits from the fleet and all too often the drafts arriving from Britain to replenish our numbers would arrive under escort and arrest to join our proud company. Rumour was that a posting to *Amethyst* was used as a threat aboard other ships and at least one ne'er-do-well was reported to have fallen metaphorically to his knees and repented rather than face joining us. Since I was primarily responsible for the discipline on board, most of the problems arrived squarely on my plate, but we managed to create that aura of predictability, and toughness but fairness, which creates the framework within which team spirit flourishes.

At about this time I fear that I added to our reputation for mindless violence. I was sitting in the wardroom in harbour, idly glancing at a six-week-old copy of *The Times*, when I read through the birthday honours and found I had been awarded an MBE. No one had bothered to inform me of this great event and at first I thought it must be a misprint. A quick check with the other papers revealed that, unlikely as it seemed, the report was probably correct.

I could not think of a nicer way to hear of an honour, for within minutes we had the most colossal party underway. Unfortunately, as naval parties tend to, events got more and more boisterous and culminated in a *mêlée* which broke the ribs of our long-suffering RNVR Lieutenant. I always thought it unfair to post reservists to Korea – arguing that it was our job as professionals – but I would have been very cheesed-off to get killed as a reservist in a minor war. To have one's ribs stove in by one's own side as a participant in someone else's war seemed an even harder fate for poor Ken.

Time rolled on and we alternated between war footing patrols with plenty of pretty one-sided action and turn-around boiler-cleans in Japan. Looking back, it is amazing how primitive conditions were in that country then. The shipyards were efficient but did not enjoy the fearsome reputation for quality and efficiency that they were to acquire later. Indeed, my main memory is of the very large numbers of very small men simultaneously deployed on board to patch us up for our return to the war.

Ashore, the roads were largely unmade and within a couple of miles of the base it seemed that we were back in the Japan of feudal times with the wooden houses and tatami floors of classical Japanese woodcuts. Sadly, our own contacts with the Japanese was minimal, being restricted largely to the shipyard management and the serving staff in the few restaurants and bars which catered for the Far East fleet's less esoteric tastes.

Anyone then who foresaw that we were in what would be, only thirty years later, the most powerful economic country in the world would have been quietly consigned to the loony bin. The few souvenirs and consumer goods available were of poor quality, and largely of that curious pre-war Japanese design which proclaims its country of origin long before you even read the words 'made in Japan'.

Despite these rather superficial views of what was to be one of the mainstream forces on my life in the future, the Japan which one could glimpse on country walks had a weird, haunting, natural beauty which seemed to grow straight out of Japanese prints. The tiny paddy fields being painstakingly and, apparently primitively, hand-cultivated, the wide peasant hats, and the windswept and gnarled trees apparently growing from natural rock, all gave an aura of immutable resistance to change and almost of a prehistory. I was not to begin to understand Japanese character for many years, for at that time the memory of the war was too recent and fear is hardly the best background for sensitive analysis of racial characteristics. That period has served me well if only as a benchmark of the nearly unbelievable progress made by the Japanese in such a short period of time. I revisited the area only ten years later, to find it barely recognisable. The simplicity of its nature was already being concealed by frenetic and, to Western eyes, ill-chosen development which succeeded in being neither good Western design or in keeping with Japanese tradition.

Our patrols continued unabated, and unfriendly Koreans and occasionally aeroplanes continued to take pot shots at us – knocking further bits off our old ship but, luckily for us, causing our people little harm. The ship was also used extensively as a front-line evacuation hospital, uncomfortably along the lines of the American television series *MASH*. We possessed an excellent doctor and trained sick-berth attendant, and could manage most sewing, amputating, and bullet-extraction jobs. So all too often our wardroom was full of silent, stoic tributes to naval medical skill, lying uncomplainingly on rows of stretchers on our deck.

The time came, however, when we required more fundamental refitting than the Japanese shipyards, which were not able to deal with armaments, could put in hand for us. The intention had been that *Amethyst* should recommission on station rather than return all the way to the United Kingdom. It was for that reason that the captain and I had already taken over and the officers were being replaced sequentially. Off we went to Hong Kong to the naval dockyard I had 'liberated' after the war. The officers and ship's company were accommodated ashore to enable the dockyard to really tear the ship apart.

It proved to be a wonderful change. Hong Kong in the early 1950s had not yet wound itself up to the business pace it was later to achieve. The island and the new territories were bustling, but the expatriates on the island were still of a number where new arrivals were noticed and of interest. I was particularly fortunate, for one of my friends at the Russian course at Cambridge had left the Army and joined Butterfield and Swire as a trainee manager. He was accommodated in their bachelor quarters and we spent much of our time together. *Amethyst's* boats were still available to us and in addition we had a motor fishing-vessel attached, so weekends were spent in picnics and parties on the adjoining islands, sailing or water-skiing and living life in a totally inappropriate style, bearing in mind the financial stringencies we were all under.

Admittedly, the Navy found all our living expenses, and duty-free drink was the real thing with gin, whisky and brandy at a penny a tot. Nevertheless, on the few spare pounds I retained from my pay, we managed a style of life which most young people would still envy today. Betty was not faring so well. Once the rent was paid, there was all too little left to do more than dress the two of them and pay the household bills. After paying my tax and the stipendiary payment to my Naval Tailor, I retained about £15 a month and sent all the rest home. The £15 had to pay my mess bill, laundry and extras and yet there was still enough left for an occasional meal ashore or a party at the Hong Kong race course.

Once the dockyard really got stuck into *Amethyst*, they soon found the magnitude of the repairs escalating at a fantastic rate. We were involved in worried conferences until, not totally to the chief's or my own surprise, the whole question of the scope of what was to be done was remitted home to the Admiralty. There, economic logic overcame emotion and it was decided that we should be patched together to return to the UK where we would be paid off into the Reserve Fleet, prior to being scrapped.

The dockyard duly bolted us together, again, albeit with a lack of enthusiasm that our eventual fate engendered, and we were ready for the off. We were all determined that the old lady should make her trip back looking as loved and in bandbox condition as she had been in her heyday. We sailed from Hong Kong with our decommissioning pennant blowing proudly astern and our friends waving us a last farewell. Hong Kong had been the scene of many of her triumphs – the welcome back, battered from the Yangtse, and so many other proud endeavours – that our final leaving left a pang in the throat. It had been decided that we should put in a couple of East Coast patrols off Malaysia on our way back and it was there we headed, and there that *Amethyst* was last to fire her guns in anger – albeit pretty ineffectual anger.

The Malaysian rebellion, or 'state of emergency' as it was called, was in full swing and the Navy's role was to intercept any supply sampans down the coast and occasionally to provide firepower in support of the troops ashore, who were smashing and hacking their way through the undergrowth. There can be few bigger wastes of time and money than firing four-inch shells into the jungle from a slowly steaming frigate a couple of miles offshore. The jungle all looks the same, there are seldom any clear aiming points, and when the shells explode, at best, you knock the tops off a couple of tropical hardwood trees. I suppose our activities were meant to bolster the morale of the poor Army who slogged on their way in the heat and humidity, seldom seeing any recognisable enemy.

We proceeded on our tropical cruise, enjoying the Eastern states in their unspoilt beauty. Kota Bahru, Trenganu, Kuantan and Mersing were all ports of call for us. On our stately progression we visited Puloa Tioman, now, I believe, a holiday resort, but then a living proof of the concept of island paradise. It was uninhabited and we glided into the lagoon, dropping anchor a couple of hundred yards off golden beaches fringed by coconut palms. Unlike practically all tropical paradises, this one was not infested with creepy crawlies, scorpions, sand-flies, or poisonous jellyfish. By universal agreement, at lunch time we packed up work and swam, sunbathed, fished and walked as the fancy took us. It is amazing how indelibly one's memory becomes imprinted with such an experience. It is, after all, a random twenty-four hours in a lifetime, and yet I can savour the sight and even the spicy scent that Malaysia always pervades to seaward. It gave some idea of the wonders that explorers like Cook must have experienced. The reality of Tioman's natural environment must have been a hard one, for it would surely have been inhabited if my sentimental and naive impressions were halfway accurate.

In a surprisingly short time we were back in Plymouth, having called in at such familiar trysting spots as Colombo, Aden and Malta, in each case for the last time as far as I was concerned, although I was not to realise it at the time. On a bleak, wintry and coldly raining Plymouth day we secured alongside at the docks and Betty was there to meet me. She looked fantastic, but we were in a curious and sad way strangers again. We had hardly parted under ideal conditions, and she it was who had created our home and life on her own. She still did not drive, and the problems of coping with a young baby, lack of money, and assembling some sort of home must have been daunting. She must have felt trapped, while I had been roaming the world enjoying a carefree existence doing what I like to do.

In addition, I found it very difficult to get to know my daughter. In the first place I was still quite frightened of her. I had never been brought up with a toddler around, and had exaggerated fears of her frailty – but even worse I found it, and still do, well-nigh impossible to put myself into a toddler's mind. This is a major failing of mine which I seem to be temperamentally incapable of overcoming. I can, I think, understand the way that animals' and even birds' minds work, but I cannot begin to empathise with the very small human being. I irrationally expect them to think as grown-ups scaled down to size, rather than as beings in a totally different stage of development with different thought-processes and points of reference.

As usual, the First Lieutenant was last to go on leave so after our pitifully brief reunion in Plymouth, it was back to decommissioning *Amethyst* – a horrid process at the best of times. Most of our people left the ship and as we off-loaded our stores, ammunition and provisions the ship suddenly began to lose her life and turned into a cold and soulless piece of fabricated steel. All the brightwork over which we had slaved was covered in thick grease and the grime of the dockyard soon turned my pride-and-joy into a desolate and rather grubby hulk. I was heartily thankful when I was relieved of my duties and handed her over, as her last commanding officer, into the tender mercies of the Reserve Fleet. Then at last it was off to our home in Sydenham Hill.

I was amazed at what Betty had accomplished, and still to this day do not know how she achieved so much with so little. Contrary to expectations, my own arrival home made only a pitifully small encroachment on our financial stringencies, for my £15 a month did little more than cover the extra expenses of another member of the family. Betty had built up a range of friends in Dulwich who again were totally divorced from the lives I had led – indeed they looked on a naval officer as an oddball and someone from the intelligence world as beyond comprehension.

Our leave flashed by and I was summoned to the Admiralty to discuss my next appointment. Bearing in mind that the *Amethyst* appointment, as well as signifying my re-entry into the naval mainstream, was meant to have represented a rest from the tribulations of my Intelligence work, I felt they could have done better. I put this point of view to the Appointments Commander and was promised 'a quiet commission'. So, indeed, it proved to be for I was appointed as First Lieutenant to *St Austell Bay*, a member of the American and West Indies Squadron, which was due to take over as Antarctic Guardship the following summer. Before this, however, I was to refit her at Plymouth and recommission her to leave in the spring. It meant yet another eighteen months away from Betty and Gaby and my heart sank at the prospect. However, in the meantime I had a three-month refit to do and would at least be in the United Kingdom.

Betty's parents offered us the use of a guest cottage in the converted mill-house which was their home in Cornwall. We gratefully accepted, and shifted the lot of us down to St Teath whence I commenced a weekly commute to Devonport dockyard, where *St Austell Bay* was being prepared for her next commission.

It was the first time we had lived in the country, and although living with our in-laws was not the easiest of lives, the location and peace were wonderful. In reality, Betty had spent almost as little time living with her mother as I had with my parents, and Eve, my mother-in-law, found it difficult to accept that as a married lady with a child of her own she was a far cry from a small child returning home. Moreover, even though she had had three children, Eve was a pretty unmaternal sort of person who looked on Gaby more as a living proof of her maturity than as a joy for the future. Yet again, of course, I got the easy end of the stick. I was away from Monday to Friday evening and was totally absorbed in ensuring that *St Austell Bay* wanted for nothing when we left.

The sort of refit you got in those days depended to a very considerable degree on the drive and involvement of the chief engineer and the first lieutenant. I was lucky in a number of ways, but perhaps above all because the naval constructor managing our refit had actually served with me in Wilhemshaven, and looked after us as though we were the royal yacht. Indeed, the royal yacht was the model I had in mind for, even though the intent of our commission was to patrol the Antarctic, our progress down and back involved circumnavigating South America and showing the flag *en route*. The boatswain and I were determined that our ship would lack for nothing, and our raiding and trading activities involved collecting, as well as spare paint, cordage and every sort of naval store, any and every 'tiddly' fitting that could be moved from any paying-off vessel.

These items, such as fancy ropework, beautifully lettered life-buoys, gun tampions with the ship's crest on them, and teak gratings of every shape and size to cover bollards and capstans were unofficial and therefore not listed on inventories. A bottle of rum here, a working party of hands there, and our 'rabbited' handcart would trundle more loot and contraband back on board from the remotest corners of the dockyard. These forays, combining (as they did) drive, initiative, commercial flair and a certain degree of single-minded unscrupulousness, kept us happily on the go. It was not just material things we were after. Constant visits to the Drafting Commander's office and endless perusal of the records, official and unofficial, went into ensuring that we collected the finest Devonport crew to man what was surely the finest-equipped frigate to leave our shores.

We took every scrap of paint off her, laying on coat after coat of our purloined beauty till she shone like enamel (which indeed she mostly was!). And all this effort could be encompassed easily during the working days so that by the first dog-watch on a Friday I was swinging out of the dockyard on my way home via Launceston and Camelford. It was a great time, but all too short. Pitifully soon, the crew joined us, the captain, 'Sharkey' Ward, was appointed and the time came for more naval farewells. I was not to know it would be my last sea-going commission, but it was already very clear to me that these constant separations made a mockery of what I thought marriage was about.

I was just beginning to feel comfortable with Gaby, and Betty and I were finding each other again, when bingo – the clock was put back. Betty returned into our little lonely flat with an eighteen-month-old toddler for company, and I was off to the four corners of the globe – albeit in the opposite direction this time.

I have never regretted my naval days – for a single man it was a marvellous life and opened my eyes to the world as it is, rather than the world as viewed by package tours or business trips. However, as a basis for a proper married life it was a complete non-starter. Moreover, I was beginning to lose my belief in the worthwhileness of my career. As the power and size of the Royal Navy shrank by comparison with the superpowers, it was more difficult to persuade myself that I represented the sure shield of my country and, therefore, of the civilised world as we knew it. I had not made up my mind to relinquish my chosen profession, for I still had some convictions about the necessity to fight the intelligence battle, but these doubts did nothing to compensate for my depression as each turn of our screws took me further away from Betty and Gaby.

The Navy recognised this problem, which I was not alone in feeling, and sought to alleviate it by the almost frenetic activity described as working-up. We practised and re-practised every manoeuvre and situation one could think of, fired everything we could lay our hands on (despite the unlikelihood of encountering a war mission in America) and, when not engaged in improving our professional competence, painted, polished and beautified our pride and home.

The major missions that lay ahead for us comprised an endless series of cocktail parties at each port we visited and here the 'rabbiting activities' of our refit paid off handsomely. Our fo'c'sle and quarter deck could be rigged for a cocktail party in such a way as to transform a functional and utilitarian man-of-war to a fairyland of coloured marquees, lanterns, fairy lights, and every decorative feature you could find in a modest palace. The guns themselves were fitted with serving tables, and it was a clearly understood deal between the captain and myself that neither fo'c'sle nor quarter deck guns were fired during our party season for fear of spoiling the paintwork and brightwork which transformed ordinary four-inch guns into *objects d'art*.

We partied our way happily down from Bermuda, the squadron headquarters, calling at all the happy hunting-grounds that I knew from my very first commission with *Diomede*, on our leisurely way to the Falkland Islands. It was sad to see the changes in only a little over ten years. The British communities in the ports we visited had shrunk beyond recognition, and even though the style and panache with which we behaved drew widespread acclaim, nothing could conceal the change in the realities of British power in South America. When I had last been in those waters, there had seemed little to choose between the South Americans' perception of ourselves and their view of the North Americans, although as a generalisation we were seen then as less imperialistic than the USA. Now, despite the unflagging hospitality of the tiny British communities and the anglophile Latin Americans we still met, no amount of difference in behaviour could compensate for the realities of the shifts in economic power.

In due course, we arrived at Port Stanley in the Falklands where at least nothing appeared to have changed since 1942, except that the islands no longer produced bunkering facilities and we therefore had the anchorage almost entirely to ourselves except for the supply ship. This ran a regular round-trip to Montevideo and also supplied the outlying settlements around the islands, for there were no roads or transport and everything had to be done by and from the sea.

Our main task, besides deterring any potential Argentinian adventures by our mere presence, was to keep an eye on the survey stations in the Antarctic proper, and to provide back-up to the Falkland Islands Dependency Survey Ship. Between us, during the short Antarctic summer when the ice broke up, we visited all the British survey sites, as well as calling on those established, despite international agreements forbidding them, by the Argentinians.

The Antarctic was, and is, one of the last unspoilt and natural areas of the world. It is indeed a terrible place – such winds and seas, and throughout it all a spine-chilling cold which even modern clothing and the comforts of our steam-propelled frigate could not allay. Yet, there is about it all a savage beauty and a total absence of other human activity, coupled with the fearlessness of the wildlife going about its business. The energetic penguins roller-coastering around the ship, the sea elephants, too large and uninterested even to move at one's approach, the unbelievable wing-span of an albatross and the constant excitement, in those days, of seeing every sort of whale, gave eternal delights. In addition, the colours of the ice in the different weather conditions were a marvel to see. The whole appearance could change in minutes as the sun came out, or as snow began to fall.

The bases we visited all had romantic and heart-stirring names bestowed by the early explorers. Desolation Bay, Deception

Island, Hope Cove, and so on, gave advance preparation for what one was to find. The whole place breathed history, immutability, and the smallness of Man in the scheme of things. Even the quite inadequate charts which we worked from breathed the atmosphere of the place. The few existing soundings showed all too clearly the tacks of the sailing vessels on whose map-making skills we relied. They showed the zig-zag courses they had followed on their precarious way into unknown hazards. The men of those days must have been a different breed, for we found the going tough enough with good food, warmth and communication of a sort with the outside world. They were working aloft, fisting frozen canvass, equipped only with peajackets and oilskins and refreshed and kept going on hard tack and salted meat.

The sheer technical problems of making one's way in those waters was daunting enough, for the size of ice floe which could rip open even a modern steel-hulled ship was still small enough to demand a constant and careful lookout. Moreover, it needed a readiness to use every trick of the trade to manoeuvre out of the way, all too often straight into the line of another floe.

It was our task to visit all the bases, including the 'illegal' Argentinian ones where, after delivering our routine protest at their presence, we would bring them on board, booze and feed them up after showing them a film and then return them to their spartan and lonely existence ashore. The niceties of protocol and international quarrels seemed a long way away from the frightening realities of trying to exist in the Antarctic, and concern for the well-being of other human beings took unhesitating priority over the posturing required to maintain our claims to sovereignty. Even though the continent was believed to have mineral wealth and even, possibly, oil and gas, the sheer problems and costs of survival would have militated against their commercial exploitation. We were then, and I am still, mystified as to why sovereign powers value their claim to these vast areas of ice, rock and wind, and are prepared to go to such lengths to protect them.

We had a good exemplar of the ludicrous effects of this competition during our period of duty. The Argentinians announced that their Navy Minister, Admiral Olivieri, was going to visit the Argentinian bases in the Antarctic in his flag-ship. This posed a few nice problems to our Government, who had resolutely refused to acknowledge that the bases existed or that the Argentinians had any position in 'our' Antarctic dependency. The visit could not be stopped short of force of arms, and the Argentinians had more and larger ships than poor little *St Austell Bay*, although we could outgun them at a cocktail party any day.

Possibly recognising this area of potential superiority, we were instructed to act as hosts to the good admiral during his visit, interrupting our hospitality only to drop off a diplomatic protest at each stop. The difficulty with the order was, of course, that the last thing the Argentinians, who were accompanied by press, film crews and the whole gamut of a modern PR exercise, wanted was to see the white ensign fluttering proudly at their bases. To add to our problems their ships had about a five-knot speed advantage over us so it was difficult for us even to follow them.

However, in the Royal Navy an order is an order, and ever mindful of the fate of Admiral Byng, who was shot to encourage the others, we set out to do our best. Fortunately, there was only one likely point of entry through the necklace of islands which stood off the main land-mass, and we patrolled miserably and slowly up and down, conserving as much fuel as possible for the events ahead. Eventually, we saw a puff of smoke on the horizon and turned to intercept them, for indeed in those waters it could be nobody else. Once in sight we signalled them a warm welcome to British Antarctica which, with a rather depressing lack of manners, they ignored as they swept past us and we sat and tried to guess their first destination. Farce then followed farce as we puffed belatedly into their first anchorage and prepared to carry out our hostly duties.

The captain, who was a master delegator on occasions like this, had left all the diplomatic stuff to me, so in full uniform with medals and sword, I went off to deliver our diplomatic protest and to offer our services, bearing in mind that I was offering them to a ship and force larger and better equipped than ourselves in every way. The first protest was easy to deliver, for the unsuspecting Officer of the Watch took it from my hand as I made my way to call on the admiral to whom, in my alternative position as Postmaster of Deception Island, I offered the same services I was subsequently to proffer as Customs Officer of Hope Bay, Officer in Charge of the Shore Facilities, and so on.

At each successive stop we went through the same charade, with the difference that the admiral became steadily shorter tempered and less welcoming, and it became increasingly hard to push my protest into any Argentinian hands at all. Eventually, the admiral earned my gratitude, relief and respect when he cut a deal with me. The discussion went something like this: you are a naval officer, I am a naval officer, we both have our jobs to do and we plainly will both do them. Why don't I give you my itinerary and I will take your protests and you take mine and we can cut out all this malarkey. The persuasiveness of the deal was enhanced by a side of fresh Argentinian first-quality beef, and three new films. I suspect that, from our point of view, this very satisfactory saving of honour on both sides was perhaps in recognition of the way we had always dealt with the poor devils stationed at their bases. It was a far cry from what I imagined Their Lordships in London believed we were actually doing, let alone the Foreign Office.

Our stay in the Falkland Islands was a marvellously happy one. We had plenty of adventures, including the salvage of a coaster which had run into difficulties and, at the other extreme, the marriage of our captain to a lady who was employed by the Falkland Islands Company as the island's sole beautician and *coiffeuse*. She was almost the only unattached girl on the islands, and at the time I thought it a little hard on the locals to have her captured and taken away by a visiting naval officer. We had a marvellous naval wedding to which the entire ship's company were invited. It took place at Government House and was, for the Falklands, a glittering social occasion. We went the whole hog. We lined the only street, we pulled the only car, we lifted every sword on the ship and generally acted as though we were the whole home fleet – which in a way we were.

To the joy of our sailors, who were growing less enthusiastic about the concentration on drinking to the exclusion of other sailor-like activities, our time came to a close and we were relieved to journey back to Bermuda up the west coast of South America. We were the first ship to have returned that way for many years and we received a tremendous welcome in Chile, Peru and Ecuador. In all three countries the navies were marvellous hosts and, since they had all been set up originally by Admiral Cochrane, their traditions and ours were very similar.

In some areas of commercial activity, equally, the return of the Royal Navy was welcome and I recall that the enthusiasm of the British ambassador to Chile, and of our captain waned somewhat when I pointed out that the showers of cards and messages thrown on board as we secured in Valparaíso were in fact the business cards and invitations of the ladies of the town. We had a further departure from normal naval routine in Ecuador when the chief writer consigned all the ship's ledgers and accounts to the mercies of the river at Guayaquil. They were speedily dispersed into the wide Pacific and the captain, correspondence officer and doctor initially accepted the chief's claim of a nervous breakdown as the cause of this somewhat unusual form of book-keeping – or, more accurately, book-losing.

During the previous commission we had had a victualling scandal so the captain had retained responsibility for the cash and accounts while entrusting the control of the victualling side (a notorious area for side-kicks and short weights) to me. I was convinced that the ledgers had gone because the chief must have been on the fiddle, and set about reconstructing the accounts to prove it. Sure enough, brainstorm or no brainstorm, nervous breakdown or not, it seemed more and more likely that the naughty ladies of Chile and Peru had exacted their toll and made off with Her Majesty's cash.

The rest of the commission was relatively tame stuff. A self-refit and admiral's inspection at Bermuda, a cocktail-party tour of New England, and off we went home again. Would I be glad to be returning, for I had every reason to expect another intelligence job where I would be with Betty and Gaby again, and would also be closer to the front line and to the task where, I felt, we were dealing with the real problems rather than firing endless salvoes of whisky-and-sodas or horse's necks.

8 Slinging the Anchor

After I arrived back from the Antarctic and had paid off *St Austell Bay* things really looked set fair for Betty and me. Perhaps most importantly of all, we settled into the home which she had so successfully made for us, and at last we started to live as a family. I was amazed at how much she had accomplished. The flat was really well equipped and we wanted for nothing. We repossessed our car, and even rented a television set (the height of luxury in those days). We did everything as a family and Gaby was a joy to be with. Not only was she beautiful to look at, but she showed all the warmth and demonstrativeness which was to characterise her future life. She was also an endearing mixture of tiny toddler and wise old head, even then showing her strength of character and determination in ways which totally defeated me and came close to testing even Betty's formidable resolve.

In my absence, Betty had made a number of friends who were to affect our future lives more closely than we could have guessed. In particular, she had become close with our doctor and his wife – they were our own age and he was the most outstanding general practitioner I have ever met. Mark Hodgson was the son of a clergyman and an open-minded, totally dedicated medical man who constantly investigated both new and old ideas in order to care for and heal his patients. His ideas were far in advance of his time and he never lost sight of his primary aim of bringing solace to those who were lucky enough to be on his list.

The grand Edwardian houses which lined our road were just beginning to be redeveloped, to take advantage of the large gardens and wonderful location of Sydenham Hill. From our position there, we overlooked the whole of South London. Fashionable Dulwich was only a step away, and yet we were able to take advantage of the cheaper shops and markets of Upper Norwood and Penge to ease our financial problems. Even these had begun, miraculously, to ease. I had reached the rank of Lieutenant-Commander, and, living together at last, we found that after paying the necessities of life there was a little left over at the end of each month which we could choose to spend as we wished. To cap everything, I was given a highly responsible job in the Naval Intelligence Department.

As always, I was in the Russian Section, and was put in charge of the 'plot'. This was really the nerve centre of the whole operation and had access to every scrap of intelligence and information from every source we could command, no matter how secret. The task was to sift, collate and monitor the order of battle and location of the Russian navy throughout the world, and continuously to update it so that we knew exactly where every ship was, and what it was doing. There were four of us doing the job, and because we were such a small team, working closely together, we soon knew everything about everything. It taught me a great deal about communication and teamwork (many years later I was to see the same effect created by a Japanese project team on a major construction project). The mere act of sitting together, hearing and taking each other's telephone calls, discussing problems as they arose, and quite often all huddling together to try and puzzle out a mystery or discrepancy, improved both the quality and speed of what we did.

Even more to the point, we got to know the idiosyncrasies and patterns of behaviour of individual ships and their captains in the most extraordinary manner. This was impressed upon me most forcibly when, after eighteen months in the job, I was sent over to Washington to compare notes with my American opposite number. Where we had four, they had vast numbers and had broken the problem into discrete chunks with a whole team of officers looking after each. The result, besides being far slower than our operation, was that it was extraordinarily difficult to discern the linkages between events and movements which continually forced themselves on our attentions.

For almost the first time since our marriage, Betty and I started to lead a normal family life on our own. As well as getting to know my daughter again, in a sad and revealing way I had to attempt to re-woo my wife. Each of us had had to make our own lives, and although it was only three years since we had enjoyed life together in Germany, they were years during which Betty and Gaby had grown close without me. I felt deeply the problems of establishing myself and, to my alarm, found myself irrationally jealous of the closeness between the two of them. A more ignoble emotion would be difficult to imagine than the jealousy of a man of over thirty for his own child of only three years of age. Sadly, emotions do not respond to logic, and the problem was exacerbated by my chronic difficulties in understanding the workings of a small person's mind.

Much of this realisation is retrospective, and I suppose in a way I was at last coming to grips with a heavily delayed adolescence. I found more and more to love and admire in my wife. Her courage, sense of fairness, and endless determination to pursue her convictions single-mindedly over very long periods, were to be cruelly tested in the future – but they were a revelation to me. She was, in many ways, the first person I ever knew in real depth, and her characteristics were not only different from those I thought I had seen in her before, but also markedly different from those of the people I had worked with. The Navy was a man's world and so were the areas of intellingence in which I had operated. My knowledge of women was not only superficial, but in many ways crass and stereotyped. From Betty I gained not only the first rags of the self-confidence that had so constantly eluded me, but also the beginnings of an understanding of how much women had to offer and the strengths they possess – which so often compensate for male weaknesses and prejudices.

Although, in theory, my work was related to normal office hours, the nature of my responsibilities meant that if there were any unusual or inexplicable Russian naval activities I had to scurry into my bunker in the Admiralty at any time of the day or night. This was where the very tight manning of our operation placed horrendous demands on the entire team. Most of our evenings and weekends were interrupted in some way or another. At the time, my background training and belief in the importance of our work made me accept these forays as normal and understandable. In a way, my war had never ended, and I continued the same, unhesitating, placing of duty before family which we had all practised during the war. In my naiveté I believed that civilian life would be even more demanding, for as a naval officer I enjoyed security of employment whereas surely in the private sector the smallest dereliction of responsibility would be instantly punished with the sack.

Even Betty, who would grumble good-naturedly, accepted that, when one of the First Sea Lord's surrogates (of whom there were apparently a great many) summoned me, we dropped whatever we were doing and I fled to respond. All too often I found myself sleeping on the camp bed in the bunker, rather than tucked up with my wife in our cosy flat. In our approach we were both rather like those Japanese soldiers who emerge, blinking, from the jungle thirty years after the end of the war, clinging on to their swords and oaths of allegiance and fealty.

Despite these vicissitudes, we managed to develop a social life which was, yet again, based on Betty's friends and acquaintances, rather than mine. A feature of naval life was that, unless you lived in a 'naval area', you spent much of your life in temporary social groupings of surprising superficiality, despite an apparent closeness. My brother-in-law had married and was living in London, and so I had the first opportunity to get to know him. He has been a lifelong friend ever since, and an unfailing support to us all both in good times and bad. Our pleasures then were simple. We entertained in each other's houses, had an occasional bottle of wine, or game of cards, and every now and then a trip to the cinema which, despite the arrival of television, was a source of continual delight and excitement.

It all seemed too good to be true. The only apparent fly in the ointment – and ever present fly in a naval career – was the knowledge that we had, at most, three years of this unaccustomed approximation of real life, before I would be despatched to sea again. Moreover, I was on the run-up to the zone for promotion – a strictly time-limited period during which one was either promoted, or destined to continue for the rest of one's naval career in the rank one had attained. The 'rest of one's career' under such circumstances was also truncated, for passed-over Lieutenant-Commanders were obliged to retire in their early fifties and precedents for developing a second career after that were not encouraging. My next appointment was, therefore, certain to be another sea-going one, and my success or failure there would decide our entire future. I always felt under intense competitive pressure in the Navy. Perhaps this was because I was conscious that my career pattern was so weird as to militate against preferment in that very traditional and conservative service – or perhaps it was because of the naked ambition and drive of many of my peers, to whom, one felt, failure to gain promotion was akin to a death sentence. However, in one's early thirties one does not allow such matters to hang over the important business of enjoying life in the present. My job represented variety and responsibility and I knew I was good at it. Our home life was idyllic, and to cap it all we had just reached that stage of financial security where, after paying for the essentials, there was a little money left over for us to spend as we wished. After the trials of completing our move and building our home on her own, at last Betty had someone to share the burdens with, and although she greatly missed the radio work she had done in Germany, she seemed contented.

It came as a shattering blow to us both when Gaby fell ill. She was a robust and happy child who had caught few of the childhood diseases which had so plagued my own unhappy youth. She was secure and deeply loved, and the memories I have of the three of us are drenched with giggles of laughter and enjoyment. It seemed to start innocently enough. One Friday Gaby apparently fell ill with a cold and, providentially, Betty put her to bed early and kept her quiet. The next morning we were abruptly shaken out of our Saturday morning lie-in by a scream from her room. We shot in to find a very frightened little girl saying she could not stand up. Betty took her temperature and went to phone

Mark, our friend and doctor. At that point we found ourselves at the start of an absolute nightmare. Mark told us to wrap Gaby in a blanket as quickly as possible and take her to Sydenham Children's Hospital, where he joined us. There we were told that she almost certainly had poliomyelitis, a notifiable disease, for which there was neither prevention (in those days), cure or palliative. To our horror she was wrenched from our arms and transferred to the Hither Green Isolation Hospital, the nearest to our home, and one of the worst-endowed places we had ever seen. Gaby, who had never been separated from her mother, was nearly hysterical with fear and unhappiness and, in our ignorance of what lay in store, there was little we could to to console her.

We followed the ambulance to Hither Green and our already low spirits suffered jolt after jolt as we watched our daughter put to bed in a Florence Nightingale-type ward built in the late Victorian era. We were not allowed to stay with her to try to settle her in and, with her cries for us not to leave her striking right through us, we had to leave. In the light of what we know now, this and the subsequent events were almost calculated to ensure that the attack was intensified. Visiting hours were one hour a day only and for a child of barely four years of age, feeling the unstoppable advance of the paralysis, there was no distraction of any sort. Even during the agonisingly short visiting hours she could not be distracted, for she would constantly burst into heart-rending sobs and beseech us not to leave her. As though that were not enough to cope with, we had by now learnt the grim truth. Nothing could be done to halt the advance of the paralysis, other than remaining quiet and still. By the end of the week the attack would have run its course, destroying the nerves it fell upon utterly, so that in time the muscles would wither, bereft of their control system. The horrible possibilities were underlined by the presence of an iron lung in the hospital, which served as a constant reminder of where Gaby could end up.

We racked our brains for things to take and things to do to show our love and attempt such pathetic reassurance as we could manage. Alas, there was no one to help her play with the toys we took, for the inadequate number of hard-pressed staff could barely even manage to maintain the execrably poor standards of hygiene that ruled there. The entry to the ward was often blocked by piles of sodden, dirty bed linen. The little girl in the bed next to Gaby sat silent, and almost motionless, staring into space. She came from a local orphanage, and did not seem to have any visitors at all. She showed every sign of deprivation and was desperate for any sort of attention. It was hard for us to give her the attention she craved, when visiting time was so limited and our own little one was so ill, but we did what we could. When Betty tried to dress her hair she found to her horror that her head was infested with nits, even though she had been in the hospital for some time. We beseeched Mark to help us remove Gaby to somewhere more congenial, but we were all powerless until the statutory isolation period of two weeks was completed.

Meanwhile, an event happened which finally tipped my resolve to leave the Navy. On the Monday, I telephoned my superior to tell him of our tragedy, and explain that I had to have the week off to be with Gaby, and to help Betty cope with this ghastly situation. I was informed that I had to report back immediately. The Russians had decided that this was an opportune moment for a foray, and my services were required. I sought an interview with my admiral, and got the same response, albeit with at least a glimmer of sympathy. The best they could or would do – if events permitted – was to try to relieve me for the visiting hour. I still find it hard to understand how they could have failed to respond in some more practical way to our desperation and, in fairness, I think today's services probably would. Even then I was not able to be there for every visiting hour and, in addition to her other burdens, Betty was faced with the problems of travelling across South London alone by public transport. How my wife retained her sanity and remained able to show Gaby serenity and calm, I shall never know. Betty has unbelievable strengths, and there is no better bad-weather sailor, but this was bad weather with a vengeance.

Meanwhile, from the Admiralty's point of view, they had an intelligence officer at work whose mind was so full of other things that my reactions and assessments must have been nearly worthless. Each day seemed to last forever and Gaby's paralysis continued its slow progress. Every day we barely had the courage to ask how our beloved daughter was. It was like watching your child being destroyed before your eyes, with the knowledge that apart from praying there was nothing that could be done. By the end of five days the worst seemed to be over, but that was bad enough. The muscles in one leg had gone completely and the other was weakened. Her hips and back were weakened, as was one arm. After a heart-stopping few hours the paralysis stopped just short of her lungs, although an iron lung had been standing by the bed, just in case. At least we now knew what the reality of Gaby's situation was likely to be. Skilled physiotherapy could help her to achieve some recovery, and to develop other muscles and nerve systems that might compensate for those which had been destroyed, but it would be a slow job. Over ninety per cent of possible recovery would occur in the year after the attack, so that the quality of Gaby's attention during that year would be critical to her future.

Meanwhile, she had to stay at Hither Green for the remainder of the statutory isolation period. Familiarity, if anything, made our dislike and distrust of the hospital even greater, and nothing and no one could console Gaby, or reconcile her to that place. Here again, Mark came to our aid. He carefully explained the procedures and difficulties involved in removing her from the hospital after the fourteen days, and warned us that there was bound to be stiff resistance from the authorities. He stressed that it might even be necessary for us to obtain the assistance of the police to get her released from the hospital, but that, provided we were strong enough in our resolve, we could not be stopped. In the event, nothing quite so dramatic was required, although the hospital which had shown so little interest in or concern for our daughter while she was so ill demonstrated an astonishing degree of reluctance to lose a patient.

The due day dawned and we were at the hospital as early as possible. We had to sign innumerable forms relieving the hospital of any sort of responsibility for Gaby, both retrospectively and for the future. We acknowledged, both orally and in writing, the strength of the advice we had been given about the bad effects on Gaby's health if we persisted in what was portrayed as our ignorant and pig-headed intent to remove her. But eventually we got her discharged and took her back to our little flat.

It seemed more like two years than two weeks since we had heard her fall, and her screams of fear, and in the interim something had changed irrevocably for all three of us. However, we clung together with joy and relief, even though the sombreness of the hospital's warnings hung over us. Our home seemed to be a haven of tranquillity, cleanliness, comfort and love, and when we shut the door it was as though the world outside had gone away – as indeed we wished it would. At last Gaby managed a whole day without tears and trauma, and one could see her, despite her incapacity, coming back to us as a person. We both believe, still, that any longer in that hospital would have damaged her irreparably, and yet who can judge? So often human beings can triumph over desperate unhappiness, but I do not believe you can fight both a physical struggle against ill health, and a mental one, when your mind is incoherent with grief, terror and misery, and particularly not if you are just barely four. We were only to have a couple of weeks respite to pull ourselves together. The problem of Gaby's further treatment now lay firmly on our shoulders, and we knew that every moment of the year that we wasted reduced the chances of her recovery. Once again, Mark came to our rescue. I still do not know what strings he pulled, for I certainly had none which I could use. Suffice it to say that he arranged for us to meet Lloyd Roberts, the orthopaedic specialist at Great Ormond Street Children's Hospital. The Great Man, and he was indeed a great man, agreed to take on Gaby's case and arranged for her to be treated further at their wing out at Tadworth.

By this time any prospect of parting from her mother instantly reduced Gaby to hysteria and, needless to say, this further enforced parting distressed us all greatly, but the differences between the hospitals could hardly have been greater. The children received constant love and attention from dedicated nurses who worked on the precept that only happy kids could cope with their physical struggles. The wards shone, and to the degree that any hospital can be a happy place, this was one. The only treatment available was constant physiotherapy and the physiotherapist, Daphne Harvey, treated Gaby as though she was her own child. Our worries lifted slightly, but our problems did not.

Travelling to Tadworth from Sydenham involved one of those curious lateral journeys which the British public transport system seems specifically designed to prevent. Except for the weekends when I could drive us, Betty found her life dedicated to endless, protracted odysseys from bus to bus, pressured continuously by the knowledge that arriving late would trigger in Gaby the terror and fears we were trying so hard to allay. Looking back on that year, I cannot begin to comprehend how my wife coped with all the demands upon her. The Navy's view that their officers were entitled to no private life, coupled with their perceived import-ance of my responsibilities, meant that there was no easement of my time commitment to my job. Even though, mercifully, I was shore-based and in London, the time I could spend with my family was absolutely minimal – or at least minimal by compari-son with the need.

The whole experience soured me. I accepted, of course, that our problems were our own, and I could not expect any employers to share them, but it seemed to me at the time that they were almost deliberately attempting not to help or show any understanding of our position. This, as much as our growing realisation that our lives had changed irrevocably, increasingly convinced me that it was going to be impossible for me to continue in the Navy and that I must seek a job where I could spend more time with Betty and Gaby.

The year progressed and Gaby made some improvement, but it was increasingly clear that the damage was too severe for complete restitution. She was fitted with a caliper – the first of many – and the hospital continued its unabated and devoted efforts to activate other channels of control to the already wasting muscles. She had caught polio the same year that the Salk vaccine was introduced into the UK, and must have been one of the last pre-vaccine poliomyelitis sufferers in the country. Our continuous treks to Tadworth continued unabated also. The relief that occurred was, however, in Gaby's mental attitude. Over time, we could leave her until the next visiting hours without being pursued and haunted by her heart-rending sobs and grief. Our visiting hours were less and less punctuated by her terrified enquiries as to whether we were about to leave.

The whole experience had a crucial effect on our lives, and even more on me as a person. I realised, as I never had before, that it was the three of us against the world, and I realised in a painfully direct way how lucky I had been to persuade Betty to marry me. A less single-minded, dogged and persistent woman could not have coped as she did and, not for the last time, she proved to be the pillar of our little world. She was always practical and unbelievably hard-working. We both share the characteristics of being poor sitter-downers. Somehow we are always active and always building for the future. Betty, however, is much more ordered in her approach than I am. When she has an objective in mind she dedicates herself to it with clarity of concentration I have seldom encountered elsewhere. I tend to be at my best when dealing with a lot of things simultaneously, flitting from problem to problem, rather like those Chinese jugglers who balance plates on bamboo canes, catching each just before it falls to the ground.

Even though it was plain that the worst was over, and that we were not to lose our daughter, it was a fraught year. Despite our energies and determination we were both tired and we seemed to have no time at all which was not already bespoken either to London Transport or to the Navy. Moreover, the happy situation where we had just begun to achieve some disposable income had left us. The cost of travelling and continuously trying to find things to distract Gaby and to demonstrate our love and concern for her broke through our fragile defences and we began to have money worries again. There was no way in which we could augment our incomes, for there was no way we would avoid visiting Gaby on every permitted visiting hour. Before the polio, Betty had just started to pick up the reins of acting for radio again, but in these circumstances she was no longer able to continue her efforts. It was a great loss, not only financially, for Betty had real talents and derived enormous pleasure from the activity.

Gaby was discharged from Great Ormond Street within the year, and although we had to continue with the physiotherapy, there was nothing more medically that could be done. The time now came to move on and to try and create the new life which we envisaged together. I was certainly not impelled by ambition, even though my dissatisfaction with the Navy's attitude to its people was pretty thorough. We just needed a new life where we could be together and face the future together. A different kind of life – I thought – where the three of us could adjust to our new circumstances, and be able to appreciate the fact that we were all still together and able to care for one another.

I made up my mind that I must leave the Navy and seek a career elsewhere. Somewhere I could do a worthwhile job but where I could be sure of getting home every evening. I did not mind what I turned my hand to and was quite prepared to start at the bottom. I was totally convinced I could earn enough to support us and we had few material ambitions for the future.

Leaving the Royal Navy was not really the great sacrifice that I have sometimes thought it to be. The Navy seemed to me to be becoming less and less relevant to the problems of the world. When I had joined in 1937 those of us who had the privilege of serving in it genuinely believed that we were the 'peace-makers'. We were by far the largest navy in the world and we had possibly ill-founded but unshakeable convictions that we were the best, and would always win through. By the time I was contemplating leaving we were already substantially smaller in size than the Soviet navy which had been to us, for most of my experience, almost a bad joke in terms of both size and effectiveness. We had long ago lost the number one spot to the United States' Navy. Increasingly, we began to wonder whether navies, on their own, were capable of maintaining the peace. Even my experience during World War

II, when I had twice been sunk through air attack, had demonstrated that the Navy's ability to rule the seas on its own was fast disappearing. Moreover, new weaponry and the advent of rockets, nuclear bombs, and so on, had also contributed to the Navy's apparent lack of relevance. I had drawn solace, in the years after the war, from my work with the intelligence services. We felt ourselves to be in the front line, and for a long time I was able to convince myself that the Soviet Union had merely replaced Nazi Germany as the ultimate threat to civilisation as we knew it. I am bound to say that, here again, my illusions had begun to wane.

All these threads had come together some weeks before, when my close friend, Derek Wilkinson, had astonished us all in Naval Intelligence Division Number Fifteen by announcing that he was resigning his commission in order to follow a career with ICI. Derek and I had known each other at Dartmouth, had been in the submarine service together, learnt languages together, and had ended up working in the same department of Naval Intelligence. We had sailed together as boys. To see him moving out, without the added impetus of my own family circumstances, really brought things to a head for me. He was followed swiftly by another lifelong friend, Colin McMillan.

I met them both often after they had left the Navy. They were both bubbling with enthusiasm and comparing, very favourably from ICI's point of view, the opportunities, pleasures and challenges of life within the company with the naval background in which we had all grown up. They marvelled at small differences, like the lack of bureaucratic supervision and the degree of trust placed in young people in the field of commerce. They were fascinated at the new skills they were being taught, and believed totally that they were more likely to be in positions of influence within ICI than if they had remained working with me in the Citadel beneath the Admiralty. They felt that they were being trained to deal with real-life problems where instant solutions were required, to produce instant results. They compared this with the slow, thorough, painful and expensive build-up of ever more knowledge about an enemy that we hoped and believed we would be unlikely to fight. Moreover, even if we were to fight the Soviets, a number of us felt that it was unlikely that the Navy would play much of a role, since it seemed probable that the war would be over long before our own fields of expertise were called upon.

Their enthusiasm chimed almost exactly with my own inclinations. In those days I believed that Britain faced a bleak economic future. I wanted a job which was close to the basis of our existence and believed that industrial power was the foundation for national wealth. I wanted to make my new living in an area which had some social relevance. I determined, therefore, to try to emulate them and seek a career in industry. I decided to make a start by approaching ICI.

Derek and Colin were well aware of my family circumstances and the increasing worries I had, and it was they who enquired whether ICI would be prepared to interview me. It was their intervention with the head of the work-study department, Russell Curry, that had opened up the opportunity for the interview for which I was now preparing myself. So in addition to my other worries I had a further one. I wanted the job, and did not want to let my friends down. Preparation for the interview was not easy. I had little real idea of the world of business, and apart from what I had been told by Derek and Colin, very little idea of what the work I might be going to do involved. I had been cheerily told that I should not worry since I would be trained, and that once taken on I would be found a 'slot' even if I didn't take too well to the job for which I had originally been recruited.

I caught the train from Sydenham Hill station to Victoria as I normally did when going to the Admiralty, turned up Victoria Street and walked for the first of many, many times along Horseferry Road to Millbank. The building looked less historic but somehow more reassuring than the Admiralty. Subsequently I have never thought of ICI's Millbank headquarters as being a warm place – but on that day it seemed so. The external appearance of the building had reassuring grandeur, but once inside the differences were immediately apparent. I arrived at ICI's front entrance and was greeted immediately with a degree of comfort and welcome that I found surprising, particularly for the lowest form of animal life about to seek a job. I was encouraged to sit down in a waiting room – where there were actually chairs and up-to-date magazines. A telephone call was made and in what seemed a remarkably short space of time an obviously extremely senior officer, who proved to be Geoffrey Choate, the head office Personnel Officer, appeared. No aged pensioner or lady civil servant dragged me, clutching my piece of paper, through myriads of passages. No, the man himself arrived, shook me by the hand, asked if I'd had a good journey and took me to his office. He then explained exactly what was going to happen, who I would see and what they did, and asked pleasantly interested questions about me. I had already, of course, filled in a form. But he had done a good deal more research and knew about my personal circumstances. He asked about Gaby's condition and appeared genuinely interested in me as a person. I was immensely impressed. I began to relax and rapidly acquired a very positive wish to be taken on by this firm.

This was a much more helpful frame of mind in which to approach an interview than the fear of failure with which I had entered the building, and I owe a great deal to Geoffrey for making that transformation. I was then taken up stairs, again through sparkling passages, everything looking extremely neat, tidy and well ordered, to my first interview. Unlike my experience at twelve years old, I was to see three individuals on their own and had been allocated about half an hour with each. No dossier accompanied me – each had their own briefing note, and none of them was sitting at a desk submerged with paper. In each case I felt much more as though I was meeting somebody, rather than being interviewed. The discussions were very relaxed. It seemed to me that they were really interested in trying to understand me and what made me tick. I actully began to ease up and enjoy myself. There were no trick questions. My experiences so far had already belied the simplistic and naive picture that I had formed in the services about what life was like outside. All of us in the services knew, of course, that the one advantage we had was security – at least until the ripe old age of forty-five – whereas in civilian life you were almost certainly fired at the drop of a hat, particularly if your face did not fit with your boss. ICI didn't seem to be like this at all – and nor did my potential bosses.

I remember working my way gradually through the interviewing process towards the boss himself. Eventually I was summoned in to Russell Curry's office. Russell was one of the biggest men I have ever met, both physically and in every other way. He was an absolutely formidable salesman. He had, as all good salesmen do, a total conviction about the bill of goods he was selling. He had a somewhat emotional and histrionic style of addressing people which did not always match the rather measured and scientific style of much of ICI's business. He was not afraid of emotion, would put his arm around your shoulder, and was not embarrassed to touch. He was a tremendous player on emotional reactions. He always appeared to know everybody's name and all about them. He was in many ways the most unlikely enthusiast for work-study, which I subsequently began to feel was rather devoid of any understanding of human motivation. The Work-Study Department of which Russell was head had been set up by Sir Ewart Smith to introduce – or perhaps, more accurately, re-introduce – the concept of 'work-measured' bonus schemes into the system.

In addition to the concept of work-measurement there was also a much more interesting and exciting field of study for the Work-Study officer, which was called method-study. This was, and remains, an extremely valuable management tool, and to this day I still, on occasion, chart out operations using the formulae that I was to be taught once I had been taken on. However, at the time, apart from the fact that I was to be trained as an 'efficiency expert' I had little idea of what lay in store.

Russell's interview with me, I remember, seemed in many ways more inconsequential than the others. The discussions became even more the sort of friendly talks that you would have with somebody you met in the bar of a club, and even less directed at acquiring information. I suspect, with the benefit of hindsight, that he had perhaps made up his mind in the first few moments of our meeting, and for that I probably have to thank

Derek and Colin. Russell had a strong predilection in favour of employing naval officers. His brother was a distinguished naval officer, and he had, over many years, known and worked with the Royal Navy. He was confident that when he recruited one of us he would be getting a reasonably trained mind and considerable reliability and dedication. He also knew what I didn't, that it was very difficult to get trained managers to take on work-study assignments. They were not seen as leading anywhere, in a career sense, and the work-study practitioners lived in a hazy world between the rock of management and the hard place of the shop floor.

Be that as it may, the time with Russell was enjoyable and went by in a flash. We had a cup of tea together and the last question he asked me was how soon I could start, at which my spirits lifted. I had expected a pretty sickening gap between the interviews and being informed whether I was to be offered a job or not. Geoffrey Choate came to collect me again and left me in his office while he went to consult the three august gentlemen I had just met. He came back a few moments later, shook me by the hand and said, 'Well, you've got a job for life if you want it.' I was shattered. I could not believe that on such a casual basis I was about to be offered a job for life. I certainly wanted and needed to step away from the Royal Navy but whether this vast company, of which I knew so little, and this weird job, of which I knew even less, provided the right place for me to dedicate the rest of my life to – this seemed more uncertain. Geoffrey said, 'Sit down, let's talk a bit about what you are looking for. What sort of starting salary do you want?'

Betty and I had discussed this at great length, and this was were I made the first of a number of mistakes. Believing, as I did, that the busines world was red in tooth and claw, we had decided together that I should seek the minimum salary at which I felt I might be able to get a job, secure in the feeling that once there I would either perform well, so that my salary would go up quickly, or would move to somewhere else where I was better paid. I didn't know, and nobody had warned me, that you were paid the valuation that you placed upon yourself. My pay as a

Lieutenant-Commander had just reached £1,600 a year, and for the first time since our marriage we found ourselves in a position where we had a small amount of money that we could spend as we wished.

Our costs and expenses had gone up enormously as a result of Gaby's illness. Constant visits to the hospital were expensive as well as time-consuming. Once she was released from hospital, taking her up to London for physiotherapy was a constant strain, both physically on Betty, and also on our meagre resources. The cost alone of fares to and from Great Ormond Street was heavy and it wasn't easy for Betty to struggle there with a paralysed four-year-old on buses, railways and tubes. We had worked out that we could probably manage to live for a year or so on the sum of £800 a year, but that after that there would have to be a rapid escalation in my pay if we were to survive. When I left the Navy I would get a small (it now seems very small) gratuity in lieu of my pension, and we had that mentally earmarked to apply to the down-payment for a house. When asked, therefore, what starting salary I would require, I replied, fatally, £800 a year. Of course, when I got my formal job offer, surprise surprise, that is what I was offered.

I remember discussing my prospects with Geoffrey, and saying that although this was what I wanted as a starting salary, I actually needed more money. I had to be sure that I could earn more than £2,000 a year as soon as possible. In the Royal Navy £2,000 represented the upper reaches of a Lieutenant-Commander's pay, and seemed to me to be at least level-pegging with what I felt I could have achieved. Geoffrey looked surprised, and replied that unless I reached more than £2,000 both I and the company would have made a grave mistake, and I remember gleefully reporting this back to Betty as an indication of the boundless opportunities that lay ahead. The time-scale of these delights was left vague, beyond the fact that it would depend upon me. The intricacies of the reward system to which I was about to commit myself were not described at that time. I was told that I would get a formal offer within a few days, and though obviously it was dependant upon their taking up my references it seemed likely that there would be no problem in that area.

That was more or less it. To my absolute amazement, before the morning was out I found myself on the pavement outside Millbank with the rest of the day free, having apparently secured a job – moreover a job with a future. I rushed to the nearest telephone and phoned Betty, who was overjoyed. There were, of course, a number of other things to be done. I had to obtain my release from the Navy, to fix a starting date, and I had to learn my trade – but the opportunity was there, and had been opened within less than two hours of discussion with three people I was to know well for many years.

The day finally dawned when I was to leave the Admiralty. It was, as I recollect it, the beginning of June, and it was a beautiful summer. I turned in for my last day, handed over my responsibilities, and left. I went home to our little flat in Sydenham Hill, and for the first time in my life and (so far) the last, I was unemployed. I had a month between leaving the Royal Navy (and being paid by them), and starting my career with ICI. A month during which I had left the 'womb' of a protective employer, and was totally on my own for the first time since I had entered Dartmouth in 1937.

I wish I could pretend, in retrospect, that it was a stirring time when I was able to put my fears for the future and regrets for the past behind me, and just apply myself to the enjoyment of a month with my wife and daughter. To start off with, we had very little money. Like most naval officers at that time, my bank balance hovered precariously around the overdraft line. I was to receive £1,200 in lieu of my pension from the Navy, and that was all. We were determined to try to hold on to that money, because it was the only capital we had and we would depend totally upon it for setting up our new world.

For the first time in my life I found myself faced with the necessity of signing on for the dole. It was a new experience, and one which I devoutly hope not to have to repeat. I used to have to collect my unemployment benefit at Catford in south-east London, and I am bound to say that those I joined on the dole queue did not seem to be in quite the same circumstances as I was. I felt something of a fraud, and yet I had contributed, and so I reasoned that I was entitled to get some money back out. In those days, collecting the dole was not designed to protect the sensitivities of those who were down on their luck. It involved a certain amount of looking down the nose on the part of the clerks who were dispensing our money to us. However, like so many experiences in life, it was a very worthwhile one.

You could not queue for the amount of time involved without talking to your companions and realising, as you talked, that they were not a bunch of hapless layabouts but people who were facing real problems. It was 1956, the country was booming, unemployment was at a very low level, and allegedly anyone who wanted to work could get it. However, with few exceptions, those who joined me in the queue were not feckless 'rippers-off' of the welfare state. My month on unemployment benefit did not shake my political beliefs, or my conviction that in any society there would always be a number of people who could not cope on their own and would need a helping hand if they were to survive.

The month passed slowly. Despite the fact that we had so many internal worries and doubts about the future it was, in retrospect, a magic period. It was a month without responsibility, we were not interrupted by my employers, and we lived, as we always had, very simply. It was a time where we were able to share, as a family, our dreams and hopes for the future. It was also a month of splendid weather, and one where we felt more involved in making our way through life together than we were to feel for many years thereafter.

9 My Apprenticeship

In trying to recount, later in this book, the effects that the problems of being chairman of ICI had on me and my family, I hit some major problems. The first was that I have already attempted to set out the development of my business philosophy at that period in an earlier book and, to a considerable degree, my business beliefs and my personal values are very closely interwoven. The second problem is, however, a more curious one. When my colleagues on the board – with whom I thought I had worked amicably and with mutual respect for many years – heard that I intended to write my memoirs, they became very upset. After interminable and, I felt, unnecessary discussion, they asked and I agreed, that no memoirs would mention them by name, or in any way that any of them could be identified as individuals.

In writing Making it Happen *I laboured under this difficulty, which prevented my paying personal tribute to their individual contributions, and in writing these more personal reminiscences I have had the same difficulty. At the time, I found the request hurtful, since it betrayed a lack of trust in my regard for them which I felt I had not earned and did not deserve. However, since it was their wish I abide by it even though I think they lose thereby. For this reason, many senior members of ICI remain anonymous, or are referred to by their first names only, in the following chapters.*

My first job was to be as work-study officer at the Wilton site near Middlesbrough. We had lived in Sydenham for nearly five years and had made some good friends in the area, although our relations with our immediate neighbours had never been very close. Maybe that was a feature of flat-dwelling, or perhaps it had more to do with the rather weird selection of individuals who occupied the house. The journey, in early 1957, from our flat in Sydenham Hill to our new home in Nunthorpe was a traumatic experience. It took place in the depth of winter and our little A30 car was so full that it was sinking on its springs. It was the first new car we had ever had and the only way we had been able to afford it was by Betty selling her engagement ring. Like most things that are hard won, it was the pride of our life. The removal van had taken the odd items of furniture that we had begged, borrowed and acquired from second-hand shops during the early days of our marriage. One of the problems of life in the Navy was that we never had any permanent base, so even if we had been able to afford them it would have been difficult to gather too much in the way of personal possessions. At the time, although we had the necessities of life, and Betty's keen house-building abilities had ensured that everything was comfortable, what little we had was very basic. Maybe it was as well, because our taste and the style of houses in which we were to live was to change abruptly in the not-too-distant future. At that time we were going through a period of modernism and our heroes in the furnishing world were Heal's. We had contrived to decorate our flat in its fine Edwardian house on Sydenham Hill with modern wallpapers and had done our best, within our extremely limited means, to give an impression of Tate Gallery elegance. In Nunthorpe this was to lead us into some determined efforts to metamorphose a house which had a specific character of its own into something which it really fought against! It was this experience which really taught us to 'roll' with the houses in which we chose to live.

Not only was the weather atrocious as we started our drive up North, but to make matters worse Gaby was taken violently ill. We had a nightmare journey trying to cope with a tiny, over-crowded car and a very unwell five-year-old. We had to stop frequently as she was sick, and finally gave up the struggle to continue when we reached Stamford. The George provided us with a dormitory of a room in the annexe, in which there were three beds, and we settled down for a few disturbed hours. Of course our various medicines were packed in cases and trunks which had gone up with the removal men, and we could only obtain aspirin to help Gaby's problems. We knew we had to be in Nunthorpe early in order to collect the key and greet the removal vans, and therefore had to start as early as possible. By the time we got to Nunthorpe the next morning we were a shattered and exhausted little group. Moving in to anywhere is bad enough in itself, but moving with a sick child, in the height of winter, with pouring icy rain and no heating added dimensions to the experience for which we were not prepared. When we arrived at what was to be our home for the next three years, the house was absolutely freezing. Our predecessors had left it reasonably clean, but of course the electricity had been disconnected, and in any event our electric fire was at the back of the van. By this time Gaby was feverish and extremely miserable and even Betty, who has always been superb in a crisis, was beginning to feel somewhat at a loss.

It was then that one of those marvellous, neighbourly North-Eastern things happened which was to brighten our whole day. One of our neighbours from down the road, and who has remained to this day one of our closest friends, arrived to see if there was anything she could do to help. Her name was Josie Horsley and she found us looking helplessly around an empty house, our teeth chattering with the cold, and our daughter lying in the back of the car, surrounded by impedimenta. Within no time at all she had the whole matter in hand. She provided the wherewithal to light a fire, hot drinks, and even went to the extent of bringing us a cooked lunch. This, we were to learn, was the way in which people in the North East helped each other, and it was a very far cry from our experiences in London and the South.

Eventually the van left, and finally the move was completed. Our house was a very well-built, solid 1930s' construction. Its real glory was that it stood on a double patch of land – not only a source of pleasure to us but also of considerable financial assistance, since we were able to grow very large amounts of our own fruit and vegetables. As time passed, we discovered that we were surrounded by ICI people. Only our immediate neighbours to the left, who proved to be Josie's parents, were not ICI employees. I still had the consciousness of rank and hierarchy which was a legacy from my days in the Royal Navy, and found it difficult to accept that I, on the lowest rung of whatever ladder I had managed to scrape on to, could possibly hope to relate to these senior, impressive, obviously wealthy and well-organised members of the company which I had joined. They all had larger cars than ours, and grandiose titles to compare with my lowly grade of work-study officer, which was hardly an Open Sesame to industrial acceptance. In time I was to find that they weren't in any way status-conscious and indeed it was I who imposed those difficulties on our relationships, rather than they. They were people with whom, in one way or another, I was to work for the rest of my career with ICI, and they were an astonishingly gregarious lot. They were united in their competence and conviction of their own abilities, and also by the assurance that they worked for the blue chip of blue chips, and that they were a special breed of industrial manager. In a funny way I had managed to progress from a branch of the armed services which considered itself to be above all others, to a company which had, at that time, a similar total conviction that it alone knew the correct way to do things and that others were in some way lesser mortals.

Our house needed a great deal of work before it became the marvellously comfortable home that it proved to be after Betty's skilful attention. We had almost nothing in the way of free-standing wardrobes and there was no built-in furniture, so hanging-space was a nightmare. We enjoyed planning how we would adapt the various rooms and conceived extremely ambitious ideas for building in vast amounts of furniture, but were at a loss to know how we were to do it. Yet again ICI produced the answer – albeit unwittingly. I found that there was a first-year apprentice in the woodworking section at Wilton who was interested in earning some extra money at weekends. Thus it was that we met Fred Airey, who was to introduce us to entirely new and different aspects of life in the Middlesbrough area. Fred came from a large family who lived in a back-to-back house in the centre of the town. He, and all his relatives, had been Middlesbrough people almost since the city had started to develop in the nineteenth century. Certainly we could not have met anybody who knew his way around the area better, and he could lay his hand on almost anything that was needed. At that time materials of all sorts were difficult to obtain, particularly if, as in our case, you had little money and needed to buy things cheaply or get special deals. Fred started working for us a couple of weekends after we moved in. He was to continue doing jobs of one sort or another with us for quite some time, and to remain a friend to this day. He certainly transformed the house, and we can still attest to the quality of his workmanship, since it is only in the last year we have finally disposed of one of the bedside tables that he built for us.

Obviously, we could not afford painters or decorators, and had to do as much as possible for ourselves, being very conscious of the need to economise. As always in our lives, we accepted the necessity to keep warm as being a first priority, and it was just as well that we did, for the winters in the area were of numbing intensity.

The time in Nunthorpe was one when Betty and I were very involved with 'doing it ourselves'. We grew everything that we needed for the garden from seed, or scrounged cuttings from friendly neighbours. Although Betty has always been a very practical person, happy to turn her hand to almost anything, I cannot say that it has ever come naturally to me. However, together we did the painting, papering and tiling, hung pictures, laid carpets and lino and so forth. We put a great deal of effort into the garden, digging, double-digging, composting, mulching, pruning and propagating – all of which were newly learned skills for both of us. Josie Horsley's husband, Arthur, was an engineer at Billingham, and they seemed to take on our problems and endeavours with the same whole-hearted involvement that we had ourselves. Of course, they did have the advantage of having done most of it before, whereas it was all new to us.

There were, however, some things that we developed together – for example the alcohol-production lines were a joint endeavour. In those days, long before brewing kits were invented, we taught ourselves to brew beer and started making our own wine. Springtime found us all out together gathering dandelion heads, burnets from the railway embankments, elderflowers, and so on, to add to the enormous range of potable and in some cases, it must be admitted, non-potable drinks that we produced. It was at this time we learnt the invaluable lesson that when you have made it yourself you somehow don't seem to notice any minor imperfections of quality. Absolute honesty and integrity in the sampling process of home-brewed drinks seems to me to be very difficult to achieve. There is such a big investment in time and effort involved that it takes a strong man to wrinkle his nose and pour the whole lot down the sink. The alcohol content (something we never had a problem with) is there, if you can only somehow get it down the throat. Over the years I have reluctantly come to the conclusion that the superb products that I thought we made at that time were not quite up to the standards of some of our industrial competitors in France, Italy and Spain. In those days such concerns did not trouble us.

I still marvel at the extremes of ingenuity, sheer hard work and perseverance that we all went to, to live on the money that we had. Meat was an almost unknown treat, and we perfected then the habit of the meatless Sunday lunch which these days we return to from preference rather than necessity. Since we grew every possible sort of vegetable, and a vast selection of fruit, we could always produce marvellous, fresh-tasting, good-quality greengrocery. The addition of gravy and a Yorkshire pudding managed to persuade us that we were not really missing a Sunday joint at all. It is ironic perhaps that in later years my daughter has become a vegetarian, and my wife and I still far prefer vegetables to the meat. Maybe it started then, although I know that my daughter's preferences are borne of conviction rather than just habits of taste.

It was an immensely rewarding time from the point of view of our home life, and a very friendly time from many other points of view as well. To save money we shared transport into the site, and formed car clubs. I do not know whether it is my imagination but the fact that we were all young and not very much in competition with one another seemed to lead to a tremendously light-hearted approach at that time. None of us was really conscious of competitive pressures in business. ICI seemed totally secure and indeed to be triumphantly leading a successful country to a great future. All the talk was of expansion. The idea of shutting something down would never have remotely occurred to us. The problems to be overcome were ones of shortages. The plant could not be put up because we had not got the stainless steel, or the trained people, or we had not been able to recruit the managers that we wanted. Looking back on it the rate of expansion was almost frightening. One or two of the construction firms were beginning to develop housing around Nunthorpe, but at that time there were no modern houses at all. The whole of the village had been built over a period of time from the late nineteenth century onwards. Virtually all the houses were different, and there were no estates, or even ribbon development of similar-type buildings. Within four years of our arrival, Nunthorpe was to be surrounded by estates developed by national and local companies, and these were occupied not only by the young managers who were coming to ICI, but also to those who were being recruited into British Steel, into the shipbuilding company, and the large number of supporting industrial concerns on Teesside. There was some cross-exchange between the steel people and ICI, but surprisingly little between ICI people and the others.

Meanwhile my work-study career, if you could call it that, was continuing apace. Looking back, I can't help but feel that perhaps the hand of fate was already at play, because the particular jobs I did during that period gave me insights and understandings into the workings of Wilton which were to be absolutely invaluable in later life. I seemed to be given all the shift studies – maybe because I did them uncomplainingly.

At this stage, to my absolute amazement, I obtained my first promotion. To this day I do not know whether the promotion was a real one, or why it came my way. I was summoned in and told that I was to become a section leader in the work-study department and that I would have two of my colleagues working for me. I was shifted up a grade in the deadly hierarchy of work-study officers and felt duly impressed. I rushed home to Betty to tell her that I was being promoted and that at long last there would be some alleviation to the grinding financial problems that we had been struggling with. I had a theory of a disposable income barrier which has remained with me ever since. I had noticed in the Navy that life looked very different when one's income reached the point were, after paying the basic necessities of life, one had just enough in hand at the end of the month to enable one to make a choice. It did not matter that the choice might be a relatively small one – between say a shovel and a shirt – but the important thing was that one actually had a little disposable money. Before you reached that stage, money seemed to be a near obsession. We worried about getting enough petrol to be able to take our share of the car club. A trip out, just for sight-seeing at the weekend, was unheard of, and anyway we had too much to do just to keep our little homestead going.

In any event, I was absolutely delighted at the promotion and Betty and I waited confidently to hear how much additional money we would get. It was then we discovered the trap into which we had fallen. The ICI system in those days was that each job had what was called a 'job maximum', the salary which was paid for the job done well and to standard. When you were promoted the maximum for your job was put up, and the difference between what you were earning then and what you would earn in the future was paid to you over a period which varied with your performance, but was generally aimed at being about five years. The effect was, therefore, that to begin with you received only about one fifth of the amount you would ultimately receive for your promotion. Far, therefore, from immediate relief from our £800-a-year stipend, as I recollect it my pay went up by £40. I suppose I should not really have felt disappointed, since to be promoted after only a year in the company was no bad achievement in itself, but nevertheless at that stage I was really rather more interested in the money than in the honour. It looked as though the money was going to be a long time coming! My two colleagues who had been assigned to my section appeared to accept my jurisdiction with more equanimity than I might have expected. Both were considerably more experienced work-study officers than I, and indeed as a trio we formed a degree of mutual interdependence, rather than any boss/worker relationship. We had a lot of laughs together because none of us took our work too seriously. I am glad to say that while each of us saw that work-study had a contribution to make, we none of us were Messianic in our belief that it would solve all the problems of industry for ever, a position which some of our more extreme colleagues appeared to embrace. When given a task we sat down together to work out how best to do it between us, and I always looked on myself as being a spare reinforcement (in fact the only spare reinforcement!), to help either of them if things were going badly. We shared the problems, and such opportunities as they gave. We also took to eating together in the canteen whenever we could, and we formed a happy working team.

The next, and nearly the last, job I was to do in work-study, was in many ways the most interesting of the whole lot. It was perhaps fitting that it taught me more about the outside world, but at the same time served to underline the absurdities of some of the things that we were trying to do. In the race to pay people more, the group that had been left furthest behind were the long-distance tanker drivers. This group were essential for ICI's survival in many ways. By definition we had limited amounts of storage for our materials, and everything depended on a constant stream of delivery, in and out of the site. As well as performing this vital role, the tanker drivers were also our ambassadors and were, in many cases, the only person seen by our customers on any sort of regular basis. We had our own very large fleet of tankers. The movement of chemicals by road has always demanded very high skills and attention. By nature, most chemicals are hazardous unless you know how to deal with them. They need to be transported in scrupulously maintained, specially strengthened vehicles, and the drivers have to know a great deal more about the products they are moving than your average long-distance man, who can afford to be relatively indifferent as to what he is carrying in the back of his van.

At that time our drivers were scheduled very carefully and indeed, years before the law required it, all ICI tankers had tachographs in their cabs, without any of the nonsense about 'spies in the cabs' which was subsequently to erupt. They were not, of course, eligible for a work-measured incentive scheme. They therefore saw their differential in pay, by comparison with all the other ICI employees, being reduced in a relative sense, and were understandably somewhat disenchanted by this situation. The actual hourly rate for a tanker driver didn't mean very much, since, within the very correct limitations imposed by the law, they worked extremely long hours. Scheduling of long-distance tankers was an absolute nightmare. In 1957 it was not possible, under the existing road conditions, to drive a tanker from Teesside to London in the time allowed. The tankers therefore had to be overnighted at Biggleswade, and taken on by another driver. The scheduling was set by one of the managers driving a loaded tanker down the appropriate route, making absolutely certain that he did not exceed the speed limit, and averaging the time that it took over about three runs. This then became the set timing for the run, and the time that the tanker driver was paid for. In a rational world, you would have thought that some means could have been found of paying the men more money. The reality was that they could not drive any faster, because to do so would have involved breaking the law and the speed limit. There was, therefore, no question of their being able to do more work within the time. There was no escape through our usual routes of writing in 'cleaning time' and so on, since the vehicle was on the move and patently you couldn't do more than actually drive the thing.

The problem blew up and up and up. ICI was wedded to a concept of only paying on work-measured incentive schemes, and were frightened that anything which broke that somewhat illusory line would open the flood-gates of demand. The drivers, meanwhile, were getting more and more upset at the decline in their relative earning power, and were demanding action. The action that ensued was that I and a colleague, Charlie Moore, were asked to try to devise a work-study incentive scheme for long-distance lorry driving. We were doomed from the start. Remember that the theory was that it was only physical work and exertion that was paid for. The whole incentive was to encourage more physical work and more exertion. One didn't actually want one's lorry drivers to be forever changing gear, or wrenching on the steering wheel. The ideal was that they got up into top gear and, with measured calm and considerable skill, touching the wheel from time to time, drove down the road perfectly safely and within the law. Nevertheless, we were committed to carrying out the studies, and a richly rewarding experience it proved to be. It was apparent that we would have to accompany the drivers on all their main runs, and Charlie and I divided them.

To this day I do not find too many managers who have ever experienced the problems of long-distance lorry driving as they existed in those days. Indeed, I recently rode in the cab of a long-distance tanker and was shattered at the changes that had been made. In those days we drove Scammell tractors and Barrel trailers and when I finally retired from ICI my friends in the distribution and transport section commissioned a picture, which I cherish, of the vehicle in which I studied. I have it before me as I write this and a handsome beast it looked in its blue livery, with the ICI badge on the side. The handsomeness of the appearance belied the appalling experience of actually driving, or even just riding in one. It wasn't just the sheer physical effort involved in shifting through the sixteen gears that were necessary to move it, or the necessity to stand up in order to get enough leverage on the brakes to stop the enormous weight that was being driven. It wasn't the muscle-wrenching force that was necessary to turn the wheel, despite the high gearing, or the number of turns required to get round the simplest corner. It was the cold, the draught and the noise which really wore you down. Although there was a rudimentary heater in the cab it was quite impossible to remain warm. In fact it was so cold that, even wrapped up like a Michelin Man, frequently I was too frozen to enter the readings of my watch on the sheets which we were marking. The noise, the vibration, the continuous juddering of the vehicle, combined with the necessity to keep the side windows open for hand signals, all made the journey very different from what I had envisaged as a simple motorist. Of course, nowadays these things are so different. Tankers of this size are automatic, with sophisticated braking systems, the cabs are immeasurably more comfortable, and the vehicle is properly sprung and insulated. In those days long-distance lorry driving was a killing operation. It made men old before their time, and what really shook me was my previous total lack of any sort of perception of these conditions. I thought then, and still do with guilt, of the times that I had obliged a large tanker to stop because I had right of way, and after the studies had been completed I can assure you that my driving habits changed markedly.

The tanker drivers were, moreover, a different breed of man. To start off with they virtually never saw their supervisors. They were masters of all they surveyed, captains of their ships, totally independent as long as they did their job, and they relished every moment of it. Despite the appalling conditions they were the most cheerful, gregarious and enjoyable bunch I have ever worked with. The art of tanker driving in those days was, of course, to hop from transport café to transport café and on the sort of regular runs that my chaps did you got to know who you would meet, where and when. Transport café memories are long, and once one has become a regular they seldom if ever forget you. One of the many things which has saddened me has been the disappearance of the many stops that I used to know, along the trunk roads of Britain, and their replacement by motorways and motorway service areas. Even when I was the chairman at Wilton there were still a few transport cafés remaining from those days, which were a joy to visit. Lorry drivers have an easy-going *camaraderie* and mutuality of respect which is a pleasure to see. It is just as well perhaps, since if anybody loses a load, or needs to change a wheel, they need every bit of help they can get, including the work-study officer, if one happens to be aboard.

The job lasted nearly two months, and during that time Charlie and I covered practically the whole of the United Kingdom. As well as learning the transport cafés and the overnight digs that were provided (which were always good for a party when we got there), we also had some other eye openers. The problems of waiting at the docks to offload have been referred to in the national press, but the frustration of actually getting to the docks and having to wait for hour on hour – moving one's vehicle a few yards at a time and having no idea when one might expect to reach the head of the queue – has to be experienced to be believed. There are no facilities for lorry drivers at docks. There is no canteen you can go to, no way of spending the time except sitting on the dock edge and kicking your heels. I used to see my watch, which was usually accustomed to recording seconds and minutes, recording elapsed times of hours at a stretch. Sometimes amusing things happened while we waited there, but they contributed nothing to the study and, apart from a certain amount of hilarity, very little to the advantage of the drivers themselves. The hours spent together and the unusual opportunity for them to have somebody to talk to, helped me to get to know them intimately. I found myself getting very close to these lonely men, and we made friendships which I have always valued. It is only very recently that I have given up staring intently at the faces of every long-distance tanker driver from the North East, as the last of my friends from those days have retired, or moved on to other jobs. They were a smashing breed of man, and my admiration for them was intense. So, indeed, was the problem of trying to ensure that we devised some politically acceptable way of rewarding them within the self-imposed limitations we had set ourselves. Finally we produced a solution which was a pretty transparent 'fudge' of the principles on which we claimed to operate. In reality the sheer problems of controlling the vehicle at all, hour on hour, was physical and mental work of a high order but scarcely measurable by stopwatch and rating. We succeeded in demonstrating this to our satisfaction and more or less ratifying the existing scheduling systems with the sanctity of our doctrine.

This was to prove to be my last work-study appointment. Suddenly, and totally out of the blue, came a completely unexpected move. I was to become the Deputy Supply Manager at Wilton. A promotion which was quite outside my wildest dreams or ideas of what might lie ahead of me. I had done almost exactly two years in work-study from my time of joining ICI and my initial training to the time that I left. What had I gained? Even though I have often been critical of the application of work-study and the way it was done then, I would be the first to look back with gratitude for the opportunity and insight it gave me. There was no other job through which I could have entered industry which would have given me such a closeness with such a variety of people on the shop floor. I learnt to see a great deal of industrial life through their eyes, and to realise the enormous gaps of perception that lay between the work people and even the most junior ranks of management. Carrying out a work-study with a small group of people forced you, whether it was in your nature or not, to be so close to them over a period of time that it was almost impossible to maintain artificial barriers even if you had wanted to. I have never wanted to.

In my service in the Navy I had always valued the closeness that one was able to establish with the men under one's command, and many of the jobs that I had done in submarines and in intelligence had put me in positions where I was working with very small numbers of ratings. It was this opportunity to really get to know people, to understand their interests and enthusiasms, what motivated them and what they saw as their problems, which I had found one of the most rewarding features of an officer's life in the Navy. I found it curious that it was not seen in quite the same light in industry. I realised that there were almost two separate worlds. A world where the job was done, day in and day out, and another world where the planning, costing, development, expansion and so on were the prime considerations. There appeared to be a practical world and a paper world. It was astounding how little interplay there was between the two, and this was in one of the best-run companies in the country, which prided itself on its labour relations. I learnt, also, the curious position that the union occupied with its members. A combination of affection and something amounting almost to fear. I learnt to respect and understand the difficulties that shop stewards had in maintaining the leadership of their people. To this day I do not understand why it is that people are willing to take on the task of shop steward in industry. Certainly in those early days the shop stewards were, almost without exception, older men who took the job on out of genuine concern for their fellows and a real wish to improve their lot. Most of them acknowledged how much ICI had done for Teesside, and there was a tremendous reservoir of goodwill for the company as a whole. This was reinforced by the differences in our approach to that of the other businesses on which Teesside had been based over the years.

We had always employed graduates as managers and, relatively speaking, a lot of them. From the very inception of the company there had been a belief in the abilities of the men on the shop floor, and indeed the Chairman of ICI at that time, Sir Alexander Fleck, had joined the company as a laboratory assistant. We were a relatively open society, albeit perhaps a bit paternal in our approach. We had a genuine belief in trying to provide the best for our people, and an equally strong belief that our people would respond. Our managers had enormous back-ups of staff and very high-level technical advice of all sorts. They had professional personnel officers, work-study officers, occupational-health specialists, really everything you could think of. They were carefully trained to carry out their jobs, and were continuously being given further training courses. They were counselled, developed, exhorted and led by example. Contrast this with the lot of our shop stewards. The shop stewards' job was very largely done in their own time, it was unpaid and with very little training available, although this situation improved greatly over my years in industry. They had no background of power to rely on in leading their men and they had to stand for election continually, so that the temptation always to pander to the popular decision when it differed from the right one must have been very strong. They had no offices, little back-up, and poor means of communication, and yet they exerted an influence and inspired a confidence on the part of the men on the shop floor that our managers all too often failed to command. It was to remain, during the whole of my industrial life, a puzzle and a problem.

During my time in work-study I had realised how hungry our people on the shop floor were for the normal features of human contact. I was saddened how little the managers 'walked the floor'. I compared this with my days in the Navy when we were taught that the officer who did his paperwork while his men were working was negligent. There seemed to be a counter-cultural belief in industry. If you were absent from your office in some way you were failing, and if you were walking around talking to your men, keeping an eye on what was happening, getting to know them all and concerned with them, somehow you were not doing the job for which you were paid. It was all the odder, since we lived in a relatively small community and it was almost impossible to drop in to a pub or a club without seeing somebody from our shop floor. Many of us used the recreational club as an alternative to the canteens, and there met the very same people that we worked with on the site.

Amongst the other great lessons that I learned was how the site was sustained. Although I had only a smattering of an idea how the various plants worked and how the various parts worked, of transformations from one chemical to another, I had a very good idea of what bound the site together, and the basic infrastructure which kept this whole complex machine ticking over. There was literally no other job that I could have done which would have given me such an excellent grounding in such a fascinating and expanding work-place. Wilton had already, by then, achieved a size at which it could begin to claim, together with its sister factory at Billingham, to be the largest petrochemical plant in Europe. To see this, and understand its workings, was an ideal apprenticeship.

Lastly, and I suppose the biggest lesson of all, was learning how much more our people knew and understood of what they were doing than we gave them credit for. We always knew that we relied on them to carry out their duties well and effectively. But we tended to believe that we, who understood the theory of what was happening, knew better in some way than those who wrestled with the practice. When things went wrong, as with the incinerator, it was remarkably seldom that we asked the people on the shop floor for their views. We tended to make our own diagnosis, supported by observation on the spot and casual comments from the troops. But it was seldom that a manager really sat down with his people and explained the problems he was dealing with and asked if they had any views. It was common practice when carrying out work-study to discuss exactly every action that was taken and why it was taken, as opposed to another. More often than not, the experience of doing the job, day in and day out, had enabled our people to learn all sorts of short cuts and wrinkles, many of them good and only odd ones undesirable. The built-in learning process and urge to simplify that everyone has, came through very strongly, and was one of the reasons why work-study schemes, no matter how excellent, continuously paid more and more money as our people learnt quicker and different ways of doing the job.

The people I had worked with during these two years were of universally high quality. They were men and women of breadth and wisdom, maturity and roundness. The range of their outside interests and their abilities astounded me then and cheers me now. Once they believed in your sincerity, they were, almost without exception, lovely people to work with. I made many friends then that I have carried through for the whole of my industrial life. I still hear from some of them, although they have long since retired. They were, and are, the true strength of a company like ICI, and although I had no standards of comparison with work people in other countries I was convinced that they would be a jolly hard team to beat, just as long as they were giving of their best. I also learnt how incredibly demoralising it was not to have enough work to do. I realised how much happier our people were when they were under pressure than when they were trying to fill the time, and how difficult it was to concentrate, hour after hour, on an instrument panel where things could deteriorate all too fast, and the only warning that was likely to appear was a small divergence on the chart, or a change in the position of maybe two dials amongst several hundred. Despite all this, in the overwhelming number of cases our people did find and detect the onset of trouble in time.

On the less bright side of the equation, I had developed grave doubts whether the work-study incentive system was the best way to motivate people. I had seen the problems of trying to apply a doctrinaire system across the piece, and had recognised the pressures that potential increases in pay, which might not be available to all of them, put on both managers and men. I had recognised that managers' priorities were not always to obtain the highest results from their men and that just keeping the show on the road was closer to their own sense of need. I had realised that never in the whole equation, at the levels at which I was operating then, was there either understanding or concern about the overall business situation. I do not think I heard the word 'customer' during the whole of my period in the work-study department, and while costs were looked at, it was always in terms of the abilities of our schemes to justify themselves from a cost point of view. I had learnt the impossibility of real control, and the futility of attempting to supervise in detail such widely dispersed activities as those on a chemical site. Although I have always been thankful that I was not asked to make the rest of my life in work-study, because I am sure that I would not have had enough inherent belief in the systems to sustain my commitment, I realised then, as now, how lucky I was to have had this entry into industry, and how much I owe to Russell Curry and his colleagues.

The job to which I was to be appointed proved to be by far the most fun of any I was to hold. It was also the area where I spent the most consecutive time, apart from that on the ICI board, of all my years in industry, and in many ways my time there still represents one of the most rewarding periods of my life. In those days the supply department was a very large one and it had the closest approach to commercial responsibility of any existing on the Wilton site. Because of the enormous variation in the factories that were grouped together at Wilton, an ever increasing range of spares and equipment was necessary to be held in store to keep the whole show running. In those days delivery times were still very long on a whole variety of items, and it was seldom that materials could be obtained from overseas quickly.

At this time the stores alone held over 110,000 different individual items, including the variety of raw materials that were necessary to keep the plants running. The range seemed to be continuously expanding by ten per cent or more a year. The amounts of money tied up in this way were absolutely mind-boggling although, since we were not charged for working capital, we were able to view it as a largely theoretical cost. In order to try to keep track of this bewildering range, which was, after all, something like three or four times the size of the stock of the largest supermarkets, we employed an army of supply assistants and an almost equally strong army of storemen. The department was responsible for the running of the stores, which alone had over a hundred storemen and, if I remember my numbers correctly, consisted of about a hundred and twenty people, many of whom were women.

The department bought and handled every sort of material you could think of, from clothing to food to every sort of tool (even the most basic, such as spanners, screwdrivers, etc.), and including the multiplicity of engineering items which were necessary to maintain the immense array of plant that Wilton deployed at that time. Many of the specialised engineering spares had a very long delivery time indeed. Woe betide the supply department and the engineer concerned if, for instance, you ran out of a special seal from Switzerland on which delivery time could be a year to eighteen months. In theory, at least, this might well mean that all production could be lost for that period. We did have a back-up, however, because we had one of the largest engineering workshops in the country, which was capable of making, on a one-off basis, practically any product, provided that it had the essential materials to hand. But even here the delivery times were unconscionable. For example, ICI was, at that time, buying nearly one-third of the stainless steel production in the country, and delivery time on stainless steel ranged from eighteen months to two years. Moreover, as I was soon to learn, stainless steel is not a single product. The chemical industry in particular used an almost infinite range of special variants, each of which was only produced on a one-off run every two years or so. The whole supply system was designed to try to ensure that the site as a whole was kept running, and while obviously there were pressures on the amount of money tied up in spares, they were nothing like as vicious as the pressures that fell upon you if all failed. Although the supply department was, theoretically at least, responsible for buying all these products, ICI, from the early days of its inception, had set up a central purchasing department in London.

But none of this was particularly apparent to me at the time I got the job. My heart absolutely sang. I was going to be involved in managing a lot of people again. I was to work for a man of about my own age, Alistair Muir, who was a most civilised person and an excellent manager. He had also been in the Royal Navy and we must have seemed a somewhat incongruous couple in our ex-naval greatcoats with civilian buttons, braving the winter snows of Teesside. In addition to the two of us there was a stores manager, a redoubtable chap called Bill Scott-Herd who also had an ex-service background, but in the RAF. This difference of service experience, coupled with the fact that he had recently joined the supply department from the transport department merely served to increase the contempt he had for the two of us, whom he considered to be theoreticians, unskilled in the arts of man management. Over a period of time the amounts of material we had purchased had broken beyond the barriers of the Dormanstown compound and had spread, in what had once been tidy heaps but increasingly became an untidy straggle, along the boundary road. There one could see enormous pipes of various sizes, girders, and every sort of structural steelwork imaginable. In fact about the only things we did not stockpile in any quantity were bricks, most of which were delivered directly to the site as needed.

It was, so to speak, the biggest builders' merchants in the world, and I found it endlessly fascinating. When I got to know more of our operations I realised that the rate of pilferage was such that we were, more literally than I had thought, the builders' merchants for Teesside. We supplied to the site enough spanners to provide one each a year to every man and woman on Teesside, while in the winter it was quite a rarity to see anyone in the area working in his garden who was not wearing an ICI donkey jacket. Perhaps fortunately for us, the local demand for hundred-ton pumps, or stainless-steel sheet was not so large, but anything which human ingenuity could turn to useful domestic purposes 'walked' through security fences, random checks, vehicle searches and so on with unbelievable ease.

The organisation of the supply department was intricate and followed the historical patterns which had operated in ICI for some time, but we were to be subjected to ferocious rates of organisational change, which were instructive in themselves. The very first thing I was asked to do was to go on a course. This I did with great willingness, since I was all too well aware that I knew nothing about purchasing and even less about the organisation of purchasing in ICI. A central purchasing course was run which showed the power of factorial analysis and the application of relatively straightforward mathematical studies to existing situations in order to trigger the imagination and an understanding of what was actually going on. The buyers in central purchasing department were men of very great eminence who struck real fear into the hearts of the suppliers. I was, some time later, to accompany one of them in a tour around the American oil companies, and we were received much more like royalty than as the emissaries of another potentially competing organisation. They were men of great experience, to whom the world was their oyster. There were no limitations to where they could look for supply, and they wielded a size of order which was enough to make vice-presidents and chairmen turn out at the trot if it was known that they were in town ready to place some business.

These Rockefeller-like individuals turned up to give us the benefit of their views and experience and fascinating it was, too. Each of them had an encapsulated view of the market in which they operated which was both sophisticated and intriguing.

Despite the fact that I had already been in ICI for two years, it was my first real introduction to the world of commerce, and the first realisation I had had that we were part of the world as a whole, and not just a large and important part of Great Britain. It became apparent, as the two weeks progressed, that there was both a great deal more to buying than I had thought and also a great deal more to running and controlling a supply department. At that time ICI was producing some fundamental thinking in the whole field of clerical and other methods, and Lord Courtown headed the equivalent of the work-study department as applied to clerical tasks. He had a formidable array of mathematicians and others working for him, who were able to cover every conceivable subject from the design of forms through to the design of control and order systems. This was, of course, before the days of computers, although Hollerith and punch-card machines were in wide use for payroll and other calculations.

The approach to stock control was an entirely mathematical one, and the course gave me my first introduction to a lady called Mary Munn who was later to work for me directly and had an enormous influence on my thinking. She had a most redoubtable mathematical mind and was an extremely clear thinker. Both her example, and that of Jeremy Bray, showed the effect that mathematical analysis could have on interpreting so much of business behaviour, showing up the defects and sloppiness of much of our thinking. Not only had she done a great deal of work on the cost of holding stock and how to optimise this, but she was also developing some radical new thinking about ways in which the administration of the work could be done. It was fairly clear, from an analysis of the actions that were carried out, that everything was done twice. A chit would be filled in to justify a withdrawal from the stores, which was handed in and the item was exchanged for it. The storeman would sign the quantity that he had delivered, and the chit would then go to the supply department where the quantity would be deducted from the ledger amount that was being maintained there. This would be done manually and a new balance would be struck. When the written record showed that the reordering point had been reached, the supply assistant would automatically send a new call-off order on the supplier, notifying the storeman that he could expect some goods in due course. When they arrived they would be added to the ledger and the process would be repeated. Once a year, at stocktaking, the effort would be made to reconcile the actual stock with the record. Not surprisingly sometimes it did and sometimes it didn't. Almost invariably it was assumed the discrepancies had occurred through pilferage, whereas equally often they owed their origins to the mathematical and other failures in the recording systems. Monty Courtown's group had worked out that if we trusted the storeman, he could see the number of items that he was holding after he had made the issue. He would then be in a position to trigger the ordering process and would also be able to see whether the stock was moving faster than usual or at the expected rate. The necessity to keep a written record of the amount theoretically in the stores would be obviated, and an enormous amount of work saved. With the introduction of computers, this whole thing has completed the circle and stock is controlled from computer records once again instead of visually. I am still not sure in my own mind whether this is an advance or a step back.

ICI prided itself at that time on having very different approaches to business in the different parts of the company, deriving to a large extent from the historical background of the businesses that we were in. Thus the Alkali division, based at Northwhich, was looked upon as being the upper-class end of the ICI spectrum. They were seen as being gentlemen playing at being chemists, and were renowned for having the finest wine cellars, the best food, the best club and the most far-reaching social connections of any part of the company. The dyestuffs division was, by comparison, looked upon as having the cleverest chemists, and being the most technically professional, but as very much the poor man's division. Little time was spent on frippery, and they were viewed as notoriously mean in their approach to such problems as offices, support services, canteens, etc. The Nobel division in Scotland was again viewed as a world of its own. They were believed to be very conservative, rigidly hierarchical, and fiercely nationalistic Scots. Many of these pictures were travesties of reality, but like so many caricatures they had a curious effect on those people who operated in the divisions which were so characterised. Rather as owners are meant to bear closer and closer resemblance to their dogs, so did ICI managers begin to bear recognisable relationships to their operational units. Experienced ICI operators would claim that they could recognise a man's division within seconds of seeing him at a cocktail party, and there were times when this seemed to me to be a perfectly possible skill to develop.

The course was to be held at Warren House on Kingston Hill which, with its splendid Edwardian magnificence, coupled with its wonderful gardens, reinforced our beliefs in the power and glory of ICI. During this visit, with my new-found interest in gardening, I viewed the grounds with much greater respect than I had hitherto. The course took place in July, when the gardens were at their best, and I wandered happily through them with a collection of small polythene bags, taking a cutting here and there to take back to Betty. After my couple of weeks induction I returned thankfully to the North and my more normal existence. The cuttings were invaluable to us. Our gardening skills were not very well developed yet, but our money was far too limited to buy much in the way of plants, so we were delighted with any addition. I was, however, to have many opportunities to visit Warren House again and it was an absolute treasure trove of plants and shrubs of every kind. In those days it would have been quite impossible to have thought of cutting back the grounds with which the building had been endowed. Detaching a couple of building plots and selling them would have been viewed as a vulgarity which a company like ours should not descend to, despite the fact that the gardens represented a continuous financial drain, employing at that time some five full-time gardeners.

When I got back to work I found myself embroiled in one of those problems of authority which were to recur so many times in the future. The experience was an extremely painful one for me, but also a very valuable lesson. My appointment as the deputy supply manager in my view meant, quite clearly, that I deputised for the supply manager himself in every respect. I believed therefore, and had been encouraged to think so by my boss, that I was responsible for the operation of the stores and that the stores manager, Bill Scott-Hurd, should accept instruction from me. This was the way that the organisation chart was drawn and this was the way, in my simplicity, I thought it would work. I was speedily disabused, however. I was determined to 'walk the floor' every day, as I had in the Navy. Each day, therefore, I set out to visit every one of my operating sections and also to walk around the stores. It was speedily intimated to me that this was not appreciated by the stores manager. I was welcome to visit him if I wished, but walking around his patch was, in his view, an intrusion on his responsibilities and a course of action which he was determined to frustrate.

As a matter of courtesy I had, from the very first day, called in at his office before going to walk around. I soon noticed that he would find ways of prolonging our discussions in the hope, I felt, of foiling my intentions. Alternatively he would ask, in very great detail, exactly where I wanted to go and what I wanted to see, in order to persuade me that it was unnecessary. If all else failed he would accompany me in a very grumpy manner. I started getting messages back that Bill would prefer that I did not visit the stores at all. I took this for some time, and eventually decided that the only way to deal with the matter was to sit down and level things out with him. We had a blunt, and not particularly enjoyable discussion. I was told that he was damned if he was going to have a manager like me, for whom he had no respect, 'interfering' in his operations. I would keep off his patch or I would learn the hard way. I was absolutely shattered, and reacted, quite wrongly, by climbing on my high horse. I pointed out that I had been appointed to do the job and that while I would, of course, take his views into account, nevertheless I would do the job in the way that I thought was right. If I wanted to walk around his stores and talk to his storemen I would do so as often as I wished. If he thought he was going to teach me a hard lesson, I had news for him, I was quite capable of ensuring that anything he did was more than reciprocated! I went home absolutely fuming with rage.

First thing in the morning I went to see Alistair, who had been watching the growing conflict between the two of us with a detached and wry amusement. I was later to find that I was treading a well-worn path, and that he had had not dissimilar experiences with our stores manager when he had been appointed as the deputy. As he had already had some experience of being an assistant supply manager somewhere else, and already knew the ropes, he had had a major advantage over me and so had been somewhat better prepared for the onslaught. I explained my problem, said that I felt that we should have a show-down, and would he please see Bill Scott-Hurd and explain to him that, as the deputy, I could do what I liked in whatever way I wished. Not only was this the way it would have been dealt with in the Navy, if anybody had had the temerity to behave in the way that Bill had done, but also I would confidently have expected to see the recalcitrant stores manager keelhauled, made to walk the plank, or flogged around the fleet, or possibly all three. As far as I was concerned, I was facing mutiny. I was therefore even more stunned when Alistair told me that he was not going to see Bill and put him in his place for me, and gently explained to me that it was my job to establish myself in the position to which I had been appointed.

Luckily for me I had not resorted to telling Bill that it was my intention to ask the boss to review our situation, so at least I didn't have to lose face by being unable to deliver the thunderbolts and rockets which I had so confidently expected. At the time I interpreted Alistair's lack of what I felt would have been the correct intervention as being based upon cowardice and fear of his alleged subordinate. I took a more charitable view sometime later, realising that if I had been able to establish my authority and independence over Bill only by the overt and continuing support of my boss I would never really have been in control. As it was I found that I had to plan a campaign both to re-establish my rights, and to develop ways in which I could work together with my prickly subordinate. After a time, of course, I quickly realised that the reason Bill reacted as strongly as he did was much more prompted by fear that I would establish a direct authority over his people and therefore obviate the necessity of having a stores manager, than for the ostensible ground on which he chose to fight. I was determined that we were going to avoid an endless round of game-playing, me seeking to score points over him and him seeking to score points over me, which would inevitably be to the detriment of our staff. I found the system which I was obliged to work one which was so foreign to my previous ideas on command that, at the time, I remember having real doubts whether such a way of working would ever suit me.

I proceeded to lay siege to Bill. I spent much time thinking about how to handle the matter. I suppose that this was the beginning of what was to become a lifelong fascination with the processes and study of relationships between groups of people and the problems of business management. I was clear, first of all, that I must be extremely careful not to overstep the bounds of authority which had been set. At the same time I was determined that I would walk where I wanted, when I wanted and talk to whoever I wanted, but I would always inform Bill after going around his patch, of anything I had found or seen. I would play every card in the open. I would make clear to him the ground rules on which we were operating, and I would ensure that I did not get seduced into playing political games. Equally, I would inform him very quickly of my own displeasure if I saw him playing such games. He was an unskilful political operator, and his reactions to situations were fairly easily predictable. Although he was a very decent man and a very good friend to have, he did not find personal relationships easy and was not good at projecting warmth to his people. I plugged away determinedly, but it wasn't until after about four months that I was able to feel that we had established ways of working together which were satisfactory to both of us. We had, and were to continue to have, many more blunt exchanges of views and in later years, when I was to have Alistair's job, Bill was both a friend and a supporter. He never, ever failed, however, to let me know if he disagreed and when he did so it would be in the bluntest terms, without any regard to the pain that he might cause, or indeed the counter-effects that he might have.

Bill's normal approach to any complaint was a violent counter-attack and a total denial that anything could be wrong in the best of all possible worlds, which was, of course, the world which he managed. This attitude ensured, as it was bound to do, that in a great many cases people would complain at the drop of a hat for the slightest malfunction or lack of efficiency on the part of the stores organisation. The continued rebuttal of complaint in return increased the vehemence of the attack and so, over a period of time, one of those situations had developed where, instead of getting good marks for what was mostly an excellent service, we were looked upon as being stubborn and intransigent in order to conceal our own shortcomings. It was obvious to me that those who complained about us had little idea either of the size and scope of what we were trying to deal with, or of the faults in their own approach to us. There was no customer awareness in our service and the customers themselves were a disgruntled lot who believed they had total rights and no responsibilities.

When we finally established a sort of uneasy truce I sat down to discuss the problem with Bill and the stores superintendent, a chap called Ronny Lynagh. Ronny had been a professional storeman in the RAF and so had great experience of the problems with relationships between stores and their customers. It was painfully obvious that the way we were handling our relationships was not improving matters, in fact the reverse. We were involved in an almost continuous battle, a sort of war of attrition, which was heightened and worsened by the fact that we worked for the Wilton central organisation, which was universally viewed as being divorced from the operational needs of the divisions and factories on the site. We decided to set up a sort of advisory group for the stores, and I duly took on the task of setting it up. We started by Bill and I going to see each of the works engineers to tell them we were worried about the relationships between us. While we took all complaints seriously, we thought that maybe we were missing some tricks which our customers could help us with. We pointed out the rate at which the whole problem of spares on the Wilton site was expanding, and the sheer size of the range that we would be carrying unless somehow we were able to get to grips with the problem together.

In the event we found, as one almost always did in ICI, that an open and reasonable approach to people produced a sympathetic and understanding response. It was, of course, very much in the engineers' own self-interest that the stores system should become better and they recognised, as we did, that the time and energy involved in fighting internecine wars and battles of the memoranda did not actually help either of our operations to become more efficient. In each case they loaned us an engineer from their organisation who would become our liaison man. These were to form our network. At the same time, Bill and I made it clear that we would deal personally with any complaints referred to us from the engineers and that they had only to call. We then took it upon ourselves to make sure that when the first cries for help came we moved heaven and earth to resolve the problems. Quite often the complaints occurred because of lack of foresight in the plants themselves, but we mutually forswore the cheap option of passing the buck back to them. We did not seek to try to establish the blame for the situation, but rather concentrated on what we and they could retrieve from the position in which we found ourselves.

It was a very valuable series of experiences. The fact that Bill and I were now operating on the same side and with a common problem forced us to bury our differences. I learned to respect and admire his competence in his own job, which was significant. We had a common objective and we brought to it complementary skills. I had the advantage of being the new boy, who was at that stage unknown and at least got some benefit of the doubt. Bill knew the reality of the problems backwards, and could quickly sort out the practicable from the theoretically desirable. Even though we had managed to establish some common ground in an area where we could be of mutual assistance to each other, it was a very long time before I was able to establish, to his satisfaction, that I could actually be a help, instead of merely a threat. This again taught me both the necessity for consistency and the difficulty of building up trust where none existed. Bill was a moody man, and although I have always rather prided myself on being relatively consistent and equable, I learnt quickly that if he caught me on the raw and I reacted in the 'wrong' way I set back the whole cause to which I was dedicated very heavily.

It wasn't until almost a year after my conscious efforts to improve our relationship had begun that I felt able to relax and believe that we had the basis for a sensible mutuality of regard. I was struck by the fact that it was only when I began to view him in a more positive light, and understood his real strengths, that I began to get back what I had hoped for for so long. There were a great many lessons in this, which were to be repeated often in the future. Perhaps the most disheartening one of all was the time that it took to sort out sensible ways of working together once one had started on the wrong foot. It would certainly not be true to say that this could be done with anybody and everybody, but over the years I found that, provided I was prepared to really work at it and to be genuine in my approach, it was very seldom that one couldn't get some sort of working *modus vivendi* over a period of time. In fact, looking back, I can only think of a handful of failures, although one of these was a serious one which had more unfortunate consequences. Patience in human relationships is not an easy lesson to learn, and a particularly difficult one if you come from a service background, where you can always take recourse in the power of authority. Nevertheless, authority is only meaningful if you have earned it, and earning it is not only extremely hard work, but also personally very testing.

10 The Buying Business

Alistair and I operated in almost complete dual harness. He made no attempt to subdivide the work between us, but used me on a sort of jobbing basis for specific tasks. The three years I spent working with him were amongst the greatest learning experiences of my life. A routine was quickly established, and as long as we were at Wilton the day always started in the same way. The mail for all the departments was opened by the secretaries and brought in so that we could glance through every letter. While this took a little time it was invaluable to us, enabling us to have an overview of what was going on in the various departments without appearing to interfere, and keeping us up to date with how any particular situation was developing. It also ensured that we were adequately informed for the inevitable telephone call that would come from the finance director during most mornings. It says something for the pace of industrial life at that time that, in addition to our surveying the whole of the mail, it was a matter of personal pride to the finance director of this enormous site that he saw every invoice that was sent to the works. He would invariably select one or two invoices, which raised a question in his mind, to ask us about.

He was a man of great experience and wide interests and there was an odd sort of rivalry between him and our own department. There was little doubt that he would have loved to be responsible for supply, and could not quite understand how it was that we remained under the control of the managing director of the whole site. The managing director, Ronny, was an absolutely outstanding engineer as well as a great manager. He was a rather typical

ICI 'product'; a man with a tremendous intellect, a great thinker, but not always the most notable of communicators. The finance director had had wide commercial experience in the Middle East and elsewhere, as well as being an extremely distinguished accountant. Since the supply department represented one of the largest single services on the site, giving rise to almost half of all the transactions dealt with by the accounts department, it would certainly have seemed logical for us to come under the finance umbrella. In any event, although we authorised the payment of the invoices, the payments themselves were made by the accounts department.

The finance director was considered to be responsible for all the auditing at Wilton, of which a substantial part involved carrying out the audits of the supply department. In addition he ran the internal audit, which supplemented the professional auditors, doing snap checks of our procedures. I never clearly found out why the managing director clung so tenaciously to our little department, but he did so until after I became the supply manager, and the eventual disappearance of the Wilton council as a service organisation. It was a great help in many ways, because Ronny Newell, our boss, had a very analytical mind and extremely clear ideas on the need to constantly improve our productivity. While he was capable of delving into extreme detail, nothing seemed to obscure his view of the broad thrust of what we were trying to achieve.

The finance director had a rather different approach to life. He loved to 'gadfly' into minutiae, and was convinced that random chasing of individual facts and items would often disclose vast wastelands of opportunity, neglect or inefficiency. Hence our daily telephone call from him. He never announced himself, so one was left to guess who was calling. Mostly he called Alistair, but Alistair had a way of showing, in a suitably discreet way, that he thought the questions were of unbridled stupidity and so, if the query was a particularly odd-ball one, he would phone me instead. The calls always took the same form. We would lift the phone and announce who we were, and from the other end would come the magic word – such as 'widgets' or 'three-quarter bolts' or 'step-ladders' or 'industrial gloves'. There would then be an expectant silence. The silence would not go unrewarded. Eventually our nerves would crack and we would say, 'Excuse me, who is speaking?' and the voice would triumphantly announce himself, sometimes with his name and his title, but on a gruff day just his title. We were then still left with the problem of our widgets. We would then say, 'What did you want to know about widgets, sir?' – or, in Alistair's case, just 'What did you want to know about widgets?' The questions would then become of varying complexity. It might be why we were ordering so many or – alternatively – so few, or why we were ordering them from a particular area or firm, but as sure as God made little apples there would be a pursuance of the 'widget' problem *à l'outrance*. The difficulty from our point of view was that, even with the precaution of having read the mail, bearing in mind our stock range of 110,000 items, there was no way in which either of us could possibly have known such detail about the stock itself. Invariably at some stage, therefore, we would have to call quits and tell him we would look into it and phone him back. Occasionally, if the call came through when we were sitting together, I would nip off and get the stock card, which contained virtually all the information we had about the product, enabling us to give a pleasing impression of omniscience which served to reduce the severity of the grilling. Usually it would end with our being instructed to look into or change some aspect of the supply system. It was a sort of game, but an incredibly time-wasting one, both for him and for us. Some years later, when I took over Alistair's job, the severity of the inquisition eased, as I think I was rather more trusted by him than Alistair had been. The interesting thing was that Neil was actually supportive and quite proud of our department, which was at least as competently run as any other in the company.

When we had finished the mail, which usually took about three-quarters of an hour, and discussed any subjects which appeared to warrant looking into, we then went our separate ways. I invariably walked through the department and had a few casual words with each of the section heads, asking how things were going and finding out about any particular problems they were grappling with. Often I would spend a bit more time in one of the sections in order to ensure that I had spoken to everybody. Later in the day I would go down to the stores and walk around there as well. Each day that I was at the works I would aim to be seen by every one of the people who responded to us. In many cases, besides asking what was going on and what the problems were, I would stop for a few minutes' chat about what I knew of the individual's interests or personal circumstances. Over a period of time I got to know each of them quite well – their hobbies, their cars, the schools that their kids went to, and so on. This was of immense help in understanding when things went wrong or some problem or other occurred.

During the rest of the day there would be a whole variety of 'normal' events. There might be works to visit where something had gone wrong, or they felt they had not received an adequate degree of attention, or wanted to procure some special item. Very frequently there was a supplier to be seen. The normal points of contact for the reps were the section heads, but if the reps were fielding their sales manager or their regional manager, it was always considered courteous for one of us to be present also. Occasionally we would be invited for a meal. The competition between our suppliers was intense. Because of the system of central contracting, their only method of competition was to give a superior 'service'. This meant, in effect, demonstrating to both the supply department and their ultimate customers, at the works, that they could supply us more quickly and reliably, that their products were better packaged, better stocked, or whatever it might be. One of the problems with which we constantly struggled was that, although the economic activity on Teesside was very much greater than that on Tyneside, for historic reasons practically all supplies came through Newcastle. We were always struggling to get contingency stocks held on Teesside, or even to have the centre of gravity of the entire operation shifted down. There was the most astonishing resistance to meet our needs on the part of the suppliers. Since one of our aims was to try to minimise our stock, and hence the capital tied up, without running the risk of shutting things down, the nearer we could have the suppliers' stocks held, the better, from our point of view. In fact the ideal would have been, if any supplier had had the imagination, for them to hold their own contingency stock in our space, merely transferring the title to us as we used the materials. We were struggling in that direction, but despite the attraction of ICI's business, there were surprisingly few British suppliers who were prepared to alter their own ways of working in order to give us, the customers, some advantage.

In addition to the more routine things that we did there were quite frequent meetings on behalf of the company as a whole, held in the central purchasing department in London, or visits to that splendid organisation. Alistair or I would go down to Nobel House, just opposite Buckingham Palace, which housed the purchasing department, about once every six weeks or so, and invariably had a great list of queries or ambitions that we wanted to discuss with the buying managers down there. ICI's buying was extremely competent, scrupulously fair and very professionally carried out. However the purchasing of general stores did not command the attention of the top brass in the same way that the purchasing of raw materials did. In this area our department was somewhat deficient, the only notable item really being the coal for the Wilton boilers. We purchased this, against the centrally negotiated contract, from the National Coal Board, and the arrangements for delivery, calling off and so on were made with the Newcastle office. There appeared, on the face of it, to be little scope for local initiative. However, we continually found areas which we could exploit. The analytical content of the coals varied, as did the delivery costs and times. Over a period of a year or two I was to get to know all the supplying collieries in the Durham coal fields. I happened to be in the area just over a year ago and felt a lump in my throat as I drove from one colliery village to another and saw how few of my suppliers were still in business. In addition to burning coal from the Coal Board we had also started purchasing a certain amount of what was called locally 'sea coal'. These were the results of the discharge of slag into the sea, and the subsequent washing up onto the Durham beaches of the coal that was sifted out of it by the action of the waves. There was a time-honoured trade in Durham of visiting the beach with horse and cart to collect the coal, which lay in a shining clear black line at high tide mark, and excellent coal it was. Of course we could buy it at a fraction of the cost of the Coal Board's own product. The extraction had, after all, already been done, and the cleaning had also been obligingly done by the North Sea, so there was really only the cost of the collection and transport. Over a period of time we steadily increased the amounts of sea coal which we bought, and introduced contractors who in turn purchased from the sturdy Durham entrepreneurs who did the collection. By juggling the supplies from the various colliers, improving the delivery systems, and steadily increasing the admixture of sea coal, we succeeded, over the years, in making a significant contribution to our firing costs at the power station.

One of the fascinations of the supply of coal to the site was that our stock was held on the ground and was moved by massive bulldozers. Most of it came in lorries and a wagonful at a time was tipped onto conveyor belts which moved the coal up to the massive hoppers in the power station, which automatically supplied the crushing mills and, from there, the customers themselves. Our stock, however, was normally meant to last for about ten days to two weeks, to cope with interruptions or potential strikes. It was held on open ground and formed a sort of mountain of coal, located near the railway siding. When it came to stocktaking, this mountain had to be measured by quantity surveyors. The shape was irregular, its compactness was variable and, as we were later to find out, the whole mountain was slowly but surely sinking into the ground. The process, therefore, was something less than totally accurate. Each year we would find substantial gains or losses of coal when it came to reconcile our stocks with the theoretical totals. The true reality of our situation however, only finally emerged when we came to convert the boilers to oil firing. At that stage our task was to utilise the whole coal stock and burn it all off before we could convert to oil, and to our slight horror we found that we ran out of recoverable stock, some thousands of tons, before we were meant to. To this day I do not know whether the resulting shortfall had been due to our enterprising work force taking the coal out in the boots of their cars, to the fact that our mountain of coal undoubtedly descended slowly into the clay burden on which it was based, or just to the inevitable vagaries and ineffectiveness of book-keeping very large quantities of products both in and out of stock over a long period of time.

In the area of coal and raw materials it was relatively easy to measure one's purchasing effectiveness, but extraordinarily difficult to do so across the full range of engineering and general stores. Here a combination of the variety of products held in stock, and the very different uses made of them, ensured that comparisons were almost meaningless. We could, however, measure the on-cost of actually handling the materials and the total amounts we were holding in stock, and it was on these measures of effectiveness that we concentrated. The whole ethos of our supply department, which has remained my business philosophy ever since, was that we simply had to find continuously better ways of doing more with less. It is easy to say this but much more difficult to do, and over the years we were extremely proud of the constant improvements in productivity which we achieved.

From the time that Alistair and I took over the Wilton supply department, we succeeded, despite the growth in range, turnover and demand for our services, to make a steady reduction in the numbers of our people, both in the stores and the supply department itself. This was no mean achievement, and was only accomplished by introducing a continuous flow of new ideas. Of course, the problems were made easier because at that time there was no general shortage of jobs; indeed the reverse was the case. In any event, improvements in productivity could be achieved merely by holding the numbers of employees steady and still managing to cope with the constant increases in demand; but we went further than that and aimed to reduce our overall numbers as well. Over the next three years we managed to improve our productivity by over ten per cent per annum as a result of all these efforts. At that time ICI measured every conceivable aspect of its activities and the central purchasing department used to issue a sort of league table of the various supply departments throughout the company in the UK, with measures of their costs per transaction, and various other gauges of their efficiency. The average stockholding, the amount of cover held and such other measures to effectiveness were all published in detail. We were absolutely determined to fight our way to the top and indeed, because of the rather curious structure of the Wilton council, we needed to be in that position. The Wilton council was, as I said earlier, a service organisation. It produced nothing except the services which enabled the operating divisions to continue in being. As such, we were looked upon by them as an overhead. They would have been less than human if they had not believed they could do our job better than we. Our lives became a constant fight to be able to demonstrate that we were the best and that we were producing the best service at the cheapest cost. Hence our position in the league table was more than just a matter of personal pride.

The individual divisions were continually chipping at the centralised services provided by the Wilton site and seeking to take back, 'all to themselves', support functions which tended to get lost within their own total operating costs. One of the constant battles we fought was to try to prevent mini stores developing in each of the works, in addition to the central stores on the site. In one case we actually succeeded in operating the mini stores through the central organisation on behalf of the works, which at least enabled us to ensure that there was a minimum of duplication between the two outlets. In some other cases, however, the rugged individualism, for which ICI divisions were rightly famed, won and we had little impact upon them.

Christmas came and with it a series of new experiences. In my naiveté I had failed to realise that the season of goodwill involved the arrival of all sorts of relatively small but nevertheless highly valuable 'Christmas expressions of goodwill' from our suppliers. Looking back, they were not of a particularly horrendous nature in terms of their ability to bribe, mostly taking the form of a single bottle of whisky or gin, or perhaps a box of biscuits. However, when the first gift arrived for me, I was horrified and went to see Alistair to ask him what our policy was. The question shocked him almost as much as the gift had shocked me! He had never considered it to be necessary to have written policy about these matters, relying instead upon the good sense and goodwill of our people not to accept outrageously large favours from our suppliers. I remember asking him what he would do if one of our buyers arrived one day driving a brand new car which had been given to him by a supplier? He replied that he would tell him to take it back. What would he do if the buyer refused? After all, since there was no financial gain within our contract, or system for favouring one supplier rather than another, the buyer could hardly be accused of costing the company money. The discussion continued for some time until eventually I was told to try to draft something which would meet the requirements of the situation. We did not wish to stop a long-established customer expressing his 'goodwill' but we also wanted to keep the thing within reasonable limits. I proceeded to try to find out what other people did, and found to my surprise that nobody had any policy on the matter and that I was, so to speak, on virgin territory. Eventually, after a lot of deliberation, we produced what we called the twenty-four hour rule, namely that you could receive anything that was edible or drinkable, provided whatever it was could be disposed of by the recipient within twenty-four hours, and that other gifts had to be clearly marked with the name of the donor's firm and be valued, in those days, at less than £5. The system was duly brought in and persisted, with minor amendments to the total value allowed, for many years to come. I suspect it was looked upon as being a rather pernickety and old-fashioned interference – and even a lack of trust, but it seemed to me a more satisfactory system than allowing each individual to make his own judgements. In the event, the presents were pretty innocuous, but it was surprising how quickly they became a valued addition to our Christmas arrangements.

Betty and I were still struggling to overcome the difficulties of pay which I had unwittingly led us into and, whilst at last we had some disposable income, our needs increased continuously. We had so little of the basic equipment of a house that every penny really counted. A real bottle of scotch or gin was a pearl beyond price, since we were still existing on home-made beer and home-made wines. Similarly, an entire box of biscuits was something we would never have dreamt of expending money on in those difficult days. If we felt that these items were helpful to us, how much more so must they have been to our buyers, who were earning quite a bit less than I was. Indeed, in any other country but this, one would marvel at the integrity of the clerical staff who worked for ICI. Although their pay may have been competitive by clerical standards, they were certainly not highly rewarded. For their money they gave absolutely unswerving loyalty and, in all my time in the supply field, I never had occasion to doubt the uprightness of one of them. The imagination they were capable of using constantly surprised me. If something was required in a hurry they would go to untold trouble to try to ensure that the item got to the site in time. On occasions we even sent people down to meet aeroplanes and bring the item back on a train. If there was a problem with an item they would stay behind, of their own free will and volition, without being asked, until the problem had been resolved, and they were unfailingly good-humoured as well as effective.

In addition to the arrival of these unexpected bonuses at Christmas, the time came for the annual Christmas review of our performance and the appropriate addition to our salary for the following year. For me it was a particularly important moment. ICI was not famed in those days for praising its employees and my boss, Ronny Newell, was even more reticent, unless one had in some way failed in one's responsibilities. I was summoned to the 'great presence' to receive my Christmas salary and waited somewhat nervously outside his door. Alistair went in first and did not look particularly pleased when he emerged. I was summoned in and handed a letter signed by the great man telling me what my new salary would be. Here the first of many problems ensued. I was capable of doing the mental arithmetic to see by how much my salary had been increased, but for the life of me I was not capable of working out whether this was meant to be a very good, an average or a bad increase. Moreover, although I had met Ronny on a number of occasions, he had never discussed my performance in my new job in any way. I therefore summoned up my courage and asked him rather nervously whether he would give me some advice. He assented, with some discomfort, and turned his back on me to look out of the window. I stammered on and explained that I had not done anything like this job before, and had received only the most minimal training. As I had little idea whether I was doing the job to his satisfaction or not, I would genuinely be very grateful if he could give me some guidance on areas where I could improve, that I was not looking for particular plaudits but rather some indication of the sort of directions in which I should be applying my efforts. There was a long and painful silence during which it was borne in on me that I had plainly far exceeded the sensible actions of a prudent young manager in ICI.

Eventually I heard, bouncing off the window pane, the immortal words, 'Trouble with people is bad.' While I had no difficulty with agreeing with the concept, I was far from clear whether this was meant to indicate that I had had trouble with people, or that I was likely to have trouble with people, or that I was at all costs to avoid having trouble with people. I clutched dismally at the fast-ebbing remnants of my courage and asked whether he felt that I was having trouble with people? 'No,' said the great man, 'you asked for advice, I am giving it to you. Trouble with people is bad!' At that, he looked pointedly at the door and I slunk away. This was to prove to be almost the only advice about how I should carry out my job that I was given by any superior during the whole of my time in ICI. I still look on the advice as sound, but I also learned, over a period of time, that no trouble with people is also bad, since the continual avoidance of any form of conflict really must mean that one is not adequately pushing the frontiers of change. However, that lesson was to come much later.

This experience made me determined to ensure that those who worked for me should at least not be left in the same state of bewildered amazement as I was. I accordingly started to instigate systems under which we fed back to each of our people, not only the areas in which we felt they were doing particularly well and showing great strengths, but also the areas where we felt there was room for improvement. This also gave me the opportunity of sitting down with each individual and spending a bit of time discussing how things were going, how they saw their career ambitions, what training or assistance they felt might be helpful, and so on. Of course we had appraisal systems but they were very rudimentary, involving little in the way of feedback to our staff. It was a totally different system to that of the Navy where, in addition to the most elaborate paper records of one's strengths, weaknesses, performances, etc., one was always handed a written summary.

When I eventually became the manager of the supply department I instituted what was the forerunner of briefing groups and quality circles. Every ten days or so, I would ask the whole of one of my sections into my office for a chat about their work and our problems. Although it was looked upon as an eccentric waste of time, the pay-off in terms of involvement and commitment was immense. I soon realised how shockingly under-utilised many of my people were. We had working for us, in clerical positions, men and women who were capable of much greater responsibilities if given the encouragement and opportunity.

My time in the supply department was of immense importance in forming all sorts of habits and ways of behaviour which stayed with me for the rest of my career in industry. The key to the job was, besides coping with an ever increasing flood of demand, to continuously improve our efficiency and our costs. I was given an almost totally free hand as long as we performed. We were a service to the site and to a site which, in those days, was not particularly cost-conscious. ICI could sell practically everything it could make, and our belief in our effectiveness bordered on arrogance. There was little foreign competition and we fondly believed that we were making most of the running in terms of new discoveries and new products. As a result, a good deal of effort was put into providing almost any whimsical requirement, regardless of cost, and the only sin was to hold up production. Many of the essential materials for chemical production were in short supply and we carried immense stocks of stainless steel and other costly items. There was very little pressure to reduce the amounts of money we were tying up in this way, for dead stock was almost unknown, and prices seemed to go only one way – always up.

Nevertheless, we prided ourselves on our professionalism, and continued our efforts to provide the best possible service from the smallest possible stock at the lowest possible cost. It was a marvellous apprenticeship. The aim of my tiny management team, four in all, was to ensure that Wilton was always at the top of ICI's constantly issued league tables – be it with the lowest days' cover for nuts and bolts, the highest productivity in order handling, or the lowest level of stock outs. The result of all this was that life was never dull. We were always striving to improve some aspect of our activities, and the fact that we were ancillary to the mainstream of the company's efforts enabled us to avoid the over-management and control which was endemic at that time.

For some time, I had been used as a sort of all-purpose interpreter at Wilton, which, as the company's showpiece, was the subject of continual visits from every nationality you could think of. It seemed to be believed that German and Russian would enable one to interpret to and from any known European tongue and so I found myself struggling to build bridges of understanding between my illustrious bosses and Hungarians, Romanians, Russians, and nationals of almost any other European country you could think of.

Fortunately, the French, Italians and Germans had the good sense to speak English, so my services were more usually required for use with Iron Curtain countries. These occasions were not without their humorous moments – the day I inadvertently put into the same bedroom a distinguished foreign politician and the lady I thought to be his wife, but who proved to be an allegedly unconnected opera star, is still etched in my memory. I had found my mistake on inspecting the visitors' book and despatched our most prized possession, the castle butler, to spy out the land for me. He reported, with his usual *sang froid*, that not only did we not appear to have a problem, but that the pair of them showed every sign of greatly appreciating the situation. I subsequently learnt that we had scored considerable marks for our subtle understanding of Eastern European ways.

The directors at Wilton used to delight in trying to catch out their acting, unpaid, unqualified interpreter. They were forever telling stories involving puns, plays on words, or *double entendres* completely impossible to translate. I soon learnt that, as long as the recipient of these gems of British wit laughed at approximately the right time, it was assumed that my brilliance had overcome the linguistic improbabilities of such humorous sallies. I therefore took refuge in the large repertoire of coarse Russian stories which I retained from my earlier existence, much to the pleasure of all concerned. I still wonder where my Eastern European friends thought our distinguished scientists and engineers had picked up such bar-room anecdotes but, strangely, their respect for our people seemed to grow through these displays of worldly wisdom.

Possibly as a result of these escapades, I found myself seconded to assist with two exhibitions ICI was staging in the Soviet Union. The first at Leningrad and the second, eighteen months later, in Moscow. These opened my horizons in quite a different way. Firstly they involved learning enough of the mysteries of plastics to be able to make some sort of fist at selling polythene buckets or washing-up bowls in a country where less than one per cent of the population had even seen such things. It broadened my understanding of ICI's business tremendously, for all the divisions were represented. For the first time, besides my activities at Wilton, I saw the organisation's ability to put together a disparate group of people who could shake down and work together almost effortlessly. Everybody mucked in, and turned their hand to anything – be it hauling and sorting the tons of Russian pamphlets on our products, or helping the contractors finish the stands on time.

Practically every Russian speaker in the company had been mobilised for these exhibitions, which were the first of their type and were the direct result of a suggestion by the company chairman himself. This ensured the maximum hierarchical spotlight on our activities, and exposed me to all sorts of the 'great' in a very personal way. I found myself speedily appointed by the manager of the exhibition, an amicable wartime sailor and second-generation ICI man, as a sort of 'Mr Fixit'. He spoke no Russian, and although he learnt on his feet very fast, had little understanding of the curious admixture of sweet talk and power play necessary to get anything done in the Soviet Union of Khrushchev's day. I was in my element. My Wilhemshaven days, and subsequent dealings with the Russians, had given me an affection for them and a tolerance of their systems which enabled me to withstand the frustrations and annoyances which drive most people round the bend in the Soviet Union. I was armoured with the knowledge that everything that could go wrong would, and that it would not be by malice or design, but caused by the almost unbelievable non-working of the Soviet system. This form of detached but involved cynicism and low expectation of success was, in those days, essential self-protection for survival. Whether it was to explain to a main board director (the nearest thing to God in ICI in those days) that he had no chance at all of getting a three-and-a-half-minute boiled egg served in his room at 7.25 am exactly, or whether it was to obtain the release of all our samples which had been impounded by bureaucracy, there was endless scope for initiative and fun.

At that time, the MVD were extremely active and we in general, and I in particular, had rather more than our fair share of attention. One of our ICI interpreters, a Latvian who had fled that country leaving her daughter behind, was subjected to the usual pressures to operate for them and had to be removed back to the UK with great urgency. Some of our men found that their masculine charms attracted some most unlikely and elegant Russian ladies at a time when the physique and dress of the average female Russian reminded one of nothing so much as a T34 tank. Such events were all familiar stuff to some of us, but were greeted with a mixture of horror, disbelief and rage by our managers, who were convinced that they were all the actions of over-zealous minions and could be stopped instantly by a complaint to the helpless Russian liaison officer.

My efforts in these exhibitions had two unexpected side effects for me. The first, and most helpful and pleasurable, was that, out of the blue, I was summoned and given a £200 good work bonus – a princely sum in those days. Within ICI's incredibly complex reward system I was not even aware that such a thing was possible. The effect of this unplanned and unexpected gift from heaven on our precarious 'non-balance of payments' was electric, and it taught me in the most vivid way the totally disproportionate effect of this type of reward. I have remained a believer in the value of unsystematised rewards ever since. In my view no reward gives better value in a large and complex organisation than the occasional personal and specific gift, and yet practically every personnel system sets itself out to prevent such actions at all costs.

The second effect, which may well have been more significant in the longer term, but made less impact at the time, was that I had attracted the attentions of a whole raft of people at all levels of the company. Two of the main board members whom I had worked for during their visits proved to be mentors and friends throughout my whole ICI career. One never failed to write to me at every move I made, and the other, I know, kept his eye on me, although less obviously. They were as different as one could imagine. One, intellectual, cultivated and a connoisseur of good living. The other, bluff, tough and immensely forceful – terrifying many of his subordinates, but underneath it all a warm and involved person. In their different ways, however, they showed concern, interest and involvement in one of the thousands of junior managers they met without behaving in a nepotistic manner.

At about this time we embarked on some fundamental changes in our home life. Much though we had enjoyed our first home at

Nunthorpe, the village was increasingly being absorbed into Middlesbrough itself. The nature of the place was changing with the development of large housing estates by Wimpey and others, and it was becoming more and more suburban in style. Our part of the village was increasingly described as Old Nunthorpe, hailing as it did from the earlier part of the century, but even so the village was getting larger at an alarming rate and its whole way of life was becoming more urban.

We had been looking further afield for some time, driving across the moors and feasting our eyes on the beauty of what is now the National Park. As always in our lives, Betty's enthusiasm and confidence was what carried us forward, and when she finally found us a house it was love at first sight for both of us. Nestling on a tributary of the Esk, at the bottom of a one-in-six hill each way out of the valley, lay Stonegate Mill – an old water-mill dating from the early 1700s and converted lovingly by a Whitby jeweller with his gratuity after the war. Although the house was tiny, only some twenty-four-feet square, and built on three stories, its location was unique. A waterfall in front of the house fed the mill pond and provided endless entertainment at all seasons of the year, as salmon flung themselves at it to reach their spawning grounds, or the trout in the mill pond itself continuously leapt to catch the midges and flies on which they feasted. A few hundred yards further up the beck lay the spawning ground for the salmon themselves. Behind the house there was a dense wood rising a hundred feet or more, and to the left of it was a densely wooded valley which was a paradise for birds – in which we never met another human being. The house itself was of stone construction and placed with such skill that the floods, which came with the spring thaws, would miss the front and back doors by inches as they swirled past into the beck which could rise eight or nine feet in as many minutes.

It took every penny we could borrow to buy the place. It was to be our home for fourteen years – the longest we have ever lived anywhere – and it introduced so many enduring happinesses into our lives. Perhaps most importantly, it brought us right into the arms of the countryside and nature. We derived constant joy from watching the dippers and the wagtails bringing up their young, the trout in the pond, and the endless varieties of birds with which we shared our blissful existence. The garden was tiny, by comparison with Nunthorpe, but we soon learnt that keeping our little valley trim and looking natural, yet cared for, was even harder work than the formal gardening we had just learnt. As far as the inside was concerned, we knew how unsuitable our mostly modern furniture was and for some months before we moved, and endlessly thereafter, Betty had been visiting auction sales in an endeavour to buy more appropriate pieces. At that time there was not the all-pervasive interest in antiques that there is now, and the sort of things we wanted and needed were often ill-considered and more or less worthless. Oak furniture in particular was enduring one of its low points in value, and copperware could be bought almost at its scrap price. Betty's taste in these things has always been unerring, and despite the absence of money, primarily through the expenditure of endless time, patience and hard work, she started to assemble the furniture which has given us so much enjoyment over the years. In fact the furniture inexorably led to our preference for living in sixteenth- and seventeenth-century houses where we bask in the strong glow of English oak with its warmth and feeling of eternal solidity. It is fair to say that now we buy our houses to suit our furniture, rather than the other way round.

I am less sure now than I was then that the move was as advantageous for Gaby as we had hoped at the time. On the good side she joined the charming Lealholm village school, a small country school with two dedicated mistresses, who despite Gaby's constant absences in hospital still enabled her to pass her Eleven Plus exam and procure a place in the grammar school. On the other hand, life for children in the country, particularly in the bleak North Yorkshire moors, is often a lonely one – or else they are forced into the company of adults. Despite her handicaps, Gaby is a gregarious girl and I think she would have had more friends had we stayed in Nunthorpe. Although we discussed these aspects at the time, we were so enchanted with the beauty and seclusion of our new home and so engrossed in building it into a tiny jewel of perfection, that we were determined to go ahead.

The rugged beauty of the location brought with it a number of drawbacks. When the snows came, as they did every year in time for Christmas, the roads were soon impassable and we would be back to our survival groceries and digging our way out of the back door. The only way to get to work was to walk across the moors to the railway station carrying a compass, for it was all too easy to get lost on the two-mile trek, since there was no sign as to where the roads had been. Despite these discomforts, which would now appal us, I never missed a day at work and very frequently contrived to arrive, smug and self-satisfied, before those coming from Saltburn and Guisborough only a few miles away from Wilton itself. In a curious way we used to look forward to being snowed in. It was an adventure. The house was snug and warm and the valley sparkled in the sunlight and had that satisfying silence that a noise-dampening fall of snow brings with it. The waterfall and the mill pond would freeze into static, shining sculptures. We would concentrate on baking our own bread and trying to succour as many of the birds and animals we could. Our love of the quiet and seclusion of country life came from those days, when we could see no neighbour and felt ourselves to be a little island, isolated from a world which we touched only at our own will. It was often very hard for Betty, left on her own with a handicapped child, but for a businessman it was a wonderful gift, and made up to me, to some degree, for my absence from the sea and all it had always meant to me. The same sense of the insignificance of man in nature's scheme of things, and the unimportance of so much which occupies us, by comparison with the never-ending stream of nature's patterns, provides a wonderful balance for those who become consumed with the importance of their lives.

Suddenly, everything seemed to be coming together. We felt settled at Stonegate, and felt we belonged in the countryside. We enjoyed our links with Whitby, York and Scarborough, all so different from Teesside and Stockton. Gaby enjoyed her school and Betty was busy from morning to night collecting and exchanging items of furniture, working in the garden or painting and repairing in the house. I felt confident in my job and enjoyed what I was doing. Life had become fairly predictable, I got home practically every evening, winging my way across the moor and getting almost drunk with the beauty of it. The ever-changing colours of heather, bracken and gorse and the endlessly different effects of clouds and sky never failed to lift my spirits. We were living well and if one 'factored in' the quality of our existence we were living superbly. We knew it, we appreciated it and we were happy.

11 Take-off and Breakthrough

The year of 1963 was to change many features of my life. Early in the year my mother died and, although my father was to live a further five years, my last real links to my youth had all been tied up with her. I knew that I meant a great deal to her and she always gave of her love unstintingly to me. At one time our relationship had been almost stiflingly close and she had never found it easy to come to terms with the fact that Betty and Gaby were now the most important parts of my life. In her latter years she moved, with my widowed great-aunt, to Henley and it was there that she died peacefully in her sleep. In reality, despite her love and concern and my love for her, in recent years we had been able to spend very little time together, and my life had moved in ways which were totally strange to her. Yet with her death I felt a terrible void and alone in a totally unwarranted way. To the degree that I have had anchors in my life she had been one, and Betty has always been the (incomparably stronger) other one.

Just as I was beginning to overcome her loss, and had coped with winding up her sad little estate, I became the subject of an experience in my professional life which is much more widely known now than it was then. The Wilton council, of which I was a proud employee, suffered a takeover bid and disappeared from sight. The council had been set up to supervise the development of the Wilton site, and administer its services. It represented, therefore, an all-to-visible overhead and had no revenue of its own to mitigate its apparent extravagances. As the newest of all the ICI sites, Wilton's style and presentation was much in keeping with the enlightened views of Brunner & Mond, our

industrial forefathers, but it seemed like ostentation by comparison with our paymasters, the operating divisions, who were
working from sites developed in a totally different era, with a
different ethos.

The fact that we were only a service organisation forced us to
seek to demonstrate superior efficiency in all our functions. Our
costs were under continual attack and, as a consequence, we
were good at our jobs and accustomed to proving our competence. None of this, however, was to save us. Eventually the
main board decided to bite on the bullet and hand over the
running of the site to one of the divisions. The choice fell to the
Heavy Organic Chemicals division, the newest of all the ICI
divisions. It had been wrenched from the heart of its progenitor
at Billingham and charged with the production and development
of the petrochemical feedstocks, which formed the basis of our
plastics and fibres production.

The adjectives which sprang to mind to describe HOC were
'brash', 'aggressive', and 'arrogant'. Their approach was, in
many ways, more akin to an oil company's than to the traditional
ICI approach, and they took a pride in doing everything differently from the rest of the company, as though to demonstrate
their contempt and superiority. They had been predictably
awkward tenants on the site, and merciless in their criticism of
our people, who they saw as a bunch of well-fed, dilettante
parasites, living high on the hog at their expense. It was to their
tender mercies that we were to be handed, and we quailed at the
prospect. The actual operation was a classic of how not to do it,
and taught me a great deal.

In the first case, our top management was, in our view, treated
badly. This did not take a financial form, because ICI's benign
personnel policy took care of such matters, but in terms of self-
respect and pride little was done to preserve the status and
positions of our leaders. In the case of Wilton, this was a
particularly unfortunate omission, since even the most junior
managers knew all their seniors well, both socially and professionally. They took this cavalier treatment as a clear sign of
the lack of regard in which we were all held, and a likely indicator

of the way in which we would all be treated in the future. There was not even a pretence that it was to be a merger, and the horny-handed and impatient HOC managers descended upon us like huns on a raid – changing our little world, and imposing their own very different culture, without apparently taking the time to find out whether it would be appropriate for our very different role.

Paradoxically, in the midst of all this carnage, I was to prosper, but the sourness of the feelings I had at that time, and my concern about the treatment of my colleagues, remained with me even when, ten years later, I was to become the chairman of the conquerors. More to the point, the wounds never healed, and when I was appointed to the chair I received letters from almost every surviving former Wilton manager exulting over what was viewed as a triumph of good over evil. I was particularly deeply affected by the treatment of our chairman who was appointed to a patently unimportant staff job at Millbank, and our managing director, my boss, mentor and friend who was unceremoniously hiked out into early retirement in his early fifties, despite his acknowledged engineering genius. He had never suffered fools gladly, and on this occasion he reaped where he had sown. But he was one of the most inspired managers I was ever to work with and I am still surprised that ICI felt able to dispense with his assistance. I wrote a sad and despairing letter of protest on their behalf, making it plain that my colleagues (the other managers) shared my unhappiness, to the ICI main board – but of course to no avail.

Almost every single one of our functions was taken over by the appropriate HOC manager who, by and large, we felt to be inferior. It was not altogether surprising that we felt superior to them because, as a generalisation, operating businesses tend to put their best employees into operations and we, as I have pointed out, were very much on the functional and service side of the business. To my surprise I became the token ex-Wilton manager, retained to demonstrate the fairness of the distribution of the spoils. Since Wilton Supply commanded nearly two hundred people in the stores and offices, and HOC's supply section comprised only eight men, it would have taken a strong stomach to put my opposite number in charge. Nevertheless, the decision was not without its courageous aspects, for Ian Mac-Arthur, my HOC opposite number, was a chemist by profession and responsible for the purchasing of the arcane but vital products which were the lifeblood of the division. My experience at running the largest warehouse in the east, and involving and developing my storemen and clerks, was no preparation for the purchase of phenol or alpha olefines in fierce opposition to the American and continental companies, who were our voracious competitors.

Not only was the action, when taken, brutal and swift, but there was little communication and even less effort on the part of the HOC directors to come and meet us to allay our fears, or even to explain what the business was about. The HOC chairman at that time was almost the opposite of our own urbane and cultured leader, with his taste for fine wines and the social niceties of life. Sammy, our new leader, was an admirable man, totally without 'side', famous for his aged and filthy raincoat (apparently the only outer garment he possessed) and for his blunt and down-to-earth approach to life and business. His very ordinariness and lack of affectation seemed to point up the fact that we had been taken over by a different breed.

The HOC division was as achievement-orientated as we were concerned with form, perfection and presentation. They prided themselves on speed, toughness and decisiveness, while we prided ourselves on thoroughness, the meticulous study of the alternatives and moving only with consensus and the avoidance of friction. We were in many ways complementary, and a more subtle lot would have used our skills to enhance their own, but of course they had just broken free from exactly this sort of environment, and were not going to subject themselves lightly to such influences again – particularly when the main board had so clearly vindicated their views.

These experiences introduced into my life a new and uncomfortable series of professional challenges which I was ill-prepared for. They caused me to reflect deeply on the whole episode and how it could have been handled better. Later in my industrial life I was to be involved in a dishearteningly large number of similar rationalisations, and never approached one without thinking back to what it felt like at the bottom of the pile. The test of any such operation is the speed with which all parties feel themselves to be members of the new organisation, rather than looking back on themselves as, in this case, 'Wilton' or 'HOC men'. Ironically, one of the first tasks I was given as a new division chairman in the 1970s was to take over the intermediate business of the Fibre and Dyestuffs divisions and my approach to that task would be guided by my experiences of the HOC takeover. Even with care and concern it is notoriously difficult to create new organisations from old ones. After sixty years, the characteristics of different parts of ICI still portrayed their historic origins. So much of today's business manoeuvres require regrouping and the formation of new alliances or new ways of working together, that the study of the processes of building new teams from old is an essential management skill. In addition, it is an area where it is possible, with forethought and sensitivity, to avoid creating unnecessary personal pain and harassment.

For the moment, I joined my new masters and found their style curious and in some ways unreal. Everything seemed to me to be high drama and pressure and every problem which we dealt with was of immediate, vital and overriding importance. A relaxed approach was taken almost as treason, and certainly as a lack of commitment and real involvement. The commercial director was an exception; a true business philosopher, he was a blessed exception to this general rule. He taught me more about basic commerce than any man I have known and did it effortlessly and apparently inconsequentially. He had surrounded himself with a tightly knit, relatively small, but highly ambitious group of career men into whose midst I found it difficult to insert myself.

My own business heroes have always been those rarer beings who appear always to have time, always to be relaxed, but by sheer skill manage to remain ahead of the game. I found some of the antics in my new job deeply antipathetic and, despite an uneasy feeling that I might well find my services dispensed with, continued to stick to my view that my job could and should be done between nine and five and that ostentatious burning of the midnight oil betokened inadequacy rather than enthusiasm. Alec – my boss – was an evening person. He tended to appear late in the morning and to puff imperturbably on his pipe throughout the day until what he considered a decent gin-and-tonic time of about 7.30 pm or so. Accordingly, all my colleagues would work industriously until the great man left, in the hope that their assiduity and dedication would be appropriately observed, as well as in the conviction that terrible punishments would afflict anybody who did not do so.

Our home at Lealholm was now an uncomfortable seventy minutes' drive from Billingham, where the headquarters were. I thus had even more cause to leave promptly at the end of our alleged working hours. Moreover, I did not find it easy to master my new responsibilities. The division looked upon my previous job at Wilton as having been a very inferior task, more suitable to a low-level administrative clerk, than a man of commerce. Meanwhile, with the aid of a Penguin paperback on organic chemistry, I was endeavouring to understand at least some of the mysteries of the petrochemical business. Unfortunately, if you are at the buying end of the business you need a rather more detailed knowledge than my studies provided, for there is always a link between price and specification which can be highly advantageous if you get it right and disastrous if you get it wrong. It is even more difficult if you don't even know what constitutes the difference between right and wrong. On at least one occasion I was saved by the skin of my teeth, when my commercial zeal for a low price had almost led me into concluding an agreement to buy thousands of tons of material containing some or other potentially lethal trace element which would have knocked out the entire plant.

Despite my uncomfortable awareness of my stylistic and technical shortcomings, at this time a new challenge was put my way which helped to establish me in the petrochemicals world.

The key raw material for our operations was naptha, and we bought some millions of tons of it every year. In layman's terms this was crude petrol, the lighter end of a barrel of crude oil. In those days it was in oversupply, for most refineries were balanced on the middle cuts, and the demand for gasoline did not match that for heating oils. When we had processed the naptha we bought, we were left, as a by-product, with some petrol constituents which our suppliers then bought back for blending into their own petrol outlets. We were, therefore, in the uncomfortable position of buying our raw materials from suppliers who both competed directly with us in the products we produced and also had a stranglehold on the disposal of our by-products. Despite the oil companies' protestations of arm's length internal dealing, we were convinced that they manipulated our naptha prices to give their downstream operations an advantage over us. We got ourselves into an unholy row with both our supplying oil companies and with the central purchasing department of ICI. Our division looked upon central purchasing as a bunch of running dogs who could not be relied upon to fight our corner with single-minded resolve. Into this brew I found myself projected to lead a joint mission of discovery as to the 'real' price of naptha, if there was such a thing. I was given a representative from central purchasing, and, thank God, a scientist/economic specialist from Billingham, and told to get on with it, and quickly. It was an extraordinary risk to take. The division's ability to compete depended totally on getting this purchase right. I had been in the company for only six years, and in the division for a few months. I literally did not know naptha from gasoil, and yet I was deputed to carry out this vital task.

The three of us flung ourselves on the problem with the naiveté and ingenuousness of babes in the wood. We did a two-day paper study of every oil company in the world which was likely to be 'long' in naptha and within a week we were on our way. We started in Finland and finished on the West Coast of America. Within five weeks, we had completed the task and our own education to boot. The sheer speed and effrontery of our efforts produced results, for we were armed with a potential £20 million worth of business, which tended to get attention, even if we ourselves did not. A number of things emerged which taught me more about the ways of the world than any MBA course could possibly have done. For a start there was a surprisingly narrow range of price variation for the basic materials we sought – and it quickly became apparent that the requirement to buy back our petrol was a considerable negative factor which predictably, complicated what was already complicated. However it was when we tried to work from the price of crude oil that the scope for real reduction in our naptha costs began to appear. It became clear that the true open market lay in crude oil and that a refinery of our own, or a joint venture with an oil company, could break the naptha price wide open. We believed that the price we were paying could be reduced by at least a quarter, and that a refinery investment would be worthwhile in its own right. This would also increase our purchasing freedom, since we could buy crude from anywhere, and if we could devise ways out of the petrol buy-back system, totally new vistas would open up before us.

It says much for the ICI senior management that they never blanched at this recommendation from such a team of innocents. Quite the reverse, in fact. After a surprisingly short decision period, I was encouraged to follow up my own recommendations and produce a proposal for a refinery venture. Fortunately for me, my inadequacies were recognised, to the extent that a splendid technical man was assigned to help, but I was still in charge and was to remain so until the final stages of the deal. Looking back on these events, I realise, yet again, that it was ignorance of the 'correct' ways of doing things which led to this outcome. If at any stage I had asked for permission, or sought help, caution and wisdom would have prevailed. However, it never occurred to any of us to do so. We were equally *insouciant* with the companies we visited. Not for us a call to the sales manager. We telephoned the managing directors and perhaps out of sheer curiosity were seen by them in every case. Of course it was a smaller world, and ICI's name and reputation was what opened the doors. Many of the distinguished men I met during those five weeks were to prove to be colleagues and competitors in later days. There cannot be many people, then or now, who have the opportunity of visiting thirty oil companies in such a short space of time. The mere fact of doing so gave me a unique perspective – a sort of snapshot view of the world of oil, frozen in one instant of time. This experience, together with the subsequent excitement of negotiating with potential partners and ultimately setting up a joint company operation with Phillips Petroleum, provided invaluable experience of the realities of commerce in this big tonnage world.

It was about as far removed from my job at Wilton as one could imagine, for while the transactions were relatively small in number, they were immense in size. Moreover, the cost of the raw materials was so large a proportion of the total cost that a purchasing mistake could vitiate all the clever chemistry and operating technology on which we relied for our competitive advantage. We could survive, and even make a modest, albeit unexciting, profit, as long as we were buying on an equal basis with our competitors. However, we were lost if we failed in that attempt. At the same time we knew, or thought we did, that no one could expect to buy with a permanent inside track on the competition, and hence our whole buying strategy was directed at achieving and maintaining parity with the market.

A year or so later this proved to be a marvellous background for me when I was appointed, in addition to retaining my purchasing responsibilities, as sales manager for the hydrocarbon end of our business. Here again, we found ourselves in a business with few competitors and only a limited number of customers. Moreover, the breakeven point of our plants was very high – in every case at over seventy per cent of capacity, and in some cases at more than eighty. I, and my tiny team of ten, faced the task of ensuring that the plants were kept running day in day out, and that we could sell everything we could make. As if that were not enough of a challenge, in the event of a breakdown on the plant or in the production flow, we had to devise ways of ensuring that our customers did not suffer.

Because of the size of the deals, despite my belief in delegation and my relative inexperience, I found myself involved in practically all the major sales, and this inevitably led to more and more time away from home and on aeroplanes – for our customers were international. We sold everywhere – in the USA, Japan, and Europe in particular – for most of our products were the sophisticated raw materials for further elaborate chemical-processing steps. I enjoyed this new world of great activity and high responsibility enormously – in some ways too much. I do not believe that my period as sales manager was a good one from the point of view of my development as a person, and I don't look back on those years with pride. I found the power and scale of the stage on which I now strutted difficult to adjust to. The lifestyle was a very far cry from the simple values of the life that Betty was building at Stonegate Mill. I began to grow apart from her, and from Gaby, and our interests became more and more separate. While I loved and appreciated the security of our retreat on the moors, I played a smaller and smaller part in it. To make matters worse, for the first and luckily the last time in my industrial career, I found myself in the grip of personal ambition.

Up to this point I had always believed it either impossible, or at minimum highly improbable, that I could progress further up the infinite hierarchy of ICI. However, with my appointment as sales manager in 1965 this situation changed. It was plainly within my scope to become commercial director when and if Alec was promoted, but to do so I had to demonstrate my superiority over my colleague, a far more experienced salesman who controlled the trickier elements of the division's commerce. He was not only more experienced than I, but I am convinced he was a better commercial man. He had a natural flair and love for the market-place, and an encyclopaedic knowledge of the products, the customers, and the personalities of the players in our curious, enclosed world. I became more and more engrossed, not just in the achievement of my selling and profitability goals, but also in constantly seeking to demonstrate my corporate superiority over my competitor. I do not think, even in retrospect, that I did anything which was dishonourable, but I know that I diverted too much of my energy from doing my job into pursuing my own personal professional interests. I also neglected my family and my home in ways I was later to regret. I found myself departing from my own standards of integrity, concealing unfavourable news and proselytising unduly and immodestly our achievements. I failed to give credit to my subordinates as generously as they were entitled to, and instead sought the limelight for myself. I became less and less involved with my family and more and more involved with my external appearance. I was forty years old, and I have often wondered whether that had any bearing on my abandonment of so much I had cherished before, and was to cherish again. If there is such a thing as a male menopause I guess I had mine at about that time. The saddest thing was that those years were wasted unnecessarily. If I had stuck to my beliefs in doing the best job I could, and letting the chips fall where they may, I am pretty sure I would have reached the same end point without compromising myself on the way. More importantly, I would have retained my position with my wife and daughter which meant so much to me.

Certainly repairing the links into Betty's and Gaby's lives took a long time and was not easy to do, for I had forced them close together and played myself out of my own role as a partner and a father. I found myself knowing less and less of their interests and and activities, and justifying my own lack of involvement by my imagined need to promote my career. Maybe every life and every career has a patch like this, but certainly in my case it is the period of my own existence of which I am most self-critical and most aware of having created my own difficulties. I was very fortunate to come to my senses before the behaviour patterns and values I espoused at that time became engrained and ineradicable. I was later to try to help others who seemed to me to be heading in the same direction as a result of too-fast promotion, and too much personal, as opposed to professional, ambition. I believe it is a trap into which many people, particularly in large and overmanned companies, can fall. It is one of the many reasons I am so keen on flatter hierarchies and fewer promotions. People can stay in their jobs longer and adjust within their own time-scales. It is also one of the reasons that I distrust excessive personal ambition. I look rather for ambition for the job, the task, or the outfit. When I see personal interests rising to the fore I know that other things are suffering. Personal ambition of this sort distorts the clarity of one's self-perception, and has a thoroughly bad effect on the individual, his family, his subordinates and his business. It is all too often confused with drive and determination, without which business success is impossible to achieve.

Despite my misgivings about my personal motivations, it was during my years as sales manager that I really began to understand the industry in which I worked. Fate had been very kind to me in arranging for the Heavy Chemicals division to take over Wilton. We were the start of all the fast-growing chemical chains being developed in the sixties, and as a result I came to know, either as a customer or a competitor, almost every other chemical company. I learnt about their different approaches to our common tasks and, even more strikingly, the totally different styles and characteristics they seemed to engender in their people. It was perfectly possible to guess, with a high probability of success, whether or not a man came from Dupont, Dow, Hoescht, BASF, or Ciba Geigy, after a few minutes' general discussion. It was not that one was good and the other bad. It was that these very strong and historic corporate cultures tended to attract similar-minded individuals, and also tended to reject firmly those who did not correspond to their behaviour patterns. Of even more value to me in the longer term, however, was the fact that I numbered practically all the other ICI divisions amongst my customers. In this way I began to get a useful inkling of the intricate spider's web of interdependency which had built up our company. This company flow-sheet had not been developed as a result of a grand design by some great chemist in the sky, but by painstakingly filling in every gap in our ability to create more value from the by-products left over from each stage of the chemical process. At about this time, the Japanese were setting up their chemical industry, *de novo*, and it was fascinating to see the way they replicated again and again (luckily for us on a much smaller scale) the patterns which ICI had evolved so painstakingly over time.

While I was indulging myself by travelling the world and playing at being a tycoon, Betty and Gaby had opened an antique shop in Whitby and were working together in their own business. Betty had a tremendous flair for antiques, and a combination of assiduous study of anything she did not understand, allied with her natural good taste, made their business a pleasure to behold. So many things were considered worthless at that time which are now treasured and valued collector's pieces, and Betty had a wonderful eye and natural instinct for such things. Gradually she improved and increased the quality of our household possessions, and brought into our lives many other areas of art and artefacts which have enriched our lives enormously. Although I gave occasional help of the carrying variety, the business and their success gained all too little from my involvement. It broadened Gaby's horizons tremendously, and helped her to learn to deal with a wide range of people from a very early age. The business was to provide her with her first career when she decided to get married some time later.

It was not long before I received the rewards of my ill-considered personal ambition, and was appointed to the division board although not, as I had fondly imagined, as its commercial director. The post I was given was the highly improbable role of Technical Commercial Director. For a technical rabbit like me to be given any responsibility for technical matters seemed as foolish as it was improbable. I found myself floundering around in unfamiliar territory to which I was able to contribute very little in the way of new thinking. The job involved the buying and selling of know-how and the pursuit of patents. I did, however, begin to observe the ways of the world from a board position which, I soon learned, was very different from the 'worm's eye' supposition of how things were actually done.

Once again I was lucky, not only in my chairman, but also in my colleagues, who were absolutely top-flight masters of their crafts. Because I was the most lightly loaded, as well as the most junior member of the group, I found myself used for all sorts of odd jobs and began to function almost as a personal assistant to the chairman. He was an engineer by training but a reflective and deep-thinking business leader by inclination, with a particular interest in personnel management and the development of people. Curiously, he was such a strong character that few perceived his sensitivity and real concerns for the processes by which decisions were taken. He spent enormous time and effort ensuring that he elicited the contribution of others, and it was from working with him that much of my own fascination with this subject derives. It was a priceless gift, and one which, at those levels of industrial activity, is the hallmark of true success. While there are undoubtedly people who have the natural ability to prepare and chair discussions, even they can gain from studying the art. Jack's concern was to ensure that he had heard every viewpoint – even if, as frequently happened, he rejected them. His primary motivation was to manage his board meetings better. Initially as the dogsbody, but later as personnel director and his friend, I played an increasing role in trying to help the process of changing a management committee into a participating board. We were in uncharted waters then, for the concepts which we developed, and which I was to refine when I in turn became chairman, were largely new ideas in the context of ICI and its decision-making process.

There were a number of further steps involved in my apprenticeship, but none more significant than my appointment to personnel. I am still mystified at the process by which I was selected to be the Personnel Director. Apart from my time in the Wilton supply department, I had had nothing to do with the unions, and only the most superficial contact with the shop floor. I had always been interested in the processes of management and developing people, but this was not perceived as being the main area of personnel activity at that time. It may be that it was my position as a token Wilton man that was the decider, for it was at Wilton, and our handling of the people there, that many of the problems which were to occupy my next years centred.

After the takeover, the division's view had been that the running of the Wilton site had been overblown as a task, and that it was, in reality, a minor administrative chore, compared with the real world of commerce and production, which was our *raison d'être*. Running the Wilton site was thought to be like running a large works, and rated about the same amount of high-level concern. It could safely be delegated down the line, while the board dealt with the technical and commercial problems which were meat and drink to us.

The difficulties with this approach soon showed themselves. In the first place, Wilton was the nerve centre of the whole company. A stoppage at Wilton could shut down the whole of the rest of ICI in days, rather than weeks, and in many cases, where key materials were moved by pipeline, alternative supplies could not even be delivered into the plants. In the second place, the organisation at Wilton had remained diffused. The divisions, of which there were five on the site, each controlled their own plants, production processes, and managers, and there was no centralised control. The unfortunate Wilton central management carried responsibility for the site but had no power at all. The divisions could appoint their own managers to the site without regard to their collaborative abilities or roles in the wider site context. We therefore had a divided and disparate management standing guard on the crossroads of the whole business of ICI, and if we lost control the company would be not be able to withstand the pressure. As a result, over the years the shop stewards' committee had scored a notable number of victories over the management, who had begun to lose their belief in their ability to manage, or to do anything other than give way as slowly as possible to inexorable union pressure.

At this time ICI was trying to introduce a far-reaching reform of its relationship with its workforce. The company was attempting to scrap the work-study based incentive schemes which had been my introduction to industry and to replace them with a salary system. Many of us believed we could achieve some even more important goals by this process. My work with junior staff had convinced me that many of the apparent differences of motivation and involvement between the shop floor and our clerical staff were related to belief in the possibility of a career as opposed to simply having a job. Even though the statistical evidence showed a modest chance of advancement from the shop floor, most people on the floor believed any significant prospect of advancement to be highly improbable. A progressive salary structure related to increased experience and responsibility could rectify this situation, and the 'us and they' attitudes which still bedevilled us. These reforms had been jointly evolved with the central unions and had largely been accepted by them, but they had run straight on to the rocks of rejection with the workers at Wilton. Every sort of compromise was rejected and they made it clear that they would have no part of it. The rest of ICI blamed, with some justice, the Wilton management for the intransigence of our troops and, to make matters worse, we were holding up many parts of the group which had done all the work and were raring to go. It was into this high-pressure scene, where everyone was blaming everyone else, and the ICI board were making their displeasures known almost daily, that I found myself projected.

There is always a silver lining to every cloud, and in my case the silver linings lay very largely in my personal life. My office was moved back to Wilton and closer to Stonegate, and I stopped my jet-set perambulations around the world. I did not find myself in a nine-to-five job, for the task would take every bit of personal dedication and most of my fairly minuscule reserves of courage, but it did ensure that I was at home in my own bed practically every night. At this time my father died, finally severing my links with the past. He had obtained a series of administrative jobs involved with education, and spent his last years happily enjoying the attentions of a lady admirer in Warwick. Over the years he had evinced characteristically little interest in us, although I knew him to be as fond of Betty as he was of anyone. Right to the end of his days I was in total ignorance of his feelings about me, and I never received the recognition or signs of approval I had so desperately sought for so many years.

The sheer scale of the problem at ICI smartly removed any

further urges I might have retained to pursue my personal ambitions. I felt, and probably was, in the most exposed position in ICI, for all eyes were focused on our success or failure. I was battling for survival on totally new ground. I was very conscious of my lack of understanding of the workings of the union world, and my lack of intricate knowledge of rule books, procedures, and the real (as opposed to the theoretical) exercise of power and influence. I lacked the long period of working together which builds trust and confidence with the shop floor and their representatives. I lacked reputation, direct production experience, and I had no standing in ICI's world of personnel – a closely knit specialist world, which rightly prided itself on its expertise and being continuously in the forefront of enlightened management thinking. And yet, in a curious way, it was as if my whole life, on a personal level, had been a preparation for this improbable job. My early naval experience, my time with the shop floor on work-study, my attempts to involve my staff in the world of supply, together with my knowledge of the wider world scene of our industry which again stressed the need for us to change, all contributed to giving me a perspective – and a chance.

It was immediately apparent to me that the problems could only be resolved by uniting the Wilton management, and building a team which could reassert its leadership of the employees. In effect we had abrogated our responsibilities which had, very sensibly, been picked up by the shop stewards. At the time there was a great belief that our shop stewards were politically manoeuvred by the Socialist Workers Party, which represented a sort of 'evil empire'-type threat. While I know that some held strong left-wing views, I do not think that was the source of our troubles. In the first place we had not utilised the considerable leadership abilities which these men had. Without any of the advantages of our managers, without the educational background, the training, or the facilities, they were accepted by our people as their leaders. That, coupled with our unwillingness ever to fight a point of principle, but always to buy off the trouble, had led us into a situation where the managers operated only within the tolerance of the unions. Moreover, the increasing power of the shop stewards had progressively eroded the positions of the union officials themselves. The problems were easy enough to see, and it was obvious that there could be no quick solutions, despite the fact that time was not on our side. Moreover, it was much easier to diagnose what had to be done than to build an effective team without any constitutional powers behind us. As so often with ICI, once our minds were made up things moved faster than anyone could have expected. I started building my team at the top with the works managers, while Jack, David (the deputy chairman), and I were simultaneously working to change our powers and controls on the site.

Within a year, I was appointed Deputy Chairman of the division, with responsibility for the site, and Chairman of the Wilton Coordinating Committee. This was made up of all the deputy chairmen of the divisions which had plants at Wilton. In addition, I had sought, and received, agreement that by means of annual reports I could influence the rewards of the works managers, and that no one above a certain level could be appointed without my agreement. We had not resolved the problems, but I was becoming more confident that we could do so. The Wilton Coordinating Committee involved many of my friends who were to serve on the ICI board with me – they were a tremendous bunch. Our success owed much to their handling of me as well as of the problems we were dealing with. It was the first committee I had ever run where I succeeded in enforcing a rule that we would never accept any presentation on more than two sides of a piece of paper. Anyone who has ever seen any paper on a personnel issue will recognise this as the nearly miraculous feat of willpower and determination it did indeed represent.

Starting from the top with the works managers, every manager on the site went on a training course, and I and Brian Jenkins, the new personnel director (also an old Wilton hand and a man with a vast knowledge of the unions) addressed every one of them. We restarted the Wilton Smoking Concert – long defunct – and played every trick we could to build up management morale. We made it known that we were determined to reinstate management discipline but that it had to be applied sensitively, and we spent vast amounts of time with our people at every level. I took a much higher-profile position on the site than my predecessors, and dropped in continuously on all the works, ensuring that it was known that there was somebody other than the works management who had responsibility for the site. These visits were observed by management and shop floor alike. I personally turned up at any accidents and generally played the obvious and open role of being the site's boss.

We then did an unprecedented thing by fighting and winning, without concession, two particularly stupid strikes on the sort of issues which no sensible shop-floor worker would support. During the first of these, I appeared for the first time on local television, sure that in that process I could talk to the strikers and their families. We had chosen the issues to fight with some care, for we knew that they had to be cast-iron, clear and simple and that the strike itself must clearly be seen to be mischievous. As is so often the case, the ostensible causes of the strike were not the real ones at all. After the strike had collapsed, therefore, we sat down with the men to discuss how, collectively, we had managed to get into such a mess, and what we could do to avoid doing so in the future.

The whole atmosphere on the site began to change dramatically, but even though the atmosphere was changing, the resistance was not. We increasingly believed that the majority of our people wanted to change to the new ways of working and payment, but there was no way we could get past the intransigence of the senior shop stewards. Their hegemony had lasted so long, and our reassertion of our managerial responsibilities was so recent, that few of our people were prepared to push the status quo. Meanwhile, we had polarised the problems with the shop stewards. Despite their willingness to talk with us, they felt increasingly threatened by our steady pressures. One of the problems with the new Weekly Staff Agreement was that it changed the role of the shop steward in a way which few of them found beguiling. Instead of the endless minutiae of our complex reward system, which provided continual opportunity for negotiation, representation, and often victory on behalf of their people, our agreement offered few opportunities for such activities. The whole basis of the agreement was aimed at individual promotions, and rewards on a salary basis, rather than haggling over a penny, or an hour, here and there.

Things followed their inevitable course until we found ourselves in a showdown with Paddy, the unofficial leader of the shop stewards who, after a heavy lunch-time session at the recreation club, challenged his management's instructions in a particularly vehement way. I suspect that this was not the first time such a thing had happened, and in the past the management concerned would have evaded the row, but on this occasion they did not. Chemical plants are a bit like ships. You must maintain a certain level of discipline, so that if things go wrong there is no question as to who is in charge and giving the instructions. This case was one for which there could be only one punishment – dismissal. Because of the possible outcome, the matter was referred to me before the sentence was passed and I agreed that we could not possibly make an exception in this case. However, I did so in the knowledge that if we had not succeeded in winning enough of the hearts and minds of our people we could lose control of the whole site, and there was no real room for retreat. If we were forced to reinstate the man and had made a mistake, my own authority would have been destroyed and I would no longer be able to run the site. This was how we reached what is the industrialist's nightmare – a one-way road with no side exits. It taught me a lot and I have never before or since felt so exposed or frightened. It was made worse by the fact that I had to radiate continuous confidence to the troops on whom we relied to win the day.

Sure enough, the members of the Amalgamated Engineering Union who had voted to strike went out *en bloc* a second time, but to my relief the other unions stayed at work. We could keep going for a fair time by using staff for the key jobs and all of our people returned after a few days except those in the fibres works – Paddy's power base – where the incident had occurred. The fitters there had a particular routine job, which was necessary in order to run the process at all and, over the years, they had developed the maintenance of spinneret packs into a black art, controlled only by themselves. Engineers from all over the site joined together in manning the pack room around the clock, working like men possessed to keep production flowing. I visited them frequently, for they were our front line, but despite all our efforts, we had only sixty of our people attempting to do the work that over two hundred and fifty fitters apparently barely coped with. The strike lasted six weeks, during which time our people not only kept the plant going, but got rid of the vast backlog of work which had accumulated over time. This was an interesting lesson for us all.

The dismissal followed through all the various levels of appeal and investigation which existed under our agreements with the unions, but our action was upheld at each stage, and Paddy remained dismissed. It proved to be the turning point for the site. It also proved to be quite difficult to restrain our managers from exploiting their new-found positions of power. Within an unexpectedly short space of time, resistance to the agreement crumbled and we were able to get ahead with the constructive work of introducing new ways of working together and improving our productivity. Surprisingly, our relationships with our shop stewards improved and we found new and constructive outlets for the energies we had dissipated by squabbling and fighting. Yet again, this demonstrated how difficult it is to work with people unless there is mutuality of respect and a reasonable balance of power. The real *machismo* lies in concentrating on cooperation rather than in spending time trying to demonstrate that you are the boss.

For me the whole period was a close encounter, in a very minor way, with the sort of problems which brought the car industry to its knees, and made me realise how testing of the human spirit such battles can be. They require a combination of toughness and softness which is a very difficult trick to turn. On the one hand, managers have to be clear where the absolute no-go areas are, and fight for them regardless of cost – while on the other, they have to be patient, leave room for the other point of view, and lean over backwards to communicate and be demonstrably fair. There is nothing sweeter than a harmonious and well-run factory, and few closer approximations to hell than one in which the management and workers are at loggerheads. The paradox is that this relationship can only work if there is genuine liking and regard between them.

I have always thought myself very lucky that these lessons were learnt in the North East. From my first days at submarine school at Blyth I have found myself completely at home with the people of the area. If I could choose, I would be reincarnated as a North Easterner. It would be difficult to find their like, with their sheer decency, fairness, hard work, and friendliness, as well as concern for their neighbours. Friendships, once given, are not easily or readily withdrawn. It was a privilege to have the chance to manage so many of them, and they taught me far more than I ever taught them. The area has a wonderful feeling of reality, and the people are the same, and no one is ever in any doubt about how he or she is viewed by their fellows.

Things really settled down after this and many of the pressures on me eased. I did, however, get an undeserved and unhelpful boost to my already inflated ego by the success of the steps which we had taken at Wilton. The changes that occurred would probably have happened one way or another without my self-acclaimed cleverness. There is often a natural time at which problems get resolved, and, equally, sometimes no amount of effort can bring matters to a head. With the benefit of hindsight I believe I was particularly lucky in the timing of my arrival on the scene and also fortunate in having some relevant background. Be that as it may, the apparent facts were that I had played a substantial role in the resolution of a recognised major problem in an area where ICI prided itself on its avoidance of such matters.

The reward came quicker and in a more unlikely way than I had ever dreamed of. I was away sailing with a friend in his company's yacht, and so was unreachable when the decisions were taken. When I arrived back in the UK I discovered, to my delight, that Jack had been appointed to the main board, and that I was apparently to take over as Divisional Chairman immediately on my return from leave. I found it hard to believe the news on a number of counts. Jack had expressed his views on the company's personnel policies in the most forthright of ways. Moreover, our divison was hardly a by-word for profitability. We had an endless appetite for capital and we were a draw on the rest of the company. The profits we achieved were, although positive, woefully inadequate in any realistic sense. I was therefore pleased that the board had recognised his real worth.

Even given all this it seemed to me that there were a number of very good reasons why I could not possibly succeed him. At that time it was extremely rare for a non-technical man to head up an operating division, and there were two very experienced deputy chairmen in the division, both with technical backgrounds and lengthy service within ICI. Both of them were to go further in ICI, indeed one, who had been my technical mentor when I was sales manager, would take over from me. I had plenty of time ahead and could have taken my turn. Indeed, I still think it would have been a better use of my talents than the way my career was to develop. Being leap-frogged over two men for whom I had worked at different times, coupled with my relative inexperience and ingenuousness, meant that I was likely to be a disturbing (and disturbed) boss. All in all, the possibility that I might take over from Jack had never even crossed my mind.

I had every sort of misgiving, even though I was delighted at the promotion and the position. It exceeded my wildest dreams of the level to which I might aspire, and far exceeded any aspirations I could possibly have achieved in the Navy. The divisional chairman's job in ICI in those days was almost the most powerful single position in the company. The main board operated collegiately and the chairman was at least theoretically *primus inter pares*. The scheme of organisation meant that the responsibility for the future well-being of the division lay exclusively with the divisional chairman. His 'board' was there to advise him, as was the main board member who carried the portfolio of his division. The position had, both in theory and in practice, tremendous power and within the chairman's bailiwick resided all the style, scope and ambition for the business and its people.

What a gift to receive in my forty-seventh year, and in my fourteenth year of service in ICI. I could not believe it then and I still have difficulty in believing it now.

12 Independent Command

The next three years proved to be probably the most formative of my life, for they were the years in which I grew up – both professionally and in my personal life. People talk of 'mid-life crisis', but in many ways this was a mid-life opportunity to redirect myself and attempt to re-establish myself as the sort of person I wanted to be.

Professionally, I was very much in command of my own show. Moreover, over the years I had worked for virtually all my fellow board members and with most of the people in the division as a whole. It was now 1970 and since 1957 I had made my life on Teesside; I knew, and was known by, the members of HOC from bottom to top. Everything I believed about business had been acquired during these years and much of it taught me by those for whose future I was now responsible. Moreover, outside the North East I had at some time or other done business with almost all our customers and suppliers and knew our competitors at every level. Starting as divisional chairman was a wonderful opportunity and I felt much as I imagine a new colonel does when he takes over the regiment in which he has spent his life. I was absolutely dedicated to not letting the side down, while I was conscious of being offered a unique chance to try and move our ways of thinking ahead.

My first problem was to reconstitute the board and establish the differences in the way we were going to work. Here I was helped immeasurably by my relatively short service in ICI. I knew that I could only hope to lead by consent, and I was also aware, despite the breadth of my training, of how many facets of the business I lacked practical experience of. Our division prided itself on its functional expertise. We considered ourselves the best plant operators in the company, and possibly in the industry. Because in those days there were relatively few operators in the world in our business or of our scale, we knew our competitors and contractors well and continuously sought to be better than they were in all aspects of our craft. Our only areas of weakness (that I was aware of) lay in our attitudes to our customers and in our research and development capability. Our pride in our professional expertise led us to tend to view our customers as the fortunate recipients of our products. Our commercial people were reasonably customer-orientated and we prided ourselves on delivery times and redistribution reliability, but the business was unmistakably production-driven. Moreover, although we sold world-wide, we produced only in the United Kingdom.

In R & D, despite employing excellent people, innovative success had largely eluded us. Mostly we used proprietary technology from elsewhere, which we then tweaked up and optimised; only two areas of our activity operated with the use of unique processes of our own devising. Strategically we were no longer tied to our original, unspecified role of being an 'in-house' sort of chemical power station, and had diligently sought to develop business outside ICI. It was as well that we had, for not only did we make more money from our outside customers than from our in-house ones, but by being a force in the market-place were able to enjoy a degree of independence which was our salvation. I was determined that we were not to suffer the same fate as Wilton and be gobbled up by customers who did not value our skills and expertise. I had not really thought my way through any of these facets of my new job, since I had not expected to find myself in this position. However it did not take me long to make up my mind on a number of the issues I wanted to try to tackle, and how to go about them.

My hand-over from Jack was one of the classic twenty-four hour desk-clearing type, and I am sure he deliberately tried to give me maximum freedom to tackle the job my way. Possibly he also over-estimated how prepared I was for the task ahead. My first necessity was to replace myself at Wilton and to tackle the problem of appointing a Commercial Deputy Chairman. In those days this required clearance with Millbank (an area where my understanding and expertise was minimal) and it was clear that I would be expected, particularly in the light of my relative youth, to operate with a full compliment of three deputies. I was lucky to be able to persuade Alec, who had been my boss for so many years, to take over as Commercial Deputy and Ken, who had been the deputy head of work-study when I joined ICI (and found the task as little to his liking as I had) to take over at Wilton. Arthur remained and, with a generosity of spirit I admire to this day, supported me through thick and thin, despite the disparity in our ages and experience. I thus had a formidable team of deputies, any one of whom could have eaten me before dinner – and still sat down for four more courses. The directors were equally distinguished and capable. Plainly the problem was to weld this disparate group together as a team, and try to ensure that we amounted to more than the sum of our parts. It was the second time I had had to try to do this, and called upon all my previous experience.

Fortunately for me, I had two advantages – we all liked each other and, almost as soon as I took over, it became apparent that the division was likely to make its first-ever loss. Talk about preparation for the future! Nothing so solidifies a group as bad news, provided they believe they can bring about their own salvation. I had decided to run our board on slightly different lines from Jack, stressing the collective nature of our responsibilities and forcing even more openness and argument. I had told them all that, while I could not change ICI's organisation, I would abide by collective decisions, unless, in extreme cases, I felt I had to back my own judgement. In the event I did so on only five or six occasions, and in each case we looked at the decisions later, to try to establish whether I had been justified or not – more often than not I might just as well have gone with the consensus view.

In the event we did just manage to stay in the black that first year, but only by selling the steam from the Wilton power station. All our other expertise, investment and operating skills just about enabled us to break even. It was a pretty doleful experience but fighting as a group had brought us together. We had reduced our numbers, improved our productivity, scrimped and saved on our costs and fought like tigers for our prices. It also taught me another lesson about ICI. We had greatly cut down the paperwork for our board deliberations, concentrating on what we felt were the main issues and noting decisions rather than arguments. When the time came for us to sit down with our main board masters and explain our stewardship I submitted a very concise five-page report outlining the key points and explaining that we would expand upon them at the meeting. To my surprise, the sub-committee declared themselves insulted by this cavalier treatment and made it clear that the worse the business situation the more written explanation they sought. Worse was to come. When it became apparent that we couldn't make our expected profit we had decided that whatever happened we would make up our cash contribution to our original budget. It had not been easy to do so, but had proved an excellent discipline for us all. However, when we laid down our offering with modest pride we were roundly berated for our efforts. When ICI needed cash, we would be told so – it was not for us to think that we could escape our prime responsibilities by offering such a stupid, irrelevant and inadequate token – and so on and so on.

Regardless of the professed attitude of our masters, however, we knew that if we had been a self-standing business we would have been obliged to contribute the cash. Our belief was that we held our businesses in custody for our shareholders and that it was our job to run them to the best standards in the world. We measured ourselves in that way and we thought that, over time, our standards would prevail over corporate gamesmanship. I am not sure that we were right – particularly since I could never elicit from the company the actual part they saw us playing in their view of the future. This was not suprising since, although there was an add-up of all the plans, and a series of proclaimed aims, to my knowledge there was never a grand design which would create the ICI of the year 2000, or even of 1980. In the absence of any overriding direction we therefore set ourselves the aim of looking at our own business as a self-standing unit, in which we both paid our way and developed our capabilities to the best of our ability *vis-à-vis* the international competition.

Meanwhile, our family life was undergoing equally fundamental changes. Gaby and Betty were running their antique business together, with considerable taste and success, but Gaby was beginning to spread her wings. She had learnt to drive, and we had bought her an automatic car and she was seeking increasingly her own friends and interests. To our mingled pleasure and concern, she fell in love with almost the first boy she met and declared her intention to get married as soon as possible. Our pleasure at this was marred by the fact that her intended husband had no job, and indeed had never held a regular job of any kind. When challenged as to how and where they were going to live, she told us Adrian would get a job hedging and ditching if necessary. At the time this didn't seem to offer a very adequate future for our cherished and well-loved daughter.

My hectic business life having created a distance between myself and Betty and Gaby, we were ill-equipped to cope with this situation. Our ultimate solution had a catalytic effect on all our lives, which was painful for all of us and might well have been avoided if I had not allowed myself to draw away from my family and home. The paradox in it all was that I knew what I valued and depended upon, and yet had risked so much for so little. This may be a problem with which all 'successful' people have to struggle and sadly few of us seem to get the balance right. I do not believe the facile explanations of 'growing away from each other' which are proffered for failure. I think rather that it is a fascination with the present to the exclusion of the past and the future. It is only when one reflects on the growth of the relationships with one's family that it becomes possible to see and acknowledge the influence they have on one's development as an individual. Time and again my wife and my daughter question or criticise positions I take and assumptions I make which, on deeper reflection, I realise to be flawed or imperfect. Such influences can so easily be relegated in one's thinking, and accorded less value and validity than is their worth. Despite a reputation for openness and bluntness, I have never found it easy to open up completely. I think I am frightened of repeating the pain I felt when a child, and I conduct my relationships on a level which still seeks to protect what I consider to be my unduly soft centre.

Our attempts to talk our family stuation through in a constructive way were probably doomed from the start. Despite the closeness between Betty and Gaby, it was hard for me to understand the depths of their individual fears and needs, and I believe that I failed them both at this time. The upshot was that Gaby was married at the age of barely nineteen, and took up a life with her husband that contained the seeds of disaster. To help them get started, Betty gave them both the antiques business she had built up with such love and success. Her loss was the greatest of all, for she simultaneously lost her daughter and her business. Worse was to come, as Gaby and Adrian struggled to make a living out of the once-thriving enterprise. Slowly Betty saw the decline of her beloved business, which had been such a source of pride and a visible demonstration of her taste and skill.

Meanwhile where was I? Following my unexpected star and striving to establish my leadership in a position where all too many eyes were upon me, and the effects of success or failure were there for all to see. It was not a happy time for any of us. As so often in my life, my early upbringing and sense of responsibility, coupled with my pride and need to demonstrate success, led me to hold the balance too greatly in favour of my business responsibilities. It seemed all too logical at the time, for our business was facing a host of real problems and the responsibility for the livelihood and future of my 17,000 employees rested heavily on my shoulders. However, whatever my excuses, my wife's needs were plain to see, and the prime one was more time, consideration and understanding from her husband, as well as a lifestyle more attuned to her needs and less to mine. I was well aware of this, and did indeed try consciously to adjust the balance – but I knew I did not do enough and a better man would have risked more of his business success. Over time, my wife and I began to grow together again and I felt I was beginning to give her some of the support and understanding I had so thoughtlessly taken away over the years. The whole experience taught me a great deal. Since my Navy days I had disliked the assumption that one should always put work and duty before all else and had defended my colleagues who had made the other choice. I know now just how much strength of character and sense of values it takes to do this and I respect those who make such a conscious decision.

I was very lucky to have a second chance, both to build a new life with my wife and also, at a later stage, with the daughter I had in reality known so little. Such good fortune is not usual, and most people are forced to live with the consequences of their actions. Business success is ephemeral and can only be achieved by continuously being put at risk. The fences get higher, the competition gets tougher, you get older, and what worked yesterday fails today – eventually almost everyone falls off. To hazard the solidity and durability of family life for such a capricious and short-term mistress as business success, seems to me to show a lack of balance in a person's make-up. It is possible to combine the two, but I am convinced that such an outcome is only possible by unswerving clarity about what is most important to oneself in the long term. When I look back on those years I can see that, while I was to learn many more lessons about running large business organisations, without question my attempts with Betty to create a new balance in our lives had the greatest effect on me, and was of the greatest importance. For a start, it punctured my belief in the vast importance of what I was doing at work. I will always need to believe that my work is worthwhile and of value – but now I know that there are many other things in my life which matter more. It was, in a way, like a reaffirmation and restrengthening of the release from ambition I received when leaving the Navy, and was almost as tangible. This feeling freed me to take risks and to stick by my beliefs in ways which I now realise actually made me more likely to move ahead rather than the reverse. Once again I found a need to press thirty hours into every twenty-four, as well as attempting firmly to separate my private life from my professional one.

It was a great learning time for me and served to be the test bed for so many of the ideas and beliefs I was to employ when I became the chairman of the company. The most important direct lessons concerned running a board in a collegiate way. From a leadership point of view, we were able to develop these ideas together in almost ideal circumstances. Since the responsibility was clearly mine, and the career development of my colleagues rested overwhelmingly on my shoulders, I had massive power. The fact that I chose to share it gave me a double advantage, provided I obeyed my own self-imposed rules and behaved as openly and trustingly as I was asking my associates to do. Things moved faster than I dreamed was possible and now I realise that the speed of change owed much to Jack, who had laid so many of the foundations. I soon found myself in the unexpected role of being the brake-man rather than the engine. The pacing of the tasks we set ourselves and the number of things we could effectively change loomed ever larger in my consciousness. The art became one of ensuring that each change we made had enough momentum to be self-sustaining before turning to the next one, and new initiatives flowed fast and furious.

At this time the main board of ICI was re-examining the company organisation and production skills and a group on the board believed a number of changes to be necessary. Despite our poor profit performance the HOC division was considered to be one of the most professional plant operators. It was decided that we should take over responsibility for the chemical intermediates production of the Fibres operation which had always been located elsewhere. The decision was probably the right one, although possibly taken for the wrong reasons. The nylon intermediate business was run, rather improbably, by the Dyes division and was losing money at a frightening rate, while the polyester intermediates, under the control of the Fibres division, was due for a major technical change. Neither division wished to lose its bailiwick and our emergence as main-board favourites was viewed with something far short of fulsome support. The only good news was that we were demonstrably as unenthusiastic as they were. The whole concept seemed to push us further back to the chemical power-station concept, as well as distracting us from our self-chosen programme of change. No one could accuse us of making a takeover bid and, after all the cries of pain and disbelief had been discarded, both the divisions could not have been more supportive and helpful.

In truth there were real advantages to us once we looked at it differently. It removed one division from the site at Wilton and gave us overwhelmingly the major role there. We were to find and develop external sales of the intermediates, which would actually take us in the way we wanted to go and, perhaps most important of all, it gave us the opportunity and grounds for altering our own ways of doing things in a fundamental way. The task was a big one. The advent of these two businesses from very different backgrounds and operating styles nearly doubled the size of our own operations at a stroke and, together with our oil refining and oil interests, placed us firmly across the base of the whole fibres and plastics operations of the company.

Yet again, the past came to my aid. The takeover at Wilton had taught me a lot about the pitfalls of this sort of industrial task and about being one of the 'taken over'. That experience and my time trying to weld the team at Wilton into a cohesive whole all influenced the key decisions. There were really three of them. The first was that we were going to treat the whole operation as a merger. We were going to change our own way of doing things more than we would ask our newly acquired colleagues to change, and we would aim to produce a new outfit with new values and a new ethos – hopefully taking the best from all three divisions. We abandoned our proud but incomprehensible name and gave us all a new one, the Petrochemicals division.

The second decision stemmed from our knowledge that the people who were joining us knew their own businesses better than we did. Despite the temptation to flood them with our own people and alleged expertise (after all, the perceived reasons for the change) we would rely on them to come to us for help in meeting the challenges we would set together. We therefore selected our best director – a subsequent chairman of the division – and gave him the task of gateman. He was the only man we put in, and he shared our collective views of the right way to go. His task was to protect the businesses from our well-intentioned invasions and to aid and assist the managers already in position to achieve what we needed. It was an organisational device I was to use many times again, and it derives almost completely from the teachings of Carl Rogers and observation of group psychology.

The third key decision was a commercial one and again proved to be a practical justification of a theory which is unarguable but nevertheless all too seldom followed. The nylon intermediates business was run as a cost centre and passed its costs on to its only customer. The customer complained continually of uncompetitive prices and the business continually 'proved' its ability to match the best yields, highest conversion factors and so on. Arthur knew something of the technology (indeed his knowledge of practically any chemical technology was extraordinary) but I knew little of the commercial side of the business, so he and I decided to visit other producers and form an independent judgement of where we stood. The differences in opinion between the Dyes and Fibres divisions amounted to over a third of the cost and, over the years, they had virtually ceased civilised relations. After only two visits in the USA we were sitting in a bar discussing our findings and both of us, coming from our different viewpoints, agreed that there was no way we could justify the price that was being paid. The problem was simple to state, but difficult to achieve. We had to take £100 a ton out of our costs if the whole business was to survive. At that time neither of us could see how to do it, although both of us thought we could achieve up to about half of what was required, with a struggle. However, at least the aim was clear. It was £100 a ton or throw in the towel.

When we got back and announced our views, the nylon managers flatly refused to believe us – and pointed out with some justice that if they had felt able to achieve such figures they would have done so already. We just kept on pushing the problem back to them, pointing out over and over again the commercial logic, and giving them the choice of the rock or the hard place. To their surprise, but not entirely to ours, once they had changed their perspective and set themselves these ambitious goals they made unbelievable progress. Rab, our 'gateman', helped in this but nevertheless the task itself was done by the very same managers who had argued with us that it was unachievable. The nylon plant was speedily littered with sacred cows who had been slaughtered, albeit humanely.

In addition to our three main aims, we had to reduce the numbers in the new division in order to achieve the savings we sought. We tried to ensure that all the constituent parts took their share of the pain. While we didn't put former HOC men in to run the Fibres business we did do the reverse. Our whole way of going about things was the exact reverse of what Millbank had expected us to do, but even though our ideas were queried we were left to get on with it. This was and remains one of the most ingrained beliefs in ICI and an excellent one it is. It is very seldom that a direct instruction will be passed to a subordinate on a matter within his own responsibility. Nowadays he will be offered lots of advice, perhaps too much for comfort, but the direct removal of responsibility would be exceptional. The onus thus lies on the individual, who runs the risk of disregarding advice, but is free to do so if he or she feels sufficiently strongly on the matter.

Before I took over, Jack had, somewhat improbably, obtained the board agreement to the building of a new headquarters for the division at Wilton. This need was based on a combination of growth forecasts for the Teesside divisions which were, in the event, heavily over-optimistic, and the scrapping of many temporary wartime offices. In addition, it was felt that the absence of our presence at Wilton had contributed to our loss of control of the site. Shortly afterwards, ICI's fortunes took a down-turn and the company became short of cash. There was a good deal of pressure from practically all the board members for me to volunteer to cancel the project, which I continually side-stepped because I had other plans for the business. We were voracious gobblers-up of cash and I doubted that ICI would continue to support us strongly enough to enable us to grow adequately and enhance our competitive position. I had sought and obtained the agreement of the board to discuss with BP the idea of putting our two petrochemical businesses together as a free-standing, jointly owned company. With hindsight I do not believe that the board had any intention of allowing such a fundamental change to occur. I was probably allowed to go ahead more on the doctrine of personal responsibility and in the unlikelihood of success than from any belief in my proposal. Nevertheless, we started down the line and made surprising progress. I wanted the headquarters building because I believed that its possession would ensure that the new company would be based on Teesside and that we would, therefore, play a larger role in its subsequent fortunes. Sadly, the project came to nothing. There simply weren't the champions available in either company and yet I still believe the concept to have been right. The building was completed, however, and is now (following the inevitable precepts of Parkinson's Law) overcrowded.

In addition to the running of the business, the chairmen of the two Teesside divisions played a very substantial role in the area. During my time as the Wilton deputy chairman I had become increasingly involved with other local employers, and also with our MPs and local government. When I took over as divisional chairman, however, we were shedding numbers even though we were still investing capital at Teesside, and the North East was going through a bad time. Our own unhappy profit experience was matched by a particularly rough time in the agricultural business. I joined the Port Authority and the North East Development Council and played a very active and public role in our regional attempts to attract new industries and develop our economic potential. The North East had relied heavily on basic industries – coal, steel, ship-building and heavy chemicals – and the writing seemed to be on the wall for all of us. Despite endless attempts, we failed either to deal with the region as a whole, where competition between the three rivers – the Tyne, Wear and Tees – was intense, or to succeed in building the spin-off businesses one would have expected. It seems to be only now, in the 1990s, that this problem is at last being successfully dealt with.

At this time the Government put in an enormous plug of infrastructure spending on roads, and we already possessed excellent ports to service the continent. The basic raw materials for a host of industries – ranging from light engineering to plastics and textiles – were available in the area and we had a super and willing workforce, albeit one with a ferocious reputation for independence. At that time, despite good educational facilities, an excellent polytechnic at Teesside and the universities at Durham and Newcastle, we did not have the indigenous supply of professional managers which we are only now beginning to develop. Most successful North-Eastern people sought their futures elsewhere, and far too high a proportion of the industrial management came from outside the area. It must have been a legacy of the history of the area, whose people pride themselves on a no-frills, blunt, down-to-earth approach to life, and are quick to distance themselves from those with inflated ambitions or opinions of themselves. Every form of local and government initiative was tried to rectify the imbalance of our industrial base, which remained stubbornly fixed towards heavy industry. The development of the Tees river banks themselves merely attracted more chemical companies and, while we had some success in transferring from shipbuilding to the construction and servicing of North Sea rigs, that was also likely to be a industry of limited life. We lacked the local entrepreneurial base to build up small businesses from totally new concepts, and even in today's much more favourable climate the North East does not seem to get its share of these leaders towards tomorrow's world.

The area remains the one in which I have lived for the longest and where Betty, Gaby and I all feel instantly at home. We love its beauty and variety as well as its friendliness and integrity, and I am sure I have gained much from its values. No man is considered to be better than another, they reject cant, show and hypocrisy, and have an innate respect for the individual and his differences. There is very little pressure for conformity, a good deal of tolerance of idiosyncrasies, and an almost automatic urge to provide mutual support in trouble. It is as though the traditions of the coal mines and the pits have run through the whole population, for loyalty to the group never lies far below the surface, and there is always a feeling of optimism and fight. People buckle down and do something about their misfortunes, and they are quick to appreciate kindred spirits. This finds an echo in my natural reaction to problems. I am never content to let things lie – I simply cannot put a problem away and wait. I have to be doing something – to have a creative plan to alleviate things or lead to a solution. I do not necessarily have to see a clear way through, but I do need to see the next steps, and the general direction in which they lead. This is a very North-Eastern characteristic and has its weaknesses as well as its strengths.

One of the many lessons taught me by my colleagues at that time was that instant action is not always the best. There are occasions when you simply have to give a situation time to develop. I find this very difficult and can only manage it if I know what I am waiting for, and what my ultimate actions will be. One has to be particularly careful about moving too fast when one is dealing with people's perceptions and beliefs. It is not only dysfunctional but actually deeply damaging to move too far against the accepted beliefs of those whose views you are trying to change. Patience and time are needed if tender flowers are to grow, but this does not mean that there is nothing you can do. People cannot be moved too far from their ingrained beliefs but, with patience, the gap between their aims and their acceptance can be narrowed. I have learnt to divert my invariable wish for instant action into the slower, but ultimately more effective, process of persuasion and discussion. The great value of the latter approach, besides the fact that the 'ownership' of the problem and its solution is transferred, is that in the process your own thinking also shifts.

The period of my life from 1968 when, as deputy chairman, I was given responsibility for Wilton, until 1973 when I handed over as Chairman of Petrochemicals, was my post-graduate course in management. This was when I first learned to lead thousands of people rather than hundreds, and the period during which all the various strands of my early life came together to create my philosophy of the management of large organisations. This was the time when I realised that the leader's job lay in three overlapping but mutually interdependent areas. First there was the need for a vision of where the whole show could and should go. While this vision has to be a shared one, its derivation lies clearly at the leader's door. It has to be a vision which is simple, stretching and above all a turn-on for all the people. It has to be qualitative rather than quantitative and to encompass values as well as achievements. I have held this belief since my earlier days in industry and I think I can trace my need for such an approach right back to my days in the Navy, first perhaps developed in Germany and thereafter. It is the most potent team-building weapon ever developed, for a clear, shared vision of where you are going, or in the German expression 'all the noses facing the same way'. Without such a vision, decentralisation, trust, speed, experimentation, tolerance and the setting of diffi-cult aims for oneself become either impossible or immeasurably more difficult. The vision for petrochemicals was that it was our business and together we would run it to be the best petrochem-ical outfit in the world. From this came our willingness to take our own initiative and look upon ICI as a resource to be managed, rather than as a master.

The second lesson I learnt at that time was that the leader could not and should not seek to manage the business in its entirety. My aim was to manage my colleagues – in this case our board – and to enable them to manage the division. I had done the same thing at Wilton, where the Works Managers' Com-mittee was the key to success. Managing a group of people is not an automatic process and all too often it is relegated in one's thinking in favour of managing the specific task or challenge. Groups do not work together by some natural law. They need help – individually, to grow and develop each person's own unique role and contribution, and collectively, to harness the group will efficiently to achieve the ordered solution of agreed problems. The leader's role encompasses both these important aspects. This should be to assist, counsel, befriend, and occasionally curb each member of the group on a personal basis. The leader should also be doing the less glamorous but even more essential tasks of getting the preparation work done, ensuring that discussions are meaningful, setting the environment and utilising time to the best effect. It rests with the leader to 'pace' the group, continuously to check progress and achievement, to hold the balance between the long term and the short as well as between the practical and the visionary.

A group that works well together is as much of a joy to see as a well-practised football team. Each member knows his own especial role but also knows his place in the team, when to move in, cover, or reinforce someone else. So it is with a management team, and the leader's role is a combination of coach, manager and teacher. When so much depends on the teacher, it is amazing what a low priority people give to this aspect of their work. Perhaps this is because when the team works well the credit is shared between them – and yet the reality is that no group of people can develop these vital skills without the help of another party, and the job calls for skill, study and practice. How fortunate I was to have these opportunities to learn, and such able people to learn from.

The third area about which I learnt at this time was the need to project the organisation's values if it was to succeed. Because I believed in involvement, and had great confidence in the ability of our people, I wanted an open, relaxed and informal style to prevail, where differences of view were aired and debated and where time was not wasted on politics and trivia. I also wanted a high achieving ethos in which anything less than the best was not good enough, and a restless dissatisfaction with the status quo. At Wilton and in the Petrochemical division I had the same concepts of the style and values which were most likely to create the results we needed, and it was evident that these could only be created by example. Fortunately, I think I work best in a stressed environment of high expectation and I am more at ease with openness and informality than with the reverse. Openness and the creative use of conflict are not comfortable ways of living and are a far cry from most corporate cultures. They need the leavening of humour and a healthy cynicism about the final unimportance of issues if the pressures are to be converted into an enjoyable way of life. Everyone wants to belong to a winning team and derives much pleasure from the belief that they are both personally and collectively the best. In both of these jobs I drove myself hard, and sought consciously to project my own ideas on how to work. I looked on time in my office as time wasted and tried to be out and about throughout the day, being seen all over the works. The process was helped immeasurably by the fact that I had worked with almost everyone on the site at one time or another – we were a closely knit team, and I knew the families, lives and aspirations of a surprisingly wide cross-section of people from the shop floor up. The loosening up of the division occurred quite quickly but introducing the same sort of ethos into the businesses that had joined us as a result of the merger took longer. As far as performance was concerned we set ourselves the aim of doubling our profit each year – a less impressive goal than it sounds in the light of our poor starting performance.

Two further professional developments at this time were to influence my future significantly. The first was that, in pursuance of our aim to be world leaders, I started playing a wider role in our international operations. I contrived to visit Japan and the USA every year and was frequently in Europe. Largely on our own initiative, we set up a European Petrochemicals Association which met annually to discuss a wide range of the international factors affecting our businesses, ranging from technical trends, the prospects for oil availability and so on. One of the problems of our business was that, consequent upon changes in distribution costs and technology, our products could increasingly be moved and sold worldwide. In addition, the unit of investment had grown steadily and there was a sort of technical race on to produce the biggest plant in the world. As a result, the business teetered continuously from feast to famine, and if a plant failed to operate, the world supply and demand balance could tip overnight. Many of the basic weaknesses of the business were concealed by a combination of high growth and inflation. As a result all too few of us reaped the penalties of our own bad decisions and it was depressingly easy to appear to prosper just by staying in the game and not questioning too deeply the underlying trends which were at work. These international contacts, and the friendships generated then, were to prove of unending value to me in the years ahead.

The other development was an internal ICI one. The board and the divisional chairmen met together only twice a year for a couple of hours. It was the worst kind of meeting – where each of you 'performed' for a few minutes only and chose with the greatest care to purvey your own version of the good news. There was no cross-table discussion and the company chairman carried out a sort of endless game of two-handed tennis – playing each division in turn before moving on to the next. At one's peril did one comment or question, even if it appeared that misleading impressions were being created, and little action ever followed from the meetings, except exhortations to do better. A number of us felt that there was a vacuum in the leadership of the company and believed we needed to work more closely together as a group. Donald, the doyen of the divisional chairmen and my opposite number at Runcorn, discussed this problem with me many times and we decided to set up a regular meeting of the divisional chairmen. We sounded out our colleagues and received their support and enthusiasm. Donald, who was more wordly wise than I, took the precaution of informing the company chairman of our intentions.

I would be an exaggeration to say that our intiative was welcomed. In fact some of the board looked on it as subversive and even insubordinate. Indeed, they were potentially right – since in those days ICI was still overwhelmingly UK-orientated and a combined policy, supported by all the divisional chairmen, would have posed some very real problems to the board. Rebellion was not our prime consideration, but effective collaboration to enable us to use ICI's strengths to greater effect certainly was. We had already created an axis of coordinated effort between our two operations and now sought how to build on this on a wider basis. As far as I am aware the meetings continue to this day. It was certainly a key part of our structure when I became chairman of the company. Moreover, in typically ICI style, it remained the property of the divisional chairmen. Members of the board, including the company chairman, could only attend by invitation, which was never an automatic right. Working together in this way gave me a second chance of working with many of the people who would in time be my collegues on the ICI main board. It taught me some very valuable lessons about the tremendously increased effectiveness of the freely given collaboration of a group of high fliers, together with an understanding of the sort of time and effort necessary to bring such a group together.

While all these fascinating business developments were occurring, Betty and I were trying to rebuild our lives in a new pattern. Gaby and her handicap and difficulties had dominated our existence for so long that the experience of not having to take her activities into account was a totally new one for us. We started having holidays away from home, and I made strenuous efforts to avoid being away at weekends. I got home most nights, but usually after some sort of evening event, and Betty spent long periods on her own. It was, in a way, a new beginning – but not entirely, for we were still living in the same place, the isolation of which was less appealing for someone totally on her own. Gaby and Adrian were settling down in Scarborough and were having their own problems of adjustment. When the business was transferred to its new location, it did not do as well as it had in Whitby and the going was hard for them, even though they started off with a house, a business and a car. Slowly Betty and I came to adjust to our new lives, and I realised how much I relied upon the security of life with my wife in order to keep up the pace of my business existence. Trying to head up a large outfit is exhilarating and rewarding, but it is also a drain on one's reserves. Careful projection of cheerful relaxed confidence, for the benefit of one's people, imposes pressures which have to be balanced out. Yet again, things seemed to be settling down well, and Betty and I began to do more and more things together, and to coordinate our visits to London so that we could travel and stay together. The business scene was settling down – our new way of working was hugely enjoyable and I began to relax as I felt more confidence in our team's ability to cope with our ambitions. We had reached the happy stage where we felt we had the initiative. We knew where we were going and were increasingly in command of our environment. There were fewer and fewer unplanned events, for we had mostly thought out the needs of our customers and the actions of our competition.

At home, Betty and I felt increasingly as we had in the early days of our marriage and, since I was well paid, we had few money worries. It seemed that we had reached the pinnacle of our ambitions. I felt well entrenched in the North East and knew a host of people from every background in the area. We both looked forward to some years of stability. I was still under fifty and there was plenty of space for the division to expand into. I reacted with mixed feelings therefore when I was summoned down to see the company chairman in order to be told I had been elected to join the main board. With my usual talent to create a gaffe, I expressed my appreciation of the honour and asked what would happen if I declined. This was apparently a new experience for him, as was my request to discuss the matter with my wife before deciding. It was made clear that if, in my foolishness, I did not accept the promotion, there was no way I would be left in the division for long. We didn't see a great deal of choice – we could move to London with more money and further prospects, or we could be shunted sideways to a business I didn't know and an area we couldn't choose. Looking at the pacing of my career, and how useful my next few years of work were, I still believe I would have been better left to complete the task I had embarked upon. I feel that you really need five years to establish change and I had only three. The operating style I had tried to introduce was highly unusual, and unlikely to be emulated by my successor – indeed why should it be? Outfits take their drumbeat from the top and it is tough to ask thousands of people to change their step because of the very short residence time of the leader.

On a personal level, we were moving way from the home where we had lived the longest period of our married lives – our modest, beautiful, comfortable retreat in the peace of the moors. We were moving away from Gaby and her husband, and no matter what we did, would inevitably feel separated from her for the first time since she was born. It should have been a time of rejoicing and celebration – for I had, in my view, achieved what I had always felt was unachievable – and yet it was not. We both felt we were leaving just when we had found a way of life we were increasingly beginning to enjoy. The attractions of city life had little to offer us in comparison to what we were losing and we searched vainly for ways of hanging on to what we had. They were doomed and unrealistic – and yet without a belief that we could somehow manage to remain linked to Whitby and the moors, I do not think that we could have contemplated the change.

So it was that on 1 April 1973 I joined the ICI Main Board at Millbank and yet another new chapter of my life began.

13 The Bored Years

Our move to London proved traumatic in all sorts of ways. ICI had provided us with an extremely elegant first-floor flat in Chelsea, which should have gladdened the heart of any ordinary folk. In our case it was more like a death sentence. Our cats and dogs were accustomed to the freedom of life in the country and had no experience of town living. Nor, for that matter did we. We were all ill-equipped to cope with the sophisticated pleasures and homogenised life of London flat-dwellers. We were able to see Gaby only occasionally and our cats and dogs had to be found homes with friends – except for our alsation, Tippy. He was an ex guide-dog, and as inseparable from us as we were devoted to him. On more than one occasion he had demonstrated his determination to avoid being parted from us. I have never thought London life suited to large dogs, even such adaptable ones as an ex guide-dog, and Tippy made it plain that he shared these views – even though he would have preferred to roast in hell with us than enjoy life in a doggy heaven on his own.

To add to our problems, the UK was in the throes of a property boom and houses within reach of London were escalating daily in price. We were not too concerned about the distance we had to travel into London but, in order to shorten our journey to visit Gaby, we wished to be on the northern side of the river. This preference was amplified by the fact that the other members of the ICI board seemed to live mostly in the Beaconsfield area, west of London. Without wishing to be stand-offish, we wanted to make our lives outside our work acquaintances, so we looked for properties on the borders of Suffolk and Cambridgeshire. We

320

felt a great sense of urgency – both because of the trends in the market, and because of our wish to be settled once again – so we both spent every spare moment house-hunting. After a number of false starts, we eventually found an adequate, if improbable, old house in the village of Elmdon near Saffron Walden, which we thought only needed some minor alterations. Despite having lived in an old house, we were babes in the wood where timber-framed dwellings were concerned. What had started as a bit of modest doddling-up and alteration became major rebuilding and restoration before our very eyes. The climax came when, the night before my departure to India for three weeks, I arrived home to find two entire external walls had vanished and been replaced by sheets of polythene. I cannot say I relished leaving my wife depending on sheets of polythene for her physical protection, even with a large and protective alsation dog by her side.

We were still trying to keep Stonegate Mill as a weekend home and a haven of peace in the Yorkshire moors but we soon found that we were unable to cope with the pain of the visits. The house which we had lavished so much love upon began to look shabby and neglected. The bustle of our cats and dogs, and the reassurance of our familiar and well-loved furniture was missing. Despite the efforts of our part-time gardener and caretaker, the grounds and the river almost immediately showed the lack of Betty's involvement and care and attention. We simply could not treat our home as a weekend cottage – it had meant too much, seen too much and been a part of us for so much of our lives that we felt the reproach of abandonment each time we stayed there. It was made worse because we had the inner feeling that we had not fought hard enough to stay. Not for the first time, I was concerned that I had sacrificed something precious to all of us for the sake of my business career, and I wondered whether the cause had justified the loss.

We probably struggled too long before we accepted the inevitable and put the mill up for sale. We sold it to a young and appreciative family, who seemed to share our enthusiasm for it and its wonderful location, but their ways were not ours. We had thought always to help and improve on nature's handiwork, so that when she sowed foxgloves by our dry-stone walls we cherished them and added to them. We trimmed the banks by the brook with care, to preserve the same look of close-cropped turf which was such a feature of the sheep-mown moor. We lovingly removed every dead branch from our oak trees and we must, over the years, have sown more than a ton of daffodils on the banks of our little valley. It was unreasonable to expect that others would operate in just that way.

During our time there, we had increasingly begun to feel part of the pattern of the moors and their timeless values. Nothing came easily, and the very hardness of the environment gave perspectives which we all valued, and which nothing can replace. I knew that I was going to miss the experience of being a contributory part of the natural world which had been so important to me ever since my years in the Navy. This realisation made losing it even more poignant, and yet I have always felt strongly that one must be constantly voyaging into the future. Above all, for an industrialist it is always tomorrow and the future which preoccupies the mind and the effort. Too much hanging on to the past and you are defeated; and yet too little regard for your heritage and just as surely all is lost.

Whilst Betty and I were battling with these myriad problems, I was also attempting to adjust to life on the board of one of the world's great multinationals. Despite my pride in understanding behaviour patterns, my knowledge of the individuals concerned, and my years of experience of the ways things appeared to work, the unreality of my new life was a surprise. Perhaps the most unexpected reaction I had was the feeling of lack of responsibility. Over the years I had become accustomed to carrying a good deal of responsibility, with clearly defined tasks, and I lived by my success or failure in their accomplishment. Suddenly I found myself the junior member of an alleged collegiate of decision-taking. I say alleged, for there was little freedom for any individual to affect the ways in which we went about our business, or even took our decisions. Even though, very properly, ICI took pains to ensure that each new board member was made aware of his (for there never had been a female on the board) legal rights and responsibilities, this seemed to be almost theoretical, since one had no feeling of carrying the burden. Almost for the first time since I left Dartmouth in the early years of the war, I felt no load on my shoulders.

Our debates seemed academic rather than real. Our deliberations were ritualistic rather than robust. It was the total flipside of what I had tried to achieve in Petrochemicals. In addition, the tasks I was assigned seemed to me to have been a somewhat infelicitous choice. To start off with, I was made the 'friend' of the Petrochemicals division. This posed major problems to Arthur, my successor, and to me. After all, the directions we had set had been taken under my leadership, but these responsibilities now lay with Arthur. I obviously could not be the divisional chairman *in absentia* without fatally damaging the very independence of view I had spent so many years developing. The alternative course, to resign myself to being the division's mouthpiece, was equally undesirable from my point of view. I felt that my years of work warranted a better reward than that, and moreover such an approach would destroy any lingering regard my colleagues might have for my possible personal contribution to the future direction of our company. This dilemma proved impossible to resolve satisfactorily. I was too close to my old division and, despite the efflux of time, I was always considered to be an expert in their affairs. This confusion and duplication of roles was difficult for me, unhelpful to ICI's interests, and probably damaging to ICI's petrochemical business. My attempts to voice these concerns were treated more as admissions of my own inadequacies than showing up an area of real conflict of interest and over-management. This experience was decisive in forming some of the views which I put into practice later. It taught me a great deal about the need for clear thinking in the areas of who does what, to and with whom, and I still have an apparently pedantic passion for getting to the roots of these situations and understanding where individual roles start.

In my other portfolio tasks I had rather better fortunes – albeit after a struggle or two. Each of us in those days was assigned a territorial responsibility as well as a business and a functional one. Not unreasonably, since I spoke Russian, the chairman assigned me the post of Eastern European Director, and was shattered when I refused it. When I had last visited the USSR my efforts had attracted the attention of my old adversaries, the KGB, who, with their usual discretion, had passed me a warning not to return or else to face the consequences. Quite apart from my own disinclination to put such messages to the test I had promised Betty, who was well aware of how real this threat was, that I would not take such a risk. I explained all of this to my boss who refused to believe that any sovereign power anywhere would dare to lay a hand on a main board director of ICI, but reluctantly accepted my decision. Some years later he and another colleague suffered an experience which demonstrated to him how wrong this view had been. However, in addition to having asked for time to reflect on my initial appointment I had now added to my reputation for bloody-mindedness by refusing this particular task. Instead, I was given the task of being the geographical director for the Indian subcontinent and the Middle East. The prospect of returning to India filled me with delight, and the future of oil and petrochemicals in the Middle East was so clearly interwoven that I felt sure there would be a constructive role for me to follow.

On the functional side of things I also had some good luck, although it was a while before I realised it. For many years, the practice had been to make the newest arrival on the board responsible for 'organisation', which I think reflected the general disdain for the subject. In addition, I collected a ragbag of tasks which proved to be of the greatest importance in the development of my future thinking. Firstly, I was made responsible for the administration of head office. This was another 'fall guy' task of significant proportions. The scheme of organisation did not allow for any boss of head office except the company chairman. Indeed the only coordinating force for the entire company was that illustrious man. Each section of head office responded to an individual director, so that all differences of view were referred back to members of the board who were often least able to judge the practical impact of their decisions. Someone had, however, to manage the despised administrative functions, which included the mail, the drivers, the cooks, the cleaners and the head office personnel function. The exercise of these were, in reality, one of ICI's glories, and the minuscule coordination which existed between them all now fell within my bailiwick.

I was lucky to be able to appoint a splendidly worldly-wise, unflappable, yet determined, general manager to do the work. I gained a great deal from having this responsibility, got to know the ins and outs of the workings of our headquarters in a uniquely personal way, and did not like what I found. In those days, head office was a graveyard to ambition. Our people worked all the hours that God sent, and to ICI's usual perfectionist standards, but all too little avail. If the board did not have whole-hearted agreement on its priorities and aims, endless problems were created for the overworked staff. Moreover, London itself placed constraints upon them which did not exist elsewhere. On Tees-side everyone knew one another, irrespective of their lifestyles. There was a family atmosphere and everyone would drop into the company club for a drink on their way home and meet their friends from all levels of the company. Moreover, almost every-one lived close to their work. Here in London sometimes as much as four hours a day travelling time was added to our working days. There was little socialising, and even had there been a club, the tyranny of the 6.25 train – or whatever it was – slaughtered such companionable instincts. There was hardly any cross-posting between functions, so each member of the staff saw themselves as an accountant, or whatever, first and last. In itself this made such collaboration as we achieved even more surprising.

My last responsibility at that time was for information tech-nology. As a demonstration of a certain randomness of allocation of responsibilities, this had a sublime side to it. I had never been a computer buff, and indeed Eric Sharpe (later to head Cable and Wireless) and I collected a joint wooden-spoon on our computer course, for a mixture of incompetence and incompre-hension. I had been trained to understand the role of computers in the control of plants, but had hitherto failed to realise the profound impact they could make on ways of doing business as a whole. My predecessor, who was a believer in orders rather than involvement, had been fighting a war of attrition to remove the division's own computers and centralise into a complex of three massive mainframes. A combination of my dislike of centralisation and my distrust of coercion, together with my conviction that enforced action of this sort would lead to the organisational equivalent of the One Hundred Years War, made me seek another way to achieve the same result. The solution we found was to insist on compatibility of systems and this proved later to be a better foundation on which to build the changes ahead. Sometimes such quirks of fate avoid major and expensive mistakes.

Although I had this curious feeling of weightlessness, during this time I learnt lesson after lesson about corporate behaviour in a large, slowly adapting and rather self-satisfied institution. In reality, a board member had greater power to influence and direct than I realised, as long as he learnt to concentrate on the 'what' and totally avoid becoming embroiled in the 'how'. This was difficult, however, because all the pressures, and our own inclinations, encouraged us to act in the executive role in which we felt more comfortable. Lack of involvement in the execution of the decisions to which most of the dialogue and discussion in the board was directed was viewed as evidence of lack of commitment. Failure to reply to some vexed question that I felt was outside my particular area of knowledge or participation was looked upon as a sign of laziness, or flippancy. This impression was enhanced by the fact that at the time I was one of only two members of the board who commuted by train, and I made a point of leaving the office rigorously at ten minutes past five every day. While my fifty-minute train journey gave me an uninterrupted opportunity to read the mountains of paper which appeared as the raw material of our tasks, and was a significant advantage to me, my punctual departure did nothing to relieve the impression of me as a rather frivolous free-loader who did not take his responsibilities seriously. It would indeed have been difficult for me to create any other impression for, if I stuck to my self-imposed decision not to do other people's jobs for them, I was hopelessly underloaded and indeed felt so.

Once I had settled in, I gradually began to feel that the whole way in which we operated was wrong and needed fundamental change. There was a minority of my colleagues who shared this view, but over time the relative ease and comfort of our ways of working wore down their feelings. The adequate, if unexciting, results which the company achieved, allied with the moderate acclaim of a surprisingly friendly press, also tended to enforce this unwillingness to rock the boat. For a long time I thought this to be a generation-gap problem and that, as more of my former divisional chairmen colleagues joined us, we would create a critical mass for change – but it never seemed to happen. I have noticed that in practically all large companies the seductive power of the status quo, combined with the fear of the unknown, work in more or less the same way. I must have been a real pain in the neck to the chairman, who patiently put up with my continual expressions of frustration and attempts to change the time-honoured ways of doing things. In reality the company was changing, but to my mind far too cautiously and slowly to cope with the effervescent environment around us. My allies in pressing for faster and more radical change were not by any means restricted to the newest members of the board, but over time each of us became more involved in dealing with our individual responsibilities rather than endlessly trying to tilt, like Quixote, at the corporate windmill.

Apart from a few trivial claims to success, I find it difficult to recall any real contributions which I was able to make to the future of the company. During my first two years on the board I and three colleagues made an ill-fated and unsuccessful attempt at proposing a new organisation of the company. However, with the imaginative and creative help of the finance director, I did succeed in obtaining the money to invest in the Ninion Oil Field in the North Sea, which ICI's consortium had discovered. It was just as well that I did, because this investment made the entire difference to our company profitability when the bad days struck.

Ironically, the board only agreed to it because we were able to demonstrate that we could tap financial resources for the investment which would not otherwise be available for putting into chemical plant. If this had not been the case, I doubt whether the board would have considered an investment in oil as being of sufficient importance by comparison with building another mighty chemical machine. I do think that I helped to make some small impact on our Indian operations, where we had a considerable pool of talent which we found difficult to stretch because of the restrictions on foreign investment in the subcontinent. We started up a research operation, and managed to get some Indian-managed project teams into Africa, to help with developments there. It remains a depressing list for a highly paid and presumably qualified industrialist, and is the root cause of my belief that I would have been better employed for a further two years as the chairman of the Petrochemicals division. Looking back, these years certainly focused my concerns, with a laser-like intensity, on the whole area of the way in which the board worked and how it related to the company as a whole.

We were then a very Anglo-centric bunch. Despite our continuous plans to grow faster outside the UK, and the devoted attempts of some of my colleagues to force us to look further afield, it was the UK and its ills which preoccupied us, followed, at a discreet distance, by the fortunes of the old Commonwealth countries. An analysis of the time spent by the board would show an overwhelming preponderance on those areas of past glory and our chosen method of direction was related almost entirely to the allocation of capital for specific projects. I do not recollect any discussion of the direction in which any individual business was going, let alone the total balance of the company, with the exception of the work done by the planning department in preparation for the capital programme. Curiously, this all-important discussion was not headed by the chairman but by one of his deputies and was compressed into a single morning. The process was curiously reminiscent of a bargaining system in a bazaar. Before the formal presentation, there was an animated period of horse trading, in order to discover those areas which individual divisions and operations believed were truly critical to their futures. Everything was contrived to avoid the ultimate confrontation, and even the subsequent presentation of the individual projects to the board were never in doubt, for the 'trade-offs' occurred in smoke-filled rooms rather than in the open.

Meanwhile, at home Betty and I had been 'nest-building' at a frenetic rate. Our house was grander than the mill but it had the same elusive character that all old houses seem to bring with them. With her usual relentless courage, optimism and enthusiasm, Betty had thrown herself into the restoration of the fabric of the building, and rapidly become an expert on the timber-frame building techniques of the sixteenth century. In the process of the work, she had revealed two early fireplaces that had been built over during the intervening centuries, often working on her own, and late into the night in order to do so. We felt we 'owned' the house in a real sense, for a tremendous amount of our efforts, but mostly of my wife's, had gone into its restoration. Eventually we even felt secure enough to get two Burmese kittens, who helped us to feel that we had transferred our roots. Becoming involved in the village and the area was slower and more difficult. For the first time, and also for the last for many years, my life was rather more predictable. Nevertheless, my various responsibilities still involved a lot of travel and a good deal of evening entertaining. Amongst the good things that had happened to me when I arrived in London was that I inherited a marvellous secretary who addressed herself, with some success, to the problems of making sure that I was able to spend as many evenings as possible at home with my wife. Edna and I were to work together for fifteen years, and I never ceased to count my good fortune at having her appointed to me. She projected so many of my own values and my way of working, and our association proved to be quite priceless.

'Farthing Green' did not boast the bird life of the mill, but, despite being nearly in the centre of the village, it had eight-foot hedges and vast walls to give it a feeling of seclusion and privacy. Once the gates were closed, we felt that we were in our own world again and seldom wanted to stray far afield. London was about fifty miles away, far enough for Elmdon to have a life of its own. In fact we seldom felt the need to visit the city – tending to go northward, to Cambridge, when we wanted something which our market town of Saffron Walden could not provide. In those days, Audley End station was an empty car park surrounding a tiny station and there was always space to leave one's car, no matter how finely you cut the timing. We travelled in 'real' trains, initially with a buffet car and bar since we were the main line service from Kings Lynn to London. 'Progress' speedily removed such luxuries and before we left, in 1981, the car park was packed, and the buffet and bar were only a cherished memory.

Most people who lived in that part of Essex did so for the same reasons we did, and were prepared to accept the extra travelling time in order to share some, at least, of the joys of rural life. Because the train came into Liverpool Street station, most of our fellow travellers were from the City and the Stock Exchange – people with whom in the past I had had surprisingly little contact. Our choice of home and my travelling arrangements enabled us to get to know quite a number of people from this very different world. I suppose that I was as much of an object of curiosity to them as they were to me, for our worlds barely crossed. Certainly in my years in the North East I had not met any of the people from the Stock Exchange who held our futures and fortunes in their grasp. I was surprised at how different our perceptions of events were, and it was almost as though we each looked at things from opposite sides of the looking-glass. My 'blooding' in the thinking of the City was to prove of great value in the future, even though drinking sessions in the 5.42 from Liverpool Street seemed an unlikely college.

At least every six weeks we went up to Scarborough to see Gaby and Adrian and of course we always spent our Christmases together. Our granddaughter, Abigail, was born some months after we moved to London, and visiting her was an even stronger inducement to head north. They were struggling to make the antique business support them, and had now branched out into antiquarian books. The antiques business was increasingly competitive and the situation was made more difficult for them by the deterioration of Gaby's health during her pregnancy. After Abby was born Gaby had to spend some time in hospital, and Adrian was struggling to look after a new-born baby, a sick wife and a business. Increasingly we felt that they needed our help and support. We found it difficult to live with the contrast between our increasing affluence and easy lifestyle and their struggles for the simplest luxuries. While they would accept presents during our visits and on birthdays and so on, financial support was something they found it difficult to accept. At the same time, we were reluctant to erode their independence, which once given up is so difficult to retrieve.

We all adored Abigail and it was a constant delight to us to see the joy which Gaby took in her baby daughter. In many ways it seemed to be a relatively happy and stable time for us all. For my part I was determined to do a better job of staying close to Abby than I had managed with Gaby. To begin with I was not as frightened of her as I had been of Gaby as a baby. She did not seem so fragile and I had learnt to have more confidence in the ability of babies to bounce back than I had had in 1951. I still had the blank spot in my mind which refuses to understand how a baby's mind works and I still expected her to be a sort of scaled-down adult – but at least I now recognised the stupidity of such an expectation. Moreover, I did not have the same fears about being able to provide for her, nor did I scare myself with feelings of extra responsibility. I determined that I would always find the time to spend with her and settled back happily to be the model of a doting grandfather. All in all, it was a very laid-back sort of time. I did not feel much pressure at work and certainly none from ambition, and as a family we seemed to be embarking on a new phase of contentment. Betty and I could indulge our interests together and we enjoyed the freedom from worry that we seemed to have in our grasp. I enjoyed my work and liked and respected my colleagues, despite my differences of view with many of them. The ICI board was a very able group of civilised men. There was little back-stabbing or political in-fighting and differences of view hardly ever spilt over into personal antipathy – even though there were as many divergent opinions on almost every situation as there were directors. Perhaps it was this very diversity that helped create an atmos-phere where you could be out of step without being out of the team. My lack of ambition at the time derived partly from the new balance we had created between our private lives and my business life, but also from a realistic approach to my probable lack of further opportunity for hierarchical advancement. At this time in ICI the chairman served for a period of only three years. His successor had to carry the majority vote of all the directors and was inevitably likely to be one of the three deputy chairmen. Based on the grounds of likely breadth of support, relevant experience and age, it seemed probable to me that I had reached my zenith. There were many less agreeable zeniths than the one I found myself in and I was aware that if I really wanted to move outside ICI I could probably do so in the late seventies.

Meanwhile, new experiences were piling up on me at a bewildering rate. I was fortunate enough to join two outside boards as a non-executive director. ICI appointed me to be one of their nominated directors on the board of Carrington Viyella. ICI held the majority of the Carrington Viyella shares, but had given an undertaking to the Department of Trade and Industry not to use its voting power. The chairman was Sir Jan Lewando, formerly of Marks and Spencer. In addition, I was head-hunted to join, again as a non-executive director, the board of Reed International chaired by Alex Jarrett, and to my delight our ICI chairman agreed to my taking the job. Although ICI had allowed its executives to join the board of financial institutions if they were asked this was, I think, the first time one of us had joined another industrial outfit. The appointment was made more piquant by the fact that Alex joined our board at the same time. The two companies were competitors in at least one area of activity, the domestic paint business. At last I had the opportunity to see how other companies were run and I joined both boards with a singing heart and high expectations. Although the singing continued, the expectations speedily hit reality.

Jan Lewando knew his market-place backwards and ran the company very much as a chief executive. For him the board was his management committee and he did not spend much time on the legal niceties of collective responsibility. As a nominated non-executive, I was viewed as an unavoidable evil and the representative of an outfit which had demonstrated its incompetence to run a market-oriented and market-driven business. We were suspected, not totally unjustly, of viewing the textile business as a convenient way of shifting our fibres into the market-place and much energy was devoted to trying to demonstrate the unsuitability of our ways of doing business. He was personally kind to me and I enjoyed working with him, but neither of us succeeded in making much progress in utilising the potential strengths of both outfits. However, it certainly gave me my first insight into the weaknesses of an autocratic system of governance. The ICI system of consensus seemed to lie at one extreme and Jan's leadership at Carrington Viyella at the other.

Reed International and Alex's style lay in between. He is a man of formidable intellect and integrity and represents one of the rare breed who have successfully made the transition from the Civil Service to industrial leadership. He had only recently taken over from Don Ryder who had amassed a formidable reputation by building and diversifying Reed with a constant flow of acquisitions. One reason I was so keen to join the board of Reed was that ICI had relatively little experience in the acquisition of companies, and those we had acquired had not often achieved our hopes for them. At that time, Reed were viewed as the masters of the art and I looked forward to rounding out my experience in this area. This was not quite what happened, although I speedily learnt a lot about the pitfalls and difficulties. In a curious way, Reed had persuaded themselves that it was possible to buy other companies from the acquired company's own money. There was little discussion of what Reed themselves could bring to the party, and there was surprisingly little inter-relationship between Reed and the businesses which had been bought. Howard MacDonald (the outstanding treasurer at Shell) and I joined the board at the same time, and with very similar misconceptions about the company we were joining. Alex was relatively new in the chair and had had little experience outside Reed itself. All three of us, coming from quite different backgrounds and experience, reached the same conclusion at about the same time – namely that we were in trouble, which looked as though it could only get worse.

The difficulty with building companies through acquisition is that it is easy to get into a situation where you see the solution to problems with the earning power of the company in undertaking yet another acquisition. As the company gets bigger, each successive acquisition also has to be bigger if it is to have any material effect, until eventually the inevitable day comes when further progress is only possible through improvement of the businesses you have. Over the next few years, I observed how few businessmen are able to do both – be succeessful predators in the exciting and dramatic jungle of buying and selling companies, and at the same time do the difficult, painstaking and protracted job of generating increasing profit from within your own business. ICI had always tended to concentrate on the steady business of generating growth through investment in research, plants and people and that is still the world in which I feel most comfortable. Quick adjustments to a company's portfolio, however, are inevitably not possible through this route and if the future has not been adequately foreseen, or you have stayed too long with a business where you've lost your competitive edge, selling or buying is the only recourse.

All this and much much more I learnt from my time with Reed. Alex was continually evolving his own techniques and skills as a chairman and was a courteous and careful listener to the ideas with which Howard and I bombarded him. Over the years I was there, we developed a closer approximation to the sort of organisation that I had dreamed of than I had met elsewhere. My fellow directors were a super lot, but as different in background and approach from my colleagues in ICI as it would be possible to imagine. The company encompassed businesses in publishing, including the *Daily Mirror* Group, in paper, paint and building materials. Most of these businesses were much closer to the customer than most of the ones I had been involved in. My colleagues at Reed were, above everything, businessmen who thought in terms of profit and growth rather than being as concerned as ICI was with its competitive position in technology and science. These two experiences as a non-executive director made me realise the value of broadening one's area of business experience, something which I have sought to do throughout the rest of my career. There used to be a view that a vast multinational like ICI or BP could produce sufficient breadth of experience from within its own group and so did not need non-executive directors, or to make its own people available for such tasks. Such ideas, however, ignore the vital differences that a variety of perspectives and viewpoints can bring to bear on business situations. While very few emperors have no clothes at all, almost all lack some essential garment or other and the outsider is often in a better position both to notice the lack and to draw attention to it.

Despite my feelings that these years were not being as productive, in terms of personal impact, or as exciting as the preceding ones, I was learning the whole time and, partly by design and partly by accident, broadening my scope and experience and forming and reinforcing my philosophies of business. In 1976 the whole of my portfolio of jobs in ICI was changed and I was given three opportunities which were to help enormously in the years ahead. For the first time since the early sixties, I was relieved of the responsibility for petrochemicals and became the board member responsible for fibres. At the same time, I was made the director responsible for continental Western Europe and appointed to the board of ICI America.

Quite suddenly the rate of my business life accelerated and I could certainly not complain of lack of opportunity. Our fibre operations, in company with practically all others in Europe, were making substantial losses. The entire industry had over-invested and expanded, while our European textile customers were increasingly losing the race against Far Eastern imports. Moreover, we had not innovated sufficiently fast to justify the massive movements of raw material across the globe and back in their new form as garments or cloth. Despite having been the first to develop the ubiquitous polyester fibre and being involved in the very early stages of developing and selling Dupont's great invention of nylon, we had been in retreat for some years. Fibres had been the apple of the board's eye for most of the sixties and had greatly contributed to our golden years. It was a shock to us all that we had fallen from grace so quickly and that we were likely to lose our position to our European competitors. We were all involved in a sort of game of beggar-my-neighbour, believing that the last to survive and hang on must reap untold benefits. The snag with this scenario was that fibres were relatively large employers of labour and a number of national governments were determined not to allow their national standard-bearers to fall.

The task that I was faced with, therefore, was an ideal microcosm of the problems of the chemical industry at the time. I had to enable change to be effected not only within the division and ICI but also in the external European environment in which we worked. I was fortunate that the new chairman of the Fibres division was a friend. We shared every aspect of the problem and the task, and almost from the beginning placed complete trust in each other. Brian is a natural leader who knew his business and all the international players in it, inside out. He was universally respected and liked, and I have never seen him lose his equanimity or his confidence. I believe we made a good team and we speedily worked out our respective roles and our strategy. We actually got our strategy almost dead wrong, for our idea was to use the cash generation of our nylon operation, where competition was somewhat less intense, to make a mighty leap ahead in the polyester technology. Despite some initial success, we were eventually defeated by the sheer scale of the problem and so ended up pushing nylon and largely abandoning polyester. I remember, about six months after taking the job on, explaining to my board colleagues what we were aiming to do and writing the fateful words that if we did not succeed we would have to withdraw altogether.

It was one of the first occasions on which we had to face up to the fact that, despite our head start, we might have lost the international race and, although my paper was accepted, I do not think any of us really believed it might happen. In the meantime, we had to cut our costs, fast. We had to rejuvenate and redirect our research towards far more ambitious and risky aims, and could not provide any back-up for failure. Brian and I explained to an initially disbelieving audience of senior managers that it was for real. If they could not make drastic improvements, we would have to take the business out. This attitude was so contrary to ICI's previous stance that it is not surprising that they gave us a tough run. I think it was the fact that we were both committed and determined that really enabled the unpleasant reality to sink in. Meanwhile, we both worked like beavers on the European scene to try and bring about the necessary restructuring of the industry. Here we were helped by two factors. I was already involved in Europe and knew the boards of most of our competitors from my position in the past as a supplier. With my new European hat on, I had access to them across the whole of our activities. My years after the war had made me a believer in a single Europe and since then my links with most of the main chemical manufacturers had been nurtured and developed. My affection for Germany, and its people particularly, helped me to build bridges which were of great importance. The second factor was the much-maligned EEC. Stevie Davignon was the Commissioner responsible for industry and, while a free-market man at heart, recognised and was determined to effect the transition from government support to a more competitive structure.

The tempo of my life mercifully accelerated to the sort of pace at which I perform best. Moreover, there was so much to do, and my knowledge of the details of the fibre business were so meagre, that there was neither temptation nor possibility of crossing Brian's wires in the running of the business. It was a happy time at work. At last I again felt some burden of responsibility and even more of expectation. In reality, all of us in the business knew we could not go on as before – so the ground was set fair for change. Brian and I knew that we sank or swam with the rest. I was better placed then he. ICI had not, as far as I was aware, sacked a main board director, although some had left. My punishment for failure would be a sort of Exile to Elba – comfortable, well paid and totally without influence or responsibility. A fate which would have led me to look elsewhere instantly. Our company was tough – as I knew from my early days. Material matters would be catered for, but the provision of a safe haven, even for a relatively short haul, was much less likely. The job needed time and the EEC intervention gave it to us. But time was only helpful if we pressed on relentlessly to use it to restructure and reposition the business, and this we did. The whole experience was a magnificent training school for us both, and eventually our people began to win. We looked anew at what the market-place needed and stopped believing that just reducing our costs would do the trick. Of course we did reduce them, savagely, but we started at the top and attacked our services and overheads with gusto before moving down the line. All of this was helped immeasurably by the fact that the rest of ICI could afford our drain on them, but even then we were constrained by the need to observe and preserve the employment practices of the rest of the company.

The real impact we made however, was the simple one of trying to differentiate our products. Since we were focusing our research effort, in an attempt to jump ahead of the competition, our product variations had to be produced on a shoe string. Yet again I was taught a valuable lesson. Technologically proud and able companies always want to make big inventions. Big leaps forward are much more satisfying than small incremental changes. Yet, making money from a great invention is notoriously slow and difficult. It is the small innovations, targeted directly to someone's needs, that produce the quick and generous pay-back. Such innovations, however, seldom come from the classically organised research department. They derive from the hot breath of the customer on your neck, combined with technical mastery of your own field.

Slowly, but nevertheless surely, Fibres began to turn round. The smaller team we had was tempered in the fire and we all worked with real commitment. The surprising thing to me was how much energy and enthusiasm was released by this fight to regain our lost position. Early on we had decided that we needed to be in a leadership position in our industry, or the game was not worth the candle. Survival on its own would not satisfy us. The difficulties we had were in knowing when to abandon hard-won positions. It is probably the most painful type of decision in business, for one always feels that a bit more effort, or even worse, a stroke of luck, can turn one's fortunes. I am afraid that in my own armoury of skills, quitting an untenable position in time is my weakest ability. It seems so awful to walk away from the commitment and work of thousands, and it takes courage, analytical conviction and cold-blooded determination to do so. Yet it is an absolutely necessary business attribute. When I inveigh against ICI's failure to change and lack of urgency during the 1970s, it is all too easy to forget that those very attributes gave us the time, headroom and backing to retrieve our fibres operation. A smaller or harder company would have cut us off far earlier.

Meanwhile, we were facing another change of chairmanship when in 1978 Roland decided to retire after three years in the chair. I felt more than ever convinced that hard times lay ahead, both for the country and the company, and our choice of his replacement was a key one for ICI's futures. It was a difficult choice, for we had two well-prepared and excellent directors of very different characteristics, both of whom were to make their marks in a national sense. In the event Maurice was chosen, and we all had every reason to bless his unruffled bravery and clarity of thought in the years ahead. For sheer calculated courage, I have never known his equal. He had fought, and largely compensated for, the almost total loss of the sight of one eye after an unsuccessful operation, and had still had the courage to have his other eye operated on in the same way. He had used every technique of technology, and his own outstanding intellectual abilities, to cope with the masses of paper which deluged us all and in many cases had to have documents read to him. It was particularly hard for him since he is the most numerate man I have known. For him numbers speak and sing and he arrives at concepts through figures. He and I made an incongruous team, for I use numbers only to check the scale of concepts, while to him the numbers steer to understanding more easily than words. When the company found itself in the eye of the storm of the 1981 recession he used these qualities to the full.

After his appointment I was chosen to replace him as one of the three deputies. I was not totally surprised at this, for in terms of seniority and experience I was well qualified for the task, but I did not assume that this put me in the running for the chair, since Ray and Bill had been in position for some time. Maurice's contract was for three years, so this meant that the next election would be in 1981, to take over in 1982. As one of the deputy chairmen, my portfolio was shifted back to the Heavy Chemicals side of things, but this time including the divisions manufacturing plastics and chlor-alkali. It was the first time I had had any influence across the three areas and I was lucky in the extreme with the directors who worked with me. Even in 1978 it was apparent that we needed to make big changes, for our Plastics operations seemed to be heading the same way as Fibres. Over the next year I put forward various revised solutions, of which my favourite was to put all three divisions together into a single company. My colleagues, however, thought it was too fast and risky and so it was almost seven years before this was carried out. I was, however, given the chance of putting together Plastics and Petrochemicals, and at least this provided the bedrock for our future changes.

Meanwhile, the external environment in which we were operating became more and more difficult, culminating in the Winter of Discontent when I found myself, not for the first or last time, the harbinger of bad news. It had fallen to my lot to announce to an unbelieving world that the current wave of strikes, even though they did not affect ICI in a direct way, would within a week force us to start shutting down our Heavy Chemical operations. This announcement was made the day that Jim Callaghan flew back to the UK and was reported as commenting,

'Crisis, what crisis?' The two comments were exploited by the press in direct opposition and proved to be the final straw. Meanwhile, as a result of our public announcement, the unions made dispositions that they had hitherto failed to make, to enable us to keep operating albeit at heavily reduced output. Sure enough when, as a result, we did not shut down within the time stipulated we were taken to task for scaremongering and worse. It was a rather frightening example of the power of the press in a whole variety of ways.

Besides my heavy chemicals responsibilities at that time I was deeply involved in Europe, and European matters. The major chemical companies met on a one-to-one basis every year, and in addition I was the ICI representative on CEFIC, the Confederation of the European Chemical Industry, so I found myself heavily involved in developments across the continent. Luckily for me I got on well with my opposite numbers and over time I was able to build valuable relationships with them. The chemical industry differed from many others in those days for we were our own best customers, and so our relationships with each other had to cope with being customers, competitors and, not infrequently, partners as well. Even though it sounds schizophrenic it actually made for a breadth of working relationships which was a real strength. From my earliest days the industry had been generous in the way competitors would help to cover others' misfortunes and help maintain supplies in situations of breakdown or unavailability of plant, where more short-termed interest might well have decreed a different approach. At the same time, we all competed fiercely in our urge to improve our products and seize technological leadership.

The advent of a Conservative government in 1979 made a number of almost immediate changes in our circumstances – initially much in our favour. Managing our interface with Government and with the Prices and Incomes Board had taken more and more of our senior management time and had almost placed a greater premium on our success in this direction than in fighting the overseas competitive battle. There was an understandable emphasis on the United Kingdom and our home market, and UK and government policies took the major share of our time together as a board. It was all too easy to be sucked into those areas where we felt we could have a direct impact and therefore to trap ourselves into the slower growth of our home market. Intellectually, we were committed to grow in America and Europe, but in both markets we sought to do so by greenfield investment, in all too many cases without a significant product or technical advantage. We were beguiled by two, probably fallacious, arguments. The first was that prices would inevitably rise to the levels at which reinvestment was rewarded. This siren song was very dangerous. The chemical industry boasted far too many aggressive and efficient companies, and was far too interested in technology to ever stand back from expected opportunity long enough to allow the rewards to come through. The whole history of the petrochemicals business – fuelled as it was by inflation – was one where in good years the industry made modest returns which could be offset by potentially horrendous losses in the bad ones.

The second, equally disastrous perceived wisdom was that as long as we were as good as our competitors we would get our share. In both cases these beliefs came from our preoccupations with production, at the expense of knowledge of our markets. The main board was then dominated by people from scientific or engineering backgrounds, whose experience of selling and marketing had been gained from their time on our divisional boards rather than in the field. Collectively, our decisions were based on a belief in numbers rather than on market knowledge, and I well remember being crushingly defeated when I objected to a mathematical formula justifying a new plant to make a product. I could not defeat the mathematics but I 'knew' that the market would never stand the predicted prices on which such a large investment was to be made. The fact that I knew the market, the customers and competitors, weighed as nothing against the equations which purported to prove a direct and coherent relationship between market price and raw-material prices. Would that life were so simple. The plant was built, and the maths proved wrong. When I was chairman I finally had to dispose of the plant we had so optimistically built.

Our profits continued in a satisfactory, albeit unexciting way, and our new chairman and his board started to put the screws on our costs. We applied these pressures in some detail across the totality of our operations and demanded improvements in a range of areas which should have improved our competitiveness quite starkly. Even though things did move in the directions we sought, our position *vis-à-vis* our overseas competitors did not. Quite suddenly, in 1980 and 1981, disaster struck us. The Chancellor, Geoffrey Howe, had increased interest rates starkly to squeeze our inflation, and as a result the pound had strengthened far beyond our capacity to compete. In three consecutive quarters our annual ratio of profit fell from £600 million a year to an annual rate of loss of £200 million a year. We were losing on virtually all our exports – certainly in my areas – and only the highest added-value products such as pharmaceuticals could jump the currency hurdle.

Maurice's strengths as chairman shone through, as did his courage and clarity of thought. One of the good results of our very detailed form of management was an extremely quick feedback of our earnings trend, so we were able to react very quickly. The decisions we took at the time were simple and stark. We decided, with some courage, to defend our export positions as long as possible, arguing, that once lost, recovery would be slow and painful. We decided to attack our cost base with renewed urgency, but as far as possible still to retain our traditional values and ways of dealing with our people – which, in effect, meant going for voluntary severance, and finally we decided to run for cash. The last decision was, for us, new ground, for cash management had been the prerogative and concern of the finance function and while we complained from time to time about stock levels, or creditors, or debtors, we had seldom looked to cash management as a total function of management.

To our relief the simple clarity of the decisions, coupled with the immediacy of the threat, and the amount we all had to do, provoked a speed of reaction which showed yet again how excellent our managers were if clearly directed. The brunt of the numbers reductions fell in the areas for which I was responsible, for indeed the brunt of the force of the storm which had hit us had struck on the commodity end of the business. As the year progressed, our discomforts were increased by the realisation that more and more of our customers were giving up the ghost, or being taken over. This caught us in another double whammy. The only escape was to export and there, because of the high exchange rate, we lost money on every ton we sold. Even if you took out the whole of our labour cost, we would still be losing money. It was doubly galling since independent surveys of the heavy chemicals businesses in Europe had shown us to be in the absolute top league technically – in fact in many cases the best – on such crucial competitive areas as on-line time and conversion factors. It looked increasingly as though we might have to shut down the heavy chemical end altogether unless the exchange rate eased back. In the meantime we addressed ourselves with even greater vigour to economising in every way we knew, and a lot we did not know, but found out on the run.

By the end of the year, one-third of all our customers in the UK had gone out of business in one way or another and of course we were incurring the additional costs of our voluntary severance policy. In terms of testing the nerves, it was as tough a time as I've ever experienced. The whole time the problem was to try to balance the present and the future. It was plain that we could not look to any return of demand – certainly in the short term – from our customers in the UK. In fact it was to take a further six years before the growth that followed brought us close to the demand figures we had previously enjoyed. It was plain that we had to try to shift our company further away from its reliance on the UK and further into the higher added-value spectrum of our business, and we set about our retrenchment with those aims firmly in mind. The time came when we had to take the forceful decision on our dividend and we had to take it against a background where no one could guess when the current pressure would abate. None of us had any doubt that we had to cut and yet, more than any other decision we had taken, this one reverberated about our ears. We who had usually basked in the approval of our countrymen, members of parliament and the press, suddenly found ourselves the butt of criticism. We were blamed for our misfortunes, for being slow, bureaucratic, uncompetitive and letting the country down. Our share price fell to levels at which we continuously feared a predatory swoop, and our external image did not encourage us that we would find many friends if someone took a run at us.

It was a tough time and we had a tough chairman, who must have been hurting like hell, but never wavered in his determination that we would face up to the nasties while retaining our ability to fight again another day. While the storm was still blowing about our ears, Maurice's contract was running out and we were obliged to appoint another chairman. There were by then three deputies, Bill Duncan, Bob Haslam and I. There had been endless speculation, inside and outside the company, as to which of us might be chosen and even – the unthinkable – whether ICI, which was considered to have so clearly failed, should seek a newcomer from outside the company. I did not believe then, and still do not believe, that it would have made a great deal of difference which of us was appointed. Bill was the most experienced, and possibly least radical of us, but the real differences between us lay in style rather than capability. This was amply proved by our subsequent careers. Bill, before his untimely death, did an outstanding job at Rolls-Royce, while Bob seems to have run practically everything in the country with his usual mix of friendly informality, clarity and determination.

The ICI system of selecting its chairmen is, as far as I know, unique. All the members of the board are consulted and vote individually. The outgoing chairman presides over the election, but has the same vote and influence as everyone else. The system has enormous strengths. In particular it is very helpful to a new chairman to know that he has been chosen by his colleagues and, at least initially, starts with their support. The system avoids 'crown princes' and allows for surprises and changes. Certainly, from my experience, each of us took the choice we were obliged to make extremely seriously and tried to make a judgement of the qualities which would be required in the future. All of us now believed that the business had suffered from the previous chairmen serving for too short a term and we had agreed that the next incumbent should be asked to serve for a minimum of five years. Having worked together for so long, we all knew each other's strengths and weaknesses intimately, as well as our ideas on the future running of the company. During the whole of my time on the board I had always argued for radical change, and that such change had to start at the board and the way we operated. I had made it clear that, in my view, there were too many of us and that, in particular, I did not like the existence of a layer of three deputies under the chairman. It did not seem to me that a promise to reduce our numbers and layers, combined with a total overhaul of our ways of doing things, was a very promising electoral position. Moreover, Maurice had always made clear his disbelief in organisational change – arguing that behavioural change was what was needed and that it could proceed independently of further upheaval. Upheaval while we were fighting for our lives was not everyone's cup of tea, and the board had already shown its unwillingness to face up to radical change by its efforts to avoid amalgamating the three heavy divisions.

One way or another, it seemed very improbable that I would be chosen to lead the company, and I made my plans accordingly. I did not want to spend another five years advocating change against the grain of my colleagues' wishes, and I believed it would be damaging and dysfunctional if I did so. I was not short of opportunities elsewhere, and had decided to leave as soon as the incoming chairman felt I could decently do so without damaging him or the company. In fact I had rather come to look forward to the change, and the opportunity to try out the ideas I had developed and grown over the years, in a new setting. I knew ICI would be in good hands and felt no rancour or ill-feeling at either of my colleagues, both of whom I liked and admired, being chosen.

It was, therefore, with mixed feelings, and considerable apprehension, that I received the news from Maurice that my colleagues had chosen me to be the next chairman. I have often puzzled over the thought processes of the members of the board at that time. I thought they had made a risky choice, and I guess they probably thought so too, but I knew that I had to try to justify their beliefs, and turned my mind on how to do so.

14 The Chairman's Time

When I was informed that I was to take over from Maurice, I had a period of some four months in a curious state of limbo. Although it was established that I would call the shots after April 1982, we both felt that until that date the company and the board should continue to be run in the style and manner it always had been. This interim period gave me a marvellous opportunity to think my way through what needed to be done and in what way. One of the first things I turned my mind to was the negotiation of my contract and terms of reference with my colleagues. Curiously the chairman's powers and responsibilities had never been specifically defined and they derived from custom and practice rather than from conscious decision. My predecessor had felt this lack and was keen to see the chairman given the powers of a chief executive. I was less convinced of this need, having seen elsewhere the difficulties of combining the two roles. However, I did not feel that it would be possible for me to accept the honour of leadership and then immediately seek to put a new chairman above me, or a chief executive under me to do the dirty work. Moreover, I believed strongly that the company should be run by the board, rather than any one individual, but that it should be a very different board which worked in very different ways. I felt that, for a business of our size and complexity, collective leadership was essential.

I therefore sought a very limited range of powers, relating primarily to my responsibilities to and for my colleagues. The chairman had always used his power to allocate portfolios and organise the board's work, but I now sought to have these powers confirmed and codified. In addition I sought the personal right to recommend, after consultation, new appointments to the board, and changes in the rewards and status of my colleagues. For their part, they had already made it clear that they wanted their chairman to have a five-year period of service. This meant that, by the end of this period, I would be almost sixty-three – which was a year past our statutory retirement age. I was concerned that my ideas might not work, or that my style might grate to a degree where five years was a disadvantage to the company. I therefore sought a change in the contract which was superficially very one-sided, but which I thought to be a necessary safeguard for us all in the journey ahead. I asked them to agree to review my contract after three years and gave them the right either to terminate at that time without compensation or if they were still satisfied, they could insist on my serving the full five-year term. Even the company secretary felt that such a contractual arrangement was biased too much in the company's favour, but I felt that at least it would give me an honourable and easy exit if things didn't work out.

Meanwhile, I was indulging myself with a rare luxury. I sat back and started to try to think my way through the changes we should make. I had made so many attempts at changing the board and our ways of doing things since joining it in 1973 that my problems related more to the plethora of views and options than a shortage of ideas. Two friends of mine, one on the board and one below board level, helped me by looking at every other successful model we could find, and together we began to get some structure into alternative models for corporate governance. Whatever we did would need the commitment and support of my colleagues, for with my new powers I intended to hone down our numbers and work ourselves at a very different pace to that which we had enjoyed in the past. I decided, therefore, that the first four days of my chairmanship should be spent somewhere away from the office, discussing and sharing our ideas on how we should do our job, the strengths and weaknesses of our company, and so on.

The models that we drew up for discussion ranged the whole way from a holding company model – much on the lines of

Hanson – right through to a centralised and managed company where we operated as before, but with even greater rigour. In all, we found six different styles we could model, and we tried to define the characteristics of each of them. It was already clear to the three of us, and became even more so when we went away, that there was no exact model which would suit us and that it would be necessary to evolve something specifically for ICI. I was already clear on certain key issues regarding the board itself. Most importantly of all, I wanted a collegiate board, which meant that it had to be substantially smaller. I also wanted a board without differentiation by titles – I wanted and sought a 'board of brothers' and my concept of my function was to manage our relationships. Above all, I wanted a board united in their responsibility for the corporation but without the distraction of operating responsibility for the divisions and overseas companies. I saw a clear distinction between the task of defining the role of the subordinate unit's contribution to the whole and the task of driving and developing that unit in its own right. Because I felt that the management of the totality of the corporation, its make-up, geographical spread and competitive position in an inter-national sense, was the really vital issue, I sought to bring this conflict into the open. As far as style was concerned, I knew that we needed less formality and a greater pressure for achievement. We and the company needed loosening up. During this period I received very great help from a few friends, and great kindness when I sought to visit other successful companies to find out their ideas and contemporary practice. However, I was also uncomfortably aware of a real build-up of expectation within the company that my taking over would herald major change.

At home our circumstances had changed radically. In 1981 Gaby had finally decided to leave her husband and very naturally she and her daughter headed home to us. After Betty's tireless restoration efforts our home at Elmdon was charming and comfortable, but not really ideally suited to house two families. Moreover, the only staircase in the house was lethal for anyone except the totally fit and so, shortly after their homecoming, we decided that we should all move to a larger house. A key consideration for us was proximity to a suitable private school for Abby and, with our customary infelicitude, we managed at first to find one which proved to be unsatisfactory in every particular. A slower, more cautious approach to the problem (which Betty advocated) would have been wiser, but Gaby and I were anxious to be able to demonstrate to a court that there had been no interruption in Abby's education or her quality of life, in case there was a custody hearing. In an almost unbelievably short time we abandoned our easy, comfortable home and friendly village and moved to a splendid regency house in twenty-four acres of land near Halstead, in Essex. Once again we were unable to achieve our cherished ambition of living in Suffolk and, in our haste, we unknowingly took on a whole new realm of responsibilities.

For the first time since we were living in Yorkshire we shifted centuries, and our beloved, worn and cherished oak furniture looked distinctly out of place in the wildly different proportions and elegance of regency living. Moreover, for the first time we found ourselves as landowners, in a small way. Sloe House had been a home of some grandeur in its day, boasting wonderful seclusion, a long tarmac-ed drive, substantial stable block and a vast, walled, kitchen garden with greenhouses. How we had ever thought that Betty and Gaby could cope with this major shift in scale I cannot imagine, for it was already obvious that it was going to be very difficult for me to make much of a contribution. The days were plainly ending when I could look forward to having every weekend at home and the chances of my taking a day off during the week were absolutely minimal. However, our move occurred at a time when unemployment was on the increase and our chances of being able to hire help seemed hopeful.

The problem was mercifully resolved for us, for as the first removal van trundled down the drive a slim, bearded, well-spoken man arrived, together with his girlfriend and a goatling, and asked if we needed help. Seldom can any man have judged his approach more skilfully, and it was the beginning of a long association. As always when buying a house, the day you move is the day that the whole thing suddenly looks different. The excellent order which one saw as a purchaser proves to be the slightly tatty edifice which one is now committed to propping up in perpetuity. The rolling acres with their splendid, long-legged, elegant horses and strong undertones of a Stubbs painting, become an endless area of mole-hill-ridden, uneven and unkempt mess. The stable block which, before purchase, looked like a pristine Newmarket trainers' equipage, suddenly appeared worm-ridden and decaying.

Mick, Penny, and the goat, Suzy, arrived in our lives just as the true realisation of the problems and difficulties of our situation had dawned on us. We even viewed Suzy with wonder, believing the layman's stuff that goats are wonderful lawnmowers, and we fondly imagined the diminutive creature single-handedly returning our acres to the sort of close-cropped springy turf we had experienced on the Yorkshire moors. One of the features of our family is that we waste no time on regrets or looking backward. Life is for living and the word 'impossible' simply does not exist in my wife's vocabulary. I had taken a couple of days off to help move in and then, not for the first or last time, left my beloveds perched uncomfortably on top of tea chest after tea chest of our cherished possessions and facing a mountain of organisation and work.

Mick and Penny saved our lives. They both knew the area and there was no unlikely need that they didn't set off, with total confidence, to satisfy. Moreover Mick was the original king of DIY. He had been a rolling stone which stopped rolling once we met and at some time or other he had earned his living in every imaginable way. He would have been ideally suited to desert-island living. He had been a decorator, a joiner, a cobbler, a boat builder and there was no practical task to which he would not turn his hand. He could weld, was a wizard with a chainsaw and was, we thought, an accomplished electrician. No mechanical device could defeat him and he was one of those natural mechanics for whom the nut never cross-threads or the bolt requires tapping out. Penny's skills were to emerge later, for she had an instinctive feel for animals of every sort, but a particularly deep-seated love of horses – later to become an affection and understanding of donkeys, as the Harvey-Jones donkey herd came into being. It was as well that she had this instinctive feeling for, when the last of the moving vans departed and we walked round our new-found estate, we discovered that we were not alone. As we walked into one of the out-houses we were amazed to be set on by a less than appreciative gander, protecting, as only a gander can, his mate, who was sitting on a nest of indeterminate age and contents. Years later we have one of this pair still.

We threw ourselves into the unaccustomed role of being country landowners with zest and enthusiasm and, as ever, our family's nest-building skills came speedily to the fore. So did many other deep-seated urges. We still had our beloved ex guide-dog, Tippy, but he was growing older and slower now and we felt that we should get another one before he left us. Bob Steele, our original friend from the Guide Dogs Association in Bolton, started looking around on our behalf and thus it was that we had the privilege of coming to know Opus. If ever there was a magnificent dog Opus was it. Massive, long-haired, great-hearted and the gentlest animal I have ever known, he had been working for a very distinguished blind owner who had suddenly died. At that point it was discovered that Opus was going deaf and could not work any more. Somehow the tragedy of his deafness brought home to us all, more forcibly than any other experience, the terrible nature of this affliction and I started an interest in the charities for studying deafness which I continue to pursue. It is only when, unthinkingly, one approaches a large dog from behind and sees him leap with alarm as one pats him, or when you are walking with him and he looks back every few paces to be sure that he knows where you are, that you appreciate more poignantly the problems that deafness brings. He and I fell instantly in love with one another and although his sweet nature encompassed all the family, I always felt an especial linkage with him in his silent, isolated world. Like all our guide-dogs, his one wish was to be with you and since, despite his size, he could tuck himself away into an extraordinarily tiny space, he was never far away from us. Later, when I started driving a pony and trap, he took on himself the role of carriage dog and would follow us, a few paces to the rear, round and round the paddocks and fields. There truly was not a bad bone in his body, but he did possess a wonderful sense of humour and a certain slyness on occasion.

It was only a matter of time before our twenty-four acres had their inevitable effect and led us into horses. It was soon plain that the two geese and one goatling were not going to mow one meadow adequately, let alone twenty-four acres of them. This seemed like a very good opportunity for Abby to learn to ride, so we found ourselves scanning the classified ads and attending the Chelmsford livestock sales, with Penny in attendance as our technical advisor. We soon started to assemble the most unlikely and unsuitable equine group possible. A former racehorse of highly nervous but very loving disposition, a fat little Thelwell-type pony of iron will and winsome ways who was, for £25, saved from the dogmeat can, and the first two donkeys, an entire male called Steven and his lady love, Sarah. Sarah was already in foal when she came to us and she suffered from the delusion that she was a person. Because Steven was so gentle we failed to realise the risks which we were running in keeping an entire donkey stallion, and it was only after a stern talking to from our vet that we were eventually persuaded to part him from his parts.

Abby started her riding career on Billy, the Thelwell, back on a leading rein. He was such a little tub that she had difficulty getting her legs across him, but he seemed at the time to be a placid plodder. Later I was to have considerable evidence of his unstoppable will and amazing turn of speed. Our donkeys instantly stole our hearts. They are always gregarious animals, who constantly crave attention, and Sarah was a queen of seduction where humans were concerned. She would bray with excitement as soon as she saw you and at the smallest opportunity would collapse her head into any willing arms to have her ears tickled. There is something about donkeys which attracts donkeys and almost immediately people would call us and ask us to give their donkey a home, or even worse, we became aware of how miserably many are treated. The donkey herd increased to ten before we came to our senses and called a halt. Fascinatingly for us, who knew so little of them, they all had totally different characters and temperaments. When they were in our largest paddock, in front of the house, they would join in our household activities with gusto, leaning their vast heads on the post and rail fence which separated them from our lawn, with its desirable grazing and interesting plants, and our kitchen, dining room and drawing room which contained, from their point of view, an endless supply of carrots and peppermints. Their less than musical calls would greet any obvious movement and they would unmistakably summon our attention if they felt neglected. By this time Penny was working practically full time with our animals, while Mick set himself on the renovation of the outbuildings. Nothing daunted him, and over the years he reconstructed, almost single-handed, the whole of the stable block and the outbuildings so that they were almost like new.

One of the sad casualties of the pressures of my work, and our absorption with restoring Sloe House to its former grandeur, was our social life. People in this part of Essex were kind and hospitable, but there were not enough hours left in the day for any of us. It was a pity, but a nearly inevitable consequence of the priorities which I had set myself. I was convinced that the changes I wanted to see generated within ICI could only be achieved by putting everything I had into the job. I thought the company needed every ounce of energy I could give it, and I was determined to pace myself so that I could just about crawl away at the end of my five years. I was determined not to stay on for more than the appointed period of time, no matter what blandishments might be on offer. I had worked out my own personal timetable which was; year one to work on the board and our organisational structures, years two and three on the strategies, and years four and five on the value systems and personnel style. In the event year one was about right, but the rest mingled in so that I was working on strategies, values and styles simultaneously. These ideas meant that, apart from the weekends and holidays which I knew I needed to recharge my batteries, my whole week was devoted to ICI, for as many hours a day as I could manage. We spent our weekends together as a family and seeing our existing friends, and found that we had very little energy left for extending our social life.

This form of compartmentalisation has always been a weakness in the way I have organised my life, and I have often envied the many people who seem to be able to combine ever-growing social interests with a business life which shows no signs of neglect or failure. The problem has undoubtedly been heightened by our conscious decision to keep our family life and my business life apart, and I have never entertained business acquaintances at home unless I considered them to be personal friends. I have always thought it a presumption to invite people to our home unless both of us like them. After all, even though my wife has put much more of herself into creating our various homes than I, they have always represented totally shared and equally treasured havens for us both. I have never taken kindly to the view that wives are unpaid involuntary employees of the company their husbands work for. I have always considered that they have lives of their own and that it should be their own unpressured choice whether to attend things or not. I am, of course, glad of my wife's company and proud of her when she does undertake things, for I am well aware that business life is not for her; but equally I respect her far too much to want to feel that she is taken for granted by me or anyone else.

Much of what I did and learnt during my period as chairman of ICI has been described in my first book, *Making it Happen*, in which I set out to define the business philosophy which I have built up over many years. Now I am making an attempt to explore my personal development and to trace the formative experiences which have contributed to this. In this respect I found my years as chairman, despite their apparent success, and the excess of praise which I received, one of the hardest and least enjoyable periods of my life. For a start I had greatly underestimated the personal pressures of being continually 'on parade'. People personalise a company in the most extraordinary ways and have a tendency to take their view of the collective abilities of 130,000 people from a brief brush with the leader. Moreover, in everything you do and say you are speaking to multiple audiences. Your own people take their pace and style from their perception of you. Your shareholders, your customers and your competitors are all listening, watching and evaluating from tiny and unconsidered 'supposed' clues. I can only cope with life by trying to be forthright and true to myself. I find it difficult to dissemble and try very hard not to pretend to be what I am not. I have always believed that people who ask questions are entitled to the best and most truthful answers you can give, otherwise you patronise them. This combination of views does not make life as the 'frontman' of anything any easier.

While this policy may be better in the long run, it certainly produces a lot of trouble in the short term, and in Britain, where we are masters of circumlocution and evasion, it is often viewed as arrogant. The continual feeling that you are speaking for your company and your people is a constant pressure. On the one hand you feel that if you don't stand up for them and argue their cause, who else can and will? If, as I had, you have spent nearly thirty years of your life with a group of people you like and admire, you worry that you will let them down in some way or other. Curiously, the area which I had thought would be the most demanding proved not to be. I had envisaged sleepless nights of worry as we faced up to the hard and unpalatable decisions we knew we had to tackle. This was where the strengths of a team such as we had at ICI really came to bear and eased the pain. I liked and respected my colleagues and had great faith in their collective judgements. The way we tried to work ensured that I was never in doubt where they stood on the business issues. While it is inconceivable that everything we did was right, our discussions together, and the time we spent discussing the issues, ensured that when we took decisions there was real commitment to carry them out. Later I came to realise that we were much less of a 'band of brothers' than I had thought at the time, but the differences between us were more about style and ambition than about business intentions. If we failed to tackle root problems, or looked at issues too superficially, that was my responsibility, for I was the conductor, but the decisions themselves were taken collectively, and our differences were explored and thrashed out until we had agreed actions we could support.

There is no doubt in my mind that the amount of attention I got from the media was a major irritant to my colleagues, even though it both saved us money and appeared to encourage the troops down the line. I had, over many years, been lucky in my relationships with the press. Bill Blakeborough, on Teesside, had opened my eyes to the problems as seen from the reporter's point of view, and I had always tried to be open and frank with them. It is fashionable now for people to slate the press and to claim that they are unreliable and twist things. I can honestly say that in all my dealings with the press, over a great many years, I have had only one experience of being deliberately misrepresented. On the very rare occasions when I have felt hard done by, I have usually recognised that it was my own imprecision and looseness of wording which was at fault. I hate 'going off the record', for I don't understand how a reporter can obliterate what he has been told from his mind, and I wish to avoid the occurrence of future misunderstandings. Despite these feelings I still believed that a high profile would probably be my downfall, since the higher they ride the further they fall, and I thought it unlikely that my relationships with the press would survive my five years as chairman. In fact they did and, partly as a result of this, ICI did not need to spend any money at all on corporate advertising during that period.

However, the area which caused me the most concern on a personal basis was the whole business of the effect of power on the individual. I do believe that power corrupts, and I can think of very few powerful people who have been improved by it as individuals. Positions of power are, by definition, ephemeral, while one's personal characteristics remain with one until death. Despite this, the pressures on the individual to change the attributes he or she has fought for all their lives are unremitting. If you appear to be successful it is all too easy to believe that it is due to your own cleverness, rather than due to the host of others who have actually done the work. As power grows, so does the chorus of flattery. Some is obvious and sickening, but much is insidious. In common with many people I am vain, and would like to like myself. I also struggle continuously to improve my own moral courage and willingness to take the unpopular ground. There are few tests for such weaknesses more profound than to be the chairman of a large international company enjoying a period of relative success. Every day brought its challenges and no matter how determined I was to face up to them, I felt the ground falling beneath me.

If for no other reason than this I was glad when my time expired. I have never been the sort of masochistic soul who enjoys tackling the Matterhorn for the pleasure of the drink in the chalet afterwards. There is a lot to be said for the latter without the former. I have spent my life trying to become the sort of person I would like to be, and it is easier to pursue that course without having to do the survival-run through a chairman's job.

Perhaps due to our careful preparation, or perhaps because we were, in fact, all closer in our thinking than we had realised before we went away for our four days of discussion, our board produced a surprisingly radical consensus of view in an unbelievably short time. We broke into groups to look at different aspects of our problems and set ourselves a swingeing deadline for completion of the work. Every member of the company was aware that we were meeting and there was a high expectation that this time there would be real changes. I had arranged for us to discuss our idea with the senior managers in October and this was also a spur in our flanks. However, long before that we had an opportunity to demonstrate our 'loosened-up' attitude to procedures by asking the chief executives to join our relaxed, 'help yourself to coffee'-type Monday meetings. We also took decisions on the hoof and forswore the luxury of avoiding making our minds up by asking for more information or yet another report.

The structural changes rolled on at a great pace, but the basic business continued in only slightly better shape. The next major move we made, which really shocked many people, was when we put the headquarters building up for sale. We had decided that our new, smaller, faster-moving board should be surrounded only by the key staff necessary for it to do its job, and that everyone else should be dispersed, away from London. Our original aim had been to reduce the headquarters staff from 1,200 to about 150, but try as we would, we could not drive the number below 400. This included a surprising number of 'foot soldiers' – drivers, telephone operators and so on. We plainly did not need so grand and large a building, and the opportunity appeared to offer itself for us to dispose of it to the Government. True to form, before the year end both the ministers concerned, and the government funds available, disappeared and we were left without our sale. Nevertheless, it had been a decision which had showed our determination to shake off the past. Few of our actions caused my predecessors more pain than the thought that we might leave our palatial, and somewhat anachronistic, home. I had always worried about the building. It had that pseudo imperial grandeur which seemed to me totally inappropriate to a modern chemical company. Allegedly, after it was built, it was the custom of the chairman of the day to insist that government ministers called on him in his office, rather than vice-versa. How times change. In addition to its image, there were other features which worried me. The space and luxury of the accommodation for the board contrasted all too unfavourably with the conditions for the staff. The building was totally inflexible and locked its inhabitants into cell-like offices behind bleached oak doors. There was no sense of movement, urgency or team work. Almost every impression it created was the opposite of what we believed to be relevant to the sort of company we wanted to be.

The trouble was that it was easier to declare our intent than to carry it out. The market for large offices in London had disappeared, and when we sought alternative accommodation for four hundred we found very little which had any style or quality. Although we could all face up to selling Millbank, we could not envisage moving into a building in which we had no pride. We found ourselves inexorably pushed to the alternative plan of redeveloping the building and selling two-thirds of it. To facilitate this we moved across the road to Thames House, which had once been an annexe to the main building.

Other events were piling on us. We found ourselves in the unenviable position of suing the Government, a case which we eventually won, but which did nothing to enhance my personal position with the Prime Minister. That relationship had started on fairly rocky ground and got progressively more difficult. After I had been appointed, but before I took over as chairman, I was in Europe on business and was asked by the press why Britain was facing a harsher recession than the other countries on the continent. I replied, I thought accurately, that Mrs Thatcher's policies were more rigorous than those applied elsewhere, and was somewhat surprised to find this reported as 'because we have Mrs Thatcher'. I had never concealed my political beliefs, and was at this time an open supporter of the Social Democratic Party, although I had never been politically active. I felt that the SDP offered a moderate, centre alternative, which would be essential if the country were to be saved from the effects of constant swings from the extreme left to the extreme right. I now found myself suing the Government for their unreasonable support for a new ethylene cracker in Scotland. An ethylene cracker is the starting point for most petrochemical operations, breaking up crude petrol into its many chemical constituents. There was no commercial basis for the cracker, and it would operate in such a favourable tax environment, as far as its fuel was concerned, that there was no way that our Teesside cracker could compete. From our point of view, we had no option. We had to show our people that we had fought, in case competitive pressures forced us to shut down. However, not for the first time, some people ascribed my actions to political malice rather than sheer necessity.

To continue my litany of finding myself on the low ground of apparent conflict with the Prime Minister, I had declined her first generous invitation to No. 10, as it clashed with a long-standing date I had made to talk to our managers. To me, of course, they came first, but I can well understand Mrs Thatcher taking a different view. I finally completed my hand by giving the BBC's Dimbleby Lecture in 1986, in which I attempted to refute the then apparently prevalent view that industry did not matter, and that we were destined for a happy post-industrial life, paying our way by selling knowledge, financial services and tourism. Mrs Thatcher always treated me politely but distantly and I was given many signs of her disfavour. Indeed at one time I thought I might achieve the distinction of being the only ICI chairman not to be given a knighthood. This reputation for being an opponent of the Prime Minister was not something which I actively sought and was, I believe, unhelpful to my company.

By the end of 1982 my two deputy chairmen had moved on to other, very successful careers and had added further distinction to the long list of former ICI board members who have performed so magnificently in British industry. Our executive members then numbered myself and seven others and we still had a very Anglo-centric bias. I therefore started the search for more international non-executives, in order to create a better balance. We ended up with the three main geographical constituents of our activities, America, Europe and the Far East, represented by absolutely splendid individuals who not only broadened our horizons in a business sense, but also gave me personally many powerful new insights and perceptions.

With just a whisker to spare, we managed to introduce our new ways of working the company for 1983 and the effect on our people was almost immediate. Despite our determination to allow all our operating units to function in the way which suited them, almost all of them began their own versions of our changes. The fact that we had not sought to instruct them, while putting them under great pressure for performance in a profit sense, led them to degrees of commitment and varieties of thinking that surprised us. The whole company began to tighten up and, for the first time in many years, the units began to 'own' their profits in a real sense. We had scrapped all our control systems and were monitoring on only three parameters: profit, cash and strategic direction. If they failed on profit they had to turn in the cash – even if it meant selling something. If they exceeded the profit and the cash, they could spend above their budget without recourse to us, as long as the money was going to support the agreed strategy.

Deciding on the strategies themselves took a very long time, since the control systems had been built on capital authorisations of single plants. The strategies for our business had never been explicit – residing more in the minds of the chief executives than as intents which had been tested and argued about. As a group we had a clear view that we needed to shift the emphasis of the company from its domination by the heavy chemical producers, more into 'effects'. In our terminology, 'effect' chemicals were those which sold, not by the chemical formula which described their make-up, but rather for the effect they created, be it a pharmaceutical, film, paint or dyestuff. It was also clear in the light of the closure of nearly thirty per cent of our UK customers, that we had to shift our attention overseas, and fast. We also felt that we were not developing enough new businesses. In the past these had grown from technological opportunity and had seldom been market-led. Developing a new business area in the chemical industry can take twenty years or more – that was certainly the time it took our pharmaceutical and agricultural chemical businesses to grow to profitable independence. We wanted to try the reverse approach – looking at the probable market trends and trying to match these back to our existing, or potential, technological base. It was obvious to us that, with the pressure for profit that we were exerting on our existing units, it was unlikely that they would provide the continuous commitment and funding necessary for such long-range activities, so we took on the task ourselves. It is still too early to know how successful this attempt will be. One at least of our projects appears to have foundered, while one looks securely set for the future.

Whenever I hear arguments on short-termism I look back with pride to our determination, even in our darkest days, to try to ensure that we were nurturing the seed corn for the future – something we could ill-afford at that time. The strategies themselves were evolved by asking each chief executive to submit a range of options for the future of his business – varying from what he could do with limitless resources, to how he would cope on just his own cash flow. Importantly, we also asked what, left to himself, he would like to do. We then assembled all these suggestions into a rough-cut of what the company could look like, and then tried to fit the pictures into our financial capability to support them. This task of assembling, reassembling, debating the risk profile and competitive position of the company, was the guts of our own self-prescribed task, and very difficult we found it. We tested each of our business strategies and the total picture against what we knew about our competitors' aims, as well as our own technological competitive ability. In the latter case, we often found it necessary to strengthen the technological profile of the businesses until we felt confident we could take on the best.

The development of the strategic aims of the company and the businesses, as well as giving us greater insights into the strengths and weaknesses of our company, gave us a shared and owned view of the future for the first time, and had a tremendous effect on drawing us together as a team. It also showed us, inexorably and inevitably, that we could not get where we wanted to be without making some sweeping changes. It would be necessary for us to buy positions in areas where we were deficient, and sell off other areas where we had plainly lost the possibility of being a power player. In the early seventies I had worried about ICI's abilities in the acquisition field, and indeed had joined the board of Reed International to try and learn more about this arcane art. It is a highly professional field, where contemporary practice is needed if one is to be effective. Therefore we set up a four-man team, responding directly to one of my colleagues, to acquire the necessary skills. For the first time we included in the team a merchant banker, who was on loan to us, and he succeeded in bracing our thinking and helping us out of our isolationist mode.

By 1984 we were really motoring, and that was the year when we hit the magic One Thousand Million Pound Profit. This dream number had emerged in something less than a disciplined manner. It represented about a ten per cent margin on sales and a respectable, but unexciting, return on capital employed. It also represented the threshold from which we could really begin to do the things which were necessary, added to which it was a pleasantly rounded number. It emerged at our annual meeting with the shop stewards, where they were asking, in exasperation, when I would be satisfied with the profit we made – since we have already doubled our previous appalling rate. I replied, to the surprise of my colleagues (for we had not discussed the issue) that we needed at least the thousand million which seemed so improbable as to be unlikely in the extreme. Something similar happened at the Annual General Meeting when one of the shareholders challenged us to get the share price to £10 and I replied that they should be worth quite a bit more. These publicly announced aims and ambitions gave added satisfaction to the troops and the management when they achieved them and in turn boosted our own beliefs in our collective capabilities.

It would be incorrect for us to claim the entire credit for these achievements, for the business cycle was turning in our favour, and our starting performance had been so poor, and overladen by the costs of our restructuring and voluntary redundancy programmes, that some improvement was not difficult to achieve. Nevertheless, the speed and dramatic nature of the changes which occurred surprised everyone, both inside and outside the company. From being written off in the public eye as 'the civil service of the chemical industry', we were bouncing back with a vengeance and, more pleasingly, our competitors were taking us seriously again. Increasingly, they were reacting to our initiatives and were looking with envy at the changes we had made. There is no doubt that adversity, as well as demanding change, also facilitates it – for everyone is all too well aware of its inevitability. The real challenge is to keep things changing when things are going well – always to be seeking and demanding better perform-ance, new products and new ways of doing things.

In 1984 I was elected to be the Chairman of the Confederation of European Chemical Industries. It was an interesting time, for the organisation was based in Brussels and carried much of the weight of the relations between the European chemical industries and the European Commission. Through holding this post I received a sort of post-graduate course in the workings of that mysterious body, the Commission, as well as a further sharp reminder of the immense difficulties of reaching consensus. Although the chemical industry shares many common values, such as a regard for science and scientific methods, concern about safety and standards, and a long-established regard for the training and well-being of its people, it is nevertheless an intensely competitive business. There are long-established connections, both good and bad, between companies and countries. In reality the common factors far exceed the differences and yet forming a common action plan, for instance, to attempt to redress the public's rapidly growing distrust of the industry remains extraordinarily difficult.

During this time I was a frequent visitor to Brussels and got to know the commissioners and their staff well. It helped that for many years I had been a dedicated believer in the future of Europe as a whole. Bearing in mind the complexity of the issues with which the Commission was dealing and the administrative difficulties of working in more than one language, I was convinced of the need for some form of super-national coalition. I was amazed at the effectiveness of the Commission's activities and impressed by the ease of access to the commissioners themselves. They were always willing and enthusiastic to discuss issues with business people who had practical experience of the inevitable ramifications of the Commission's actions.

As ICI's internal position improved, I felt more able to involve myself in external matters which I believed would benefit the company and also broaden my own interests and experience. I left the board of Reed International and joined Grand Metropolitan as a non-executive director. I represented ICI on the Chairmens' Committee of the CBI, and joined the European Round Table as well as the Council for Large Companies of Europe. In addition I joined the board of the International Management Institution in Geneva, and the International Council of the European Institute of Business Administration. All of these activities followed concerns I had developed over many years, such as the combination of a European future and the problems of improving standards of management and management teaching.

During the period from 1984 to 1985 I was probably at the height of my attainment and effectiveness in a professional sense. The company and the industry were going well. I thought we were operating effectively and happily as a team, and new opportunities appeared to be opening up every day. Our very ably-led acquisition team started turning up opportunities for us to fill in the missing gaps in our portfolio at an increasing rate. World industry was rearranging at a frantic rate and there were continuous opportunities for those with money and clarity of purpose. It had long been apparent that organic growth and asset swaps on their own would not achieve the radical reorientation of our business which we believed we needed. We had to reduce our dependence on the very heavy-capital, commodity chemical business which, even in good times, made somewhat unexciting returns and was chronically subject to cyclical behaviour. Instead we needed to grow what we described as 'effect business', selling chemicals for the effect they created. Such businesses required faster movement than ICI was used to, and a much greater closeness to the customer and his needs. Although they fed off the same scientific and technological base their orientation and behaviour were very different. The capital outlay did not go into ever vaster plants, but into ever more expensive research and development. Their customer patterns were different and we needed an encyclopaedic understanding of industrial processes, opportunities and problems around the world. We wanted to become the 'chemical problem solver' and we wanted to do it fast.

During its first year in existence, the acquisition team helped us to acquire more business than we had bought in the whole of the previous decade. Moreover, we developed very sophisticated techniques of buckling them on to the group. After all, we were buying successful businesses in order to learn from them and enhance our own capabilities. We saw them as being the catalysts which would release more of the potential in our science base and help us to apply these skills to the markets of the world. The last thing we wanted, therefore, was to subject them to the same regimes and ways of doing things which we had developed for ourselves. This gentle approach to integration worked well, and we began to find that good money could be earned from technically modest but well-targeted inventions. Indeed it soon began to seem as though it was hardly worthwhile trying to develop new markets for novel products and processes.

As our team began to work better, my own role changed more and more to that of being the conductor, and tempo setter, rather than manager of my colleagues. They required less and less intervention in their areas of interest and gradually I began to become a sort of 'spare man' – covering for each of them. There was plenty to be done and the role was, I am sure, of use, since few of us are so self-contained that we can manage without advice or a sounding-board, but I found myself being drawn more and more into the outside world, almost on a compensatory basis.

Meanwhile at home we were settling down to our new lives as a reunited family. Gaby was going through the inevitable aftermath of a broken marriage, and while I know that she had no regrets, she was tortured by a sense of failure, and having difficulty dealing with the changes in her life. It took a while for Abby to settle down, and she had to cope with yet another change of schooling. The private school we had chosen for her had not been a happy choice and so we wasted no time in moving her to the splendid local state primary school at Gosfield. Because of the pressures of my work I was not able to play as active a part in our home life at this time as I would have liked. Even when I was able to get home in the evenings it was often not until very late, and I had to leave again at a highly uncivilised hour in the morning.

We loved our new home, but it was an immense burden to have taken on. The house and grounds were not in the condition we had imagined them to be when we first cast our rose-tinted glasses over them. Betty's time was, as usual, completely taken up with restoring, rebuilding and redecorating and planning how to create yet another silken purse from yet another sow's ear. From our earliest times together I had reaped the benefits of her tremendous talent for producing tasteful comfort out of very little, and she has always ensured that we have lived in warm and

attractive surroundings. Sloe House was a typically convenient
regency living-machine, and one of its great joys was a wonderfully large kitchen with the most marvellous views over our own
land. At the weekends I could work in the kitchen, while
watching our donkeys happily grazing under the magnificent
spread of an immense chestnut tree. Cooking has always been a
form of relaxation for me, and at Sloe House it reached new
heights of pleasure. The kitchen was well fitted with cupboards,
work surfaces and enough electric points to accommodate even
my assiduous collection of gadgets. It was light and airy, with an
Aga cooking and heating range and an enormous centre table
which had plainly been built in the room for, apart from its
weight, it could not be manoeuvred out of any of the doors to
reach freedom. The kitchen naturally became the focal point of
the house. It was the obvious gathering point, both for the family
and for anyone who was working for us, and it was a delightful
place to cook in. Gaby was also an accomplished cook, and we
found that we were able to work together very harmoniously and
with a great deal of enjoyment.

It may seem curious, when we were all so settled at Sloe
House, that we should elect to move, but Betty and I felt that we
had a number of good reasons. We were all living together and,
although there was plenty of space, it was inevitable that Gaby
and Abby should feel that they were living in our house. We
needed somewhere more easily divisible, where they could have
a wing of their own. Moreover, I did not envisage myself working
in London for much longer and did not wish to live within easy
reach of it when I retired. Finally, even though we enjoyed living
in a regency house, we still hankered after a timber-framed
house, where our oak furniture, collected so painstakingly and
lovingly over the years, would feel more at home. My contract as
chairman expired in April 1987, just before my sixty-third
birthday, and despite some soundings about my staying on, or
splitting the job of chairman and chief executive officer, I was
determined to leave on the due date. There were younger, able
men waiting to make their mark and I did not find the image of
a sixty-three-year-old grimly hanging on to his position an

edifying one, when so many younger people had been forced to leave.

I wanted us to have completed our move of house while I was still with ICI, since I believed the 'shelf life' of an ex-ICI chairman to be about six months – so for about eighteen months we had been looking for a suitable house. In 1985, in thick snow, we had found a house near Ross-on-Wye in Herefordshire. As always with us, our emotions blinded us to the obvious problems we were about to take on. The house was run down almost more inside than out, and the garden and grounds had a bedraggled and uncared-for appearance – which we soon found to be a great understatement of the facts. Our bewitched eyes overlooked, as trivial details, the ghastly, grease-covered, 1940s kitchen, the smell of decay and the obvious signs of various forms of rot – which we had tackled in various other houses. Instead all we saw was the ornately carved barge boards, the wealth of exposed beams, the magnificent eighteen-foot-high great hall, the medieval roof and all the other charming period features. Once again it was my long-suffering wife who bore the brunt of our folly. Honesty compels me to admit that my infatuation was the most complete and, indeed, lasts to this day. Betty came to her senses quite rapidly, and foresaw our trials and tribulations, while Gaby, who didn't really want to leave Essex, never really succumbed. To me the house still represents everything I had desired as a child – roots in the countryside and history, a solidity and tranquillity which it feels as though nothing could ever change, and an ability to shut out the rest of the world and retreat into my own Garden of Eden. We bought it, hired builders and architects, and started to contemplate our move. This was quickly completed and we found ourselves, once again, living in a building site.

Our rather hastily undertaken change of address had a number of unexpected, and to some extent, undesirable features. It was plain that I could not expect to commute to and from Ross-on-Wye on a daily basis. However, as I had not been managing to get home to Essex more than about once a week, other than at the weekends, it did not seem too much to forego for eighteen

months, in order for us to live in our 'dream house'. How wrong
we were. I found the impossibility of getting home during the
week almost insupportable. I felt totally isolated. At least in
Essex, if there was a crisis, I could be home in an hour and a
half, but now we all felt as though I left home each week to go to
the moon. The whole situation caused us far greater pain than
we had expected, but it did have its limited good side. At least
once I was at home there was no way I could be expected to pop
up to town for a weekend discussion.

Nineteen eighty-five saw changes in every aspect of our lives,
both in work and in our family. Our change of address entailed
yet another move of school for Abby, who had almost completed
her first year at a private local coeducational secondary school in
Essex. Abby, herself, stated that she wished to go to a girls'
school, and we found one just half an hour away from Ross, at
Malvern, which she started attending in September. I know that
at the time Gaby had great misgivings about yet another change
of school, but this one has proved to be a truly fortunate choice.
It also led, in due course, to my becoming chairman of the board
of governors of the school, which rekindled my interests in
education in a most practical way. Gaby's wing of the house was
completed first and she set about trying to build herself a new
social life. Betty almost disappeared from sight – if she wasn't
throwing her energies and creative abilities into the very complicated and technically difficult restoration and rebuilding of a
Grade One listed house, then she would disappear into the almost
impenetrable wilderness which had once been the gardens. Betty
has put all her formidable energy and enthusiasm into making
the gardens a delight – and they are a testimony to her dedication.
The lakes have now become a haven for birds and waterfowl of
every type, and they give me more pleasure than it is possible for
me to express.

Meanwhile, at work, a number of events occurred which vitally
affected my last year at ICI. To my grief, my oldest colleague
and friend on the board, Phil Harvey, died tragically and
suddenly on his return from a short business trip to Spain. We

had known each other since my earliest days in ICI and our paths had crossed again and again. Our views and values were similar on a whole host of subjects and he had been the most marvellous supporter, confidant and constructive critic. I realised at the time the role he filled in our group, but I did not realise how critically important it was to my leadership. He was as interested as I was in the processes of work, and was a tremendous team-builder. He was brilliant at foreseeing and forestalling emotional and other difficulties and was liked and respected by us all. While I am sure that we all missed him, for me his loss was irreplaceable. Shortly after this, Brian Smith decided to leave. He had concluded that he was unlikely to be elected chairman and, understandably, wanted to run his own ship while he still had time. One of the difficulties of the ICI system is that no one can know whether or not he is likely to be elected and so each individual has to chart his own course.

Brian and I had worked together since the seventies, firstly in Fibres and then as colleagues on the board. Again, although we were totally different in our approach to our work, we shared ideals and views on how to get the best from people. Brian was another person that I knew I could depend on to tell me when I was going wrong, and of course both of them had been involved from the very earliest days in setting up the ways in which we operated as a board. Both men were internationalists, known and liked throughout the world, and Brian has gone on to do a superb job in the Metal Box company. Simultaneously, therefore, we lost a quarter of our original team and in my particular case I lost my two closest friends, on whom I relied for candid personal advice. I count myself very lucky to have known them and I doubt whether we could have made the mileage we did without both their professional and personal contributions.

Professionally, our problems in replacing them were ones of choice, since all our chief executives were very highly qualified and the difficulties related more to the order of their preferment than their relative competence. As long as I can remember, ICI has always had a plethora of talent at the top and all too often the choices of whom and when depend on extraneous factors rather than business capability. The team was speedily reconstituted and brought up to strength. In retrospect I feel that I made a mistake in not recognising that this made us into a new team and paying more attention to rebuilding it from scratch. Instead, while plainly we could not expect the same personal involvement in our strategy that we had had from Brian and Phil, we did expect these new members to join with us and quickly assimilate our ways and values. The problem was exacerbated by the planning for my own succession. I was determined that I would not allow the sort of long-drawn-out, debilitating leadership contest which had happened before. In particular, I disliked the speculation before the event and the often damaging publicity for those who were not chosen. I had decided, therefore, to nominate my successor a full year before my departure and for us to split the chairman's and chief executive's roles between us. We held the election in March and the result was announced shortly afterwards. The election was for the post of Deputy Chairman and Chairman Designate.

Our election was carried out in the usual way and I was not surprised at the result. My successor was admirably qualified and in fact probably had the widest experience of the multiplicity of ICI's activities of any previous chairman. I knew that we could work together since we had been doing so for many years and, while our styles were very different, our approach to business situations was often similar. In any event, I believed that ICI needed a change of style. My own had been too highly personalised and too high-profile. I think it had been appropriate for the bad times, but I was much less sure of its desirability when things were going well. I was confident that the processes we had followed to devise our strategic aims would ensure that these were not lightly abandoned, and all in all felt pretty secure for the future of my company and colleagues. I set to, thereafter, to work myself out of my job and began to think in terms of my future – after ICI.

The year 1986 proved to me yet again that I had not yet succeeded in 'getting it together' in a personal sense. Maybe one never does, and perhaps the apparently mature, well-adjusted and secure individuals that one is constantly aware of are still trying to find themselves, just as I feel that I am. No matter how hard one tries it is almost impossible to see oneself through other people's eyes. I think that we fondly imagine that people see and appreciate our own perceptions and our motives and actions and that it is a great source of disillusion and disappointment when this is proved not to be true.

The announcement of my successor went well and we appeared to gain approval both within and outside ICI by planning such an orderly and well thought-out handover. The pair of us worked well together, and lost none of our carefully built up momentum. We had planned that, in effect, apart from chairing the board meetings themselves, Denis would supervise the budget process for 1987 and would effectively have taken over completely by the end of the year.

I had never wanted to make a grand farewell tour of the overseas companies and the home divisions, for I felt that it was important that our people should not be looking back to the past. I also felt that this sort of tour placed unfair expectations on the divisions, as they had little option but to proffer their hospitality, whatever they might feel about the outgoing chairman. There was one exception, however. During all my years in ICI I had never felt able to take time out to renew my memories of India – concentrating instead on the work in hand and the industrial areas where we had our operations. I asked for a valedictory tour of some of the parts of the subcontinent I had not visited since I was a boy and planned a trip for January – the best season for such a visit.

Meanwhile, I had been approached by Ian Chapman of Collins publishers, and June Hall – who was to become my literary agent – and asked to write two books for them. I found it immensely flattering that anyone should believe I could actually write, let alone have anything interesting to say. I had dreamy and inaccurate pictures of sitting overlooking my garden and reliving my experiences of the past. I thought it would be a sort of double re-run, enabling me vicariously to enjoy again sensations and pleasures that had passed too quickly to savour in full at the time. After a little thought I agreed to their proposal, and it didn't occur to me to discuss my plans with my colleagues, whose first intimation of my intentions was a report in the press. It was then that I discovered how deep the resentment of my high profile had become and how little my colleagues trusted my regard and esteem for them. All hell broke loose and I was asked to undertake not to write any memoirs at all. Apart from the fact that I had no obligation whatsoever to desist from my announced intention, I was deeply hurt that they should consider that I would write adversely about them, either individually or collectively.

I had considered myself fortunate beyond my deserts in that I like them all and had always admired their very different attributes and contributions. Even though I continually praised them publicly, and made it clear that ours was a team effort, the publicity had become more and more personalised on me as an individual. Without doubt I had enjoyed such acclaim – even though I tried to keep a sense of proportion. Also, without doubt, a combination of the loss of Brian and Phil, and my own failure to rebuild the team differently, had paved the way to this painful dénouement. Like most pain, however, it was a salutary reminder to me, again, that relationships must never be taken for granted and that I had, albeit inadvertently, assumed compliance without discussing it.

I had in any event been looking forward to retiring and doing new and different things, but this experience made the process of saying goodbye a much easier one. I left ICI without too many regrets, and full of ideas about how to utilise my time. Retirement is, after all, the only time you have a completely free hand to design your life. You have a pension, a home and a family, and together you can go anywhere, do anything, and learn anything you wish.

From my early boyhood, when I spent so much time living in my imagination and the world of the great adventure books of the 1920s, I have had a picture in my mind of the sort of person I wanted to be. A sort of *Boy's Own Paper* composite, archetypal British gentleman – simultaneously strong and compassionate, stiff-lipped yet emotional, courageous both physically and morally, doing incessantly to others as you would be done to yourself.

The nice thing, if you start from this viewpoint, is that there is always more to aim for, so life is never without purpose. The problem is that, no matter how much you do 'get it together', there are always other bits to be gathered in.

I do not believe that the purpose of my life was to lead ICI, nor to help to try to arrest Britain's industrial decline. All those years ago I believed that life was about continuously trying to grow – to develop one's talents, such as they are, and to try every day to do a little better. Maybe that recurrent belief is actually what 'getting it together' is really about.

Index

Abigail (granddaughter), 330, 350–1, 368, 371
Airey, Fred, 229
Antarctic, 200–3
Argentinians, 201–3

Bahadur, Maharajah, 9–27 passim, 83–4, 95–6
Bray, Jeremy, 246

Cabinet Offices, 161–2
Canada, 105–6
Carrington Viyella, 332, 333
Cean Naat, 10–19 passim, 26, 28, 29
Choate, Geoffrey, 219, 221
Christmas gifts, at ICI, 262–3
coal supply, to ICI, 259–61
computers, 325 6
Condor, Eric, 153, 154
Confederation of British Industry (CBI), 366
Confederation of European Chemical Industries, 341, 365
Coronation of George VI, 77, 82
Courtney, Tony, 146, 152, 160, 171
Curry, Russell, 218, 220–1, 242

Dartmouth, Royal Naval College, 69, 75
    H-J at, 84–99, 100–2
Deal, see Tormore School
Devon, 32–5, 42–3
Dhar State, India, 9–27
Dimbleby Lecture, BBC, 361–2
Duncan, Bill, 345

European Commission, 365–6
European Community, 337–8
European Round Table, 366

Falkland Islands, 200–3

Gieves the tailors, 78–80
Government policies, and ICI, 341–5
Grand Metropolitan, 366

Harvey, Phil, 371–2
Harvey-Jones, Betty (wife), née Mary Evelyn
    Atcheson, meeting H-J, 122–4; courtship,
    133–4, 159–60; marriage, 166–7;
    homebuilding talents, 88, 168, 196, 205, 226,
    368–9, 371; in Germany, 176, 183–5; in UK,
185–6, 195, 197–8, 205, 207; broadcasting,
183–4, 215; antique shop, 287, 303; life with
H-J, 195, 317–19; character, 215, 272
Harvey-Jones, Eileen (mother), née Wilson, 7–8,
14, 17, 27–9, 33, 41, 76, 78–9, 95–7, 167–8;
death, 275
Harvey-Jones, Gabrielle (daughter), birth, 184;
childhood, 195, 272–3; illness, 209–16;
antique shop, 287, 303; marriage to Adrian,
304; problems, 317–19; daughter Abigail,
330; leaves husband, 350–1; unsettled, 368
Harvey-Jones, John: events
    birth, 3, 7; family background, 1–5; childhood,
    7–8, 15–17; in India, 3–4, 9–28; return to
    Europe, 28–31; in Devon, 32–5, 42–3; in
    London, 36–40; school in London, 39–40; at
    Tormore, 40–1, 44–6, 47–65, 66–77; naval
    career envisaged, 74–8, 80–3; at RN College,
    Dartmouth, 84–102; naval career, 103–223;
    submarine service, 119–45; in Australia,
    138–9; and the Japanese, 140–3; in Hong
    Kong, 142–3; at Cambridge, 145–9; in
    Germany, 149–52; at Wilhelmshaven,
    152–60; in London Controlling Section,
    161–72; in Intelligence, 160–72; return to
    Germany, 171; Kiel, 171–82; Hamburg,
    182–5; back in RN, 185–206; awarded MBE,
    191; in Naval Intelligence, 206; RN
    prospects, 209; decision to leave RN, 211–12,
    214, 216–7; leaves RN 223; on the dole,
    223–4; joins ICI, 222–3; work study officer,
    225, 231–8; tanker driver's pay problem,
    233–8; Deputy Supply Manager, Wilton,
    238, 242–77; man-management problems,
    249–54; under HOC Division, 277–87; Sales
    Manager Hydrocarbons, 283–7; ambition,
    284, 290–1; Technical Commercial Director,
    287–8; Personnel Director, 288–92; Deputy
    Chairman, Division, 292–7; Divisional
    Chairman, 297–319; Petrochemicals Division,
    309–19; Board member, ICI, 318–19, 320,
    322–9, 332; Director for Indian sub-
    continent and Middle East, 324; responsible
    for Fibres Division, 335–9; Director for
    Western Europe, 335–7; responsible for
    Heavy Chemicals, 340; Deputy Chairman,
    ICI, 340–6; Chairman, 347, 348–50, 355–68,
    371–5

ships served on
  Amethyst, 186, 188–96; Diomede, 103, 105,
  106–12; Duke of York, 118–19; Empire
  Fowey, 187–8; Ithuriel, 114–16, 120; Pasteur,
  103–4; Quentin, 116–18, 120; Royal Rupert,
  153; St Austell Bay, 196–204; Sea Scout,
  135–45; Sturdy, 128; Trusty, 125–8;
  Voracious, 128, 134
home life
  first meeting with Betty, 122–4; courtship,
  133–4, 159–60; marriage, 166–7; problems
  in family life, 207, 303; home life in North-
  East, 227–31, 270–4, 317–19; relations with
  family, 285, 304–5; loss of Stonegate Mill,
  321–2; home life in Elmdon, 329–31; life at
  Halstead, 351–6, 368–9; to Ross-onWye,
  370–1
personal (in alphabetical order)
  ambition, 284, 290–1; brass bands, 42–3,
  61–2; character, 21–2, 56–7, 303–4; donkeys,
  353, 354; gardening, 18, 228, 229, 248;
  handwriting, 50; ineptitude, 88–9;
  languages, 93–4, 145–9, 267–8; leadership,
  views of, 91–2, 102, 104, 238–9, 299; man-
  management, 249–54; media attention, 358,
  374–5; pipe-smoking, 109–10; politics, 361;
  reading, 58–9, 68, 77; relations with
  children, 195, 207; relations with ICI Board,
  225, 375; and sex, 71–3, 98, 113–14, 151–2,
  155–6; sporting ineptitude, 24–5, 50–1,
  70–1; teashops, 37–8; writing books, 374
Harvey-Jones, Mervyn (father), 4–15 passim,
  20–2, 24–5, 36, 75–6, 95–6, 170–1;
  character, 6–7, 22; death, 290
Haslam, Bob, 345
Hervey, Romaine, 64–5, 66
Hodgson, Dr Mark, 205, 210–13
Hong Kong, 193
Horsley, Josie and Arthur, 227, 229

ICI (Imperial Chemical Industries), joined by H-J,
  217–21; as a company, 239; nature, 247–8;
  Warren House, 248; Wilton site, 255–6, 262,
  275–6, 289, 306–7, 313; Heavy Organic
  Chemicals Division (HOC), at Wilton, 276;
  Fibres Division, 335–9; financial problems,
  343–5; sale of HQ, 359–60; thousand million
  profit, 364; chairman, succession process,
  372–4
ICI America, 335
India, H-J family background, 3, 8–9; removal
  from, 169–70; H-J in, 3–4, 9–28
Indians, character, 26–7
Indore, 23–8
Italy, childhood visit, 28–9

Japan, 188, 191–2
Jarrett, Alex, 332, 333, 334
Jenkins, Brian, 292
Jones family, 4–5

Klose, Hans Helmut, 180
Korea, 188–9, 192
Küchler, 174–5

Lewando, Jan, 332, 333
Lynagh, Ronny, 252

McMillan, Colin, 217–18
Malaysia, 194–5
management, at ICI, 255–9; good, 266–7, 270; H-
  J's views, 238–41, 312–15; man-management
  problems, 249–54
Manka, 10, 16, 20, 21, 23, 25
Maye, John, 182
Moore, Charlie, 235–8
Muir, Alistair, 244, 250, 255
Munn, Mary, 246

Naval Review 1937, 82–3
Newell, Ronny, 255–6, 264–5
Ninion Oil Holdings, 327
North-East, love for, 121, 125, 227–8, 296,
  311–12
North-East Development Council, 310
nylon fibres, 336

Parkinson, C. Northcote, 94–5
petrochemicals, 280–3
polyester fibres, 336

Reed International, 332–5, 364
Royal Navy, H-J's first ideas of career, 74–8;
  interview for, 80–2; Dartmouth College,
  84–99, 100–2; RN career, 103–223; views
  on, 216–17
Russia, visits to, for ICI, 268–9
Russians, H-J and, 153–9, 163–6, 206, 269–70,
  324

Scott-Herd, Bill, 244, 249–54
Sharpe, Eric, 325
Smith, Brian, 372
South America, 199–204

Tees and Hartlepool Port Authority, 310
Thatcher, Mrs Margaret, 361–2
Tormore School, 40–1, 44–6, 47–65, 66–7

Unions: relations with management, 293–5; shop
  stewards' task, 239–40, 291–2
Uruguay, 111–12

Wilkinson, Derek, 217–18
Wilson family, 2–3, 32
  grandparents, 2–3, 32–5, 42–3
Wilton site (ICI), 255–6, 262, 275–6, 289, 306–7,
  313
work study and incentives, 234–5, 242, 289–90
World War II, 98–9; life during 100–1; naval life,
  104–41